The Big Dictionary of
Dreams

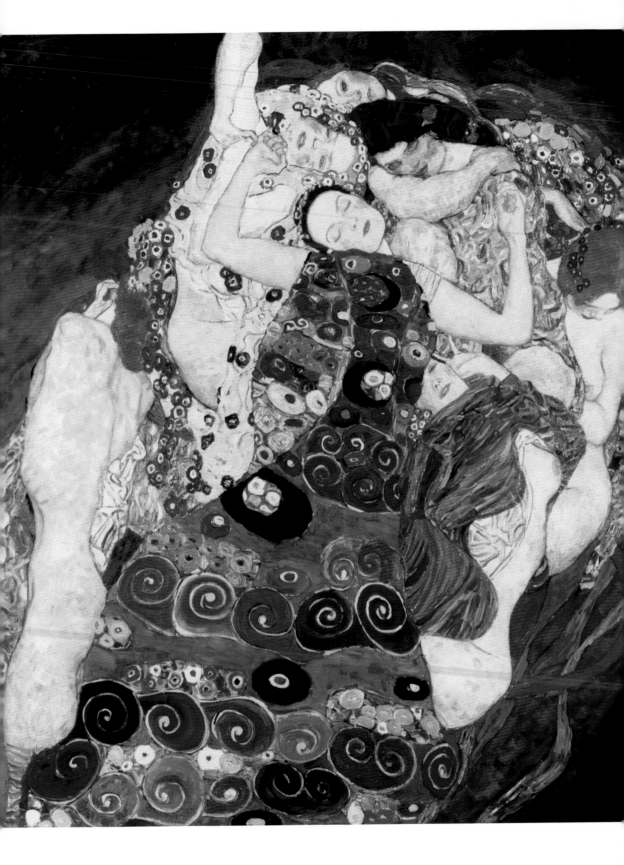

The Big Dictionary of
Dreams

The Ultimate Resource for Interpreting Your Dreams

Martha Clarke

More than 1,400 entries

Keys to understand the meaning
of thousands of dreams

Skyhorse Publishing

Original Title: GRAN DICCIONARIO DE LOS SUEÑOS © Editorial Océano, S.L. (Barcelona, Spain); Martha Clarke, 2000, 2009

Redaction and additional texts:
Martha Clarke, Ignasi Gaya, Sergio Alvarez, Maria Leach, Mario M. Perez-Ruiz Rodolfo Roman, Claudia Ponte.

Skyhorse Publishing books may be purchased in bulk at special discounts for sales promotion, corporate gifts, fund-raising, or educational purposes. Special editions can also be created to specifications. For details, contact the Special Sales Department, Skyhorse Publishing, 307 West 36th Street, 11th Floor, New York, NY 10018 or info@skyhorsepublishing.com.

Skyhorse® and Skyhorse Publishing® are registered trademarks of Skyhorse Publishing, Inc.®, a Delaware corporation.

Visit our website at www.skyhorsepublishing.com.

10 9 8 7 6 5 4 3

Library of Congress Cataloging-in-Publication Data is available on file.

Cover design by Brian Peterson
Images selected by Oceano Ambar
Images cited in the final page of this book.

Print ISBN: 978-1-63450-460-7
Ebook ISBN: 978-1-63450-477-5

Printed in China

Table of Contents

Editorial Note

Before beginning

We have developed this dictionary as a navigational map to help the reader unravel the valuable messages in dreams. In the first part, you will find an overview of the different approaches to the world of dreams; these will help you understand the multiple meanings that dreams contain as well as the importance of always singling out those meanings. It is best to not just personalize the message, but also to take into account the circumstances that produce the dream. The same dream, dreamt by the same person, could have a different meaning depending on the moment or personal experiences. Therefore, we should evaluate the importance of each interpretation carefully, as much with the details as overall.

This book contains the tools to start down the path to discovery, in a way that person can find their own interpretation of their dreams. Although, as Jung asserts, "human beings share a broad spectrum of symbols and archetypes," the concrete significance of each dream can be very different depending on the personal circumstances of the the subject. Therefore, whether alone or with the help of a specialist, each person should take on the task of deciphering their nocturnal episodes.

And for that there's nothing better than to get a little practice with concrete themes from the second part, in the form of a dictionary, where many themes of the oneiric world are explained and can be linked together, giving birth to thousands of combinations and interpretations. We hope that it will provide plenty of hints so that the adventure of dreaming is even more intense and enriching.

Sweet dreams.

Prologue

How did Jules Verne dream up his magnificent Nautilus? How did he traverse the depths of a world inhabited by other civilizations, dinosaurs, and flood-proof birds and plants? How did Leonardo da Vinci design the first known bicycle in history? How did he predict flying machines? Their visions don't belong to the left- or right-brain hemispheres, but rather they connect to another cerebral organization that resides in the soul.

The effort to understand the mysteries of life, with the physical, moral, and linguistic limitations of human thought, moves us to "seek," in the mystical ascension of sleep, the higher faculties that mature the mind past adolescence.

The activities of the "higher mind" never rest, and even determine our destiny. The clairvoyance that connects to other worlds is a marvelous experience; in connection with the invisible, in the words of R. Taylor, "Poets call these enormous powers 'golden chain,' because those powers are connected to one another and because the chain's nature is incorruptible. They are rooted in this supreme principle like trees in the earth, which have a distinct energy within themselves but also give energy to their cause."

To walk, cars instead of legs; to look, glasses instead of eyes; calculators instead of our mind; mobile phones over taking ancient telepathy . . . Will we one day substitute our dreams with movies in our minds? Will they put ads in them? The dream guarantees us a phenomenal reality; an umbilical cord that unites us with the passions of nature; the arts are unleashed, and when we commit evil, nightmares invade us. The latter ones could—if we don't reflect and fix our mistakes—distress our conscience.

The human being visits his ancestors in words of Pythagoras and Socrates. In the case of metempsychosis, vices change men into beasts. Virtue, on the other hand, makes them closer to the god that lives in every person.

Each of us can look like either of the two, since these two "beings" form part of our human nature. But at the same time, to regain our childhood integrity is to recover health, "the state of perfection, innocence and light," according to the *Golden Verses* of Pythagoras. The following self criticism—a sort of a Freudian self psychoanalysis of the fourth century BC, in times of "ancient mysteries"—would evaluate our own behavior:

"Never sleep before mentally reviewing the events of the day.

Where did I go wrong? What did I do? What did I leave for later?

Examine yourself.

If you've done badly, reproach yourself; if you've done well, rejoice."

The dream used to be invoked with songs, music, incense, milk, honey, and cashews to make the journey to the world of the gods. Our baggage for this journey should be a clean conscience, which would allow us to remember our adventure without regret on the return journey: 40 percent of our lives we are held accountable for our actions. For example, bad behavior is often the foundation of a stupid future, a future we deserve because of our ignorance.

The pomp is the scourge of insomnia, isn't it? With these simple proposals, can we make our intelligence move with that of the universe? In a way that our mind is, in the words of Philo of Alexandria, "possessed and inspired by God; able to predict and foresee the future."

Posidonius would say: "The gods themselves converse with those who sleep"; and in his treaty on divination, Cicero spoke of three types of dreams: those sent by God, those sent by angels, and those experienced by the soul itself. "Life is short and art is grand," he would say. Or Hippocrates' statement: "He who knows the dimension of dreams sinks into it without falseness and digs in it like a well."

Leaving behind the weight of the senses, we can go inside the unexplored regions that live in us, deciphering the meaning of the lived story while we sleep. The symbols of that story, once understood, will fill us with knowledge and wisdom. In this way, a huge number of books accumulates in our invisible inner library. Furthermore, by understanding those signs, by unraveling the writings—the colors, the signatures, the temporality far from earth—we make ourselves immensely blissful. Scheduled at the pace of another dimension, each night we move to a parallel universe that is available for all of us. We can all benefit from that world, you only need a responsible and intelligent attitude; there you can smell the orange blossoms, the olive oil, the incense, strawberries . . . and upon waking you will begin to harvest the fruits, which is nothing more than putting together the pieces of a great puzzle.

This dictionary, without a doubt, will help us to decipher such strange hieroglyphic that dreams are—abstract of realities and dimensions of ourselves.

Mario M. Perez Ruiz

PART ONE

Understanding dreams

Introduction

The fascination with dreams

Why do dreams fascinate us? Who wouldn't like to understand their true meaning and the personal message they contain? A dream is a different state of consciousness in which anything is possible; in dreaming, we exchange day-to-day reality for a world of endless possibilities and it is within everyone's reach.

The interest in dreams has always existed, but in the last few decades new ways to study them have emerged, with interesting results: remote knowledge about the role of dreams and their interpretation unites with the classic scientific approach. This has deepened the analysis of oneiric symbols and archetypes; neurology adds explanations about the modified states of consciousness; the study of the sleep process is complemented by an integrated, holistic approach. The possibilities of dreams, mainly beneficial and favorable to self knowledge, are definitely more well known. In summary, given that dreams make up part of human existence and accompany us our entire lives, it is worth while to discover the potential they contain.

Dreams have been given different degrees of importance throughout history. Each culture has valued them and considered them differently, and they have been the subject of many

For some cultures, dreams are divine messages, premonitions, or signs from the subconscious mind.

interpretations and hypotheses; they have been considered divine messages or premonitions of events, or as representations of sin or signs from the subconscious. However, this oneiric portion of our daily existence still retains much of its mystery.

Normally, an adult sleeps about eight hours a day, or a third of their life, which is a rather significant proportion. A seventy-year-old person, for example, has slept for twenty-seven years. And of those twenty-seven, he has dedicated five to dreaming. In short, we are talking about vital periods extensive enough that they deserve our attention.

Although we don't remember, we always dream

Although we are not dreaming the whole time we are asleep, throughout the night we pass through various cycles of sleep, as we will see further on. Some people totally forget what they dream and claim they never dream; others remember their dreams entirely. The majority of us remember a few elements or occasionally retain a detailed memory of a dream that, for some reason, strikes us or seems especially important. And nearly all of us have the feeling that certain dreams have something interesting to tell us.

Dreams don't have to be prophetic, although some can be and premonitions do exist. They don't have to warn us of a coming illness, but sometimes they do. They're not necessarily related to the problems or worries of our daily life, but frequently they are. And most of us have the impression that our dreams have a meaning, and we would like to know what it is.

The interest in knowing the meaning of dreams has survived far beyond the age when they were thought to be divine messages. The work of Freud, Jung, and others has made the analysis of dreams an important part of psychotherapy and our understanding of the subconscious. There is no doubt that we can enrich ourselves and learn more about ourselves if we remember and examine our dreams, and if we learn to discover what they might mean for us.

Sometimes, remembering a pleasant dream is like getting a present. What a joy it is to wake up and be able to reconstruct, more or less precisely, the story that our mind created of its free will! If, on the other hand, we've had a nightmare, remembering is the first

Part of abstract art is related to images from the dream world.

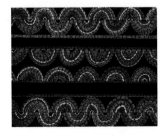

Sueños. Grabado del siglo XVI.

From divine messages to representations of sin, dreams have been subject to numerous interpretations throughout history. "Dreams," sixteenth century illustration.

step to releasing built-up tension and will probably give us some clues about an aspect of our day to day that worries us or isn't going well. The universe of dreams goes beyond simply sleeping, dreaming, waking up, and remembering or not remembering the dreams, because it contains a valuable source of information about ourselves. Although the framework from which dreams originate cannot be explained from a rational perspective, it is a different— and apparently much more reliable—way to get to know a person.

Despite the scientific and technological advances, the human mind still contains many enigmas to be discovered. Even today, the same essential questions that human beings have had since the beginning remain practically without answer.

For some strange reason—or maybe intuition—we want to believe that life is more than being born, growing, eating, enjoying a more or less sophisticated personal well-being, and then dying. We need to search for a meaning, a deeper significance. People possess an incredible capacity for adaptation and can resist the most adverse conditions, but they are incapable of going on without purpose or motivation.

Finding a single meaning in life is, of course, complicated, since there is not one single definition that applies to everyone; the implications change depending on the person, the society, the

The universe of dreams goes beyond simply sleeping; it contains a valuable source of information about ourselves.

Danae is fertilized by Zeus, transformed into a golden rain in a moment of reverie. "Danae" (Gustav Klimt, 1907).

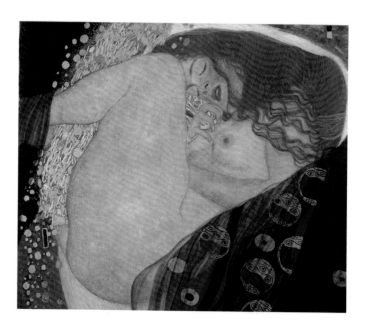

religions. Even more, it's impossible to explain rationally or scientifically but, there it is, fluttering around our minds. It's like when someone questions the existence of God: on the empirical plane, no one has been able to prove it, yet no one is able to disregard it either.

A dose of mystery

In any case, there is a generalized sentiment in human beings: the sensation, great or small, that there must be something above reason, beyond the pure sensory and physical perception of the world. In each person's life journey toward discovery of the unknown, there may be religion, intellectual knowledge, work, solidarity, etc. In the spiritual search other elements appear, among which dreams are a good "raw material."

Independent of the relationship we have with the spiritual, there is a plane that reason and sense don't reach . . . and there are dreams. Maybe this is why they've been considered divine messages for centuries; it's impossible to confirm what they are but they aren't easily ignored either. What we know for sure is that dreams take us to a *different* plane of reality, where things work differently and are out of our control and common sense. Amazingly, in this *strange* plane, we still feel the same feelings, slightly or intensely, that we experience when we're awake.

However it is, the presence of these paths to the interior world have a different importance depending on the culture or social group of the individual; in some, this may come to occupy much of waking life, while in others, like in the majority of the contemporary Western world, the frenetic activity and need for instant gratification don't leave much room or time for reflection.

Now, is it possible to predict the future through dream reading? Although there is still a lot to discover about the power and abilities of the human mind, there is sufficient evidence to confirm this. According to common sense or certain forms of rational thought, it's not easy to accept or understand. However we can't turn a blind eye to the evidence: other ways of perceiving reality exist that surpass our limits of space and time. And a way of foreseeing events before they take place in our ordinary notion of time also exists.

The thing is, we still don't know how or why this is.

In one way or another, through symbolic images, dreams reflect the vital necessity of finding a unifying meaning of life.

Dreams pulsate with connections to other elements, such as premonitions, precognition, and clairvoyance. Beyond the rational mind there are mechanisms to foresee events before they happen in real life, and dreams are proof of this.

The potential of the human mind is such that it's also possible to recreate situations that one has seen in a dream exactly. Finally, there are those that believe—and they are within their rights—that premonitory dreams are simply coincidence. Maybe they are all right in some ways...

In any case, what's certain is that paying attention to our dreams helps us understand ourselves because it brings us closer to our desires, faults, or fears. We will see this a little more closely.

1. What are dreams for?

"Trust in dreams, for in them the gateway to eternity is hidden."

KHALIL GIBRAN

Dreams and their purpose

Consider dreams like home movies that each person produces in response to their daily experiences. These movies are meant to clarify certain situations and support the person. With sufficient knowledge, they can become a sort of spiritual guide, since oneiric thoughts are a window to the subconscious where, frequently, hidden feelings and repressed needs are stored without us realizing.

Even then, there are people who question the importance of dreams. Some scientists, for example, believe that the content of dreams is simply a random mix of the many electronic signals the brain receives. Others, however, find all types of messages in even the simplest dreams, and end up distancing themselves from daily reality in favor of oneiric activity.

Neither extreme is advisable. Each dream is undoubtedly a journey into the unknown, but, at the same time, modern psychology has allowed us to understand a good part of their structure. One of the conclusions drawn from the study of dreams confirms this: dreams can be a priceless aid to the imagination, but above all when it comes to solving problems. You just have to know how to listen to them, because their content tends to have a direct relation to the emotional challenges you are experiencing.

With sufficient knowledge, dreams can be a useful spiritual guide; they are a window to the subconscious where hidden feelings and repressed needs are often stored without us realizing.

Each dream is a journey to the unknown with an implicit personal message. Although it is the content of the episode that determines our emotional state, dreaming in black and white indicates a possible lack of enthusiasm or nostalgia for the past. These dreams are an invitation to live with more intensity and enjoy the present. Still from the film Viaje a la Luna *(Méliès, 1902).*

In dreams, relationships with others are a recurring theme. The people that appear in our dreams, especially strangers, represent facets of ourselves that the subconscious is showing us.

It is known that in times of crisis, our oneiric production increases significantly, both in quantity and intensity. Should we consider this "surplus" to be positive? Yes, as long as one makes an effort to remember and interpret the dreams, since, as we will see further on, they have a valuable therapeutic potential.

For example, if a couple is going through a critical phase, remembering and analyzing usually helps them understand the subconscious reactions they have to the situation. In other words, dreams are an excellent tool to get to the bottom of emotional conflicts. Knowing the causes is an essential step to resolving the problems, regardless of what course you take.

The English psychologist David Fontana, whose books have been translated into more than twenty languages, said it clearly: "In listening to my patients' dreams in therapy sessions, I have observed how, often, these can take us right to the root of the psychologic problem much quicker than other methods." Although, we shouldn't fool ourselves: dreams are a mystery that can rarely decipher *everything*. But if a certain level of interpretation helps us understand ourselves better, what more can we ask for? From a practical point of view, our own oneiric material can be very useful.

Well-known writers such as Robert Louis Stevenson, William Blake, Edgar Allan Poe, and Woody Allen have had faith in this, acknowledging that part of their works have been inspired by dreams. The discoveries of Albert Einstein or Niels Bohr (father of modern atomic physics), among other celebrated scientists, had the same origin. In any case, these examples shouldn't confuse us: no dream can tell you what path to follow through symbolic images without the intellect to decipher them.

Prosperity, precognition, and pronostics

What's more, judging by some documented cases, we can even reap material gain from dreams. There is proof of some people that had premonitory dreams managing to earn significant sums of money thanks to their oneiric "magic." The most spectacular case was in the fifties, when an Englishman named Harold Horwood won a considerable number of prizes betting on horses. His dreams transmitted clues as to the winning racehorse to bet on. Unfortunately, these types of premonitions don't come to everyone. However, anyone has the opportunity to discover the greatest treasure of all—knowledge of one's self—through their dreams.

We've all experienced the feeling of having lost control of our lives at some point. We might feel like others are deciding things for us or that we are victims of our circumstances.

Our "dream-scapes" contain valuable information about our desires and concerns; they could also function as a forecast of some aspect of our future. According to ancient tradition, dreaming of stars predicts prosperity and spiritual wealth. "Starry Night" (Van Gogh, 1889).

However, many psychologists disagree with this. That is, they argue that daily events are not coincidences but rather meaningful deeds that reflect the inner state of the individual.

Dreams and thoughts

According to these experts, luck is a pipe dream, something that does not exist, since that which we consider the result of coincidence is none other than the natural manifestation of our thoughts and attitudes. We are basically creator, not passive receivers or victims of the events that unravel in our lives.

An example that illustrates this idea perfectly is the story of the old man who threw rocks into the sea. One day, someone asked if he ever got bored of the simple game. The old pebble thrower stared at his questioner and gave an answer he'd never forget: "My small stones are more important than they seem, they provoke repercussions. They will help create waves that, sooner or later, will reach other other side of the ocean."

What does this have to do with dreams? It's simple: as we've just seen, we are the only ones responsible for our daily experiences, no matter how hard that is to believe. Therefore it shouldn't be too difficult to take control of our lives; we just have to listen to the messages in our interior, that is, our oneiric thoughts, of which we are ultimately the authors.

Visualizations

In the bottom of the lake of our thoughts is a jewel...

In this way, thanks to dreams, our two existences—conscious and unconscious—can work together to make our lives more creative and free. An important part of this process is getting to know and understanding better the process of thought. One of the most beautiful and commonly used visualizations in yoga reminds us of this: "In the bottom of the lake of our thoughts is a jewel. In order for it to shine in the light of the sun (the divine), the water (the thoughts) must be pure and crystal clear and calm, free of waves (excitement). If our water is murky or choppy, others can't see this jewel, our inner light..."

But it's not that simple: it's often difficult to discern the connection that unites wakefulness with sleep, between what we think ourselves to be and what our oneiric fantasies say about us. In any case, if our search is passionate and patient, constant and conscious, it will result in the discovery of our true Self. Therefore the

The rooms in our dreams reflect unknown aspects of our personality.

interpretation of dreams cuts right to the heart of the message conceived by and for ourselves (although not consciously). It is important to learn to listen to them (further on we will discuss techniques for this) when it comes time to unstitch their meaning and extract the teachings that can enrich our lives.

In this way, when we have to make an important decision, we can clear up any doubts through a clear understanding of our most intimate desires. Although it may seem like common sense, this is not that common these days, since most people make decisions at random, out of habit, or by impulse.

The meaning and psychic effect of some deities in Tibetan Buddhism can be linked to the monsters that are so popular today.

Dreams allow creativity a free rein and free us from worry, sometimes resulting in surreal images that would be impossible in waking life.

Put simply, the idea is to find your true identity and recognize your wounds, fears, and joys through dreams. Never forget that the subconscious, although hidden, is an essential part of our personality. Dreams are fundamental for understanding the Self, since they are a direct path to this little-known part of ourselves. Their symbolic content allows us to recover repressed emotions and gives us a map to the relationships that surround us.

Nightmares that put us to the test

Sometimes the messages they bring us are not so pleasant and take the form of nightmares. However, although it may be hard to accept, these nightmares are valuable warnings that some aspects of our life are not in harmony with our deepest Self and thus need our prompt intervention. Nightmares are proof that self discovery is not always pleasant. Sometimes it's necessary to feel this pain in order to find out what you really are and need.

On the other hand, dreams give creativity a free rein because, when we sleep, we are free from our day-to-day worries. Therefore, even if you don't consider yourself a creative person, keep in mind that all the scenes, symbols, and characters that appear in your dreams have been created solely and exclusively by you.

It's often very helpful to record dreams in a notebook (we will explain how further on) in order to later analyze them and apply their teachings to daily life.

How to remember dreams

It is quite the paradox; the human being awakens their most intimate reality precisely when they are sleeping.

Carl Gustav Jung, who dedicated his life to studying dreams, developed this metaphor: "People live in mansions of which they only know the basements." Only when our conscience is sleeping do we manage to unveil some of the rooms of our magnificent house: rooms that may be dusty and inhospitable and fill us with terror and anxiety, or magnificent rooms where we want to stay forever.

Given that they all belong to us, it is reasonable to want to discover them all. Dreams, in this sense, are a fundamental tool.

At this point, you're probably thinking, "Sure, dreams are really important, but I can't use them because I simply don't remember them." That's not a problem, there are techniques you can use to strengthen your memory of oneiric thoughts. Techniques that, when applied correctly, allow us to remember dreams surprisingly well.

The use of these methods is indispensable in most cases since people tend to forget dreams completely when they wake up. Why? Because, according to the hypothesis of Sigmund Freud, we have a sort of internal censor that tries to prevent our oneiric activity from becoming conscious material.

Sometimes the message of dreams turns unpleasant and takes the form of a nightmare…

Relaxing in bed and going over the events of the day helps free the mind and foster oneiric creativity.

Yoga exercises, such as the savasana pose, are great for relaxation, restful sleep, and a positive outlook.

However, we can laugh in the face of this censor with a few tricks. The most drastic is to wake up suddenly when the deepest sleep phase (REM phase) is just about to end, so that you can rapidly write all the details of your mind's theater in your notebook. Waking suddenly will take this censor by surprise, stopping it from doing its job. The best time to set the alarm is for four, five, six, or a little more than seven hours after going to sleep.

If your level of motivation is not high enough to get up in the middle of the night and record your dreams, there are alternatives that let you sleep for a stretch and then remember what you dream with great precision.

First of all, it's helpful to develop some habits before going to bed, such as waiting a few hours between dinner and going to sleep. Experts recommend avoiding foods that cause gas (legumes like green beans, raw vegetables, etc.) and foods high in fat.

You must also keep in mind that, like tea and coffee, tobacco and alcohol alter the sleep cycle and deprive the body of a deep sleep (the damaging effects of a few glasses on the body does not disappear for about four hours).

What is recommended is to drink water or juice, or eat a yogurt, more than two hours after eating, before going to bed. There are two main reasons for this: liquids facilitate a certain purification of the body, and because, most interestingly for our purposes, it causes us to get up in the middle of the night. As we said, this will catch the internal censor by surprise and allow us to record our dreams easily.

Relaxation

It's important to surround yourself with an environment that stimulates oneiric activity. You should feel comfortable in your room and your bed. The fewer clothes you wear to sleep, the better. Practicing relaxation techniques, listening to calming music, or taking a warm bath a few minutes before getting into bed will help relieve stress so that you enjoy a deep restorative sleep.

There are good books on relaxation on the market, both autogenous and yogic; we recommend one of the most practical, *Relajacion para gente muy ocupada* (*Relaxation for Busy People*), by Shia Green, published by this same publishing house. However, the real key is to concentrate on remembering dreams. When you go to bed, go over the events of the day that were important to you. This way, you will increase the probability of dreaming about the subjects that most interest or worry you.

So, let's suppose you're asleep now. What should you do to remember dreams? First, try to wake up naturally, without external stimuli. If this isn't possible, use the quietest possible alarm without radio. Once awake, stay in bed for a few moments with your eyes closed and try to hold your dreams in your memory as you gently transition into wakefulness. Take advantage of this time to memorize the images you dreamt. The final oneiric period is usually the longest and these instants are when it is most possible to remember dreams.

The dream notebook

Next, write in the notebook (that you have left beside your bed) whatever your mind has been able to retain, no matter how absurd or trivial your dreams seem, even if you only remember small fragments. This is not the moment to make evaluations or interpretations. The exercise is to simply record everything that crosses your mind with as much detail as possible. Giving the fragility of memory, it's okay to start off with just a few key words that summarize the content of the dream. These words will help you reconstruct the dream later in the day if you don't have enough time in the morning. Ideally this notebook will gradually become a diary or schedule that allows you to study, analyze, and compare a series of dreams. Through a series of recorded episodes, you can detect recurring characters, situations, or themes. This is something that's easy to miss at first glance. One important detail: specialists recommend you date and title each dream, since this helps you remember them in later readings.

Remember that it's best to write the keywords of the dream immediately upon waking. It is convenient to keep a notebook on the nightstand and reconstruct the dream during the day.

It's also interesting to complement your entries with relevant annotations: what feelings were provoked, which aspects most drew your attention, which colors predominated, etc. An outline or drawing of the most significant images can also help you unravel the meaning. Finally, you should write an initial personal interpretation of the dream. For that, the second part of this book offers some useful guidelines.

While we dream, there is a sort of safety mechanism that inhibits our movement. Therefore, sleepwalkers don't walk during the REM phase. This protects us from acting out the movements of our dreams and possibly hurting ourselves. Still from the Spanish movie Carne de fieras *(Flesh of beasts) (1936).*

As we've seen, there are a series of techniques to remember dreams. This is the first step to extracting their wisdom. Now, given that oneiric thoughts are a source of inspiration for solving problems, wouldn't it be great to choose what you dream about before you go to sleep? Rather than waiting for dreams to come to us spontaneously, try to make them focus on the aspects of your life that interest you.

Let's imagine that someone is not very satisfied with their job. They'd like to get into another line of work but are afraid of losing the job security they enjoy. On one hand, they're not so young anymore, they should take the risk to get what they really want. But they don't know what to do. They need a light, a sign, an inspiration. In short, they need a dream. But not just any dream, a dream that really centers on their problem and gives answers.

However, if you limit yourself to just "consulting your pillow," you won't get the desired results. There is a possibility you will be lucky and dream about what you're interested in, but more likely you will dream of anything but. If we are really prepared to dive into that which worries us most intimately, we can direct our dreams to give us concrete answers. Just like the techniques to remember dreams, the process is simple: before sleeping, we must concentrate on the subject of interest.

It's also best to write in your notebook all the events and emotions of the day that were most important before you go to sleep.

Once your impressions and theme to dream have been noted, concentrate on the subject that most bothers you. Think about it carefully; propose questions and alternatives, "listen" to your own emotions. It's best if all possible doubts are noted in the dream notebook. This way you're more likely to receive an answer.

In order for it to be an effective answer, the question must be well defined. The fundamental idea of the problem should be summed up in a single phrase. Once you've reflected on the problem, it's time to got to bed. But the "homework" is not finished yet. Before going to sleep, you need to concentrate on the concrete question. You need to forget everything else, even the details. Just "visualize" and repeat the question, without thinking of anything else, until you fall asleep.

Oneiric thoughts are a source of inspiration. Annotating and analyzing them carefully fosters a process of self discovery.

Writing a dream notebook

You should always have a notebook and pen near your bed to write down dreams the moment you wake up. Don't forget to always write the date. What details should you include in this kind of diary? As many as you remember, the more the better.

- Note the events of the dream in order. It may not seem important when they appear unrelated. However, when analyzing them you can establish a chronological relationship between distinct elements.

- What characters appear in your dreams? Was someone important missing? If one of them reminded you of someone you know, note that. Don't rely on your memory.

- If a familiar sight appears, analyze the differences between the dream and the real world. Were the doors/windows in the same place? Were they the same size and color? And so on. This is especially important if you want to practice lucid dreaming.

- Also note the differences between familiar people in dreams and how they are in real life.

- List the non-human characters that appeared, as well as any objects that behaved as if animated.

- Take special note of recurrent themes, scenes, or characters. Do they always act/happen the same way?

- Write down all the colors you remember.

- Note your emotional reactions: if you feel happy, scared, nervous…

Don't let any theories about the meaning of dreams interfere. You run the risk of skipping details that might be very significant.

Finally, don't trust your memory. After a time, you won't remember a thing about some of the dreams you wrote down. No matter how clear they are in the moment, write them down.

Dreams are "signs," messages from our subconscious, and the study and interpretation of them helps resolve the problems that worry us.

Nocturnal sleep puts us in touch with the deepest level of being, which allows us to approach our problems with a wider perspective. And induced dreams tend to be easier to remember than other oneiric activity.

2. Why do we dream? Physiology of dreams

"Everything serious comes to us at night."

Cicero

What happens when we sleep?

Why do we sleep? The answer is not as simple as it seems. We sleep so that our body can rest, we think at first. However, science has not been able to prove concretely that sleep is necessary for physical recuperation of the body. Experiments performed on rats have proven that when deprived of sleep, these animals die.

But human nature is not as simple as that of rats. Everyone knows people who barely sleep. The most extreme case, published in some scientific magazines, is that of a man who claims not to have slept since contracting a serious illness. In a similar vein, some individuals with a highly developed spirituality are able to remain conscious all night. We're not referring to a student during exam time drinking coffee or taking stimulants to stay awake more than twenty-four hours straight. We're talking about people who can achieve advanced levels of relaxation through deep meditation.

It is known that anxiety and lack of concentration increase considerably after a night or two without sleep. One theory related to sleep affirms that we sleep to conserve energy. However, another suggests that we rest to conserve our food stores, since when we lose consciousness, we repress the hunger mechanism.

When we dream, we enter a marvelous world that escapes the laws of spatial and temporal logic.

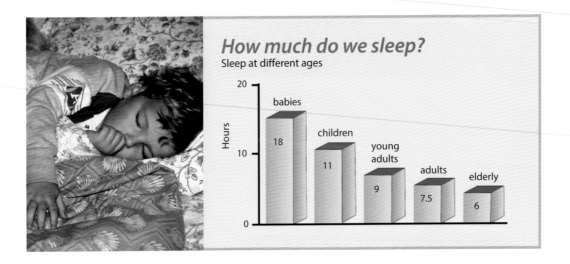

How much do we sleep?
Sleep at different ages

Hours

- babies 18
- children 11
- young adults 9
- adults 7.5
- elderly 6

In the course of his life, a person has, on average, 300,000 dreams. As we age, both the time we spend sleeping and the time we spend dreaming decrease gradually.

Newborns sleep almost all day, alternating hours of sleep with short spells of wakefulness. By one year of age, they sleep fewer sessions but for longer in total: they have cycles of 90 minutes of sleep followed by another 90 minutes of waking time. Gradually, the child will sleep more at night and less during the day. By 9 years of age, most need between 9 and 12 hours of sleep a day.

The average for an adult is between 7 and 8.5 hours. But after age 70, we return to the sleep phases of childhood and sleep fewer hours continuously.

There are arguments that even claim we have slept since ancient times in order to appear a less tasty snack for nocturnal predators (when we sleep, our body looks like a corpse).

There are theories to suit everyone, but we shouldn't forget the fundamental: for almost all of us, sleeping is a relaxing and pleasant experience that lasts between six and eight hours each night, an experience that is utterly necessary to "recharge the batteries" of our bodies.

It's no coincidence that we choose nighttime to sleep. In the darkness our vision is reduced, the world becomes strange, and as a result, our imagination runs wild. Our minds remain occupied with images (that is, dreams). At night, our eyes don't work, but we have a need to create images. If for some reason we are deprived of sleep, the following nights our dream production increases, since we spend more time in the REM phase (the period of sleep when oneiric thoughts are most active). Therefore it seems evident that we need dreams to live.

Some ancient civilizations believed that dreaming served, more than anything, to be able to dream. They were convinced that oneiric activity wasn't the result of sleeping, but rather the reason for it.

Cold-blooded animals never dream; the cold temperatures at night cause them to hibernate and all their vital functions, including the brain, slow down. Only when the sun comes out or the temperature rises to an acceptable level do they recuperate all vital functions. The only cold-blooded animal that has shown signs of dreaming is the chameleon.

On the other hand, we know all warm-blooded animals dream, since REM-phase activity has been detected in all of them. Birds dream only about 0.5% of the time they spend asleep, while humans dream up to 20% of the time. There are exceptional cases, such as that of the Australian platypus, that never dream.

Some scientists, however, don't share the theories of our ancestors when it comes to the reason behind our dreams.

There is a scientific school of thought that asserts that oneiric thoughts are simply a neurophysiological activity that comes with sleep. According to this theory, when we sleep we generate spontaneous signals that stimulate the sensory channels in the mind. The brain transforms these signals into visual images and induces the dreamer to believe that he is living real experiences.

Up to that point, perfect. But, why do dreams have such an interesting narrative? Why do they so often express metaphoric language? Why do they narrate stories that directly affect us? There is no concrete or scientific answer to these questions.

Other theories suggest that dreams serve to eliminate unnecessary facts from memory, since we can't store everything that happens every day. According to this thesis, at night we erase the "archives" we don't need, just like a computer. The sleeping mind tests the process of erasing in the form of dreams, which would

Do animals dream?
Percentages of REM sleep

| 0 | 0,5 % |
| reptiles | birds |

| 17 %   6,6 % | 55 %   15 % |
| rodents | ruminants |

| 50 %   20 % | 50 %   20 % |
| carnivores | humans |

newborn   adult

explain why they're so difficult to remember. There are obvious limitations to this theory if you keep in mind that, occasionally, oneiric thoughts work creatively (they go beyond the information that we give them). These don't have much to do with the merely "hygienic" function that the aforementioned scientific community claims. Often, dreams don't eliminate the useless leftovers of daily experiences. Quite the opposite: they give them a surprising new shape, so when we wake up, we can reflect more deeply on their meaning.

The phases of sleep

Even though we don't realize it, when we sleep at night we pass through four different phases of sleep. Each phase is distinguished by the deepness of sleep. That is, when we are in phase 1, it is a fairly light sleep; during phase 4, we reach maximum intensity.

When we go to sleep, we enter a period in which we gradually pull away from the exterior world. Little by little, our sleep

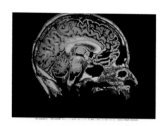

Certain areas of the brain are associated with different functions and human skills, translating external sensory stimuli into a well-organized picture of the world. In dreams, those same stimuli produce different reactions. If a sleeping person hears a sound or touches something repulsive, those stimuli will probably be integrated into their dream before they wake up.

deepens until finally (phase 4) our breathing slows and becomes regular, our cardiac rhythm slows down, and our body temperature decreases. Therefore the body's metabolism also reduces its activity.

More or less an hour after falling asleep, your body has already gone through the four phases. At this point you begin to go back through the levels until you return to phase 1. This brings along an increase in respiratory and cardiac rhythm. Parallel to this, brain waves once again start to register an activity close to that of consciousness. You are therefore in a moment of transition, demonstrated by the fact that at this point the body tends to change position.

All signs indicate that any noise might wake us. But that's not the case: since your muscle tone has been reduced, this is actually the moment when it's most difficult to regain consciousness. At the same time, your eyes begin to move behind your eyelids (up and down and side to side). This ocular phenomenon, which anyone can observe easily, is known as the REM phases, which stands for "rapid eye movement."

The REM phase

The REM phase is particularly important for those interested in dreams. All studies indicate that during this brief spell (from five to ten minutes) we typically experience the most intense oneiric activity. Some of these studies, done in a sleep laboratory, have observed that eight out of ten individuals relate very vivid dreams when woken up right at the end of the REM phase. These periods alternate at night with what we could call non-REM phases, that is, periods when no ocular movement is registered.

How many times do we reach a REM stage at night? It is estimated that each cycle is repeated four to seven times. As the hours pass, each phase gets longer. This way, the final REM stage might last twenty to forty minutes. On average, an adult enjoys an hour and a half of REM sleep each night, although for older individuals it may be less than an hour and a quarter. Babies, on the other hand, remain in the REM phase for 60 percent of the time they spend asleep.

In any case, let's make this clear: not all dreams are produced during this period. It has also been demonstrated that humans

The oneiric images produced in the most intense phase (REM) are more difficult to remember. One method to remember them consists of waking up just after each REM phase.

generate images in other stages. However, these are dreams of a different quality, since during the non-REM phases, our oneiric activity tends to generate only undefined thoughts, vague sensations, etc. Nothing close to the emotional content that characterizes dreams produced in the REM phase.

As we've commented already, those who wish to read their dreams have to first do the work of remembering them. If we want this work to be 100 percent effective, we can use a method that, although uncomfortable, almost never fails: wake up just after every REM phase. If you want to try this method, set your alarm (without music or radio) to go off four, five, six, or seven and a half hours after falling asleep. You can be sure that if you wake up just after one of the REM phases you go through each night, you will enjoy vivid memories.

This is the process used in sleep laboratories, where oneiric activity is studied through encephalographic registry of electrical brain activity.

The people in the study—who are volunteers—sleep connected to machines that register their physiological reactions (brain waves, cardiac rhythm, blood pressure, muscle activity, eye movement, etc).

At certain points during the night, these reactions indicate that, if you wake them, they will be able to tell you what they dreamed.

This is because the phase that produces the most intense dreams (REM) is characterized by a physical reaction easily observed: the rapid movement of the eyes of the dreamer.

With this method, sleep laboratories can collect proof of precisely when subjects are dreaming. And given that oneiric images are difficult to remember, the lab techniques have been a great advance in dream research. Some experts assert that thanks to the scientific advances of the second half of the twentieth century, we have learned more about sleep processes in the last fifty years than in all the history of humanity.

Hypnagogic images: between waking and sleep

As we've seen, throughout the night our sleep is divided into four distinct phases. But what happens just before we sink into the first phase? Are we still awake? Not exactly. In the moments when our mind decides between wakefulness and sleep, we begin to lose contact with the world around us, without the characteristic physiological changes of sleep.

This intermediate point has been called the "hypnagogic state" by psychologists. This is a period when, despite the fact that we're not asleep, our brains generate images that can sometimes be very

What do we dream?
A wide study done in France on the subject of dreams produced these results:

-Relationships with partners (18%)
-Home, especially that of our childhood (15%)
-Aggressors, thieves, being chased, etc. (10%)
-Missing the train; embarrassing baggage (8%)
-Water, wells, tunnels; traffic accidents (6%)
-Forgotten children or babies (5%)
-Snakes, fires, stairs (5%)
-Negative animals: spiders, cockroaches, rats, etc. (4%)
-Clothing or lack of clothing; nakedness (3%)
-Losing teeth or other alarming situations (2%)

Hypnagogic images of great visual beauty evaporate like bubbles when we wake up and are barely remembered.

Salvador Dali, painter of dreams.

beautiful. In some ways, these images rival those found in our dreams.

However, the hypnagogic state cannot be considered a truly oneiric state. Among other reasons, the scenes produced in this phase are unrelated to the episodes with a more or less coherent plot that characterize dreams.

In the hypnagogic state we produce unrelated images that hardly connect to each other and that, unlike dreams, are not linked to our daily experiences. This phenomenon occurs not only before sleeping but also in the moments before waking up, when we are not yet conscious enough to be aware of them.

Sometimes, before falling asleep we also experience a curious sensation of floating or flying, or we may see very sharp scenes, with a clarity comparable to that of real visual experiences. These types of images, like dreams, evaporate like bubbles when we wake up and we barely remember them, which is a shame because their

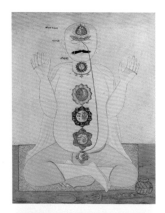

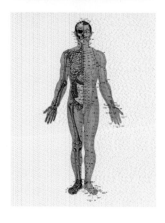

The seven "chakras," or centers of subtle energy in the ayurvedic hindu medicine (1). The nadis according to Tibetan tradition (2). The meridians of traditional Chinese medicine (3).

beauty slips from our minds. In any case, unlike oneiric thoughts, the hypnagogic state is little use for understanding the messages our subconscious wants to send us, and we should value it more for its beauty than its transcendental content.

To remember them you must not lose consciousness during the apparition. That is, you must observe the process of the hypnagogic state without falling asleep. It seems simple but it is not, because you must submerge yourself in sleep while the mind remains aware of the events happening in its interior. With a little luck, we can see some of the marvelous "paintings" of our private museum.

The surrealist artists of the 20s and 30s knew all about this. This is how Salvador Dali, fervent lover of hypnagogic scenes, turned to what is known as "the monk's sleep." He went to bed with a large iron key in his hand. With the first dream, the key would fall to the floor and he would wake up suddenly. In his mind he recorded the hypnagogic images he would later transfer to the canvas in his masterful style.

If you have difficulty retaining the hypnagogic state, try centering your attention on a concrete point. For example the "third eye" of the yogis (that is, between your eyes), in the area of the heart, or in the top of the head. These three positions are, according to the philosophy of yoga, the centers of subtle rather than physical energy in the human body. You need a place to direct the mind. Another trick to hold attention without effort is to think abstractly about the name of the object you wish to see. This doesn't mean you have to "create" the images; you just have to induce its appearance during the hypnagogic state. Entering through meditation is also very useful and beneficial.

Sometimes, the hypnagogic scenes are not as pleasant as we would like, but we must confront them in order to strengthen our ability for self-control. If they persist, try following the previous advice. Think abstractly about the name of what you want to see, resisting the temptation to construct it in a certain way from the conscious mind.

The main advantage of the hypnagogic state is that it brings us progressively closer to our deep Self . . . and all that helps to understand and better benefit from dreams.

3. Different types of dreams

"The interpretation of dreams is the real path to knowing the soul."

SIGMUND FREUD

Clear and personalized messages

Before jumping in to discover the hidden messages that filter into our dreams and appear in the dictionary in the second part, it's best to keep in mind that not all oneiric thoughts can be analyzed with the same pattern. Therefore, psychologists and analysts distinguish between three classes of dreams:

Readjustment dreams
Satisfaction dreams
Premonitory dreams

In the interpretation of dreams, we work from the base knowledge that the same subject can have very different meanings depending on the circumstances and personal situation of the dreamer. Because of this, this dictionary offers abundant explanations (psychological and esoteric) from very distinct viewpoints, although the boundary is often blurred. This is meant to show the melting pot of possibilities for discovery and prediction if one atunes their sensitivity and perceptiveness in each interpretation.

But back to this chapter, where we have compiled a series of recurring themes as examples, and touch on erotic dreams, another way in which the subconscious offers information to be analyzed.

The same subject can have very different meanings depending on the circumstances and personal situation of the dreamer.

Although these belong in the group of satisfaction dreams, their details warrant a separate explanation.

Readjustment dreams

In this type of dream, the oneiric images are provoked by merely physical causes. Readjustment dreams can be of internal origins—that is, generated by the body due to factors such as indigestion or a headache—or of external origin—heat, noises, the feel of sheets on the body, etc. A typical example of a readjustment dream with external origin would be that of a person who, due to the weight of the blankets, dreams of carrying a heavy load.

Where do these types of images come from? It's simple: when we close our eyes, we have the sensation of being isolated from the world because our consciousness of the exterior world is so linked to visual perception. However, the other senses remain in contact with the world. Therefore, even though when we sleep we appear to lose consciousness, this information continues to be collected in the brain (this is why loud noises wake us up). This is why we prefer darkness and quiet to sleep.

However, we can't always control our surroundings. When situations arise out of our control (the sound of a siren, a change in temperature, etc.), these sensory impressions become integrated in our dreams and can take surprising forms.

Premonitory dreams

Abraham Lincoln, president of the United States, dreamt of his own death by assassination.

These oneiric episodes dream of something that will become reality in the future. In the majority of cases, these are negative dreams that tend to warn of a coming danger. As a paradigmatic example of premonition, take that of Abraham Lincoln, president of the United States, in 1865. A few days before being assassinated, Lincoln saw his own death in one of his dreams. Even though this mythical case of the US president indicates the opposite, let us be clear that dreaming of a death does not necessarily imply that a tragic event is imminent.

In these dreams, death can mean many different things; for example, some psychologists interpret it as marking the end of a life cycle. This is why we insist on the importance of personalizing the dream interpretation.

Be that as it may, premonitions tend to be hidden in a symbolism that is difficult to decode, since it does not refer to past experiences. They are messages that try to warn us of dangers that face us on the physical or emotional plane. For this reason, eastern cultures have always valued them highly, as we will see later on.

Satisfaction dreams

Satisfaction dreams constitute the basis for the main theories of oneiric interpretation. They deal with those images in which we fulfill the desires that we cannot satisfy while awake. Therefore, this huge category includes everything from erotic dreams to the worst nightmares. In some cases, a certain satisfaction dream may repeat for years. This means that the person's subconscious is warning them of the importance of something they may be trying to ignore. The part of this book dedicated to interpretation refers to this type of dreams.

Sexual dreams

There are dreams that have the capacity to excite us, intrigue us, make us tremble, embarrass us . . . These are the ones that we never, or almost never, share with others. These are erotic dreams that, generally speaking, have nothing to do with the social or sexual conduct of our waking lives.

Sexual dreams are not necessarily the result of accumulated sexual tension that needs to be released, but rather they usually refer to inner conflicts and hidden needs, or a desire to enjoy sex more freely.

"Dreams manifest the desires that our consciousness does not express."

Sigmund Freud

Erotic dreams join other sensations that, in waking life, we probably wouldn't relate immediately with sex. Therefore, these dreams, which could be violent, passionate, perverse, romantic, etc., tend to refer to inner conflicts and hidden emotional needs. Therefore they belong to the classification of satisfaction dreams.

On some occasions, they reveal a fear of intimacy or warn against certain relationships. In others, they illustrate situations and behaviors that we cannot normally exhibit. The dream represents everything through symbols or a strong sexual connotation. Its themes and languages, often dark, can confuse us or make us doubt because each individual has their personal symbols (just like with other types of dreams). It's interpretation, therefore, should be performed according to the situation of the individual.

Dreams are escape routes for sexual impulses that social conventions repress; in erotic dreams everything seems permissible, so they are the best way to bring our most secret emotional desires to light. For Sigmund Freud, dreams manifested the desires that our consciousness does not express, and that was all.

Dreams contain valuable information about ourselves. But their meaning is often far from what it seems.

Therefore, it's important to pay attention to them because they contain valuable information about ourselves. However, their meaning is often far from what it seems. They may just as well symbolize tension in our daily lives as the desire to have a good time.

Erotic dreams and fantasies

Erotic dreams are also related to a person's physical and emotional development. During puberty, for example, these kinds of dreams are very common. Others that are more unpleasant are related to episodes of abuse or sexual assault. In some form or another, almost everyone has had some type of erotic dreams because at the end of the day, they are natural occurrences that are part of our lives.

They deserve our time and attention. For example, it's important to discover when they refer to sexual issues and when they refer to other aspects, because erotic dreams often bring us valuable clues about intimacy with a partner. If something is not right in the relationship, they probably indicate the path to resolution. There should not be any difference between the erotic dreams of men and women, just between different people. However, various

While men dream of anonymous kinky women succumbing to their fantasies, women usually dream of erotic encounters with men they know.

studies done in the United States have demonstrated the opposite. While women usually have erotic dreams with someone they know and go all the way from flirting to coitus, men dream of anonymous kinky women that succumb to their fantasies. Obviously this is not always the case, but it is undeniable that a personal relationship is highly valued in the feminine psyche. The masculine, on the other hand, opts for pleasure and domination.

The education one has received, the latent sexism of the collective subconscious, and that of the media are all factors that dreams cannot bypass. These dreams can provoke even decisive, strong women to feel more vulnerable during dreams. Fortunately, as our customs are changing, the dissimilarities between masculine and feminine erotic dreams are gradually shrinking.

Finally, erotic dreams, like all dreams, can hide fears, anxieties, and needs that you repress due to inhibitive situations or a lack of time to face the problem. With the interpretation of erotic dreams, we can find many clues to understand our emotions better.

Dreams of duality: masculine-feminine

Dreams of duality are those that refer to our double identity: masculine and feminine. These dreams translate the union of our two elements: animus and anima, two notions defined by Jung that appear constantly in dreams. The majority of these oneiric episodes are characterized by the denial or rejection of one of the two parts of our being—and what each one represents—creating a tension or internal conflict that can even show through in our personality. In order to help us regain balance, the dream tries to make us understand how and why we've forgotten the other side of ourselves.

In this way, when a man dreams that he is a woman, the message is not necessarily about a conflict of identity or sexuality; more likely it refers to a lack of attention to the more sensitive, intuitive side of his personality. Equally, when a woman sees herself as a man in her dreams, her subconscious may be appealing to her more energetic and rational side.

Dreams in which the left (feminine) or right (masculine) side of our bodies are hurt or immobilized (for example, an arm or leg) warn us that we are repressing or denying our masculine or feminine development. It is difficult for us to accept our duality and we reject this aspect that we don't know how to express.

Dreams of houses

The great oneirologist of ancient times, Artemidorus of Ephesus (second century BC) said: "The home is us"; and the most recent research on oneiric content confirms it. Buildings in our dreams are a reflection of our personality. Therefore you must pay attention to all the details that appear, which give you reliable hints about your desires, fears, worries . . . Each place and element of the house refers to a personal aspect of the self; the kitchen represents our spiritual or intellectual appetite; the oven is the alchemic place of transformation; the basement represents the accumulation of riches; the bedroom, conjugal difficulties, etc.

However, dreams in which different rooms appear can also refer to different areas of real life. If, for example, you find yourself cooking in a kitchen, it may be a reference to a plan that you are "cooking up" in real life. If you find yourself locked in a dark basement, perhaps you feel guilty about something and think you deserve a punishment. Lying in a bed or on a sofa can be a sign that you need a break from your exhausting daily routine.

When the doors of the dream house are shut tight or covered with brick, or there are signs on doors to the rooms prohibiting entry, you should ask yourself what is blocking your evolution in real life. It may be part of your own personality or some basic inhibition.

The buildings in our dreams are a reflection of our personality. "The Splash" (David Hockney, 1966).

47

A pleasant, organized room reflects mental order and spiritual serenity. If it doesn't have windows, it is a sign of isolation, fear, and insecurity. "La habitacion" ("The Room") (Van Gogh, 1889).

Nightmares and anxious dreams

Many people dream that they discover new rooms in houses that they know well. In general, this points to unknown aspects of their personality that are about to come out; but it can also indicate that they are ready for a new intellectual challenge.

The feelings that emerge when we find ourselves inside an oneiric building are very significant. If you feel brave and curious while exploring every nook and cranny of the house, it means that you are not afraid of what you may discover about yourself, you act assuredly, and face your problems with confidence. On the other hand, if you feel afraid it is a sign of inhibition and insecurity.

Nightmares are terrifying dreams that usually stay in our minds when we wake up. They usually occur during the REM phase and, on occasion, are so distressing that they wake you up and torment you for a few minutes. The fear is often accompanied by cold sweats, dry mouth, heart palpitations . . . and the sensation of having lived a terrible moment.

Sometimes, traumatic events that happen to us in waking life (an accident, a robbery, a sexual assault) revisit us in dreams. Our mind needs to free the tension caused by the event and it does it while our consciousness rests.

These dreams typically disappear with time. If they persist, it may be a major trauma that requires professional help or, at least, and understanding friend to listen; talking about it is the first step to overcoming it.

Many cultures share the belief that nightmares are nothing more than malignant spirits that attack their victims in their sleep with terrifying thoughts. Some research on oneiric content concludes that these scary dreams are more common in childhood, and if they persist into adulthood it usually indicates a deeply rooted problem.

Research in sleep laboratories has demonstrated that often nightmares are triggered by a sudden noise, which detonates a distressing oneiric image. Therefore, for people who suffer from frequent nightmares, it is advisable to wear earplugs.

Worry dreams

Dreams in which we feel worried about something are more frequent than nightmares, and sometimes the pressure we feel to resolve a problem in the dream wakes us up. Once awake, the oneiric worry may seem trivial compared to our real problems, however we should not ignore the importance of these dreams; their analysis will reveal areas of our lives that require attention or make us insecure.

Worry dreams reflect subconscious doubts and fears about events in our lives that have been saved in our minds but not our conscious memory. They deal with minor preoccupations that we haven't consciously given attention to, but our subconscious has recognized.

According to Freud, dreams that generate anxiety or worry are the result of trying to repress an emotion or desire, usually sexual. Freud also highlighted the importance of finding the source of that worry in waking life, since these worries left unattended can degenerate into worse traumas.

To analyze this type of dream you must pay attention to all the elements that appear in the episode, since it is symbolically giving you hints about what worries us.

Worry dreams reflect subconscious doubts and fears about events in our lives that have been saved in our minds but not our conscious memory.

Dreams about angels are usually messages of inner exploration. In some oneiric episodes they appear as spiritual guides and protectors that try to show us a path.

Dreams of inner exploration: forgotten babies and angels

The cartoons of "Little Nemo"(Winsor McCay, 1905) always ended with the images of Nemo falling out of bed. His incredible stories revolved around his fascinating dreams.

Dreams in which forgotten babies or angels appear are very common, and meaningful for our personal and spiritual evolution. But what is the meaning of this baby that screams to be held and fed? It represents, symbolically, the spiritual seed inside of us that has been left to languish without nourishment. This sacred seed, the divine Self, the "philosophical child," as the alchemists said. It has trusted us and we must help it grow.

Dreams about angels or spiritual entities tend to be messages of inner exploration. We see various examples collected in an "office of dreams."

"I am in utter darkness. I am surrounded by silence and emptiness. Suddenly, a shape appears, white and slender, pure, almost surreal. The features of the face are erased. A pure oval, the svelte body, without a definable sex. There is only the impression of extreme sweetness and deep harmony; but this character causes me such an impression of abandonment that it seems like a cry for help. I wrap it in my arms and want to save it at all costs."

This is a dream of protections, of contact with the invisible world. In this oneiric episode, the androgynous character is recognized as angelic. This fabulous vision is none other than the person's angel showing him his ailment, found in the darkness.

In other dreams, angels appear as spiritual guides or personal guardians:

"I had died on a golden carriage decorated with blue velvet; to my right, a feminine angel, all white, smiled at me . . . she held before me the reins of two white horses, while ahead of us, an unending path bathed in sunlight opened to us."

Travel dreams

One of the most pleasant and stimulating oneiric experiences is traveling to a far-off place and waking up with the sensation of having returned from a great vacation. Without a doubt, this often means a deep desire to travel that you have not been able to satisfy; but it can also hold other interesting readings.

On occasion, you remember precise details about places and settings you have never been to. This could be due to photographs, movies, or television reports that you've seen and that your subconscious has saved for some special reason.

These journeys coincide, sometimes, with moment in real life when we are about to begin something new (a change of job or location…). Just as the landscape and feelings of the dream can indicate our real emotions about this change, the circumstances of the trip are also revealing. If it is a bumpy trip in which it is difficult to get to your destination (because you lost the tickets or bags, or crashed the car…), the dream may be encouraging you to weigh the pros and cons of the situation, and warning you about obstacles ahead. Perhaps you are not mentally prepared for the change.

On the other hand, dreams about remote and exotic places are warning you that your lifestyle is claustrophobic and repressed, and that you need a change or to broaden your horizons.

The mode of transportation that you use to travel in the dream is very significant. If you travel in plane, for example, you should ask yourself if you have your feet firmly on the ground or, on the contrary, if you feel more comfortable "in the clouds." Escapism in real life tends to appear symbolically in travel dreams. Trains are symbols of new and exciting opportunities; missing the train or letting it leave is a clear symbol of a fear of change—and the insecurity that goes along with this. The station, or point of departure, is a symbolic place of transformation. The predicament of not having a ticket or money to buy one is related to some type of deficiency. However, if you manage to arrive at the destination despite it all, the dream is reflecting a certain amount of self satisfaction.

4. Creativity, psychedelia, and shamanism

"If a craftsman could dream every night, for twelve hours, that he is a king, he would be almost as happy as the king that dreams every night, for twelve hours, that his is an craftsman."

PASCAL

Surrealism and dreams

Andre Breton published *Manifeste du surréalisme* (*The Surrealist Manifesto*) in 1924. It was a revolutionary document that proposed a new way of understanding the world and interpreting reality: life, art, and the creative process could focus a different way.

For Breton, the systems of power, the moral prejudices, and the social norms were barriers for the individual. Similarly, he rejected the censorship one imposed on oneself in daily behavior and, above all, in artistic activity.

The fundamental support for Breton's thesis were Freud's studies on psychoanalysis and the interpretation of dreams, which was published shortly before Breton's manifesto. Freud's studies come from the historical context of the controversial transition from the nineteenth to the twentieth century. Alongside his studies, the exploration of the subconscious Self served as a tool and inspiration for artistic movements such as Dadaism or Surrealism, so revolutionary

Surrealism was a revolution. The world of the oneiric, the subconscious, the paranoid ... become a new way of seeing and exploring life. Its influence is still seen today.

Surrealism was considered one of the most important advances in the oneiric universe. Cover of the album Elegy, by Nice. (Hipgnosis, 1971).

at the time. The majority emerged after living the horror of the First World War, at the beginning of the twentieth century.

Within the intellectual elite of Europe, there was in those days an air of discontent and deception caused by the results of materialism and excessive faith in science and reason. Humanity was decaying. Therefore, the creative minds soon wanted to distance themselves from the established mechanisms and looked for a breath of fresh air in places far from rational discourse. In order to avoid disaster, they had to seek new and pure sources.

Curiously, these were found within the individual himself, in the deepest part of his personality, and could be the key to change. These creators thus discovered the irrational side of existence: the subconscious.

"I believe in the future harmonization of these two states, apparently contradictory, that are dream and reality, into a type of absolute reality, a superreality, or subreality, if it can be called that. This is the conquest that I seek, with the certainty of never attaining it, but too forgetful of the prospect of death to deny myself the anticipation of the pleasures of such a possession."

ANDRE BRETON, *MANIFESTE DU SURRÉALISME*
(THE SURREALIST MANIFESTO)

To reach the subconscious, the surrealists followed in the steps of the Dadaists, performing a series of practices that submitted the human mind to altered states of consciousness. However, these mechanisms did not always bring the participants to a true trance state. Sometimes it only increased their aggressiveness, turning them into violent beings. On the other hand, dreams turned out to be a more innocuous resource available to all. Better yet, they did not cause any danger or side effect. Exploration was served.

Psychedelia

Judging by the transcendence that Surrealism had in art, politics, and twentieth-century life, it is considered one of the most important and emblematic advances in the universe of dreams. In any case, that experience was not so new. In primitive cultures, other civilizations, and creative talents there is a wealth of evidence and artistic samples that express some form of the so-called "peak experiences," related to what are known as "other realities" which we will see further on.

Let's pause for a moment one afternoon in April of 1943 in the laboratories of the pharmaceutical company Sandoz, in Basel, Switzerland. The researcher Albert Hoffman (who had already discovered some interesting applications of ergot) was working with a series of derivatives of lysergic acid. By chance, his skin absorbed a miniscule quantity of a diethylamide from the series of failed tests (marked 25°), producing a slight hallucinogenic effect. This was the first LSD "trip" in history. After a series of tests and investigations, he officially published the results in 1947 (Stoll, University of Zurich), and up until the seventies access to this important discovery was limited to researchers and institutions.

Lysergic acid

LSD became popular in the West when it came to the US: in part thanks to the birth of pacifist and countercultural movements, but mostly from the phenomenon of mass communication among the majority of people in developed societies.

Parallel to LSD appeared the debate about the use and possible legalization of certain psychoactive substances that still is ongoing today. For example, it considers the legalization of tobacco and prohibition of cannabis incomprehensible, fruit of international agreements promoted and directed by US politicians. The appearance of new psychoactive substances, as well as traditional ones, and the

Pop art from the late seventies was clearly influenced by the use of LSD and other hallucinogens, as we can see from the album art of that time. From left to right: "Blowing in the Mind" (1967), "Middle Earth Club" (1968), and "5th Dimension Club" (1967).

diverse effects they produce, have not helped the government—fearful and conservative to an extreme in this territory—to establish definitive conclusions.

The effects of lysergic acid, or LSD, go beyond those of a traditional hallucinogen and are difficult to describe, although those who have "tripped" tend to describe a heightened sensitivity and altered sensory perceptions. Others compare it to mystic experiences of authentic "communion."

LSD and other hallucinogens also contribute to the reconsidering of the concept of reality as we know it. The range of hallucinations is broad and can oscillate from the highest expression of beauty to the deepest reaches of hell, but they contain sensations and perceptions that we can compare to the world of dreams. It has been written that: "The world of the twentieth century has known two phenomenons, one terrible and one hopeful: the atomic bomb and LSD."

Shamans

The anthropologist Carlos Castaneda studied shamanism with notable works in the field. A series of books published from

Primitive cultures captured in art the oneiric images and "peak" experiences from the use of peyote cactus (Lophophora williamsii). Shamans and many artists often used peyote as a means of inspiration and to experience "astral journeys." Painting from the traditional huichol culture.

Castaneda considered dreams to be an open door to the unknown, which once revealed could be marvelous or terrible. "Bond of Union" (M.C. Escher, 1956).

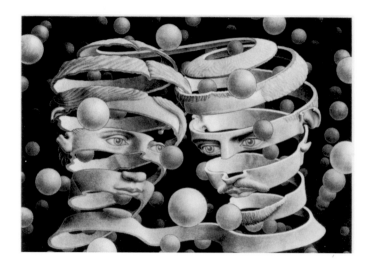

the seventies up until his death was the fruit of his experience. Castaneda spent a good portion of his life compiling the teachings of his master, a Mexican yaqui sorcerer named don Juan Matus. Castaneda lived with him for a long time and, thanks to the lessons he received, developed the necessary passion and practice to become a *nagual*, or wizard, himself.

For Castaneda, the work of interpreting dreams could not be approached from a rational point of view. He considered dreams to be an open door to the unknown parts of ourselves, which once revealed could be marvelous or terrible. It is also difficult in this case to describe the career of this anthropologist from an empirical standpoint, because his studies never appealed to reason. But it is worthwhile to see the value in his work, full of experiences and lessons of unquantifiable interest.

Las enseñanzas de don Juan (*The Teachings of don Juan*), *Una realidad aparte* (*A Separate Reality*), or *El arte de ensoñar* (*The Art of Dreaming*) are books based on the hours that Castaneda spent as apprentice to don Juan. They are written in the form of Socratic dialogue and slowly unravel the hidden worlds of the oneiric universe. Castaneda stresses the need to ingest mushrooms and hallucinogenic plants. Something similar to what happened with the practices of the Surrealists, in which the human mind was subjected to altered states of consciousness to reach what some call the subconscious. In this aspect, peyote or *toloache* make it easier to access the mental condition in which one attains a different perception of reality. However, later on, after the apprenticeship, Castaneda insisted he had been wrong.

He determined that the use of hallucinogens was only one way to reach the teachings of his master. The other, was dreams.

Semi-consciousness

During semi-consciousness, we are conscious that we are dreaming and able to voluntarily intervene in the events of the oneiric scene. "Philippino Food," comic by Ed Badajos (1971).

Once he established dreams as a path to exploration, he divided them in two stages: the ordinary and that of semi-consciousness. The first refers to common oneiric activity in any person, any night. Semi-consciousness, on the other hand, is comparable to a lucid dream, when the dreamer is conscious that he is dreaming and able to voluntarily intervene in the events of the oneiric scene. Castaneda ended up becoming a nagual thanks to the step he took by practicing semi-consciousness.

Through sophisticated techniques, the dreamer has total jurisdiction over his semi-conscious state. As you gain more control, you get further from the conscious world and reach deeper states. According to Castaneda, you must pass through various gates before you can totally dominate the semi-conscious state. Once passed, these become vehicles to take you to other realities. According to a nagual whose lineages is that of don Juan, the conception of the universe is that it is made up of layers, like an onion. They are infinite in number, and each one contains a different reality.

Our rational and conscious perception is only able to discern one layer, that is to say, it is stuck with only one way of understanding the world. However, it is possible to access the other layers if you can change or move your pivot point (that which remains fixed within the individual and leads him to a determined system of perceiving reality).

Don Juan asserted that we are born with a fixed pivot point and that all our efforts unite, through the process of education and socialization (from both our educators and ourselves), so that everything we perceive fits in the same system.

In the end, we train ourselves so well that we end up trusting more in the system than in that which can truly capture our senses.

Due to the shroud of mystery that surrounds shamanism, the work of Castaneda is often complex and difficult to understand, above all because he does not explain it with scientific rigor, as we said. The practices of Don Juan were based in the exact opposite: unlearn what's been learned rationally and thusly enter in different worlds. It is a fish that bites its tail. Despite this, it does not diminish how fascinating Castaneda's tales are. Quite the opposite, his works continue to be very attractive.

In the end, the most important thing is that his experiences with traveling to worlds far from conscious reality are added to the numerous accounts throughout history about the search for other levels of perception.

Creativity

After that quick look into the world of dreams and other reality, let's get back to its relationship with creativity. Dreams possess all the information that our intellectual, emotional, kinetic, instinctive, and sexual processes contain. Therefore they are considered an authentic source of creativity, leading some to compare the subconscious with the mythical role of the muses. Thanks to it, everyone possess their own campus of thoughts.

Does someone with an intense mental and intellectual activity while awake increase the frequency and intensity of their oneiric

Dreams have been a source of inspiration and creativity for many artists, musicians, writers…
Above: "Wish you were here," the title of this image and the song dedicated to Syd Barrett in a Pink Floyd album. Hipgnosis (1975).

activity? Yes, and there is evidence to prove it (and the opposite happens just the same).

Therefore, the less you separate dreams from reality, the more marvelous the creative results and more passionate the creative process . . . Something that Breton definitely understood when he wrote the Surrealist manifesto mentioned before.

Famous dreams

Throughout history, we find numberless dreams that have become famous, whether because of the social status of the dreamers at the time, or because the dreams themselves made the dreamers famous thanks to the wisdom or prophecy of their message. That is how so many have ended up impacting, in their own way, the course and growth of humanity.

In the Bible, many stories deal with oneiric content. On one side are the dreams that God uses to communicate his will. The chosen communicated with Him, obtaining predictions and revelations that would impact the future. On the other side, it gives evidence of the priceless information dreams can contain. In this sense, one of the most well-known biblical dreams is that of the Egyptian pharaoh who saw a vision of seven beautiful, impressive cows being devoured by seven thin, smelly ones. Next he saw seven lush, green wheat heads absorbed by seven limp, weak ones. Joseph, son of Israel, interpreted these symbols as seven years of great abundance for Egypt, followed by seven more of scarcity and famine. As a consequence, they could predict the unfavorable times and avoid the disaster that would have befallen them otherwise.

The Greek philosopher Plato (fifth century BC) already held the modern opinion that dreams show our true nature. Believing in dreams and their potential was a trait of cultured and intelligent Greeks.

Like the Bible, Greek myths contain many such dreams. The hero Ulysses, for example, was able to stay one step ahead of the real events because in his sleep he received wisdom from the goddess Athena.

In fact, believing in dreams and their potential was a mark of cultured and intelligent Greeks. The kings of Ancient Greece usually had their own oneiric translators and interpreters.

And dreams have played a big role in the historical development of humanity, radically changing the lives of many. In the following pages we offer some of the most emblematic cases, which have been studied as proof of the incredible power of the hidden and mysterious universe.

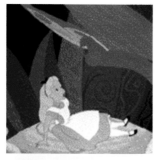

Some authors converted their oneiric episodes into inspiration and plots for their works. This was the case of the writer Lewis Carroll, who reflected part of his oneiric material in Alice's Adventures in Wonderland; or that of the director Luis Buñuel, whose work was characterized by Surrealist elements, such as this famous sequence from the film Un chien andalou (1928).

Germany, 1890. The illustrious scientist Friedrich August Kekulé is preparing to give a conference to equally distinguished members of the German Chemistry Society. Kekulé is the guest of honor, since who could forget that twenty-five years before he discovered the molecular structure of benzene, a discovery which revolutionized modern chemistry.

Kekulé began to speak. He wants to explain, finally, how he achieved this feat. The attendees listen attentively; everyone is paying attention to the man on stage. And suddenly, a surprise. Kekulé, the great scientist, asserts that his famous theory was conceived . . . in dreams!: "I was writing, but I realized that my mind was elsewhere. I returned to my chair by the fire and fell half asleep. The atoms began to dance about before my eyes (. . .) They formed long chains of atoms, all in movement, rolling and twisting like snakes. And suddenly, what was that? A snake biting its own tail. As if struck by lightning, I awoke; I spent the rest of the night working." Of course that work culminated in great success.

This example shows that creativity, like dreams, is deeply seated in the subconscious. Many scientists and artists have realized the phenomenon, but you don't have to be a genius to realize that sometimes, when one is stuck on a problem, the solution finally appears out of nowhere some time after. Everything indicates that the subconscious continues working while the conscious mind rests.

The most curious part is that we never know what the result will be of this creativity that manifests in dreams. When writers are asked why their characters behave in such a way, they often respond with something along the lines of: "Because they decided to." That is to say, they talk about their creations as if they had acquired a life of their own that the writer could barely control.

In other occasions the dreams themselves have been converted into the inspiration and theme of the work, such as with *Alice's Adventures in Wonderland* by Lewis Carroll, "Ojos de perro azul" or "Me alquilo para soñar" ("Eyes of a Blue Dog" or "I Sell My Dreams") by Gabriel Garcia Marquez, or *Un chien andalou* by Luis Buñuel, among many.

Some musicians have also received oneiric inspiration. The case of Tartini, an Italian composer from the eighteenth century, is a paradigmatic example. Tartini claimed that the devil had appeared

Still from one of the movie versions of "The Strange Case of Dr. Jekyll and Mr. Hyde" by Robert Louis Stevenson.

in his dreams and played a sonata on his violin that, according to Tartini, he could have never composed. When he woke up, he desperately tried to remember the melody from his dream. It was in vain. However, he did end up writing a work in which the devil was a protagonist. Tartini never doubted that it was the best piece he'd ever created. The phenomenon of musical inspiration (Mozart, for example, said he "heard" his famous works first) has been subject to periodic study, more or less related to dreams.

Robert Louis Stevenson, author of the famous novel *The Strange Case of Dr. Jekyll and Mr. Hyde*, said that his creative work was done by what he called the "small inhabitants" of his dreams.

In his own words, they are "close connections beyond the doubts of the dreamer. God bless them!, since they do half my work while I'm sound asleep (. . .) all of my published fiction is the product of some 'benevolent little elf,' of some invisible collaborator who works without any help, who I keep locked up in an attic while I get all the praise."

There is a common trait among many great creations that came as a fruit of dreams, and that is that they appear to be the result of intense intellectual effort done during waking hours. The important part, with everthing, is that the oneiric activity has gone above and beyond, producing solutions that seem unattainable.

Many great creations that came as a fruit of dreams are also the result of intense intellectual effort done during waking hours. The important part is that the oneiric activity has gone above and beyond just dreaming and produced solutions that seem unattainable.

In art, the theme of dreaming has also inspired numerous creations, some romantic such as this work by Brewtnall, "Sleeping Beauty."

One of the roads to independence in India came from Ghandi's dream.

Still from the movie The Great Dictator *(1940) in which Charlie Chaplin parodies Hitler.*

Is it possible to work consciously to make our dreams help us resolve problems creatively? Yes, but in order to do so you have to prevent your thoughts from obsessing on the subject in question. A focus based on curiosity, or on a playful point of view, gives a better result.

Mahatma Gandhi practiced the art of meditation, but he also tended to use his oneiric thoughts as a source of creative and spiritual inspiration. Thanks to his dreams, Gandhi was able to embody a non-violent response to the Rowlatt Acts of England, which cruelly stamped out all public unrest aspiring to the liberation of India. As is well known, one of the most important manifestations of Gandhi's pacifist doctrines was the mass strike as a weapon of civil disobedience.

Mahatma, after meditating for weeks, found the solution to his problems in a dream and that non-violent response to that act was one of the steps that finally led the country to independence.

His oneiric "muses" suggested that the people of India suspend all activity for twenty-four hours and spend the day fasting and praying. Gandhi put his dreams into practice, organizing a series of strikes that, in 1919, became vital in the fight for India's right to self determination. In this way, Mahatma's dreams contributed decisively to changing the destiny of a subcontinent.

Given the facts, the mythical Gandhi probably would have endorsed the words of Voltaire: "I have known lawyers who have argued in their sleep, mathematicians who have solved problems, and poets who have composed verses. I myself have done a few that are fairly good. In dreams, constructive ideas present themselves."

During the First World War, Hitler, at twenty-eight years of age, was just another corporal in the German army fighting the French. One night, sleeping in a trench, he dreamt that he was buried under an avalanche of earth and melted iron and that his mouth filled with filth. He could even feel the terrible pain of his wounds. Alarmed, he woke up and quickly left the trench. Just at that moment a bomb fell and all his brothers in arms died under a mountain of rubbish, hot metal, and blood. Hitler attributed this to "divine intervention." Unfortunately, this convinced him of his invulnerability, making him believe his future was full of greatness.

Alexander the Great granted a lot of importance to his dreams; he even had a private dream interpreter.

During the siege of the Phoenician city Tiro in 332 BC, Alexander the Great acheived his goal thanks to dreams. One night, a satyr dancing on a shield appeared to him. His private dream interpreter, Aristandro, recognized this images as an ingenious play on words: "satyros"—satyr in Greek—could refer to "sa Tyros," meaning "Tiro is yours." Aristandro therefore recommended that Alexander the Great continue his campaign. Tiro became one of his many conquests.

This example precedes the Freudian theory that the subconscious is a practical joker and can make rather capricious plays on words in dreams. The truth is the hidden codification that offers riddles and guesses, and is very useful in this sense: they can express repressed impulses and get around the censorship that the waking mind imposes.

Charles Dickens also had a strange prophetic dream in which a woman appeared, covered in a red shawl with her back to him. Suddenly, she turned toward him and told him she was Miss Napier. Although the images was clear and evident, it didn't seem to make sense. However, the next night, Charles Dickens gave a reading and at the end, some friends went to congratulate him and introduce him to someone who wanted to meet him . . . Miss Napier.

Constantine the Great (312–337) was the first Christian emperor and, thanks to dreams, he was a great influence on the development of the Church. During a stay in Germany, he had various oneiric visions in which Christ appeared on a cross bearing the inscription: "With this sign, you will conquer." Constantine deduced that he should use the cross as a symbol of protection against his enemies. From this dream, he ordered greater tolerance toward Christians and strengthened the conversation with Romans of his faith.

According to historical accounts, Dante Alighieri got inspiration for his masterpiece, *The Divine Comedy*, while he slept on the night of Good Friday. When he died in 1321, part of the manuscript of his great creation was lost. The sons of the Italian poet searched the house up and down looking for it, but finally gave up, thinking it was impossible. However, months later one of the sons, Jacoppo, dreamt of his father dressed in white and bathed in light. The oneiric specter was pointing to a corner of the house that hadn't been searched: the place where they found the lost manuscript of *The Divine Comedy.*

Elias Howe owes his greatest achievement—the sewing machine—to dreams. The inventor had been stuck for a long time on a prototype that he could not fix.

One night, he dreamed that the king of a wild tribe ordered him to make a similar machine, but when our protagonist answered that he couldn't, the tribe attacked him with spears. Just before the moment of his dream death, Howe noticed that each spear had a needle in the point. This was the key he needed to perfect his commercial sewing machine.

Much of the inspiration of the famous novelist Graham Greene came from his dreams. It seems that Greene's oneiric scenes usually contained prophetic messages and, according to his diary, he predicted the sinking of the Titanic when he was just five years old. There are nineteen other known cases of people who experienced premonitions related to the tragedy of 1912. For example, the London businessman J. Connon Middleton had a ticket reserved a month ahead of time for the transatlantic voyage. However, at the last moment he sold it because he dreamt two nights in a row that

Much of the inspiration of the novelist Graham Greene came from his dreams. Still from The Third Man, *a movie by Orson Welles based on the novel of Graham Greene.*

the Titanic was found in the middle of the ocean, upended, with passengers and luggage floating all around.

This testimony was written by J. Connon before a notary, three days before the shipwreck, including proof of the reservation and the cancellation. Some of his friends signed the document to corroborate his story.

It is believed that Joan of Arc fought against the invaders of France because she obeyed the divine orders of her dreams. As a young girl, she was in the country one day and heard a voice say to her: "Daughter of the Church, go, march." She looked around and didn't see anyone. The scene repeated on many occasions until the Archangel Michael appeared to her dressed as a soldier and said: "Don't be afraid, the Lord has given you a great mission to free the people." All of it seemed like a dream . . . and effectively, it could have been. A little while later, two elegant ladies (Saint Margaret and Saint Catherine) visited and advised her to follow the oneiric signs she had received: it was her duty to save her people from slavery to the English.

Nineteen centuries ahead of the curve, the Roman emperor Julius Caesar exhibited the theories of Freud. It seems that the night before taking his troops down the Rubicon River to attack Rome, he had a dream in which he saw himself sleeping beside his mother. Julius Caesar interpreted this to mean that in the future, he would be together with his "mother Rome," and that the invasion would be successful. History confirmed it.

There are at least twenty known cases of people who experienced premonitions related to the sinking of the Titanic in 1912. Still from Titanic *(James Cameron, 1997).*

The famous actor Kirk Douglas had a strange dream in which a tunnel of light appeared as he debated between life and death in a hospital. After waking up, he described this oneiric episode as a divine experience that brought him closer to God.

The actress Marilyn Monroe had dreams as a girl that foretold the great fame and admiration she would be the object of.

However, his trajectory and career failed later on for failing to heed a second premonitory dream that his wife Calpurnia had, who warned him to be careful during the month of March. Ignoring this advice, Caesar was assassinated in the senate by republicans on the 15th of March, 44 BC.

In 1991, the movie star Kirk Douglas suffered a helicopter accident that left him gravely injured. As he debated between life and death in a hospital, Douglas had a strange dream in which he felt his body become weightless and float in the air. For him, the concept of time no longer existed and he could see splendid colored lights. After waking up, he described this oneiric feeling as being in the most glorious tunnel of life, very close to God. This experience profoundly changed the character of the actor who, after his recovery, began to live more graciously.

The ex-president of the United States Lyndon Baines Johnson had multiple nightmares during his presidency (1963–1969). As the Vietnam War was escalating, one night he dreamt that he was swimming in a fast river and couldn't reach the shore no matter how he tried. He changed direction to see if he could reach the other side, but that was also out of reach. After these images, Johnson realized that they perfectly represented the professional bind he was suffering in reality: he lived trapped in an impossible political situation. The dream therefore held the answer he needed to hear and, after finishing his term, he decided not to run for reelection.

The night before her beheading, the queen Marie Antoinette, wife of Louis XVI, dreamt of a brilliant red sun at the top of a column. Suddenly, the sun disappeared behind the horizon while the column split in two and crashed to the ground. Posteriorly, this dream was explained as a symbol of the end of the monarchy.

Marilyn Monroe had a recurring dream as a child: she entered into a cathedral where a crowd of worshippers was looking at the altar. However, when she appeared, they all turned to look at her: she was the goddess they were waiting for, and Marilyn had to walk on tiptoes to avoid their heads. Oneiric interpretation considered this dream a prophetic sign of Marilyn's triumph and the admiration she would receive worldwide.

In the 1850s, the author of *The Adventures of Huckleberry Finn* worked with his brother Henry for four years as a steamboat captian on the Mississippi River.

From left to right: Mark Twain, Napoleon Bonaparte, Paul McCartney, and John Lennon (two of the band members of The Beatles). Four examples of famous people whose dreams changed their destinies.

One night, Mark Twain dreamed that they pulled his brother's lifeless body from the river. Then they put him into a metal coffin resting on two chairs, and on top there was a bouquet of white flowers with one red one in the middle. Weeks later, he was notified that the boilers on Henry Clemens's boat had blown out near Memphis. The bodies of the crew all had wooden coffins, except his brother, who had one of metal. When the writer came to look at the body, he noticed there was nothing on his chest. Moments later, shockingly, a woman entered and left a bouquet of white flowers on the body . . . and in the middle was a red rose.

Napoleon Bonaparte habitually wrote down all his dreams. In fact, he used keys and signs to plan military campaigns. Before the battle of Waterloo, it is believed that he had an oneiric vision of a black cat running between two opposing armies. As this happened, his own soldiers were defeated. The 18th of July, 1815, Napoleon was finally defeated at Waterloo by the British, Dutch, Belgian, and German forces commanded by the Duke of Wellington.

The physicist Niels Bohr was trying to understand the nature of the atom when, one night, he dreamt of a sun composed of burning gases surrounded by various planets, each of them joined by very fine lines. Upon waking, he realized that this was the precise solution to the problem he had been pondering for so long. He explained the structure of the atom to the world and thus atomic physics were born. Similarly, Albert Einstein's theory of relativity was inspired by a series of dreams the genius had in 1905, between the months of April and June.

The former member of The Beatles, Paul McCartney, confessed on Larry King's television program (CNN) that the song "Yesterday" came from a dream. The singer told how he woke up one day with the melody in his head without knowing where it came from. Curiously, this began his most famous song.

It seems that the same thing happened to another former Beatle John Lennon, who composed "Imagine" after hearing its musical composition in a dream.

Dreams helped Saint Francis of Assisi when it came time to reaffirm his pledge of poverty and establish the congregation of Franciscan monks. The chronicles of Saint Francis tell that one night he heard the voice of Jesus in his dreams: "Go and fix this house," and so he founded his own order. In order to do so, he had to attend a critical interview with Pope Innocence III, who had the bower to give approval, or not, to his ideas. Just before, Saint Francis dreamt of a great tree with very wide branches. In this oneiric scene, the longer he observed the tree, the taller he grew, until he ended up at the same level. When he touched the branches, the tree bowed to him. Upon waking, Saint Francis interpreted this dream as a sign that the pope would accept his proposal. And so it was.

The most curious part is that Pope Innocence III also had a rather revealing dream just before: the Lutheran Church was falling and Saint Domingo and Saint Francis of Assisi were holding it up. Upon waking, the Pope decided to authorize the founding of both congregations.

The Greek philosopher Socrates, shortly before dying, described to his disciple Crito a dream he'd had. He told how a beautiful woman called him by name and recited the verses of Homer: "Within three days you will see the fields." And, as the dream prophesied, three days later the hemlock poison brought his death.

One day, Thutmose IV, still a prince before ruling Egypt, was hunting on his land when he decided to lay down at the feet of the Sphinx of Giza to rest. After a bit, he fell asleep and had a dream in which the sun god appeared promising him a rise to power if he removed the sand from the monument he rested under. He did so, and Thutmose IV was elevated to royalty, a position that was not his by birthright. His reign was long and fruitful, as the dream had predicted.

According to the chronicles, Saint Francis of Assisi received a divine decree from Jesus in his dreams to found his own order.

Image from the film Brother Sun, Sister Moon *(Franco Zeffirelli, 1973), based on the life of Saint Francis of Assisi.*

5. Interpretation, divination, and prediction

"I dreamt I was a butterfly.
But now I don't know if I was a man
who dreamed he was a butterfly, or if I am
a butterfly who dreams he is a man."

CHUANG TSE

Telling the future through dreams

Rider Haggard was a novelist who gained certain popularity at the beginning of the twentieth century. But the fact that Haggard was a writer is not important in this case. We mention this character because in 1904 Haggard had a nightmare that bears explaining. In one of his dreams, the novelist saw his hunting dog Bob lying in the weeds on the bank of a river. The dog tried to tell him something but couldn't, and Haggard had the impression that he was communicating that he was dying.

When Haggard woke up, he discovered that Bob was not in his usual place. Fearing the worst, he quickly organized a search. Just like in the images created by Haggard's subconscious, Bob was found dead on the bank of a nearby river.

This true story illustrates how sometimes extraordinary things happen in dreams. You probably know someone who was perceived, in their sleep, an event before it happened in real life, or perhaps it has happened to you. But how do we explain it? There is no scientific answer, but the facts are facts. And these indicate that countless people have seen or directly experienced extrasensory

Dreams can contain premonitory messages about our future in the form of symbols.
Oneiric doors are signs of the opportunities that are opening or closing in our lives.

Predictive dreams

There are people who use their oneiric lucky numbers to bet on races or play the lottery. Oneiric lucky numbers are determined by translating the essential theme of the dream in ciphers. For example, if the theme is "burial," according to the table below, the oneiric number would be 25 (B=4 U=2 R=5 I=6 A=5 L=3).

5	4	3	2	1	9	8	7	6
A	B	C	D	E	F	G	H	I
J	K	L	M	N	W	O	P	Q
R	S	T	U	V		X	Y	Z

perceptions. That is without accounting for the tests—with interesting results—that professionals have done in special laboratories.

At this point, it's reasonable to conclude that there are a small number of people who, through dreams, obtain knowledge through means that are still unknown. In the majority of cases, this knowledge has a direct relations with future events. In other words, individuals that experience premonitions see events that take place *after* they have been dreamed. Evidently, in many cases these dreams are nothing more than lucky supposition. The dreamer's subconscious, having access to memories forgotten consciously, is able to produce oneiric thoughts that can seem premonitory but in reality are not.

However, on other occasions this is not the case, like we saw with Rider Haggard's dream. There is no theory that can explain this phenomenon, but it is known that the extrasensory perceptions that manifest in dreams are in the form of telepathy (direct communication of impressions from the mind of one person to another, or maybe some form of energy from one living thing to another) and premonitions (knowledge of a future event that cannot be deduced rationally).

Tests of dreams and telepathy

One of the most common laboratory experiments on telepathic dreams consists of observing a volunteer sleep for several nights. When the volunteer enters into the REM phase (something easy to verify, since the dreamer's eyes begin to move noticeably), another person in another room is asked to concentrate on a randomly chosen photograph that neither volunteer knew about before. At the end of each REM cycle, they wake up the sleeper and ask them to relate their oneiric thoughts. It has been demonstrated in these tests that often the dreams they tell are directly related to the image that other volunteer was focused on.

From prophecies to quantum physics

In reference to premonitory dreams, one of the few conclusions that has been drawn is that disasters and accidents are a recurring theme in this kind of extrasensory perception. What's more, the tragic events are usually related to someone close to the dreamer.

On the other hand, it is known that many animals are able to predict earthquakes.

Therefore it shouldn't be too surprising to find that there are people who, without any information on the sickness or danger approaching their loved ones, are able to know about these misfortunes ahead of time. Some researchers are beginning to ask if the fact that these premonitory dreams appear very rarely is part of

Although the prophetic character of each dream depends on the dreamer, there are some general beliefs about certain symbols. For example, seeing your reflection in a puddle predicts rapid gains; falling in one, tough times; and jumping over one, the end of difficulties. "Puddle" (M.C. Escher, 1952).

their exceptional nature, or if this fugacity is evidence that humans remember only a minimal part of our dreams.

To promote this type of experience, the only recourse is to seriously and consistently interpret your dreams, following the techniques explained in this book. It is important to relate the dreams to each other, connect them to your experiences, and interpret their symbols. This allows you to propose the questions you want to resolve and then, posteriorly, solve them through your dreams. If you get answers from this work, these will have become your "personal prophecies." Now, can you think of another type of prophecy?

The esoteric side

Before we go further: it is a long road, about something intangible, and it's something that requires prudence, patience, and consistency. Being in an invisible world, we are facing a terrain difficult to perceive in ordinary states of consciousness, in which it is best to proceed with caution and not do anything crazy.

Experiments of extrasensory perception

1. Solving of puzzles
Ask a friend to give you a puzzle that you can't normally solve. For example, tell them to hide something of yours (something special that you want to recover) someplace you would never look for it, or to draw or write something on a paper and seal it in an envelope kept someplace safe. Each night, before sleeping, try to keep the puzzle in mind and ask your dreams to help you solve it. Do this for several nights and be patient.

2. Synchronized dreams
Try to dream the same thing as your partner or friend. You can, for example, agree to meet each other in your dreams at a specific place. Publications about this phenomenon tell of many successful cases using this technique, although, due to its unpredictable nature, it may work the first night or not for weeks.

3. Psychometry of dreams
This is the practice of trying to discover information about an object you know nothing about. Hold the object in your hands before sleeping and keep it present while you sleep. You can practice the same exercise with a photograph of someone you don't know. Sometimes it helps to keep the object or photograph under your pillow. In the morning, write down what you dream, no matter how irrelevant it seems; then study its meaning as usual.

"To go where you don't know, you must go where you don't know."

Saint John of the Cross

It's not possible to approach it with logic. Remember the words of the great mystic Saint John of the Cross: "To go where you don't know, you must go where you don't know." In this case, the most sensible is to accept, and perceive what comes, leaving reason aside. There's always time after living the experience to analyze how things are and what really happened.

All of these reflections are related to the astral world, paranormal phenomena, trance and medium states, the materialization of energy, or the explanation—rationale—of determined phenomena. This is the esoteric side of dreams. It is enough just to think that, just a few decades ago, by the approximation of our grandparents the phenomenon of the human body was like "a great machine," while now we can say without pause that it is like "a hologram of light."

Any one can accept in today's world that there was an original wisdom, a primogenial, echo of an aureal age, the remains of which persisted in the form of small glimmers in ancient cultures. The poet wrote: "He broke the mirror of Truth into millions of tiny pieces, and he gave us two in our eyes." But as John Lennon sang: "Living is easy with eyes closed . . .".

The step toward logos, the way of thinking that we live today, erased the magic, destroyed the miracle. In the last twenty centuries that humans have documented, the materialist phenomenon has grown incredibly.

The scientific method is powerful and science is working hard to break certain barriers. However, the ancient arrogance of scientists is shifting toward much more open positions. But in this case, we insist, only a slow and patient study of both points of view will help you obtain results, whether it is through quantum physics or a long voyage as a psychonaut to the akashic records.

The study of dreams, a profession?

The return to the origin demands a more rigorous and studied worldview. Rereading the works of the great esoterics, such as Rene Guenon, Withall Perry, or Frithjof Shuon, allows us to rediscover not only the answers that the symbolic world offers——and they are there, within anyone's reach—but also the importance of recovering, through dreams, this wisdom lost along the road to knowledge and personal development. And from there, the serious fight with psychologists over themes such as the "unconscious" or "subconscious" emerges.

For our purposes, the origin of the visions of the great prophets does not matter as much—if they fasted a lot, received a divine

The figure of a sleeping person has appeared many times throughout history in art. "The Sleeping Gypsy" (Henri Rousseau, 1897).

"The dream of Mohammad" on a half-human mare represents the journey to the center of the world, the depths of hell, and the seven celestial spheres.

Interpretation

revelation, or knew the secrets of some hallucinogenic plants or substances (such as that found in the chin of some toads), or if "it was all a dream."

You have to respect that those ancient prophets quieted their minds repeating a mantra or praying a rosary, or entering a trance through dance. What's important is the here and now: before you try to interpret dreams you must maintain a personal compromise with the phenomenon and follow a serious path.

Doctors study and practice for years before intervening directly with patients, right? Well, whoever wants to go deep in this field (whether as a psychologist or therapist, or not) must study a lot, including interdisciplinary studies and continuing throughout their life. On only when one's practice—on oneself first, then on others—shows a solid basic preparation, can one think of passing one's knowledge to others. This is not a game. Others may need serious help, not fireworks. Remember: study, study, and study, and the inspiration will come.

There exists a way of perceiving reality, in which the eyes are not necessary, nor the precise notion of space and time we normally use. Is it possible to enter into it? Of course, but it is easier if you do so during the so-called "peak" experiences (other states of consciousness, ecstatic experience), a state of conscious rest (deep meditation), or unconscious rest (sleeping). This type of perception can take form through dreams that can be later understood and interpreted from the three-dimensional or terrestrial plane.

Almost all of us have dreamt at some point that we were both the protagonist and observer of our own dream. Equally, we have dreamt of being in a place that, without knowing how, changes to another place magically. Sometimes, people and places get crossed. An old friend can be someone we've never seen before, or a place we've never been could seem familiar.

With the conscience distracted, our personality reveals its deepest level, and from this new perspective we almost always can observe our daily activities more objectively and frankly. Unlike the state of waking, when the conscience lets its guard down and we

"Un poquito despues de la muerte" ("Just After Death") (Vincente Pascual Rodrigo, 1989). The spaces, colors, objects, people, events . . . our dreams are the work of the selective subconscious.

start to dream, the subconscious symbolizes and expresses our worries more clearly.

And what or who gives us more headaches than ourselves? It has been determined that the majority of characters that you see in dreams are nothing other than other representations of yourself or your personality. It deals with the parts of your life you can only see *with eyes closed*. These types of images are called projections. We will get back to these later on.

We may also dream of people we interact with in our daily lives, or with characters who had a more or less decisive influence on our lives—although it may have been at a subconscious level. It may be someone who impacted your childhood or adolescence. The mind sometimes brings these characters back in order to highlight an aspect of the relationship you had with them, whether positive or negative.

Remember that experts consider each dreamer unique and ultimately responsible for the fabrication of their dreams; nothing that appears in them is casual. Selectively and minisculey, your subconscious controls every element contained in a dream. The spaces, colors, objects, people, events, and even dialogue (everything you say or hear) is your work. The subconscious is careful to choose the sensations (pleasant or unpleasant) and feelings (happiness, sadness, fear, plenty, discomfort, anxiety...) that you experience in this surreal reality of the world of dreams.

Pure consciousness

Sweet dreams, pure consciousness? Nothing is certain, but the sixteenth century Taoist poet Huanchu Daoren wrote about consciousness: "the substance of the mind is the substance of the sky. A happy thought is a good luck star or a cloud of happiness. A choleric thought is a thunderstorm or violent downpour. A friendly thought is a gentle breeze or sweet dew. A severe thought is a fiery sun or fall frost. Which of these could be eliminated? Let them pass as they come, open and without resisting, and your mind will meld with the vast sky. If you can find some tranquility in the middle of hurry, you must cling to it before when you are calm.

If you want to trap some of the calm in the middle of the uproar, you must first obtain dominion over stillness. Otherwise, anyone could be influenced by the situation and passed over by the course of events."

The best interpreter, yourself

Thanks to an exhaustive and carefree analysis of each of this mysterious pieces, searching for the meaning they represent in our lives, we can understand that dreams are for communicating concretely everything that our conscious state cannot, or does not want to see.

When an architect designs a house, who knows the foundations better than he? Who better than he will know the dimensions and materials used in its construction? The same thing happens with oneiric activity. Dreams blossom from the minds of each person. We create them ourselves. So there is no one better than yourself to unravel their meaning. Everyone should know what it is they want to communicate with themselves, since as we've seen, dreams appear to show the individual something they have not realized. It doesn't matter if you forget some of your subconscious thoughts once you are awake. A good interpretation can help clarify what they are trying to tell you.

To analyze your oneiric activity, all you need is curiosity and the will to ask questions. Dreams are usually rich in nuances, and the true message often does not appear in the first level of interpretation. Ask all the questions you think are necessary, as if you were an alien who had just landed on the planet.

It is always easier to interpret dreams when a specialist asks you these questions. But even if that's the case, don't forget that the answers belong exclusively to the dreamer.

Dreams blossom from the mind of each person. So there is no one better than yourself to unravel their meaning.

Dream dictionaries, like the one you have in your hands, help clear the path and elucidate the possible answer, only you have the final answer.

Before all else, you must be aware that almost all dreams concern you directly. Except in rare cases, we tend to see people, things, and events that portray some aspect of ourselves, whether subjectively (each person represents an aspect of the dreamer's personality) or objectively (the people have their own entity).

Projections

When you see other aspects of your personality that you don't accept (when your internal censor is relaxed, that is when you dream), it is called projection. Projections, in general, allow us to express feelings that we can't show consciously.

Another characteristic of most dreams is that they use images collected from recent experiences. Even though each person's dreams are non-transferable, some of their images have similar meanings for many individuals. This doesn't mean that all dreams can be interpreted by a universal catalogue of symbols, such as that which appears in this dictionary.

As we have said, each person produces their own images, so ultimately no one but them has the cipher to the messages. However, do not underestimate the role of culture in our subconscious, since, thanks to the universal character of some symbols, these can manifest aspects directly related to our own lives.

Oneiric projections allow you to express feelings that are difficult to show consciously.

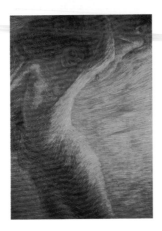

An example: a dog can be considered the most loyal companion to humans, so it symbolizes friendship and faithfulness. However, if the dreamer has suffered a negative experience involving a dog, it's likely that the presence of a dog in their dreams does not transmit any of those feelings of loyalty.

Should you then reject any general interpretation based on universal symbols? No, not at all. An exhaustive dictionary such as this can serve as a guide to complete the personal interpretation of your oneiric images. All told, the majority of them utilize symbolic metaphors to transmit their message. Nightmares and recurring dreams are, in this sense, the final recourse for the subconscious to communicate something that the dreamer has not yet understood or recognized.

From symbolism to Tarot

Sometimes, however, they have a more literal than symbolic interpretation. For example, scenes where you appear very tired could be advising you to slow down your pace in life.

How to interpret each dream? If we ignore for the moment professional psychology, we remember one of the techniques is similar to that of people who practice Tarot. Basically, the so-called "machine of imagining" offers potent and moving resources if one knows how to read the "answers." Each card is an icon whose arcana shows a clear and simple meaning, but in relation to the rest of the card thrown suggests more and more answers and ideas linked to each other that fit our reality. Who hasn't experienced this at one point?

Well, with dreams it is the same; each dream can be like a card, and they can be related to other events and personal experiences "in relation to." It's as simple as that, except that here is where the adventure begins...

6. Freud and psychoanalysis

"The dream is the expression, and even the fulfillment, of a rejected desire."

SIGMUND FREUD

A little history

The majority of civilizations have considered oneiric thoughts to be an important source of knowledge. In ancient times, they used basically two types of interpretation. The first consisted of extrapolating the dream to a real event. This is the case of the interpretation of the Egyptian pharaoh's dream about the seven fat and seven thin cows. It was an omen that predicted seven fertile years and seven of famine.

The second method consisted of analyzing every oneiric image as a separate sign from the rest. Evidently, these signs have their own symbolic significance.

From there, every culture interpreted dreams based on their own particular beliefs. The Babylonians, for example, believed that positive dreams were sent by gods, and negative dreams by demons. The Syrians, on the other hand, were convinced that dreams were omens. For them, they interpreted nightmares as warning messages.

Later on, the Egyptians used guidelines for interpretation that powerfully influenced many civilizations that came after. The inhabitants of Ancient Egypt believed that dreams could be interpreted as a game of opposites. That is to say, that a happy dream portends unhappiness, while an unpleasant one augurs good luck. The

Freud arrived at the conclusion that dreams express our aggressiveness, repressed desires, and hidden fears. In psychological terms, stairs symbolize the connection between our true Self and the Ego. "Shaft #6" (H. R. Giger, 1966).

For Freud, dreams are the images that make up the subconscious, free of censorship and the negative judgments of reason.

The Bible is full of divine dreams sent to teach its followers. These examples are found in the writings of saints such as Saint Clement, Saint Augustine, and Saint John Chrysostom. San Jeronimo, on the other hand, altered this belief. Tormented by dreams that seemed to go against Christian morals, he asserted that they came from the Devil. The Church declared that dreams did not come from God and should be ignored.

analysis of the Egyptians also was based on the search for similarity between words. If the term that designated an object from a dream had a similar phonetic sound to a word for another, it meant that the dream was pointing toward this second element. It was similar to the act of displacement, described by Freud in *The Interpretation of Dreams*, as we will see in this chapter.

The expansion of Greek culture marked a crossroads in the interpretation of dreams. The Hellenes, unlike the Egyptians, Syrians, and Babylonians, did not consider dreams divine. They believed that the origins, and thus the key, of oneiric activity was found in each person, not in messages from the gods. Aristotle asserted that if dreams were divine messages, they would only be sent to wise people who would make good use of them. The Greeks used oneiric activity as a therapy to cure illnesses, since they believed dreams could have physical repercussions on people.

In the second century BC, the Roman sophist Artemidorus came to the conclusion that the events of dreams should be seen as a continuation of daily activities. This theory allowed the study of dreams to advance greatly. The works of Artemidorus were very important in later centuries and influence the interpretation of oneiric activity until the revolution led by Freud in the early twentieth century.

The expansion of Christianity and the Catholic church was not very positive for the study of dreams. Even though, in the beginning, God spoke to men through dreams, with the passing of time this idea lost validity. The Church made itself the sole receiver of divine messages, so it was a grave sin to look for another road to the word of God through dreams. Therefore, dreams were scorned for centuries. Saint Thomas Aquinas recommended they be ignored completely and Martin Luther asserted that oneiric activity only served to illustrate our sins.

However, in the fifteenth century, the appearance of the printing press revolutionized the way of acquiring knowledge and allowed for a boom in access to information. All types of dream dictionaries were printed, based on the system of Artemidorus, and were widely distributed. Other than the inconsistencies and lack of rigor in those publications, for the first time the possibility emerged that each person could interpret their own dreams.

That, plus the interest the oneiric activity inspired in philosophers like Fichte, formed the foundation for the interpretation of dreams in modern psychology.

The father of psychoanalysis

Sigmund Freud (1865–1939) is the most well-known name in modern psychology. After him, nothing was the same in Western culture. Among other reasons, this was because he elevated the status of dreams to an important subject of scientific study.

Freud dedicated himself first to neurology. However, he soon abandoned physiological study of the brain in favor of psychology. Although being a Jew in a Viennese academic environment was not favorable, Freud overcame social obstacles to become a world-renowned character, whose theories provoked famous scandals. Starting from the intuition that oneiric activity could give us hints about our mental state, he began to follow the thread until he reached the conclusion that dreams express our aggressiveness, repressed desires, and the fears that dwell in us.

With his innovative proposals, Freud brought about a great deal of knowledge of the subconscious, since he believed that everyone was born with strong instinctive impulses that, initially, operated on a subconscious level. These impulses, which manifest through assertiveness, aggressiveness, sexual excitation, etc., are repressed from the early days of infancy when the child is taught to adjust to social norms. Therefore, adults are not able to free their primal emotions without reservation and these become a flow of energy in desperate search of expression. The way out is in dreams, in the images that make up the subconscious, free of censorship and the negative judgment of reason.

Sigmund Freud, founder of psychoanalysis

During the time period when Freud wrote *The Interpretation of Dreams*, between 1895 and 1899, his methods of psychoanalysis were solidified and began to be widely recognized. The free association of ideas was one of his tools. The technique consists of proposing a word or idea, which provokes a chain of associations that allows one to recover forgotten memories or repressed emotions.

What's more, Freud had also discovered that the behavior of obsessions and pathologic deliriums were very similar to that of dreams. Both seemed equally strange to the the normal conscience. In a waking state, no one could notice them.

The objective of psychoanalysis applied to the interpretation of dreams was to free the unconscious from the repression of the conscious. "Pallas Athena" (Gustav Klimt, 1898).

Because of this, he decided that free association, which had helped so much in psychotherapy, could be useful for the interpretation of dreams. Thanks to this discovery, Freud began an analysis that started from a collection of facts, ideas, or emotions, which seemed unconnected, but which presented elements in common.

In this way, the path to analysis and interpretation of dreams was the opposite route that the subconscious takes to elaborate dreams and oneiric scenes—something immensely complicated and difficult. The objective was to free the unconscious from the repression of the conscious to break barriers of judgment and criticism imposed by reason. So, it allowed the individual to express their deepest feelings completely uninhibited.

Upon analyzing an oneiric scene, we may encounter elements that have nothing to do with each other. To explain this fact, Freud compared the formation of an oneiric scene to a painting. He cited the example of a painter that represented in a painting all the poets reunited in the Parnassus. This did not mean that the poets had been together on the same mountain, yet it had a logic coherence. The dream has the same system when constructing a scene. In order for the result to be understandable, Freud divided the contents of dreams into two groups:

The first contains the manifest content, and reproduces elements exactly as they were recorded in memory.

The second is the latent content, the series of threads that connect the elements of dreams, appearing disassociated to

The unconscious

Frequently the human mind is compared to an iceberg: we only see a small part that protrudes above the water, that is to say, the conscious mind. Everything that remains hidden under the water would be the subconscious. When we sleep, the conscious thought remains in a state of hibernations and the subconscious takes control of the dreams. Psychologists consider the human psyche in three levels.

- Conscious: what we think in the current moment
- Preconscious: information that we have in our memory accessible at any time.
- Unconscious: forgotten or repressed material that is stored in our minds and influences our behavior, but which we cannot freely access.

On occasion the most imprecise, superfluous, or incomprehensible element of the oneiric scene represents a very important latent idea in conscious reality.

us. Contact with this second group is only possible through analysis.

After this analysis and the conclusion that dreams are the fruit of our unconscious state, Freud identified four activities developed by the unconscious. These are:

- condensation
- displacement
- visual arrangement of oneiric material
- organization of elements

When an oneiric element can relate to, in different ways, many real-life situations throughout time, it is called **condensation**. This phenomenon is discovered through analysis and refers to those oneiric scenes that condense different experiences into one.

Dreams sometimes interchange the intensity of ideas and representations. That is, they may give greater relevance to that which does not have it in the conscious plane, and vice versa. This **displacement** of priorities, according to Freud, is the most effective and intelligent method that dreams use to hide their content. Normally posterior analysis demonstrates that this element—which seemed imprecise or superfluous in the dream—represents a very important latent idea in real consciousness.

The act of **visual arrangement of oneiric material** refers to the mechanism that the unconscious uses to transform thoughts, emotions, feelings, and sensations into images. Since the content is almost always visual situations, this deals with translating a discourse in graphic representation.

Free association

This technique used by Freud and Jung consists of taking an important element of the dream—with a strong emotional or symbolic content—and from this creating a chain of different associations to bring out repressed emotions, forgotten memories, or even past dreams that had great significance. Imagine, for example, that you dream of a mountain. Keep the word mountain in mind. What associations do you make with this term or image? Hold on to this new concept and repeat the process. Keep going from one concept to another, and pay attention to everything that comes up. The deeper you go, the shorter the distance between conscious and unconscious. Unlike Freud, Jung was not in favor of getting too far from the original concept.

Once all the material of the dream has been formed, the activity of organizing the dream elements begins. This ordering is necessary to make the resulting composition something legible that the dreamer can perceive.

Upon observing these activities performed by the unconscious, you see that it's not the dream that has the creative capacity necessary to develop its own fantasies, it is more like the vehicle for oneiric material already present in the mind of the dreamer. The dream is limited, as we've seen, to condensing these ingredients, displacing them, making them ready for visual arrangement, and organizing them.

The dream therefore doesn't create itself, but rather is the pretext through which certain information that is is wandering around the mind and which the conscious, tied as it is to repression and judgment, is unable to perceive. Occasionally, this information can reveal things we ignored completely. So, dreams combine two functions: they allow prohibited desires to be expressed under cover and, upon recognizing the true nature of these desires, allows the dreamer to sleep peacefully.

One of the most criticized aspects of Freud's work is his insistence on the sexual symbolism of dreams.
For him, a snake, a complicated machine, or any pointed object were always phallic symbols with a clear sexual connotation.

As far as premonitory dreams, the popular tendency of the time was to give them divinatory status. Freud, following the trajectory of his theories, observed on the subject: "It's interesting to observe that popular opinion is right in considering the dream as a prediction of the future. In reality, it is the future dreams show us, not the real one but the one we desire."

The work of Freud was continued, although with substantial variations by many other psychologists. The most notable, and initially a student of his, was Carl Gustav Jung, who believed, among other things, that dreams brought the human psyche closer to the concept of totality. We will see a little about Jung's focus in the following pages.

Freud's theory that dreams are ciphered messages from the unconscious has been the starting point of a large part of the modern analysis of dreams.

7. Jung and the archetypes

"The dream is the self representation, spontaneous and symbolic, of the current situation of the unconscious."

CARL G. JUNG

Sleep and conscious life, one and the same

Studies done throughout the twentieth century have demonstrated that we only take advantage of the tiny percentage of the capacity that our minds really hold. Between those that believed in the extraordinary potential of the human mind, Carl Gustav Jung (1875–1961), the celebrated disciple of Sigmund Freud, stands out.

Jung considered dreams, in addition to manifesting our most intimate problems, have the capacity to develop our full potential as human beings.

For Jung there was no difference between dreaming and living conscious life. He considered that it was an expression of individualism just as important and real as anything else they did in a waking state. So, the interpretation of dreams is personal and intimate to each individual and should be done by highly qualified professionals. And, although he believed that the unconscious communicated through common symbols, he asserted that the ultimate meaning varies according to each individual's values.

Jung also maintained that the human being, in order to integrate itself, become fertile, and be truly happy, should complete a process of individualization. The end of this process comes when the conscious and unconscious become compatible and are able to mutually complement each other. Only then will they be able to live in peace with each other and the person will begin to feel well.

Freud's theory that dreams are ciphered messages from the unconscious has been the starting point of a large part of the modern analysis of dreams.

The era of the dream

The Australian aboriginals—one of the oldest cultures in the world—believe that the world is full of spiritual signs. Given that for this group, material dominion is under spiritual authority, its members try to live in harmony with the latter. Where is this authority found? In the "all." That is to say, in any part of nature. And how does it express itself? Through oracles. Therefore the aboriginals believe that the world is a living oracle.

As a consequence, for this group everything—absolutely everything, from an animal to a cloud—has a concrete implicit meaning.

In some way, this puts the aboriginal beliefs and the dreams found in this dictionary on the same plane. Not in vain, starting with the interpretation, you have the chance to explore the subconscious subjects that dominate your life, which can help you become an active creator of your own destiny.

In other words, dreams and aboriginal oracles have in common the potential to take you from a passive and defenseless position to another in which you enjoy more control over your life.

The Aboriginals define the "all" we alluded to with the word "Tjukurpa." An "all" that represents existence itself, past, present, future, and that is at once the explanation of existence and the rules that define it. Tjukurpa encompasses all the accidents of nature such as men and their actions. Tjukurpa represents a mythical time that some have defined with a very poetic concept: the age of the dream. However, do not be fooled: Tjukurpa does not refer to the images projected in our minds while we sleep, but rather to those that the aboriginal tribes recover each time they practice their rituals to recreate the origin of the world. You must keep in mind that for them, animals, plants, and other creatures are their ancestors, their brothers, and their parents. If one respects them, they offer protection and contact with the spiritual, which is why they are a guide in the search for all those answers and vital alternatives hidden inside each individual.

As far as the interpretation of dreams was concerned, Jung distanced himself from the Freud's method of free association, since he believed that this sometimes diverted the interpretation away from the real content of the dream. Keeping in mind that dreams are messages sent by the unconscious, Jung rejected anything that could interfere with their pure meaning. He only focused on the content. For this reason, symbols play a fundamental part in his work.

The role of symbols

No one *invented* symbols, they are natural and spontaneous produces. No one created them, or filled them with meaning. However, through centuries and centuries, they have been assimilated by humanity as their own. Symbols come from very ancient times. They have been used since before we were conscious of them, and now, they form part of the collective memory. Throughout centuries they have gained value and significance, representing much more than what they express at first sight, in the immediate range. This double or multiple meaning has always generated controversy and shrouded them in mystery. In fact, the meaning of symbols varies according to the context in which they are analyzed (place, social conditions, age of the individuals, etc.).

When the mind explores a symbol, it must go beyond reason, since there it will find definitions that can't be understood from a rational perspective. One example is the language used by religions. The divine, the idea of God, is only expressed through symbols. The great questions and spiritual problems of man have needed, since the dawn of time, symbols to manifest them.

Dreams symbolize events that we perceive consciously in the form of images. Curiously, in a waking state we also make unconscious perceptions. Sometimes, we have the sensation of having seen something we thought was forgotten, or having heard sounds or words that appear in our minds, without reason. The desires, impulses, thoughts, inductions, deductions, and premises the dreams contain can just as easily come from a rational place or the unconscious.

Two approximations

Freud and Jung differ when talking about the content of dreams. The latter claimed that they not only include memories, but also the seeds of future psychic situations. He backs up this claim by pointing to the new thoughts that dreams express, previously unknown

Carl Gustav Jung (1875–1961), student of Freud, used dream analysis to develop his theories of archetypes and the collective unconscious.

to the conscious. For Jung, the oneiric capacity of each individual serves to compensate for their psychic organization and the imbalances in their personality, as well as warn against potential dangers in waking life.

He illustrates this concept with some examples, such as that of the person who dreams of flying and then falling. Or that of the individual who often dreams of a risky situation that ends in death and then, later, without any explanation, it happens in real life. Specifically he told the case of a man who frequently dreamt he was climbing a mountain and, just at the top, fell into the void and died. Months later, that exact thing happened. He died scaling a peak. Jung asserts that, in these cases, dreams are not entirely premonitory. What happens is that personal crises come to pass unconsciously and gradually.

These dreams are just warnings about an extreme situation that we can't receive consciously. The fact that the situations happen in real life, just as they were presented in dreams, shows definitively that the individual was searching for a way out of his difficulties.

In Jung's thesis, studies of mythology and primitive cultures play a fundamental role. He advocates for a state of primal civilization, like the groups that have greater contact with nature and are more open to their instincts and the emotions of their ideas. Unlike the Western man, the inhabitants of these cultures interpret their obsessions as manifestations of spirits and gods. Therefore, their oneiric language is loaded with symbolism that represents them and has so much energy it is impossible to ignore. Modernity, on the other hand, has preferred to bury the gods and place all its faith in reason. And still, the obsessions continue just the same.

Archetypes and the collective unconscious

Jung establishes a difference between natural symbols and cultural ones. The first are variations of basic archetypes, whose roots can be traced to images in very ancient stories. Cultural symbols, on the other hand, are used to express eternal truths. Throughout time they have suffered transformation and more or less conscious development, but, in the end, they have become collective images accepted and integrated in civilized societies. From there, his concept of the collective unconscious.

Jung defends the evolution of the mind, conscious, and unconscious, just as Darwin proposed the evolution of life forms. A quote from Jung in *Man and His Symbols* helps clarify this idea: "We don't suppose that every new born animal creates its own instincts as individual acquisition, and we should suppose that human individuals invent their specifically human forms, every time one is born. Similar to instincts, the model of collective thought of the human mind are innate and inherited. They work, when the occasion arises, in approximate the same way in all of us."

Jung's theories ares closely related to a broad philosophical tradition that began with Plato's ideas. That is, with the proposal that, essentially, reality is formed by innate preconceptions of human beings, rather than those that we perceive with our senses. An idea also developed by Kant, who affirmed that it was impossible to know reality, since our structure of knowledge only allows ups to see representations of the real, not the real itself.

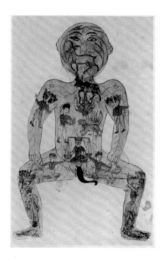

For those who ask if they can find a revelation about the meaning of life in dreams, the answer is yes. Many people who previously did not express much interest in their spiritual dimensions have discovered some fundamental truth in their dreams. And in many cases, these experiences have helped them realize and revitalize their existence.

Dreams can supply us with some of the most beautiful experiences of our lives. If you remember and value this type of images in the right measure, transcendental dreams will visit you more frequently and serve as a guide and inspiration.

What is an archetype?

In Jung's theory of symbols, there is a vital piece to its development: the archetype. Archetypes are not individual elements, they do not come from any personal experience. They are instinctive guidelines with a universal character that are expressed through behaviors or images. They seem to be innate aboriginal forms, inherited from generation to generation, and thus are common to individuals of all time periods, cultures, and civilizations. However, despite the universality of these symbols, Jung emphasized that the interpretation of dreams and symbols depended mainly on the circumstances of the dreamer and their state of mind. It is also necessary to clarify that archetypes are not the images or different representations of things, but rather the things themselves. For example, regarding the figure of the hero, his meaning is identical for any modern human. This also happens with the idea—ancient but still current—of death and resurrection; or that of destruction for later rebirth. Or with the idea of the divine, as we emphasized before. These are archetypes represented by symbols.

Dreams can provide us with some of the most beautiful experiences of our lives. "The Kiss" (Gustav Klimt, 1907).

Freud and Jung have been the most influential psychologists in Western thought in the field of the interpretation of dreams. It would still be unfair to omit the work of other analysts who have also developed interesting theories.

Fritz Perls and personal projections

One of them is Fritz Perls, whose theories are based on the idea that the characteristic symbolism of dreams is the personal creation of each individual. This psychoanalyst was convinced that, in order to interpret dreams, you must work from the assumption that every person and object that appeared in them was a projection of the same individual. It's like saying that all the symbols are representations of portions of our personality that we are incapable of recognizing in a conscious state.

Perls asserted that, on the other hand, dreams are directly linked to accumulated experiences, rather than innate instinctive impulses as Freud believed. In this case, oneiric activity would

According to Jung, the circle is an archetypal images that has important associations with the idea of plenty, totality, and consummation.

be similar to the material that many writers use in their works, derived from their own experiences that possibly remained unfinished.

Perhaps the most interesting part of Perls's work is his system of interpreting dreams. Given that, according to his theory, each symbolic element represents a part of the dreamer's own personality, he himself is the only person with the true ability to sufficiently analyze his oneiric thoughts. Therefore, if someone dreams they spend a day in a country house, only they will know which aspects of their personality are represented in the smoking chimney, in the farmer who keeps mumbling, or in the hoe hanging from the barn wall.

Perls's ideas opened new perspectives in relation to the theories of Freud and Jung, given that, for the first time in the history of modern psychology, *he gave the individual freedom to interpret their dreams through their own symbolic language.* Despite all this, it is important to note that Perls did not mean to eliminate the therapist, simply convert his role to that of an accessory who makes suggests but never imposes his analytic criteria.

Perls's method of working centered on a series of exercises he called "role play," which anyone can put into practice. It consists basically of mediating closely on the most meaningful character or objects of the oneiric scene and trying to discover their relation with more hidden aspects of your personality. This technique is very practical for gaining awareness of the images in your dreams and learning why they sometimes cause such impact.

Existentialism and emotions

Another psychologist who took a different route than Freud and Jung is Medard Boss. Boss rejected the idea that dreams are expressed symbolically, as Jung had concluded, and denied that they had one latent content and another manifest content, as Freud said. Boss belonged to the existential current and believed that each person chose what they wanted to be. He was convinced that dreams are able to make the existential state of the individual blossom. He thought the the only possible interpretation of dreams was a literal reading, of the scene just as it appears, without trying to get any different meaning from it. This method was useful for dreams that exactly reproduced real-life situations.

However, studies done by his predecessors indicate that there are dreams that require a deep analysis to understand their meaning. If the interpretation is based only on that which is present in the oneiric scene, one runs the risk of missing the most important meanings of the dream.

Is it necessary to be a specialist in order to interpret your dreams? Jung thought that it was essential, as he wrote in *Dreams* (Princeton University Press, 1974): "It would be impossible for someone without knowledge of mythology, folklore, psychology of the primitives, and comparative religion to capture the essence of oneiric processes." What's more, Jung was of the opinion that a modern person could not interpret their own dreams because they dealt with parts of the dreamer that they themselves did not know. His thesis, therefore, did not leave much hope for the neophytes to aspire to understand themselves better through dreams.

It's not a matter of refuting Jung's thesis here, however, we have seen that other studies on the material present different opinions. On one side, Freud's technique of free association can be practiced by anyone without danger. On the other side, existentialist psychologists consider that interpreters of dreams should deeply study the manifest content, disregarding any theoretic construction about the human mind. According to Boss, Craig, and others, these theories are not totally necessary for understanding dreams.

Mystery forms part of the essence of dreams and it is difficult to unravel all of its meaning. "House of Stair" (M.C.Escher, 1951).

It is impossible to find a definitive answer when we ask ourselves who to believe. A good option is to heed your own logic. It's clear that specialized knowledge is very useful for a deep analysis of oneiric thought. It would be foolish to deny that the study of religious history, anthropology, psychology, and human mythology enriches the evaluation of its content. But it's unacceptable to think that a modern person would not want to use all possible means to better know himself.

In any case, the mystery is part of the essence of dreams, and it's very difficult to every unravel all of their meaning. Psychology is not an exact science, and in this field, many times two and two is not four. What we are left with is to be guided by what is useful to us. If a method of concrete interpretation without digression

Getting an interpretation right gives us a similar feeling as that of discovering the truth to a suspenseful mystery.

helps you understand yourself better, this is the correct path for you. Jung himself said that, in psychology, the truth should compare to usefulness.

One option is to be attentive to your own emotions and the psychical representations they have in you. If you guess right with the interpretation, you will have a similar feeling as that of discovering the truth to a suspenseful mystery. The same pleasant tingling feeling will run through your body. Although it doesn't have to be like that, since it depends on each individual and it is very difficult to describe these sensations, it is certain that a correct interpretation will make us feel a certain way: like a mixture of knowledge and ignorance at once. In this case, you are correct. This new information will come to you and you will have it latently.

It is also possible that sometimes, the analysis does not lead anywhere the dreamer recognizes as their own. There are dreams that are very difficult to interpret. It may be a good idea to let several days pass so you can analyze it more objectively. With the distance of a few days, you can distance yourself from the impressive elements of the dream and capture its essence. Even if it is just partially, we can almost always obtain useful information about ourselves through dreams. Sometimes, the interpretation of a dream seems to be guarded until certain events in real life occur to clarify it.

8. Lucid dreaming

"In waking, the dream gains impercep-
tibly on the subject and engenders a
forgetting, or rather a memory, whose
contour is transferred to a plane of the
conscious that cannot accept it. But if
it reaches an appropriate plane of the
conscious, where it and the soul enter
into symbiosis, it becomes an element of
creations in the process of personal life."

MARIA ZAMBRANO

The technique of "lucid dreaming"

The life of any individual can be improved by sleeping, since making direct contact with unconscious material makes it easier to discover oneself and progress interiorly. "Flaming June" (Frederic Leighton, 1895).

Broadly speaking, this type of dream permits the dreamer to consciously participate. That is, realize suddenly that they are dreaming and that they can use the elements of the oneiric scene to their advantage or whim. In this aspect, lucid dreams have a greater potential for creativity; it is the ideal occasion to invent, conceive, and formulate without any type of limit or restriction. The main course of these dreams are the curative properties they offer. The life of any individual can be improved by sleeping, since making direct contact with unconscious material makes it easier to discover oneself and progress interiorly.

But what is a lucid dream? You may have experienced it before. You are sleeping and your mind enters into a dream in which a stranger, for example, yells at you to go home. The inverosimile of the situation makes you suddenly say to yourself: "This is a dream."

Lucid dreams are very stimulating, above all because they allow the dreamer to control their reactions within the oneiric episode, even if it is a nightmare.

Experts define this phenomenon as "prelucid oneiric activity." But this situation can manifest in a much more evident form. In this case, you not only know you are dreaming, but you can also use your conscious to change the dream as you wish. In the example given, you could ask the stranger who he is, or why he is throwing you out of your own house.

It must be said, however, that oneiric lucidity is not common, even though surveys have reported that 70 percent of people claim to have had this type of dream at some point. It is possible that many are confusing lucid images with prelucid ones, in which they only had the vague sensation of dreaming.

Keeping the conscious awake for a long time as you navigate your oneiric oceans is complicated. When one has lucid dreams, normally you either wake up shortly after, or quickly fall back into an unconscious state. Lucidity is only intermittent. And once you've had a dream of this type, it could be years before you experience another one. This exceptional character is why many people consider lucid dreams to be the most stimulating, above all because they allow the dreamer to control their reactions within the oneiric episode, even if it is a nightmare.

Unfortunately, not much is yet known about this type of oneiric process, although it is believed to occur more frequently in the early morning hours, since this time period makes it easier for the individual to realize that the mind is conceiving something improbable or outright impossible (for example, seeing yourself lift an airplane with one hand).

Are lucid dreams beneficial? Of course, since the individual who experiences them, upon realizing their mind is conscious, has the satisfaction of the sensation of freedom increasing as their self-control does. In this sense, some experts go beyond and claim that when one has learned to control oneiric events, it is much easier to solve daily problems and face anxiety. Lucid dreams, therefore, can contribute to our spiritual growth.

In another way, their potential can help us to treat the most terrifying nightmares. Lucidity allows you to face the threatening images in order to understand them, not obliterate them. According to some psychologists, such as the reputable American analyst Gayle Delaney, the best way to deal with a nightmare is not to turn it into a pleasant dream. Quite the contrary, those who dream lucidly have a better option: directly ask the oneiric characters that so terrorizes them what it is they want, or what they represent.

This experience can not only help transform the evil figures into friendly characters, but also allows one to discern what parts of the dreamer's personality are represented by the original threatening images. With proper training, the individual will report feeling more secure and confident upon waking.

How it all began

The term "lucid dream" was coined by Frederik Van Eeden in 1898, using the word "lucid" in the sense of "mental clarity." So we can say that a lucid dream is one in which "the dreamer becomes conscious that they are dreaming." This definition, given by the researcher Celia Green in 1968, is the most widely accepted today. In any case, the study of this type of dream has been ongoing since Ancient Greece. In the fourth century BC, Aristotle makes the first written reference to a lucid dream in his *Treatise on Dreams*: "When one is sleeping, there is something in the conscious that reveals that what is present is nothing more than a dream."

In 415 AD, Saint Augustine used the story of a lucid dream to justify life after death. Later on, in the seventh century, Tibetan Buddhism studies the yoga of dreams, in which the monks train

In lucid dreams we are conscious that we are dreaming. The sensation that time has passed, in a normal dream, is due to the sudden change of setting. In a lucid dream, however, the critical sense of the dreamer makes them question passing of time they did not live.

themselves in lucid dreaming as part of their spiritual development. Despite these precedents, the study of lucid dreams, as we understand them today, does not emerge until the nineteenth century, by the hand of Marquis d'Hervey Saint Denys. This researcher published the book *Los suenos y como controlarlos* (*Dreams and how to control them*), in 1867. In this, he demonstrated that it is possible to learn to dream consciously. This fact converted him into the founder of the first line of study on lucid dreams, although his discoveries were put into doubt by many researchers afterward.

Much more systematic and objective than Saint Denys, was the English psychologist Mary-Arnold Forster (1861–1951). In her book, *Studies in Dreams* (1921), she describes techniques of lucidity and control over dreams she herself experienced. The researcher was especially interested in "learning to fly" in lucid dreams, a practice which she had done since childhood.

Another very important aspect of her work was her nightmare therapy. She learned to recognize that her terrifying dreams were "just dreams." So she helped many children overcome their nightmares through lucid dreaming, teaching them techniques to change an unpleasant dream to a pleasant one. The fact that she criticized many Freudian theories, especially those about pretending and censorship, relegated her brilliance to obscurity. It wasn't until many years later that the true value of her discoveries was recognized.

Meditation is a good resource to stimulate lucidity in dreams.

Through the techniques of lucid dreaming, we can overcome nightmares by transforming them into pleasant and agreeable dreams.

The lucid dream, today

Modern research on lucidity has advanced a lot in the last fifty years and has come to dismiss old theories. Traditionally, it was thought that dreams happen in a moment, although long stories occurred within them. However, after studying in a lab the subjective experience of the dreamer, in all cases the estimated time of the lucid dream was very close to the real time (LaBerge, 1980–1985). The sensation that more time has passed is due to the sudden changes of scenery during dreams. In 1982, a study by psychologist Stephen LaBerge and William Dement demonstrated that, in the lucid dream, respiration was controlled voluntarily. They confirmed it with three lucid dreamers, who could breathe rapidly or hold their breath during the experiment without suffering any alteration of the dream.

On the other side, one of the most common themes of lucid dreams is sexual activity. LaBerge, Greenleaf, and Kedzierski (1983) completed a pilot experiment on the physiological response in lucid dreams of a sexual nature. The experimental protocol required the lucid dreamer to make ocular signals at the following moments: when he entered lucidity, when the sexual activity of the dream began, and when he experienced orgasm. The investigators discovered that the body reacts the same sexually during a lucid dream as it does while awake.

The situations, characters, or objects that are present in dreams but impossible in real life are precisely those that awaken the dreamer's critical sense and brings them to lucidity. "The Meaning of Life," Hipgnosis.

Meditation is also a good resource to stimulate lucidity in dreams. Before going to bed, find a quiet place and sit in a straight chair or on the floor with your legs crossed. Close your eyelids until only a faint fringe of light enters your eyes, or close them entirely if it won't make you sleepy. Then, try to relax for five minutes (as you practice, you can lengthen the sessions). Concentrate in a single stimulus, focusing your attention on a specific spot. When you finish the exercise, go directly to bed, trying not to lose the relaxation you attained. Meditation will help you concentrate as you sleep, allowing you to recognize the incongruencies in your oneiric thoughts. This is the starting point of lucid dreaming.

Another method for inducing this type of dreams consists of proposing to complete some sort of assignment while you sleep. When dreaming, you will try to finish this job, something that will remind you that the activity you are doing (if you do in fact dream about what you proposed to) is nothing more than a dream.

A variation of this technique (also implies taking on a task) consists of leaving a glass of water in the bathroom and eating something very salty before going to bed. If you follow this method, you are likely to be thirsty but, given that your body is reluctant to get up and go to the bathroom, the displacement will end up incorporated in your dream. The coincidence will make you realize you are dreaming.

Am I dreaming or not?

When in daily life, if a person, feeling, or thought appears repetitively, there is a greater chance you will dream of it. The content of dreams is always influenced by the content of your day. The more often you do a certain task, the more likely it is to appear in dreams. Therefore, if you ask yourself "am I dreaming?" frequently, you will end up asking this question in dreams. The problem comes when the sensation of reality in dreams is so strong that it tricks you. It is necessary to repeat the reality test we show later on.

Dr. Consuelo Barea notes that there are two primary techniques to induce lucid dreaming at night. It has to do with self suggestion and direct entry into dreams without losing consciousness, which comes from Tibetan yoga.

The number of times that stimuli repeat in a dream has a great impact on the content. However, the same happens with the quality of these stimuli. An event that impresses you, that hits you hard, that causes a big impact, is much more susceptible to appearing in your dreams, even if it only happened once. The way in which people talk to you or in which you receive information can be very suggestive and enter directly into your unconscious.

The prospective memory is a variation of this ability. It consists of giving yourself an order, forgetting it, and then completing it when the opportune moment arrives. We see an example of this memory in people who are able to wake up without an alarm at the hour they want. When the order of oneiric lucidity is given intensely and with force, it can directly reach the unconscious. Some people are able to have a lucid dream just by hearing about it for the first time; this seems interesting, but it's more useful to educate one's prospective memory, so that one knows how to give the order effectively.

Training

The process of training in lucid dreaming requires a gradual increase in oneiric experience. It is possible to advance suddenly to a much higher level of lucidity and control but, if this happens by chance, without having worked for it, you will not be able to maintain this achievement. Advances remain fixed when you work

When in daily life, if a person, feeling, or thought appears repetitively, there is a greater chance we will dream of it; this happens because the content of dreams is very influenced by the content of our waking day. "El voyeur" (The voyeur) (Carles Baró, 1996).

Practicing lucidity gives us the keys to discovering everything that worries us and stalks us in nightmares.

for lucidity, persisting with the techniques for induction. Then, the accomplishments are incorporated with your normal oneiric repertoire. In this way, you can reach a point where, in non-lucid dreams, you still act spontaneously, following the lessons learned from lucidity. For example, if you train yourself in lucid dreams to confront an oneiric character that terrorizes you, you will end up responding bravely to this person automatically, even if you are not having a lucid dream.

This practice will give you the keys to discover all that worries you in waking life and ends up represented in worry dreams and nightmares. Upon practicing with oneiric lucidity, you will learn to reap maximum benefit from this source of inspiration and creativity.

In the box we show the steps to follow to train yourself in lucid dreaming. The information comes from the studies of Dr. Consuelo Barea that appear in her book *El Sueño Lúcido*, (*The Lucid Dream*), published by this same editorial.

How to live "lucid dreams"

1. Development of induction techniques. Practice some of the techniques described earlier with the intention of having a lucid dream (for example, self-suggestion). You can practice it during the day, before going to sleep at night, or in the morning before a morning nap.

2. Gradually increase the level of oneiric astonishment.
- Level 0. No surprise about oneiric signs.
- Level 1. One-time astonishment without seeking an explanation.
- Level 2. Astonishment and superficial search for an explanation.
- Level 3. Lucidity: "I am dreaming."
The objective is to reach Level 3 through practice of the prior techniques.

3. Reality test. Once you've reached at least Level 1, you must get used to practicing the reality test in a dream. This can be visual, of laws of physics, or temporal. To do so, question for a moment the reality or coherence of that which

you are seeing or what is happening, according to your notion of time and space. If you find something strange in the evaluation of one of these factors, it will set off an alarm for you.

4. Prolongation of lucidity. Once you've reached lucidity, you must extend the time as much as possible to better obtain more information. The way to do this is by internal dialogue with the people in the oneiric scene, and with the thoughts you have during the dream.

5. Control. When you've achieved lucidity for a while and it seems like it will continue, you can begin to practice control:
- Space-time orientation
- Changing your own behavior
- Changing settings, people, events…

6. Entering and exiting a dream. After achieving all of the prior steps, you will encounter oneiric moments that you want to remember.

9. Kabbalah: dreams in the Hebrew tradition

A remote wisdom

For centuries, the Kabbalist tradition has remained closely linked to the Hebrew culture, thanks to which it has survived to the modern day. However, although Judaism has been one of the main influences in its development, the most meaningful archaic sources of the Kabbalah also come from the ancient cultures of Egypt, Chaldea, Persia, and even Greece.

The Kabbalah is a simple and precise method that explores and defines the position of the human being in the universe; it teaches what the spiritual world deals with and how to establish contact with higher states. Its wisdom explains why man exists, why he is born, why he lives, what his purpose is, where he comes from, and where he goes when his life is finished. Basically, the Kabbalah is concerned with finding the inner and hidden meaning of things, among them, also those transmitted by dreams and everything that is mysteriously related to them.

From the beginning, the Kabbalists have believed that the act of sleeping and dreaming play a fundamental role in our lives, and are a direct contribution to our physical and emotional health. In accordance with its conception of the human body, the Jewish mysticism considers sleeping—like eating or drinking—as a great spiritual intention; while we sleep we reinforce the body's defenses and are able to perceive elevated influences.

The Kabbalists associate dreams with the central symbol of their tradition: the Tree of Life. "Tree of Life" (Gustav Klimt, 1909).

For Kabbalists, while we sleep our mind is more receptive to creativity and our conscious closes to let divine inspiration in.

According to the Hasidic masters, maintaining satisfactory rest is necessary for a harmonious existence; certain moments have to serve us to take a breather and keep our interior powers in good condition. Going without nighttime rest also punishes our physical integrity.

Today, we have almost forgotten how to sleep, and the use of sedatives and sleeping pills has increased. For the Kabbalists, this denotes an obvious interior imbalance. However, one of the most common and ancient practices of Kabbalah is to pray at midnight. This originated in the Middle Ages and many followers of the esoteric Jewish tradition still favor it. Just at midnight, after a few hours of sleep, meditation through chants and hymns begins, deepening into the mysteries that the sacred books narrate.

One of the advantages of this technique is the silence we enjoy at this time. What's more, it's proven that our creativity and efficiency increase considerably after periods of rest or napping. However, the practice of midnight prayer should not be done if you feel exhausted or if you have to force the mind too much; in both cases, it's better to leave it for another time and rest.

"A dream uninterpreted is like a letter unopened"

One of the best Kabbalist books is the *Zohar*, or *Book of Splendor*, whose lines highlight the importance of dreams, putting them at the level of our conscious state. In the same way, it demonstrates that the interpretation of a dream is almost more valuable than the dream itself; therefore, there are a series of guidelines to follow at the time of deciphering our oneiric messages, which we will look at briefly further on.

The *Zohar* says that "a dream uninterpreted is like a letter unopened." Instead of ignoring them or discarding them as irrelevant to real life, we should honestly face our dreams. "A dream that is not remembered may not have been dreamt." So it's essential to keep in mind the oneiric messages we receive. Besides, for the Kabbalist dreams are not something ethereal or the culmination of unexplained experiences. Quite the opposite, they are a reflection of our mind in its waking state. The things that we think throughout the night occupy our oneiric thoughts and it's precisely these that reveal our true daily emotions. In this way, they become a way to discover the depths of our being.

"The temple of Solomon" was constructed from the measurements that God gave to David. Since he had blood on his hands, Solomon built a temple where all the materials and geometry have meaning. The Kabbalist doesn't just contemplate the city within the physical walls, but also on a metaphysical and spiritual plane in which seven different visions of Jerusalem appear.

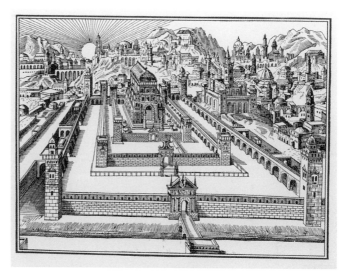

According to the Kabbalist character—a curious mixture of reason and poetry—dreams should be interpreted from a few unique rules: the same method works for any human being, regardless of his condition.

The key to this interpretation is to understand each aspect that makes up the dream separately. Similar to the Freudian theory, the Kabbalah indicates that, while we sleep, our mind works with symbolic meanings. The figures that appear to us represent our most intimate emotions and thoughts abstractly.

The *Zohar* interprets many oneiric symbols. For example, it specifies that "all the colors that we see in dreams enjoy a good omen, except for blue." In this sense, Kabbalah was way ahead of modern psychology in affirming that colors have a close relationship with the depths of our feelings. In fact, it is said that people who dream "in color," and remember it, are more in touch with their inner world. Equally, as the *Zohar* observes, dark colors are associated with sadness.

From the Kabbalist perspective, dreams are associated with the central symbol of their tradition: the Tree of Life. If we refer to the descriptions from *Sefer Yetzirah* or *Book of Creation*, a mystic text more than fifteen hundred years old, the Tree of Life is comprised of ten independent, but interconnected, forces, called Sefirot (singular: Sefirah). These are hidden in all aspects of the cosmos and originate from God.

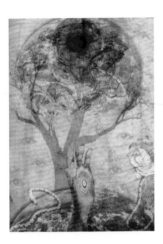

The Tree of Life according to Kabbalah is divided into five levels: the first and highest is Keter (crown). In a lower level, on the right and left respectively, are Hokhmah (Wisdom) and Binah (Understanding), and just in the middle is Daat (Knowledge). The following level is composed of Chesed (Compassion) and Gevurah (Sense), and, between them a little lower, Tiphereth (Beauty). In the third triad are Netzach (Victory) on the right, Hod (Glory) on the left, and Yesod (Foundation) in the middle.

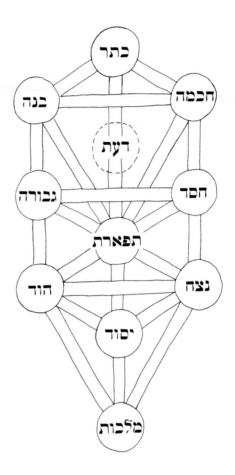

The term Sefirah, which does not have an equivalent in any other language, comes from the Hebrew word "to count" or "to number." *Book of Creation* confirms: "Only ten Sefirot: ten and not nine, ten and not eleven. Understandable with wisdom and wise with understanding."

In the majority of Kabbalist systems, each Sefirot is linked to a wide array of attributes and symbols, as well as a color, a musical note, and a specific place in the human body. In general, the structure of the Tree of Life is divided into five levels.

The five oneiric levels of the Tree of Life

The first and highest is Keter (Crown), the greatest of the forces, the principal generative power of the universe. One level down, on the right and left respectively, are Hokhmah (Wisdom) and Binah (Understanding), which correspond with the active and receptive qualities of intelligence. All these form a triad of qualities that, just in the middle, has a receiver of energy known as Daat (Knowledge). Often, this last one is considered an intermediary that unites them, or the synthesis of the joining of their attributes.

The next level is composed of the second sacred triad of the Tree of Life: to the right, is Chesed (Compassion), to the left Gevurah (Sense), and in between the two, a little below, Tiphereth (Beauty). The attributes of Compassion and Sense are necessary to maintain the balance of the universe; Beauty, on the other hand, is the vital sphere of energy—described as the greatest presence we can witness of God on the earthly plane.

The third triad is Netzach (Victory) on the right, Hod (Glory) on the left, and Yesod (Foundation) in the middle. Normally, Yesod is defined as the material generative power of the universe; in change, the other two Sefirot do not have such concrete definitions. One of the existing ones says that Netzach refers to the flow of physical energy—like the corporeal euphoria experienced when running, jumping, or laughing—and Hod has to do with the containment of this energy, including denial and asceticism of the body itself.

Finally, we find the Sefirah that completes the structure: Malkuth (Kingdom). This essence usually symbolizes the field of nature and humanity, as well as relating to Shekinah, the feminine Deity figure. According to ancient teachings of the Jewish mystics, every time we act with the correct devotion and attention, we call the divine presence to our surroundings.

The Kabbalists also identify thirty-two "paths," or vital situations (such as ecstasy, challenge, obstruction, and harmony) that connect with each Sefirah. Curiously, although it is not a mere coincidence, the number thirty-two is the exact sum of the twenty-two letters in the Hebrew alphabet and the ten Sefirot. From a numbered value of Hebrew words (each letter has a number associated with it), a dominant oneiric symbol is deduced and the psychological characteristic that goes with it (the crown, for example, represents wisdom). In this way, one can connect each dream to one of the thirty-two vital situations mentioned.

The Jewish candelabra or "Menorah," made from a single piece of gold, is for Kabbalah an object of contemplation as much as worship, and symbolizes the Divine World of Emanation.

Six steps to exploring our dreams

Following these six steps from Kabbalah, we can easily analyze our own dreams:

1. Always keep a notebook and pen beside your bed. This way, independent of the time you wake up, you can write down your dream and go back to sleep. No matter how interesting the dream is, don't be fooled into thinking you'll remember it the next morning.

2. Write down the dream as specifically as possible. Although something seems trivial at first glance, with time it could become an essential reference.

3. Describe the dreams in the present and be sure to include the emotions you experienced. The feelings that oneiric scenes provoke are vital to the reading of dreams. So, if you describe that you are walking down a street and suddenly reach a wall, also add what you felt when you saw it in your path.

4. Once you've written the dream, make a list of symbols that appear in it (mountain, flying, love, baking…); and note beside each one the emotional impact it had on you (use a scale from 1 to 5; 1=minimum emotion, 5=intense emotion).

5. Begin with the symbol with the highest emotional weight and look it up in the list of Kabbalistic interpretations included at the end of this chapter. Each symbol is presented with a triple description: its particular meaning, its meaning with respect to the forces of the Tree of Life, and the advice it offers for daily life. All this will help you clarify the oneiric message and act accordingly.

6. Reflect for a few minutes on what you learned from the Kabbalistic interpretation of your oneiric symbols. Then, think of one concrete, defined message of the dream. Keep this in mind and continue your normal activities based on this idea and new purpose.

The Zohar or Book of Splendor recommends giving our dreams outlet by sharing them with those who can help us elucidate the oneiric messages.

When a dream fits with a determined interpretation, it becomes a trampoline oriented toward the attainment of our goals. According to Jewish mysticism, we live in a sphere of action, and what we do is the most important in the earthly life. Once our dreams are understood, we need to act based on them, bringing their message into our routine, plans, and daily goals. One way to put this into practice is writing down what we do each day in a notebook and observing our evolution. We can also solicit the help and advice of people close to us, who accompany us in our waking journey.

Sharing dreams

When it comes to sharing your dreams, you should be selective. For Kabbalists, the subject of oneiric material cannot be discussed with just anyone, since strangers or casual acquaintances could distort or confuse the importance of the messages. The *Zohar* advises that we should only reveal dreams to our true friends, but also talks about the importance of giving dreams an outlet and not keeping them buried in ourselves: "When someone has had a dream, he must vent it to his friends."

There is an ancient Kabbalistic practice, known as the "dream fast," which is practiced after oneiric experiences that foretell disadvantages. Since the bad omen is not irreversible, it is recommended to fast and meditate the following day in order to recover your inner balance, the instability of which caused oneiric anxiety. This will help you to better tune in to your hidden feelings. Normally, in these cases, when the dreamer finishes a day of fasting and meditation, he gets together with three good friend. Then, they recite hopeful phrases from the Scriptures out loud, to attract positive vibrations to the conscious.

The Kabbalah also explains that dreams referring to illness, death, or destruction should be taken very seriously, because they refer to emotional conflicts we suffer in ourselves, and we can understand and resolve them through correct interpretation. According to *Book of Radiance*, "a man is not warned in a dream without cause." In the same way, advances in modern scientific and oneiric research demonstrate that, often, our dreams warn us about the state of our health even before doctors can.

The star of David, or double triangle, is called "Solomon's Seal" by Kabbalists and symbolizes the harmony of opposite elements, superhuman wisdom, and governing by divine grace.

"Oneiric incubation": How to obtain advice from dreams

The Kabbalah also teaches us to ask our dreams for advice: before getting into bed, write down—as concretely and briefly as possible—a question that summarizes your worry or dilemma. Immediately afterward, concentrate on it for a few minutes and ask your dream to bring you an answer. This is called "oneiric incubation" and was used in Ancient Greek and among Native American communities in North America.

It is also employed today in some psychologist offices. Remember that the answer you seek may not come the same night, it could be that you see everything more clearly in another dream, a few days later.

The *Zohar* also says: "There is no dream that is not mixed with some false subject, making it a combination of truth and falsehood." In this book, we do not reference the supposed "messages from outer space" that can manifest in dreams. Not because they don't exist (although in a miniscule proportion) but because their explanation would require another book this size.

For Kabbalists, dreams are the origin of paranormal knowledge. According to the *Zohar*, "a dream is more precise than a vision, and can explain what the other hides." While we sleep, our mind is much more receptive to creativity and our conscious closes to let divine inspiration in. This happens when we are sufficiently open to it and have stopped confusing ourselves with doubts and desires from daily life.

The Jewish mystic tradition connects extrasensory oneiric perception with our emotional state, and affirms that the calmer we are inside, and the less we are affected by worry and anxiety, we will attain "elevated" dreams of knowledge and our psychic abilities will become evident.

The factor that determines the visionary power of dreams is the state of your mind during waking life. The Jewish mystic tradition connects extrasensory oneiric perception with our emotional state, especially the degree of satisfaction, calm, clarity, and compassion. Because the calmer you are inside, and the less you worry about unfounded fantasies, like worry and anxiety, the sooner you will attain "elevated" dreams of knowledge: your psychic abilities will become evident.

Freud and Jung also kept in mind the clairvoyant capacity of dreams in their research. Kabbalah maintains a direct contact to modern psychology.

What is clear is that a lot of information is hidden behind dreams. The Kabbalists have always seen oneiric experiences has a great source of understanding. As the *Zohar* says: "At night, all things return to their roots and origins."

A brief dictionary of dreams from the Kabbalah

ABYSS. Danger related to an intense emotional situation. You should be cautious when interacting with others in very emotional circumstances.

ACADEMY. Denotes knowledge, especially of a philosophical and metaphysical nature. Intensive study will favor the dreamer.

ANGEL. An elevated characteristic, like friendliness, compassion, or healing, is found in the dreamer's life. A direct encounter with an angel indicates that you should strengthen said quality.

ARM. Strength and great achievement. The dreamer has power in a particular situation. If the arm appears wounded, it symbolizes that this power grows weaker.

BABY. Something is born, possibly a relationship.

BRIDGE. Transition from one situation or point of view to another. The dreamer is experiencing a positive change in his life and attitude.

BRIGHT STAR. Divinity. Proximity of favorable events and good luck.

BLINDNESS. The dreamer cannot, or does not want to, see the truth about a part of their life. Dreams in which you are surrounded by darkness have the same meaning.

BOOK OR PARCHMENT. Knowledge is near.

CANDLE. It is the human soul. A candle that burns represents a strong soul; one that is dying little by little indicates a weakness of character.

CAVE. A place to take refuge from a threatening or stressful situation.

CHILD. Represents innocence and ingenuity, the desire to learn which benefits intellectual development. Sign of the importance the dreamer places on this virtue.

COFFIN, TOMB, OR CEMETERY. Something has died in the dreamer's life. Everything will be fine if you accept it and move forward strongly.

COMET. A great change is coming in the life of the dreamer. It will be beneficial, but could bring a sudden loss of something, a disruption, or an unexpected turn.

CORPSE. Something has died and is rotting in your life. You should determine what it is and act immediately to "bury" it.

CLIMBING. The dreamer is searching for greater satisfaction from life. This image is very positive and signifies inner growth and advancement.

CRUISE. Higher spiritual growth and transformation. If the ship moves quietly over calm waters, the dreamer will find little stress in their life. If the waves are rough, on the other hand, it foretells tensions.

CUP or CHALICE. Divine blessing; very positive if it is gold or silver. If it is broken, it means the blessing will be rejected.

DANCING. Happiness and fun in the dreamer's life.

DAGGER or WEAPON. Personal violence. Denotes that the dreamer is furious and holds feelings of aggressiveness inside.

DAWN, SUNRISE. A new start, either in a relationship or a job.

DEAFNESS. The dreamer is ignoring the good advice of a friend or loved one. Indicates that you don't want to hear a truth you are being told in real life.

DEMON. Symbolizes the lower passions such as jealousy, resentment, or vengeance. The dreamer should remove these from their life as soon as possible.

DESERT. Spiritual aridity in some aspect of the dreamer's life. A way of avoiding it is to find a manner of achieving more productivity and spiritual wealth.

DARKNESS. Absence of divinity and saintliness. Ignorance. The more darkness that appears in the dream, the less spiritual illumination the dreamer will have.

DOOR. A barrier that can be overcome with willpower. Closed doors symbolize a lack of the right attitude when approaching a certain situation.

DOVE. Peace in general; pacific resolution of a particular situation.

DUST. Humility before the greatness of God. Associated with destiny. It reminds you that you should cultivate qualities of deference and submission.

DRAGON OR MONSTER. Demonic or spiritually negative forces, such as black magic or malevolence. The dreamer should avoid any matter in life related to such aspects.

EAGLE. Imagination and creativity. If it flies very high it represents a greater emergence of these qualities; an eagle nest is safe place to strengthen them.

EARTH. The world is means of life, where all creatures must fight for their existence. Indicates that the dreamer has too many mundane worries.

ECHO. Everything you do echos and has repercussions in the hidden worlds. Dreams of this kind remind you of said spiritual truth.

ELDER. Eternal wisdom, especially religious. The dreamer should seek this quality in their life.

EYE. A human eye represents that the dreamer has a correct judgment about some matter or situation. If the eye is wounded or blind, it means the opposite.

FALLING. The dreamer is falling in a lower level of consciousness and feels negative emotions such as rage, pride, or fear. Without exception, it is a negative symbol.

FISH. Abundance and material blessing in the dreamer's life. Money, properties, and other possessions will increase.

FIRE. Divine judgment of the imperfections and bad acts of the dreamer. Fire also indicates a need for exhaustive moral cleansing and self purification.

FIRMAMENT. Divine order in the universe that translates to the dreamer's life.

FLYING. Freedom from mundane worries. Also means that you should use your imagination to experience a greater sensation of freedom when facing trivial problems.

FOUNTAIN. A good emotional state, vitality. The more water that flows, the greater capacity you have to express positive emotions, such as gratitude and compassion.

FUNERAL. Something has died in the dreamer's life; a job, a relationship, or even an important belief.

GAZELLE. Precise and elegant decision that the dreamer should make. A very positive symbol.

GARDEN. Liveliness in attitude and beliefs. Reveals an excellent perspective and spiritual growth.

GENITALS. Generative capacity, the dreamer's potent creativity.

GETTING LOST. The dreamer has gone astray, has diverted from the soul's mission and his purpose in life. You must regain your spiritual orientation, above all.

GIANT. Egomania, pride, and arrogance. The dreamer or someone close to them is behaving ungenerously.

GOAT. Great ability to overcome and resist. The dreamer needs to develop other elevated qualities such as imagination or esthetic sense.

GREEN FIELDS. The dreamer's life is full of vitality and good intentions.

HAIR. Virility and sexuality. If it is thick and voluptuous, it denotes sensuality; the opposite if you lose it. Brushing your hair is a sign of vanity.

HEBREW ALPHABET. Each of the twenty-two letters has a specific meaning. In dreams, they indicate elevated communication.

HIGHWAY. Symbolizes the road or life journey. If it is well traveled, it means the dreamer enjoys a close relationship with others. If the opposite, it denotes loneliness.

HORIZON. The near future. A clear horizon represents good luck; a hard one, on the other hand, indicates problems.

HUNGER. Physical or emotional deprivation. The dreamer feels some bodily or personal need unsatisfied.

ILLNESS. The dreamer lacks balance in their life and soon could experience physical or emotional disorder.

JEWEL. Divine illumination. The more beautiful or brilliant it is, the greater the spirituality that will shine in your life.

JOURNEY. The present path of the dreamer. If the setting of the dream seems strange, it indicates a new situation or challenges. The presence of companion is a good sign; their absence denotes isolation.

KING. Power and divine judgment. Emphasizes the importance of these qualities in the dreamer's life.

KISS. The taste of the transcendental soul. Whether consciously or not, we experience said condition in some aspect of life.

LAMB. Submission and sweetness. A shepherd directing his flock signifies that you are taking special care with a certain situation.

LAMP. Spiritual knowledge and wisdom. The *Zohar* speaks of a lamb of darkness, which is associated with evil and discord.

LEG. Resistance, especially in journeys by foot. Signifies that the dreamer has the strength necessary to successfully resolve a problematic situation.

LIGHT. Divinity, saintliness, and wisdom. This is a superior symbol.

LIMP. Inability to resolve a certain situation, caused by yourself or by external circumstances.

LION. Courage and spiritual strength. Traditionally, the lion also represents the Jewish community. The image of a lion nuzzling its cubs indicates that you give courage to others.

MARKET. Sustenance of human existence. Indicates your worries about how to earn a living.

MAKING LOVE. Ecstasy of the soul when it refers to a union with God.

MOON. Fantasy, intuition, and receptiveness in the soul of the dreamer. Traditionally, it is related to other hidden aspects of the soul, like imagination and creativity. Equally, it is associated with femininity.

MIDNIGHT, however, represents a time of mystic study and contemplation.

MORNING. State of spiritual satisfaction and happiness. Also associated with physical pleasure, well-being, or healing.

MOUNTAIN. Place of divine inspiration and revelation. Indicates that the dreamer needs to find this place in real life.

MOUTH. Human speech and the capacity to create harmony or conflict. The dreamer should pay attention to the effect their words cause. A wounded mouth symbolizes a lack of communicative skills.

NIGHT. Judgment and dark qualities. Night is usually associated with demonic forces and emotional negativity.

OASIS. A place of rejuvenation and replenishment. Indicates the end of the feeling of spiritual sterility in the dreamer's life. It is a positive symbol.

PALACE. Dwelling of the divine. The dreamer should seek more consciously the sacred side of daily life.

PLANETS. Subtle, hidden forces in the life of the dreamer. Traditionally, the vision of this symbol was astrological and it was believed that it exercised a concrete influence on our daily experiences.

PLAYING AN INSTRUMENT. Exaltation and spiritual pleasure; also, experiencing the sacred through an esthetic activity.

QUEEN. Divine love and compassion. Her oneiric presence confirms the importance of these characteristics in the dreamer's life.

RAINBOW. Protection and divine security. A hopeful and encouraging symbol for the life of the dreamer.

RIVER, STREAM. The vital spirituality is flowing correctly. Soon a positive change or great experience will arrive.

SNAKE. Deception and malevolence, disguised as sincerity and attention. Warns that there is someone or something in your life that may be dangerous.

SINGING. Gratitude. The act of singing, whether it is the dreamer or other people, means that you will soon have something to be grateful for and to celebrate.

SKY. The spiritual world; the intangible, pure, subtle, and mystic part of life. A cloudless sky signifies clarity; if it is clouded, it means there is confusion.

SLEEPING. Ignorance, passivity, and withdrawal. In its most positive interpretation, it represents waiting without hurry. Falling asleep symbolizes loss of consciousness and acuity.

STAIR. Character development and personal growth.

STAGNANT WATER. Blockage in the life energy, especially in the spiritual sense.

STRONG WIND. The force of change. To dream of this element means your life will undergo a complete metamorphosis. Hurricanes indicate that said change will be very violent. STUDY. Acquisition of knowledge, above all spiritual. It is a positive dream that indicates the dreamer is developing internally.

SUN. Will and intention. The sunrise represents the birth of something new in your life. The sunset indicates that some matter is ending. Traditionally it is also associated with masculinity and it's most characteristic traits such as stubbornness—in a positive sense as well as negative.

TEETH. Physical vitality. Losing teeth is a warning to the dreamer about their health.

THIRST. Spiritual desire. Represents that the dreamer is not receiving the spiritual satisfaction they desire.

THRONE. Physical manifestation of the divine. Indicates that the dreamer must be more conscious of the sacred side of their body.

TREE. Life and spiritual knowledge. A flowering tree also represents deserved success; a bare tree denotes a lack of achievement.

TRIPPING. Impatience and too much hurry in daily matters. You need calm and balance to avoid the possibility of a serious fall.

TURTLE. Good luck in life.

UNOPENED LETTER. The dreamer did not heed a very important message. It is necessary to pay attention immediately to any communication received in real life.

WAKING UP. The dreamer is recovering clarity, acuity, and personal energy to complete some personal matter.

WAVY OCEAN. Pride and arrogance. This dream indicates that the dreamer must cultivate humility.

WEDDING. Spiritual compromise, possibly related to a field of study, training, or an effort in the long term.

WILD. The absence of civilization. A place of power and potential danger.

10. Analysis and interpretation

"If a man traveled through Paradise in a
dream and they gave him a flower as proof
that he had been there, and upon waking he
found this flower in his hand . . . then what?"

SAMUEL TAYLOR COLERIDGE

**A custom-made
mythology, a
personalized
symbology**

As message generators, dreams have their own symbolic language. It
is a language that is difficult to understand, as much due to the apparent irrationality as to the difficulty of illuminating *dark corners* (no
matter how colorful or brilliant they seem to us). No matter if it is for
objective issues or subjective ones, if we are the protagonist or not.

Why such difficulties? Why such interest in deciphering them?
Some experts point out that it is probably due to "the complex,
emotive, and vectorial nature of the symbol." And also because it
"symbolizes the individual adventure and is one of the freest and
most shameless expressions of the self."

It is even claimed that dreams complete such a vital function that
a total lack of dreams would cause death or dementia. Additionally,
they serve as an outlet for repressed impulses, bring out unresolved
matters or problems, or suggest solutions by representing them.

Their selective function, such as the choices of memory, alleviates
conscious life and often helps to establish a sort of compensatory equilibrium. One of the tasks of therapists or dream interpreters is to discover all this and work with these connotations to find the relationship
between the conscious situation lived and the images of the dream.

*The dream symbolizes an
individual adventure and is one
of the freest and most shameless
expressions of the self.*

123

The dream is one of the best elements of information that exists about our psychic state. To dream of blurry or unclear images indicates an inability to understand and decipher what happens around you.

Sometimes the separation between dream and reality can take on unhealthy tints and reveal excesses. The compensation produces, according to Freud, "horizontally and on the same plane as sexuality," while Jung said rebalancing occurs vertically, "as if this were a ship between sail and keel."

The dream is one of the best elements of information that exists about our psychic state, since it offers us and instantaneous images of our existential situation at the present time though living symbols. For the dreamer, it has to do with an image—often unsuspected—of him and his self. Well, at the same time, all this information is veiled, with other images and themes, much like a symbol.

During a dream the processes of identification flow without control. The person identifies with another being, man or woman, animal or plant, vehicle or planet. A serious analysis of dreams obligates you to precisely discern these identifications and clarify them, discovering causes and ends, and helping the you return to the path to your own identity. The dream activates the processes of individualization and contributes to the formation and expression of the whole person.

Analysis of dreams

To study and understand dreams, in the West we base ourselves on **analysis** and **interpretation**. The analysis of oneiric symbols rests in a triple examination:

- The **content** of the dream (the images and their drama)
- The **structure** of the dream (a collection of certain relationships between different images)
- The **direction** of the dream (its orientation and end intention)

The content

Originates from five types of spontaneous operations:

1) **Elaboration of facts** from the unconscious to transform them into images.
2) **Condensation into an image**, or a series of images.
3) **Displacement of the emotional nature** (transference) of these images by substitution, by way of identification, of rejection, or of sublimation.
4) **Dramatization** of this collection of images and emotional charges in a portion of life that is more or less intense.
5) **Symbolization** which hides other realities behind the images of the dream than those directly featured.

The oneiric analysis should find the latent content of similar psychic expressions that hide needs, repressions, urges, ambivalences, conflicts, or aspirations buried in the depths of the soul. Together with this expression and their dynamic appears their tonality, that is, the emotive and anxious burden that affects us.

The structure

Establishing the structure of a dream tends to be a complicated task because various phantasmagoria can mask identifying structures (adjusted according to the same deep outline) and equally, similar images can appear in different structures. To facilitate the study, a structure in the form of a drama in four acts has been conceived:

1) **Exposition** and characters, geographic location. Time period, decoration.
2) **Action** and drama that emerges.
3) **Unexpected turn** of the drama.
4) **Evolution** of the drama up to resolution, detente, correction or conclusion.

One of the difficult parts of studying the structure of dream is that you must explore different planes that are not without interference between them. In the deepest one appear common questions that symbolize such basic, universal fears or worries such as survival, death, pain, loneliness, and madness. Or also about the complexity of the world and the difficulty of adapting, or about the meaning or destiny of existence, in which dreams also intervene and interfere.

In the middle of the symbolic universe some relationships appear with clarity, such as that between ascension and light, or between integration and heat.

In any case, the studies assure us that, intuition aside, there is enough information to form a framework code with which to explore the oneiric symbolism in a rather scientific fashion.

The direction

All dreams are believed to have a direction, and therefore you can look "backward" to the cause of the dream (the Freudian or retrospective method) or "forward," investigating the intention of the dream (the Jungian or prospective method).

Interpretation of Dreams

Freud asserted that "the interpretation of dream is the true path to knowing the soul." Today that seems exaggerated, although it is still a very important tool for individual self knowledge; the dream's drama, spontaneous and uncontrolled, "does not depend on the subject's will," as if it existed outside the subject's imagination for real, with a dissolved sense of identity, and the prospects and perceptions of reality transformed.

Ethnologists have fully brought to light the secrets of dreams: "The dreamer will find all the accessories of dreams in the vast panoply of collective representations that civilization provides. Thus, the door between the two halves of human life is always open, through which constant exchanges made between dream and myth, between the individual's fictions and social coercion, occur. It allows the cultural dimension to penetrate the psychic dimension, and the psychic to be framed by the cultural" (Roger Bastide).

The interpretation of a dream, like decoding a symbol, does not answer the mind's curiosity. It elevates to a higher level the relations between the conscious and the unconscious, improving their communication networks.

Even if it was only in this sense, and in terms of more conventional psychism, the oneiric or symbolic analysis is one of the many methods for the integration of the personality, a more lucid and balanced individual with the one who was divided between her desires, aspirations, and concerns (the latter does not understand herself). "The synthesis of conscious psychic activity and unconscious psychic activity is the very essence of the creator's mental work" (CA Meier).

"The interpretation of dream is the true path to knowing the soul."

Sigmund Freud

For interpretation it is important and very useful to be familiar with the symbolic and mythological universe of different cultures—both past and present. This is because all these elements, artistic or religious, are fundamentally the same in the dream world. However, you should remember that all those images and symbolic values are in symbiosis within the psychic medium which is also a holder of symbols. This forces you to organize and synthesize all these elements if you want to establish a serious interpretation. Additionally, you must take into account that:

1) **The dreamer is at the heart of the dream.** "Dreaming occurs because of the subject and through the subject; the dream is the theater in which the dreamer is at once actor, stage, prompter, producer, author, audience, and critic" (Jung).

2) **The dreamer is at the heart of a story.** The interpretation of oneiric symbols requires each element of the analysis to: belong to a context, be clarified by spontaneous associations, and even be amplified—as is done in a movie.

In order to have a serious interpretation it is important to be familiar with the symbolic universe of all different cultures, both ancient and present. Likewise, the individual's psychic symbolism is equally important.

"The dream is the theater in which the dreamer is at once actor, stage, prompter, producer, author, audience, and critic" (Jung).
"Forks on the back" (Hipgnosis, 1982).

There are two very useful resources:

Associations. The dreamer is invited to spontaneously express everything the images, colors, gestures, and words of her dream evoke in her, both separately and all together. Thus, unsuspected latent ties or emotional traits are manifested. However, these are often not very reliable regarding a strict dream interpretation.

Amplification. This is about providing maximum resonance to the analyzed dream; magnifying it to "see it" better, like an enlarged projection of a snowflake crystal structure or veins in marble.

This amplification to penetrate the secrets of dream can be done by the dreamer, in a minimally guided manner. Nonetheless it can also be undertaken by the interpreter, based on the treasure trove of ethnological, mythological, and symbolic resources of the humanities. Such resources—derived from both folklore and religious traditions—allow us to place the content of the dream in relation to the psychic and human heritage in general.

Therapy with dreams

The oneirotherapy, or therapeutic practice of **daydreaming,** has generated the "oneirodrama." This technique consists in a dream guided by the therapist—or the interpreter specializing in dreams—by suggesting an image or theme as a starting point. Themes extracted from symbols of ascent and descent are generally proposed. As André Virel says:

"It utilizes the human condition of hypo vigilance which allows the subject to live an archaic world—whose existence she does not even suspect during wakefulness and the nighttime dreaming only provides a very inaccurate and disjointed idea of it.

"The technique first involves a scientifically conducted relaxation time that causes the appearance of alpha waves. The subject verbalizes, step by step, the images that appear to her or what she feels. Experience shows that such states are vivid. In other words, the subject has an imaginary corporeal Self that acts on a ghostly world and projects the structures of her archaic Self on that world. It is one of the ways that exist to encourage—in someone less inclined to fantasy—the recreation of sequences and situations that may overlap data from mythology or social psychology of the most primitive stages of mankind."

Classification of dreams

This is a simple classification designed to facilitate their study:

- **Prophetic or didactic dream.** More or less disguised warning about a critical event, past, present, or future; the origin of these dreams is often attributed to a celestial type of force.

- **Initiation dream.** The dream of the shaman, as described in the Tibetan Buddhist book by Bardo Thödol, full of magical efficacy and intended to bring the dreamer into a different world by knowledge and an imaginary journey.

- **Telepathic dream.** This allows for communication with the thoughts or feelings of faraway individuals or groups.

- **Visionary dream.** It takes the subject to an *imaginary* world (H. Corbin), whose full consciousness has been lost in the West, except among very few testimonies of the mystical variety. Omen is discarded in this case: this is a *vision*.

- **Premonition.** This dream allows the dreamer to sense one single possibility out of a thousand.

- **Mythological dream.** Version or reproduction of some great archetype; it reflects a fundamental or universal distress.

In visionary dreams we are transported to an imaginary, almost mystical, world.

11. Living your dreams

"—'The king is dreaming now,' [. . .] 'and what do you think he's dreaming about?'
—[. . .] 'Nobody can guess that.'
—'[. . .] about you!' [. . .] 'And if he left off dreaming about you, where do you suppose you'd be?'
—'Where I am now, of course,' [. . .].
—'Not you!' [. . .] 'You'd be nowhere. Why, you're only a sort of thing in his dream!'
—'If that there King was to wake,' [. . .] 'you'd go out just like a candle!'"

LEWIS CARROLL, THROUGH THE LOOKING-GLASS

The spiritual side

We've given a brief, bird's-eye view of different approaches that, in different times and cultures, have served humanity to bring them closer to the world of dreams and to try to understand its meaning and significance. Before concluding this short tour we will stop for a moment on the spiritual side. Some people believe that dreams tend to lead you into the depths of your being, where you may drink from the fountain of sincere spirituality. The purpose of this source is not to discover yourself, but to remember who you are and why.

We have discussed and analyzed various dimensions of dreams: their somewhat scientific explanation, studies on their mysterious character, and their amazing ability to give us a different view of ourselves. At the end this first part it seems fitting to include, in brief way, some notes on the relationship that some of your dreams have with the ultimate meaning of life, either because you can learn something that enriches your soul or because they complete your knowledge.

Dreams tend to lead you into the depths of your being, where you may drink from the fountain of sincere spirituality.

131

According to ancient Egyptian culture, the gods created dreams to show mankind some paths, when it is unable to know or to see the future.

For Native Americans, dreaming is the last and most decisive sign of experience. Dreams are in the origin of liturgy: they are the basis of the priests' election and consolidate the shaman's authority; medical science is deduced based on them, as well as the names for newborns, and taboos. Dreams order wars, hunting parties, death sentences, and aid given. Only dreams penetrate eschatological darkness. The dream, as confirmed by tradition, is the hallmark of legality and authority.

For the Bantu of Kasai (Congo), some dreams are referred by souls that separate from the body during sleep and go to chat with the souls of the dead. These dreams have a premonitory nature concerning the person or may constitute true messages from the dead to the living ones, making it of interest for the whole community.

Dreams and meditation

For many people, the dream is a vehicle of the spirit that resolves internal conflicts. Furthermore, it provides peace and gives hope and vitality to the dreamer, expressing a strong bond with the sacred.

Eastern cultural tradition relates differently with the dream world. For example, the yogis' (like Sri Chinmoy) teachings suggest the practice of meditation as the most appropriate means to broaden the horizons of our consciousness and, therefore, to increase the quality of our relationship with dreams.

The meditation technique we propose is simple, but it must be consistent and be taken seriously. The best time to meditate is early in the morning (at three, four, or five in the morning). After a shower, you should sit or lie down and concentrate on your navel. At no point should you think about your dreams. Then, imagine a wheel on your navel, that will be constantly spinning at high speed, for half an hour. Then sleep for about forty minutes. If the meditation has been strong and comes from the deepest part of your heart, dreams will be divine, dynamic, beautiful, poignant, and full of color. They will be about angels or deities, about your spiritual life, or inspiring things.

Another possibility is to meditate about ten minutes before bedtime. What is clear is that while you experience these *divine*

To start meditating, you just need to choose a comfortable position and to control your mind, avoiding any thoughts that could distract you.

The dream is a vehicle of the spirit that resolves internal conflicts. Furthermore, it provides peace and gives hope and vitality to the dreamer, expressing a strong bond with the sacred.

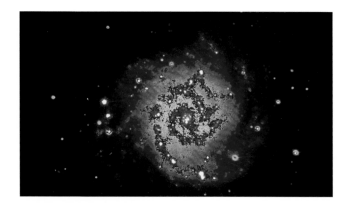

emotions, doors that lead to higher worlds or planes open for your consciousness.

As a preliminary step to meditate it is advisable to relax, for which there are few very useful and simple techniques, like autogenous training. We recommend Shia Green's book *Relajación para Gente muy Ocupada* (*Relaxation for Busy People*), published by this same publisher.

It also describes various techniques for meditation: making the mind go blank, focusing on your own breathing, focusing on a single object ... We chose the latter, which is very easy to learn and practice.

Meditation with the mind focused on a single object

First, you must choose a quiet place where you can be quiet and still between fifteen and thirty minutes at least. Also choose a position where you feel comfortable, for example, sitting; you do not need to pretend to be holy men in the Himalayas, sitting in perfect lotus posture, with a few weeks of fasting and about to attain enlightenment. In this case it is enough to just control your mind and avoid any thought that may distract you. Sounds easy? Try it ...

1) Place a flower, a candle, or a pleasant object in front of you, at some distance (a little more than 3 feet might be good). The idea is to focus all attention on the chosen object as you become aware of your own breath. You do not even have to breath purposely, just look how the rib cage goes up and down without trying to control it.

2) Focus on the object. If there are some thoughts going through your mind let them flow—do not fight them—while focusing on the object without getting distracted for a moment. Observe its

details and slowly close your eyes until the image disappears. If your eyes are closed and you do not clearly see the object of meditation, repeat the process.

3) With eyes already open, do a couple of breathing sequences, slow and deep, before beginning to slowly move the body prior to ending the meditation.

For all the Indians of North America, the dream is the most important sign of experience and determines the appointment of priests and the title of shaman or man of knowledge. The dream determines the authority.

The "dream catcher" is a beautiful handcrafted *healing wheel* that is a common gift to lovers or friends, or on the occasion of a birth or a celebration. According to the legend, they are used to trap nightmares and dissolve them in the web.

The dreamcatcher's legend

Long ago, when the world was young, an old Lakota shaman had a vision while he was on top of a mountain. In his vision, Iktomi, Grand Prankster and Master of Knowledge, appeared in the form of a spider and spoke in sacred language. While the spider was

In ancient cultures that are close to nature, like native tribes from North America, "tools for protection" such as the "dreamcatcher" (or dream catcher) are often used.

According to the native elders from North America, the dreamcatcher holds the destiny of each person.

speaking to him, it took, from the oldest willow, a hoop that had feathers, horsehair, beads, and offerings and began to weave a web inside. Iktomi told the shaman about the cycles of life, about how we begin life as babies, how we walk through childhood into adulthood and then into old age, a stage at which we must be treated like babies, thus completing the circle. "But at every stage of life," continued Iktomi while weaving the web, "there are many forces, some good and some evil. If you listen to the good they will guide you in the right direction. But if you listen to the evil forces they will hurt you and guide you in the wrong direction. Thus, these forces can help or interfere with the harmony of nature." While the spider was speaking, it continued weaving the web to the center of the hoop.

When Iktomi was finished speaking, he gave the elder shaman of the Lakota the web that he had woven and said, "This web is a perfect circle with a hole in its center. Use it to help your people achieve their goals by making good use of their ideas, dreams, and visions. If you have trust in the Great Spirit, the web will catch the good ideas while the negative ones will meander through the hole."

The elder shaman communicated this vision to his people and, even today, many Indian tribes hang a dream catcher on their bed in order to protect their dreams and visions.

The good forces are caught in the web and placed next to the people, while evil originated in their dreams seeps through the hole and is no longer part of their lives.

How to make a dreamcatcher

If you are interested in making a dream catcher will you need:

- 1 wooden ring, diameter 8" (you can buy it in a crafts store);
- 6 feet of 3-strand embroidery floss;
- 1 fine needle (to go through the beads) but with a wide head.

For decoration: crystal or wooden beads; feathers; marine coral or shells; dried leaves of different colors; dried or artificial flowers; wood chips; bows; etc.

• Divide the wooden ring into eight equal parts and mark them out with a pencil.

• Thread the needle and tie firmly at mark # 1. Always make sure that the thread remains tense.

Figure 1

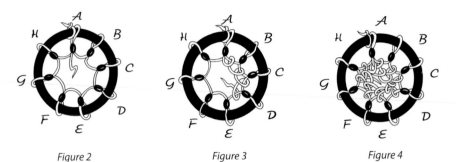

Figure 2   Figure 3   Figure 4

- Introduce two beads and pass the thread through mark # 2 going clockwise. Insert the needle into the second bead, so that the end of the thread goes through the bead (Figure 1). Repeat this operation along the wooden ring up to mark # 8.

- Next, get the needle through the the first bead and slide the thread again by mark # 1 and the first bead (Figure 2).

- Keeping clockwise direction, get the needle through the first and second beads, drawing a bow with the thread. Then, get the needle through the second and the third bead. Keep making these knots up to mark # 8.

- After the first ring of thread is finished, repeat the same steps above to make a second ring inside (Figure 3).

- Continue to weave smaller rings.

- When the dreamcatcher is completed, you will see a perfect circle in the center. Tie the thread with a last loop (Figure 4) and let hang about 12 inches so you can add the beads, feathers, etc. by making bows and knots.

On the left, "Mystic Dream," painting by Dwarbankind. On the right, a "dreamcatcher kite."

A pillow to facilitate sleep

These pillows reduce stress and help you get to sleep.
You will need:

- 2 pieces of soft natural fiber fabric (about 24"x12")
- 2 pieces of muslin for the sack of medicinal plants
- needle and thread

For the filling: cotton, capoc (impermeable natural fiber)

Medicinal plants: chamomile, lavender, and rose petals in equal parts; a few drops of lavender essential oil.

• Put all the herbs in a container and add a drop or two of the essential oil. Mix well.

• Sew the two pieces of muslin for the little bag, leaving one side open. Put the herbs inside and sew it completely shut.

• Sew the two pieces of cloth with the outer side facing in (as shown in figure 1), leaving one side open to add the filling.

• Turn inside out and fill with impermeable material. Add the sack of herbs in the center of the pillow, finish filling, and sew completely shut.

The dream test

What is your level of oneiric lucidity? Are you a distant, realist, or lucid dreamer? With this test you can discover how you relate with your dreams and the degree of importance you place in them.

1. **Do you usually remember your dreams?**
   a) Almost never.
   b) Only when one makes a strong impression.
   c) Pretty frequently.

2. **What do you remember from these episodes?**
   a) An isolated image.
   b) Concrete scenes, not always defined.
   c) I remember quite a few details of what happened.

3. **What are the images like?**
   a) Always in black and white.
   b) Sometimes black and white, sometimes in color.
   c) Always in color.

4. **Who is the protagonist?**
   a) A third person.
   b) Sometimes I'm the observer, sometimes the protagonist.
   c) I'm almost always the protagonist.

5. **Are you conscious of what you're doing?**
   a) No, the dream dictates my movements.
   b) Only in certain moments.
   c) Yes, I'm conscious of my actions.

6. **Are the settings of the episodes very detailed?**
   a) No, they are vague and undefined.
   b) I recognize the places but don't notice much detail.
   c) Yes, exactly like real life.

7. **Do you notice strange or incoherent elements?**
   a) No, while I'm dreaming everything seems normal.
   b) I notice some incoherencies: doors or windows where they shouldn't be, people who change roles, distortion of measurements and perspective, etc.
   c) Yes, that's how I realize I'm dreaming.

8. **Do you have the power to change the course of the dream?**
   a) Never.
   b) In certain moments—for example, at the critical point of a nightmare—I can interrupt the episode.
   c) Yes, sometimes I have autonomy to decide my movements inside the dream.

9. **Do you sometimes dream that you wake up, only to realize later you were still asleep?**
   a) Never.
   b) Sometimes.
   c) Often.

10. **Can you determine the theme of the dream?**
    a) Never
    b) Very rarely.
    c) Yes, if I'm very interested in something concrete.

> Points: A: 0 points   B: 1 point   C: 2 points

Less than 10 points
Your relationship with dreams is distant. You experience the episodes as if they were blurry images or sensations. In order to deepen your oneiric journeys it may be very helpful to write a journal.

From 10 to 20 points

You are a "realist" dreamer. The scenes in your dreams are pretty solid, although not lucid. If you want to improve the quality of your dreams, you can practice meditation before sleeping.

More than 20 points

You may be a lucid dreamer. You have an advanced level of consciousness during the episodes, so you can travel through them almost at will. You are prone to have premonitory dreams or communicate with other people in dreams.

PART TWO

Meet the dreams
Dreams from A to Z

The interpretation of dreams: how to use this guide

Subjective messages

As we commented in the first part, this dictionary cannot simply be applied to the letter. The dreams of each person are completely individual, and no book can tell you exactly what a certain dream or symbol means to you. You must make the interpretation for yourself; this is the attitude that this manual is trying to inspire, since the objective is for it to be a useful orientation and point of departure.

The factors that influence the interpretation of dreams are aspects such as the quotidian context, memories of the past, personal aspirations, fears, worries, and character . . . And although many things coincide with the collective experience, the language of each person's dreams is particular and nontransferable. In this way, any differential element, no matter how small, can change the final reading, or at least give it considerable context. The oneiric meaning that we offer for each symbol will help you orient your interpretation and decipher what your subconscious is trying to tell you.

In order to make the analysis simpler, we've also included some interpretations of specific dreams, in which we keep in mind not just the elements of the dream but also the moment in time the dreamer was living—their fears, worries, the external circumstances at the time of the dream, etc.

The language of each person's dreams is particular and nontransferable. The daily context, memories, aspirations, fears, worries, character . . . are all factors that influence the interpretation of our dreams.

To correctly analyze your dream, first you must take note of the most significant element that appears in it; it could be an object, a story, a character . . . Often, you know instinctively what to center on. However, if after reflection you can't make sense of this element, change your goal.

143

The language of your dreams

When we discover the most important element of a dream, look up its meaning in the alphabetical list in this book. Keep in mind that the atmosphere of the dream is often as important as the theme: if you dream, for example, that you've lost your suitcase and are searching without success, the element of loss and the idea of searching could be just as important as the fact that it is a suitcase—and not another object—that appears. The sensations that the dream produces are also very meaningful: do you feel anxious? Lost? Or do you stay calm the whole time?

You also have to distinguish from the start what of that information is related to recent events (saved in your immediate memory). What happened to us the day before, or what we are preparing to do the next, can appear reflected in our dreams and thus distract us. In this way, cases which are directly connected to current events usually don't mean much beyond the literal.

Finally, it is helpful to talk about your dreams with intuitive people who are close to you, since their opinion could open the doors of the dream to you. Often, a more objective vision can reveal things about yourself that you are not conscious of.

Two interpretations: psychological and esoteric

The interpretation of dreams is helpful in getting to know yourself and understanding your current psychological state better. Of course, there is not just one correct form of interpretation for everyone. Depending on the dreamer and their circumstances, the reading will go one way or the other. With the help of common symbols, we begin to discover the message that our subconscious wants to transmit.

In the next pages, we offer an extensive list of entry, along with the meaning and symbolism that they communicate. You will observe that some words include, in addition to the common psychological explanation, another more enigmatic interpretation: the esoteric point of view.

On one hand, the psychological meaning of figures comes from the theories of Freud and Jung (explained in the first part of the book), also keeping in mind other advances in the field of psychology. On the other hand, the esoteric meaning comes from the traditions and beliefs of ancient civilizations. These deal with the omens recorded in old books about dreams: the premonitions and superstitions that we have been able to find.

A

Abacus ▪ Represents a mental effort to develop intellectual activities. On the other hand, it is an element indicating the need to organize or review finances. It may be considered the desire to take inventory of possessions, both material and spiritual.

Abandonment ▪ This dream relates to leaving something behind and opening new horizons. Many times, the feeling of abandonment is linked to escape, which indicates cowardice regarding a given situation. Conversely, if the abandonment produces a feeling of joy, it is a sign of hope in the future. Dreaming of being abandoned generally predicts problems and difficulties; it means you feel uncared for or emotionally neglected. It may be due to a grudge you have kept since childhood. Usually, it reflects a need for self-expression or being understood by others. If the person who leaves is your mother, these problems could be of material nature; however, if the one who leaves is your father, it usually means unwillingness to achieve your goals. You may also be seeking advice about an aspect of your life or someone with authority to show you the way forward. In contrast, if it is your partner who says goodbye, you must face all kinds of problems of your own making.

❖ When abandonment is the protagonist itself, the dream indicates insecurity caused by the desire to possess the person who is turning their back. Finally, if it is you who abandons someone or something, the unconscious is pushing you to change environments or habits, because you are too attached to certain principles or settings. When this kind of dream comes after the death of a loved one, it means you are starting to recover from pain and to accept your feelings of anger, depression, fear, or even abandonment.

❖ If you leave something unpleasant, you will get good economic news. When you leave someone you value, the times ahead will be difficult. If you are the one abandoned, reconciliation will arrive soon.

Abbey ▪ All religious buildings in dreams can be interpreted, roughly, in the same manner. The abbey symbolizes questions or concerns—in the intellectual, moral or spiritual realm of our life—that are about to emerge. When a building appears in a dream, it usually represents the dreamer herself, her body, or the different levels of her mind. An abbey is a sacred place and not lavish, like your true Self. If the abbey is old, it is advisable to consult the old stories of the Celtic tradition and the first Christians; their valuable knowledge will favor your spiritual awakening.

❖ Although almost all faiths believe dreaming of an abbey is a good omen, there are some different superstitions. When the dreamer is a young woman, this dream predicts disease. And, if the abbey is in ruins, it means that your plans will fail. However, if the path to access it is blocked, you will be safe from a painful mistake.

Abbot ▪ The figure of the monk or abbot is associated with wisdom. It appears in moments of doubt and can signify the need to go to a person willing and able to listen, understand, and guide the dreamer (who cannot solve the problem alone).

❖ Ancient traditions claim that dreaming of an abbot means sickness is near or someone is hatching a conspiracy. Dreaming of an abbess, however, denotes good friendships.

Abdomen ▪ The cause of this dream may be physiological: heartburn or indigestion. From an emotional standpoint, it represents something that you can't stand anymore and wish to get away from. The interpretation varies according to the size of the abdomen. Thus, a heavy one shows that the subject is conscious of her personal or social duties; a slim one symbolizes losses or economic issues; if it is growing, it is because the loads get heavier by the day and you can't foresee how to deal with them; and a wrinkled one predicts betrayal. If the abdomen is bleeding there is a chance of an accident or tragedy within the family; and if it belongs to a child, infection may occur shortly. It also has sexual connotation. On a woman, it predicts longing for maternity.

❖ According to traditional folklore, dreaming of your own abdomen is a sign good things are on the way, but you will have to work for them. Likewise, it predicts infidelity. An image of a worn abdomen warns against possible lies.

Abduction ▪ Dreaming that you are victims of abduction signifies that you should quickly mobilize yourself if you do not want to be trapped in distressing situations that will limit your liberty to make decision. The dream could also be warning you of someone (possibly your dream abductor, which could also symbolize a part of your personality) systematically imposing their expectations on you. You have to try to fix the most pressing problems instead of lamenting in silence. The key is not to permit others to decide for you.

Ablutions ▪ Ablutions (a ritual consisting of bathing in clean water) symbolize purification. In ancient times, this practice was considered to help eliminate

inner demons. In the oneiric field, ablutions are a sign that you are in a great position to conduct business in which entrepreneurial spirit is required. Of course, if the water is cloudy it is a sign that, despite your best intentions, you will have to overcome all kinds of adversaries.

Abortion ▪ An abortion (your own or someone else's) signifies that the situation that is worrying you will not end happily the way you are approaching it. It is advisable, then, to change tactic, to build new projects on stronger foundations, and to plan again without trusting appearances. No wonder abortion is a synonym for failed plans.

❖ It indicates liberation, the end of a penance, troubles that will no longer weigh on the dreamer.

Abscess ▪ It may be the cause of a real physical discomfort. This is the first choice to rule out. In other cases, abscesses are always something undesirable. When they appear in dreams it can be a sign that there is something inside yourself that makes you uncomfortable. It can also be interpreted as a warning about forthcoming problems or issues that must mature before they are resolved.

❖ It predicts wealth for friends and relatives. But for the dreamer, it is a sign of health complications related to sleeping itself.

Absolution ▪ Dreaming that you are absolved (by a person, a tribunal, or any other institution, either religious or secular) predicts that others will improve their attitudes toward you. It can even be that you forgive yourself. It is important to keep in mind that many individuals find the most severe judge inside themselves.

Abstention ▪ Dreaming that you are in front of huge amounts of food or beverage but unable to try them represents a situation of abstinence. It is often a recurrent dream, especially, while dieting or for individuals that are trying to overcome an addiction. It represents the enormous effort the dreamer is exerting in order to achieve their goal. Sometimes, a former smoker dreams that he holds a cigar and, without even realizing, has smoked half of it. Frequently, the dream ends violently. The dreamer wakes up terrified, feeling that all her effort was in vain. This type of dream seems to be a signal from the unconscious not to trust your self-control entirely and remain alert to avoid falling back into such a vice.

Abundance ■ As it occurs with some symbols, the interpretation of abundance is the opposite of its literal manifestation. Dreaming of material wealth provokes a very nice and pleasant feeling but this kind of oneiric image should be taken with due precaution. The temporal possession could lead you into think that it is permanent and will last forever. However, as is widely known, that is not the case. Judeo-Christian tradition clearly understands this as Joseph explains the dream of seven fat cows and seven gaunt ones (the parable symbolizes the alternation between prosperity and poverty). Ultimately, this kind of dream could be reminding us we must not get used to any particular condition of abundance because chances are high it will evolve into a period of famine.

❖ This dream provides a false certainty, an external abundance that, in fact, only hides misery. In case such fortune is shared with a friend, it is a happy prediction of achievement, satisfaction, and joy.

Abyss ■ The majority of primitive peoples understood abysses as various deep marine or terrestrial features. To the Celts, the abyss was found inside the mountain; in Ireland and Japan it was located at the bottom of the sea or lakes; and among the Mediterranean peoples it was beyond the horizon. Each individual has their own problems and own daily abyss (in which they occasionally fall victim to anxiety). Conflictive situations, if not addressed promptly, can become "abysmal." Thus, this dream represents you are on the verge of something but you are afraid to take the plunge. It is important to find out what that fear is about and why you feel so bad. When the abyss is dark it likely symbolizes your unknown Self. If you are also anxious, you will not be pleased about what your feelings and hidden fears have to tell you. Dreams about abysses are often accompanied by vertigo. This vertigo can be physical if you are lying on the edge of the bed; emotional, when you are unable to control your feelings about others; existential, due to absence of goals that give your life meaning; or directly related to your circumstances, perhaps because you need to make a decision without knowing which option is best. In the latter case, it is advisable to take enough time and choose well, thus avoiding any type of precipitation.

❖ Usually an abyss forecasts financial difficulties. You must be very careful with any deals being considered in the next few the days. According to ancient beliefs, this dream portends problems in love, work, or health. It is recommended to be cautious.

Acacia ■ It is a tree of high symbolic importance. Both in ancient Egypt and Christianity, it has an spiritual character tied to the immortality of the soul. Depending on the plot of the dream, seeing or being close to a blossoming acacia represents a moment of calm and spiritual growth. On the other hand, if the acacia is losing leaves, it may indicate a fear of aging or a feeling of loss.

❖ It suggests internal strength. The person who dreams of an acacia will not be defeated by adversity and will receive good news shortly.

Academy ■ If the dreamer is not of school age, the academy suggests frustration due to a failed project, as well as the need for news on pending subjects from people around them. Dreaming that you are the owner of an academy shows that, though lessons will be learned in real life, they will not be clearly assimilated or properly applied.

Acanthus ■ A plant with delicate flowers and thorns. In the middle ages it was considered a symbol of pain and sin. In dreams, it indicates a situation that is both difficult and pleasant. Another possible interpretation is a triumph after much effort.

Accident ■ Studies have verified that some individuals have premonitory dreams, many of them about disasters or accidents; despite this fact, our oneiric activity is often an expression of our fears and secret anxieties. Therefore, dreams that portray accidents must not necessarily be taken literally because they tend to highlight a conflict in which we are immersed. So, if you are victim of an accident maybe there is something in real life that is not going well or you are taking too much risk. Sometimes it is necessary to review your existence and try to avoid making mistakes. When it is a car or train accident, the incident indicates that your judgments are precipitated, which may portend future arguments. But if you dream of a plane crash, the unconscious is transmitting a clear symbol of irrationality (the dreamer refuses to see reality as it is). If you are driving at high speed, maybe the dream is telling you to take everything more calmly and to avoid rushing. When the accident victim is someone else, you must find the answer in your feelings. Perhaps, the envy or hatred you feel for that person can only find an outlet in your dreams. In the case of a home accident, the conflict is not far from the everyday environment of the person. Lastly, disasters caused by natural elements, such as fire or water (fires, floods, earthquakes), are usually related to a fact that has recently impacted us.

❖ It is recommended to be cautious for twenty-four hours following this dream. According to some oneiric traditions, accidents in the sea represent matters of love. On land, they symbolize business problems. Witnessing an accident denotes cowardice; helping the injured, betrayal of a friend. According to gypsy tradition, this dream is a warning so the accident can be prevented.

Acclamation ▪ If you are acclaimed but unable to see the face of those who do so, it means you are in danger (vanity is hurting you). On the other hand, if cheers are scarce and you can identify the faces of those who praise you, success will be brief and will only serve to flatter your ego.

Accordion ▪ If you are playing a monotonous melody on the accordion, the unconscious is probably warning you that you complain too much, which in turn puts off people who might help you. If you listen to someone playing this instrument it means that you are the subject of someone else's unfounded complaints.

Account ▪ Its symbolism is similar to the ABACUS. It is interpreted as a warning sign. It is commonly said that when there is little the subject counts. So it may be indicative of a point in life where you feel you need to control your expenses or the delivery of your affections.

Accumulating ▪ Such images have a reverse meaning. So, if you dream of accumulating money you must be careful—economic losses are approaching. If it is about collecting objects, the episode might predict scarcity.

Accusation ▪ If in dreams you are publicly accused, it is likely you feel guilty about some matter of ethical or moral character. If this occurs in front of your family, it will be because you are not sufficiently consistent. If the charge occurs in private, you may be carrying a small remorse.

Acid ▪ This corrosive substance may indicate complicated and even dangerous relationships with the environment. Thus, caution is advised when relating to others; advice could be interpreted as criticism and turn against you.

❖ If a woman dreams of acidulous liquors it means that she will soon be immersed in distress.

Acorn ▪ This fruit is a symbol of prosperity, physical health, and spiritual well-being. Its appearance in dreams indicates that the dreamer goes through a fortunate time of greatness and spiritual strength.

❖ According to gypsy tradition, an acorn in dreams indicates health, vigor, and material gains.

Acrobat ▪ An acrobat symbolizes inversion—a need to reverse the situation in all crises (personal, moral, collective, historical). Therefore, to see yourself, or an acrobat, pirouetting in a dream warns you against a situation of instability, because this type of dream involves risk. If it is an uncomfortable feeling, it might mean the instability happening in real life could end negatively (for example, economic losses). In these cases, the resolution of the dream will match future events. On the contrary, if these stunts are pleasant from an aesthetic point of view, the conflict you are worried about will probably make you stronger. And the most important is that you will clearly discover your true direction in life.

❖ Popular tradition attributes the acrobat to inversion, the turning of a situation: adversity turned into joy, and vice versa, happiness turned into obstacles.

Actor/actress ▪ Dreaming that you are an actor or actress indicates that you feel dissatisfied with your personality, and might need to perform or pretend in order to be successful. The mask intrinsic to the figure of the actor might be useful to prevent being hurt by the attacks of others, but this attitude often hides your authenticity. Dreaming that you have forgotten your role in a play is a sign you have a hard time adjusting to everyday situations. If it is not you who is playing a role but someone else, you will have to watch out for deceptions; it is likely someone around you is hiding their true intentions.

Adam (and Eve) ▪ The figures of Adam and Eve predict that a memorable event will dash our hopes of success. Seeing the two of them in the garden means that betrayal and treachery will plot together in order to banish good fortune.

Admission ▪ This dream is a warning that calls for rectification of attitudes, judgments, or dreamer's actions during waking life. The mind of the individual is not satisfied with itself and the unconscious manifests so in this way.

Adoption ■ If the dreamer does not have children in real life (but the individual does want them), these types of oneiric thoughts will simply reflect such unrealized wishes. Otherwise, the adoption may mean that you are accepting responsibilities that do not belong to you. Although you might receive admiration by doing so, it really makes your life harder. On the other hand, these images are also related to infertility and distrust in your own capabilities. Therefore, you should rely more on yourself and try to develop the creative aspects of your personality.
❖ Dreaming that you are being adopted ensures a profitable future, while adopting a child predicts wealth accumulation during old age, or an inheritance if it is a relative's adoption.

Adultery ■ Dreaming that you are cheating on your partner means that your relationship does not satisfy you at all and you may be having difficulties that go beyond your emotional level. Maybe you are concerned about your sexuality or you want something that is not as convenient for you. Adultery may also reflect the need to overcome certain prejudices or repressions, so it is very helpful to look at the characteristics of the person with whom you are unfaithful to your partner. These traits will reveal your current needs and, thus, the causes of insatisfaction that produced this type of dream. Likewise, it is important to remember that during the days before a wedding, the bride and groom tend to experience dreams about adultery. Thus, as you approach the date of the big day, the bride and groom often imagine themselves, while asleep, having sex with third parties. These scenes are directly related to the fear and anxiety experienced by many individuals due to the imminence of a commitment like marriage.
❖ When a man dreams he is an adulterer, there will be an action of legal nature. If it is a woman, she will lose the love of her husband.

Adversary ■ Confronting an adversary reflects fear and, at the same time, the decision to address your personal issues or limitations. It is probably representative of an aspect you dislike about yourself and that has created an inner conflict. It is important to be attentive to the way the conflict resolves because it will be indicative of how you feel in real life.
❖ It is said that beating an opponent in dreams brings misfortune because it means negative friendships will end up hurting you in real life.

Adversity ■ Adversity means that, in real life, you need to respond rapidly to a situation or challenge. In oneiric terms, it usually means creative momentum and positive energy. It can also be attributed to the fact that you are tired and need to recover.

Advice/council ■ To give advice announces a break-up; to receive them, reward and faithful friends; to ask for them ensures a triumph. A family council is a sad omen of struggle; a war council denotes painful memories; a State council ensures protection. (See GRANDFATHER)

Agate ■ Dreaming of an agate is a sign that you feel helpless, so you seek help from others in order to solve certain problems. If in real life the dreamer is dedicated to agricultural activities, then this promises good harvests.

Age ■ Poet William Blake stated that "progress is the punishment of God." The life's path is a personal experience that often involves gradual loss of childhood's values. Age-related dreams can have several different meanings. Dreaming that you are younger indicates the need to review the past. Some aspect of childhood or adolescence that has not been settled is emerging now. However, if you dream of being older than you currently are, you may be anticipating events. In this case, the unconscious is reminding you to live day by day, intensely, without thinking too much about the future.
❖ Dreaming of senior citizens reports good luck. If you grow older, a failure is announced. If it's a friend who gets older the dream tells that she will let you down. Dreaming of young people, however, is a sign of family reconciliation and favorable time for launching new companies. Dreaming that you become young again predicts you will make great efforts to regain lost opportunities. If a mother dreams that her adult child is a baby again the dream announces healing of old wounds and revival of youthful hopes.

Aggression ▪ Situations in which we attack others or are attacked by others represent a difficult time and a hostile environment around us. It is possible that the dreamer is refraining from openly expressing negative opinions due to fear.

Agonizing ▪ This dream portends a radical change in the life of those who experience it. So, if you are sick and agonize in a dream, it is likely that you will recover soon. On the other hand, if you are perfectly healthy, it is a sign that you are threatened by a disease. If it is a different person who agonizes, that person's attitude towards you will turn around.

❖ To see oneself dying is, for some, a key sign of illness, pain, or loss of inheritance. And for others, a prediction of longevity. To see somebody unknown agonizing indicates unexpected benefits.

Air ▪ Out of the four elements, air and fire are considered active and masculine, while water and earth are passive and feminine. In elementary cosmogony, sometimes fire is considered the primordial source of all things, but the belief in the air as foundation is more widespread. At the oneiric level, air refers to communication, reason, logic, and, above all, imagination. Dreaming that you are being transported through air indicates that you begin to clearly see your own issues and that you are moving away from those problems. Air, in fact, helps to establish a balance between actions and emotions. If the air is cold, you might be unfairly judging someone close who appreciates you. On the other hand, if it is humid air (or steam) it means that you are not thinking clearly so your decisions may be wrong. Breeze, moreover, is inspiring spirit and life-giving force.

❖ Clean and clear air, since ancient times, is an omen of serene prosperity, happiness, and luck, as well as friendship and reconciliation. However, for some old books of dreams, dreaming of air means our hopes will vanish.

Alarm ▪ As in real life, alarms that appear in dreams are warnings against danger that must be taken into account to avoid unpleasant situations; especially if these images are frequent.

❖ The oneiric alarms can be sirens, whistles, shouts, or light signals. In the latter case, if they are located in a door or window it means that people that you trust could betray you. If it is yourself who sets the alarm off, then you must take on your projects as soon as possible; situations that could alter those plans may appear later.

Alchemy ▪ For Carl Jung, the art of alchemy was a system of symbols. The transformation of the subject occurred through them: the subject's personality would go from a basic state (lead) to a different one (gold). So, he considered that the symbols from alchemy were archetypal images of the unconscious. If you have this dream, therefore, it is possible you will go through an internal change.

❖ Alchemy was, in the Middle Ages, what psychology is for us today. Its symbolism still identifies with internal success throughout the unconscious.

Alcohol ▪ Its figure represents the union of two opposite elements: water and fire. The vital force of both complements to one another and produces an explosive result. It is a purifying element, but is also a way to drunkenness.

Algae ▪ Algae that appear in oneiric thoughts may have very diverse interpretations. If they are collected or simply found, the subject is not acting sensibly, so you should reconsider your ways. When others are those who collect them, it means that some of your secrets will be made public by close people who want to harm you. Dreaming that you eat algae implies gathering forces to address adversity. If you only taste them, wasting them, there is the possibility that a business fails.

Alien ▪ It marks an encounter with a part of you that you find strange or incomprehensible. It may feel hostile or contrary to you. First, you need to figure out what it is, and also, why you reject it. Perhaps, you have been behaving in an unusual way lately. It is a mistake not to accept this fact. What at first seems terrifying, over the time can become a great help for success. In addition, the alien can be yourself. The cause may be a recent event, such as a new job. Getting used to a new environment often makes us feel like real Martians.

❖ Many people believe that aliens are another product of modernity, so there are no traditional interpretations of this dream.

Almond tree ▪ The blossomed almond tree announces the beginning of spring. Its white flowers are beautiful but at the same time delicate and fragile. The almond tree is associated with feelings of rebirth and renovation. Despite all that, this tree flowers' fragility indicates projects may not be long lasting.

Almonds ■ If you dream of almonds it means that you will enjoy pleasant moments after overcoming some difficulties. However, if they are bitter, you may face disappointment that will bring you sadness during a certain period of time. If this dry fruit appears damaged, you will go through disillusion regarding the achievement of your desires.

Alms ■ If you are given alms in a dream, an economic project that you have underway may fail. However, it also means that you get by with little. Although a dream about alms seems to have only connotations related to money, it may also be linked to the spiritual realm. If you ask for alms but do not receive them, it means you are going through a precarious time. But if you give alms to another person, it may be an omen of unexpected gains.
❖ Alms are an omen of triumph over the difficulties and of longevity.

Alphabet ■ To recite the alphabet while sleeping indicates not only the need to organize the ideas, but also a waste of the subject's talents in the past, through neglect or indifference.

Altar ■ An altar could suggest acknowledgement, adoration, or exaltation for the most religious people. Altars also predict forthcoming weddings, although if they are ruined it is a reflection of grief and loss of moral values. From a religious standpoint the altar has different meanings. It is a place of sacrifice, so this dream could refer to a sacrifice you need to make or something that you have sacrificed for a good cause. It is not always related to something material. Sometimes it is necessary to sacrifice your own ego and to express your own real feelings some more. An altar is also a symbol of a marriage between the conscious and the unconscious. The union of this opposing elements favors the creation of a unique and strong personality.
❖ Dreaming that you are in a church is a bad omen because it represents mistakes and signs of repentance. If there is a priest by the altar, it warns against disputes and domestic or professional problems. However, if you look at this church from the outside, blessing and fortune are coming soon.

Altar candle ■ An altar candle symbolizes the efforts you have to make to get to know everything around you, the passage of time consumed slowly. It conveys a sense of heaviness, slowness.

❖ A lit candle is an announcement of marriage or birth. To see that it is slowly burning indicates good health; but if it is quickly consumed it predicts disease.

Altitude ■ Dreaming of altitudes without feeling vertigo means that the dreamer is courageous and undertakes any given challenge. In other words your unconscious is telling you that you are hard to scare. On the contrary, once on the top, dreaming that you get sick indicates that you are still not prepared to face the issues you have to deal with. To the ones that experience this dream it is advisable to wait a prudent time before beginning any given project.

Ambulance ■ The ambulance is a symbol of help, so it is a positive omen. If you perform a dangerous job in real life, the meaning of the ambulance has no premonitory character, but it simply advises that you observe maximum security measures.

Ambush ■ It usually indicates fear of unexpected changes that can have negative consequences on the dreamer's life. It denotes insecurity and precaution toward the surrounding environment and also an inability to control a situation. If the dreamer is the one who prepares the ambush the meaning is the opposite: it reflects confidence, tact, and boldness to manage dangerous situations.

Amputation ■ Dreaming that you have a limb amputated represents the inability to perform some of the activities that you usually perform with it. Behind this situation, there is a fear you should try to overcome.

Amulet ■ It shows that the dreamer believes in fate, fortune, and, therefore, bad luck. This image also indicates that, at the time, a "childish spirit" dominates you, so it is better not to make practical decisions of high impact. Instead, it is a good opportunity for games and fantasy. The amulet is also a symbol showing the impulse to control or manipulate anything or anyone.

Ancestor ■ See GRANDPARENTS

Anchor ■ An anchor transmits stabilizing force. It usually appears when you need confidence and a decisive influence in life. On the other hand, it also has negative connotations, as it may represent something that is holding you back and limiting your freedom. Perhaps, in this sense, you feel stuck in a relationship or a problem. Dreaming that you drop the anchor advises that you must pause to meditate. And if you pull it out you are ready to get going. According to the Freudian interpretation, dreaming of an anchor indicates that the subject is chained to the figure of the mother (the sea would represent the mother).

❖ Old superstitions claim that if a woman has this dream, one of her sons will become a sailor. In addition, it is said that it brings good luck to the sailor who dreams of it. For the rest, it denotes a change of residence or travel abroad. Typically, such omens are always good, but if the anchor appears hidden underwater, it expresses disappointment.

Angel ■ Angels have always been considered the messengers of God. In psychological terms, this dream could be a message from those parts of your inner self that want to lead you towards satisfaction and happiness. Angels also symbolize the invisible, the hidden forces. Dreaming of them, in this case, indicates that

Analysis of the dream

A N G E L   A L O N G

Ruth dreamed: At night I was on the roof of my house when I saw an angel flying. He was very handsome, measuring more than 6 feet, strong build, and long blond curls. The only outfit he was wearing was a long transparent tunic so I could tell he had a muscular body. I was impressed by his presence and in that moment, I felt a deep love. I never had that feeling in a dream. He remained suspended in the air, looking at me and smiling; and then he said, 'Ruth, open the door. I want to come into your house.' I woke up with a very pleasant tingling belly."

The oneiric angels are often carriers of divine messages. For more than two years Ruth had kept her heart doors closed. Someone **broke her heart** and she was not receptive to love at all, so she was not able to fall in love again. At the time of this dream Joe had appeared in her life, and with him, a whole torrent of romantic feelings. However, she remained hard and contemptuous to him. She liked him a lot but was **afraid to fall in love**.

The angel asking for permission to enter her house represents her unconscious willing to accept love again. To fall in love in dreams reflects the subject's desire to achieve a deep and sincere relationship.

you have embarked on a new journey in the course of personal evolution. So, it announces that you have great opportunities for self fulfillment and you must not waste them.

❖ If the angel looks sinister, you must look for something that is wrong in real life. It is important to take note of it and to dedicate yourself to fix it. Finally, dreaming of the angel of death is not a bad omen. Chances are it is related to your own anxiety that is looking for a way of expression.

❖ The oneiric angel predicts good luck in love, relationships, and friendships. When there are more than one it means that you will receive an inheritance; when it comes into your house, you will be healthy.

Animals ■ Animals often represent, in general, the qualities or defects with which they are traditionally associated. So, the dog may represent loyalty; dove, peace; turtle, longevity; tiger, power; etc. However, like in the other entries of this dictionary, you must always take into account the personal circumstances of the dreamer. If, for example, the dreamer has been bitten by a dog, her unconscious would hardly associate the figure of the dog with fidelity. On the other hand, animals refer to our most primal instincts and our basic desires. The dream may be calling attention to some aspect of your nature that you repress or underestimate. In any case, it is advising you to try to be more spontaneous and less rational. If you dream of eating an animal, it means that you are assimilating natural wisdom. If you fight against it, it means you are having trouble with your hidden self, rejected by the conscious. If the animal is guarding a treasure then the material passions are preventing you from spiritual fulfillment.

❖ Its meaning depends on whether it is about domestic or wild animals. While the wild animal is indicative of secret enemies and professional problems, the domestic one announces the return of absent friends and reconciliation. To own, feed, and care for them, especially if they are ruminants, indicates wealth and good businesses. Those endowed with horns predict happiness.

Antenna ■ Through an antenna you can increase the number of perceptions received. Thus, if you dream of this element, you should be aware of information that can be very useful.

Ants ■ When they are associated with pleasant oneiric images, ants are synonymous with difficult preparation work. But on many occasions, their multiplicity provokes an unfavorable meaning. If you see them invading your house, it demonstrates stress you suffer from problems that worry you. The most serious is to dream that they cover your body: this could reflect certain mental disorders. To dream of ants can also be a sign of a cutaneous eruption.

❖ Winged ants augur dangerous journeys. To squash them, destruction of your own fortune.

Anvil ▪ The anvil is made to support the blacksmith's blows as he molds iron. Dreaming of this tool indicates that you should endure the pressure of the thing to which you are submitted. Your strength will be compensated generously in the long run.

Anxiety ▪ No one has yet discovered the function of dreams in our lives. Some scientists believe that we sleep in order to dream, because dreams tidy all our emotions. Different experiments have shown that people who are sleep deprived present greater emotional disorders (for example, a disproportionate anxiety). Dreams, therefore, bring the psychological balance back. It is very common to have dreams that express anxiety and emotions that you cannot channel in real life. According to Freud, they show repressed aggression and resentment. Many of those, in fact, come from the subject's childhood. So wherever this oneiric anxiety appears, it is advisable to seek the hidden feelings that really cause it.

❖ Some beliefs state that anxiety dreams indicate exactly the opposite. In other words, it won't be long until your concerns are resolved. And, in a sense, when the individual expresses their fears in dreams, they get closer to their dissipation.

Ape ▪ The character of the ape tends to be gentle, so this dream could symbolize that part of your interior that wants to have a more simple and natural behavior. If the ape gives you fear, it represents the dark and repressed side of your personality.

❖ This dream denotes that there will be people who deceive you, so you will soon suffer trickery. In business, you should be very cautious with the promises that people make, as they could be false. If the ape is in a tree, one of your relatives will lie to you which will create large problems in the future.

Appetite ▪ This dream could take place when you have gone to bed while still being hungry. However, dreams that refer to appetite may reflect a need for more love and affection, as well as the need to express emotions. In any case, dreaming that you have an appetite is evidence of a desire to live and an important stream of energy.

❖ Having a lot of appetite is a sign of growing apart from family and friends. Not having it presupposes the arrival of bad news.

Apple ▪ The apple is related to sex; it symbolizes pleasure and sensuality. It's the forbidden fruit, the sin that Adam and Eve committed in paradise. In oneiric terms, it reveals a desire to enjoy earthly pleasures. If it is tasty, it indicates emotional satisfaction; if it is green, difficulties; if it is rotten, frustrations. From a Freudian point of view, eating an apple is synonymous with sexual appetite. The apple, however, also represents knowledge and freedom of choice. Just what Adam and Eve obtained when they left behind their innocence.

❖ Especially if they are red, dreaming of apples is a good omen. If they are ripe and sweet, you will be rewarded; if they are sour, you may suffer losses because of your own foolishness. Apples lying on the ground predict the dishonesty of your friends. Finally, if they are rotten, all your efforts will be in vain.

Apron ▪ The apron is usually synonymous with attaining the most secret desires. However, you must address its features to fully decipher the dream's meaning. Thus, if the apron is clean, those wishes will be achieved thanks to good luck; if it is broken or dirty, after hard work; and if it is white, with the help of a friend. If a woman dreams of an apron, the dream is a sign of a marriage full of hardships and difficulties.

Aquarium ▪ As always, the correct interpretation of such dreams depends on the details. So, looking at an aquarium with clear water and fish swimming inside reveals a happy and peaceful mood. However, if the water is dirty or the fish are nervous, the oneiric scene might be giving you clues about your repressed impulses. If the fish are dead in the aquarium it is a sign of vain hopes and disappointments.

Aqueduct ▪ If you dream of a well-preserved or in-use aqueduct, you can expect a prosperous future, full of all sorts of goods. If, however, it is incomplete or damaged, it can be a sign of poverty and a period of difficulties.

Armor ▪ If you dream that you are wearing armor it should be interpreted as the way you defend yourself from external influence. You fear getting hurt and therefore, you protect yourself, hiding your feelings. Armor can also symbolize strength and resistance against adversity. This is not always positive because in these cases the dreamer is often too enclosed in her own shell. It is likely that an individual with armor or shield is incapable of spontaneous interaction with people. In dreams, both protections are symbols that demonstrate anxiety. You must ask yourself what is it you want to defend yourself from. If you question your motives a little, you may discover you do not need to be so sheltered. With a little self-confidence and trust you can overcome it. In the case the armor refers to something that you will face in real life, it means that you are brave and well prepared.

❖ If you dream of carrying heavy armor it means you are taking life too seriously, without enjoying it. Those who believe in reincarnation interpret it as a vestige of past lives. If historical facts are revealed during the dream it will be interesting to prove their authenticity. Perhaps, you are remembering facts from your ancestral past . . .

Arms ■ Arms symbolize friendship and your ability to relate to others. To see yourself without arms reveals a serious emotional problem.

Army ■ An army means that you are trying to evade your responsibility to your community. Such images can also represent your employees or friends. Depending on the army's condition, you will know how much you can rely on them, if necessary.

❖ According to gypsy tradition, to see a victorious army predicts victory; defeated, bad news.

Arrival ■ An arrival is an event that marks the start of new situations. Whether the dreamer arrives someplace, or someone or something arrives suddenly, this dream could be caused by a prolonged state of lethargy and monotony. Perhaps, the dreamer desires an unexpected event to change the course of his life.

Arrow ■ Dreaming that you shoot an arrow suggests that you must be precise in your objectives. If you hit the target it means that you will achieve your goals. Instead, shooting an arrow upward is a sign of great hope and projects, which are likely to be spoiled by excessive ambition. A Freudian psychologist, however, interprets this image as a clear masculine sexual symbol.

❖ A medieval oneiric source claims this dream portends travel, entertainment, and celebrations. If you dream that an arrow is shot straight through your body it means you have a secret enemy. A broken arrow augurs disappointment in love or business.

Artist ■ Everyone, without exception, needs to be loved and recognized by others. This dream can represent your most creative and intuitive side. Maybe you need to express yourself from a creative perspective. For those who dream of being artists, this ambition is even more apparent. It may also tell you how to sublimate passions that you are not able to manifest. If you are painting a picture, it may represent the description of your own situation at the time. So, soon you will see things more clearly.

❖ Probably, you need to brush up your plans in order to gain recognition. If in the dream you talk about art, you might be promoted at work.

Ascension ■ Rising to a place in dreams indicates that you are capable of overcoming any obstacle that life puts in your path. This type of image reveals ascension to a superior plane. Such a situation permits you to improve your personal relationships. (See ELEVATOR, HILL, and JUMPING)

❖ This dream foretells economic losses.

Ash ■ Once the fire is out, ashes remain. Perhaps, you feel that all the good deeds in your lives have already taken place and there is nothing left. On the other hand, you can be too anchored to the past or overthinking something that is already over. Ashes can represent failure of a relationship or a business. Also, they are often identified with death and dissolution of bodies. Everything that comes into contact with the fire of life is submitted to ashes. For the Hindu tradition, ashes are a symbol of indestructibility. In a dream, they portray the irreducible part of yourself.

❖ Ashes predict disadvantages: bad harvests, unsuccessful businesses, and children who cause problems to their parents. According to gypsies, however, this dream means that you will finally stop lamenting opportunities lost a while ago. In many tribal societies ashes are also a symbol of fertility and good fortune. In England and the United States, in fact, it is believed they protect against evil spirits.

Asparagus ■ Its phallic shape makes it an undeniable symbol of the male sexual organ.

❖ To see asparagus out of the ground is a promise of prosperity; to cultivate them is synonymous with future happiness; and to eat them predicts domestic joy.

Assault ▪ This type of dream signals the need to change your lifestyle or moral beliefs. If you are the victim of an assault it means that, even though you want to experience a profound change (your existence does not satisfy you), you are not able to carry it out. If this attack produces a positive feeling, you should be alert to proposals or your own intuitions. On the contrary, if the feelings are unpleasant, you must avoid rushing into taking initiative in real life. It may also be the fact that you are the one who assaults someone else. If the action ends successfully, it indicates the time is right to make changes.

Asthma ▪ See DROWNING

Athlete ▪ Dreaming that you are an athlete means that you should help others without expecting retribution. If the oneiric athlete trips, it is a possible sign for alarm.

Attempt ▪ Indicates the intention and decision to get moving. It is almost always a positive dream that signifies you have lost the precaution and fear of the unknown and you are willing to start a new path or begin some type of project. The dreamer has enough self confidence to take initiative and accept the risks that come with it.

Attic ▪ Dreaming of this room is a negative sign because it relates to darkness and fear. Living in an attic, therefore, denotes a bad time in the economic field and lack of support to overcome such a situation.
❖ Dreaming that you are in an attic advises you to be careful; the dreamer is in serious danger.

Authority ▪ The dreams in which authority appears symbolize the degree of repression of the dreamer. Almost always, they indicate the existence of a conflict. (See STABBING and MURDER)

Autopsy ▪ An autopsy is a sincere desire for personal introspection. Such images are an invitation to better know yourself, taking full advantage of all experiences. Whether the autopsy is performed on you or someone else is irrelevant. In any case, the body represents the dreamer.

Autumn ▪ A serene season suggesting peace and melancholy. Autumn invites reflection, knowledge, inner maturation. After the splendor of summer, this season inspires some elegant decadence. Gradually, the winter is approaching, or the end of life, which is the same. Autumn given to introspection, allows you to face this inescapable end positively valuing that which you have had, without thinking about what you will soon lack. Consequently, this dream urges you to use knowledge and past experiences to solve the problems of the present. Dreams that refer to this season of falling leaves are often related to the next stage of life before old age or a fear of the arrival of that stage. These dreams usually occur to people of middle age, and although they are often melancholy, rarely are they deeply sad. They symbolize a reconciliation of age as a natural part of the cycle of nature.

Avalanche ▪ This type of dream reflects contingencies that may arise along the way. The subject dreams of avalanches when she is afraid of a disaster or failure. Intuitively, you might have discovered a flaw in your planning that needs to be fixed. It is advisable to try to identify the rest of images that appear in the dream to give them a sense within your fears. If the avalanche is made of dirt or rock, it would be best to keep an eye on your finances. Conversely, if it is a snow avalanche it means that the relationship with your partner is at risk of being buried. A veritable storm of passion is on its way.
❖ Some traditions say that this dream brings good luck, especially if you end up buried under the snow. It promises health and benefits. In the case it is other people who suffer the avalanche, it indicates a change in the environment.

Avenue ▪ The wider the avenue in the dream the more satisfied with life you are. It may also indicate the quick resolution of a conflict.
❖ A straight avenue is a symbol of hope; it announces prosperity, birth, and lasting love. But if it is angular and curvy, it announces disappointment and bitterness in some aspect of life.

Awakening ▪ This dream may symbolize a rebirth in your life. However, it may also mean that you are about to experience a lucid dream. In this case, your consciousness awakens in the oneiric scene and you can be part of it at will. Lucid dreams can help you increase your creativity or solve your psychological problems. For example, if someone is chasing you, you have the option to turn around and face the fear that haunts you. Native Americans applied this technique centuries ago to promote self-knowledge.

❖ Dreaming that you are walking through a beautiful landscape denotes better times after a difficult period. Many people cultivate the ability to wake up in dreams in order to gain information about the future. One method of achieving this is to imagine that you are in a time machine. The dream will come on in the calendar as you indicate, and your mind will receive relevant premonitions.

Axe ■ This is a symbol of power and authority. Dreams in which a axe appears reflect a latent aggressiveness that comes out in primitive acts. Scenes in which the axe is the protagonist manifest sickness and a lack of control of the senses. They can announce an encounter with someone conflictive and even fights that threaten the stability of your familial relationships. An axe that is used to cut firewood can express that you need to divide a problem into small parts to resolve it better. To cut down a tree, however, means that you are getting rid of old things so new ones can emerge.

❖ Apart from warning about some danger, this dream has different popular interpretations. If the blade of the axe is shiny, you will receive a pleasing reward. If the opposite is true, you will lose prestige. Equally, an axe foretells that soon you will have news from friends. Finally, for a woman, this dream augurs that she will find the man of her dreams but she will be forced to live in poverty.

B

Babble ■ When you are babbling in dreams, the unconscious is telling you to watch your words. It is also possible that you are talking casually about things that are not completely clear to you. If it is someone else who babbles it denotes you have a pejorative opinion towards that person or you are unable to understand her arguments.

Baby ■ Dreaming of a baby means that you are happy and alive, wanting to create. It represents something new in your life that is calling your attention. It also denotes that new ideas or feelings are rising from your inner self. On the other hand, it might reveal a deep desire to return to your origins and discover your true personality. In this regard, it symbolizes the pure and uncorrupted nature of the subject. Perhaps, the dream manifests that you are innocent of an indictment that concerns you. If you are turned into a baby it may reflect need for love and protection. Of course, this dream can also express the paternal or maternal instincts and the desire to make them come true. (See MOTHER, WIFE, and CHEST)

❖ Amazingly, most old books about dreams do not relate babies to pregnancy. On the contrary, if a woman dreams of raising a child, someone she trusts will disappoint her.

Back ■ The back symbolizes physical strength and endurance. However, if it is curved it reflects weakness of character or emotional dissatisfaction. According to other interpretations, the back is where we keep our secrets or those aspects of our personality that we do not want to hear about. If, in this case, the dream gives you an unpleasant feeling, traits that may have hidden in your back contain a good dose of guilt, shame, fear or disgust.

❖ Traditionally, it is said that evil is right behind. Therefore, to scare it off, many superstitious people throw spilled salt over their left shoulder. This dream may also point to a problematic situation that you have overcome, something that you have left behind.

Backpack ■ The backpack has several possible interpretations. On the one hand, it is a symbol of travel that reflects a provisional situation. You probably feel overwhelmed and exhausted by routine and want a change in your life. On the other, it also represents the burdens you carry day to day. The condition of the backpack and how heavy or light it is will be key to the correct interpretation of the dream.

Backwards (walking) ■ Dreaming that you walk backwards means that you are regressing in life. What you are looking for is increasingly farther away. You may feel unsuccessful, unable to achieve goals. Thanks to the warning sign of this dream, you must begin to take action. On the other hand, perhaps it expresses that the best option is to withdraw. Sometimes you waste time fighting for something that is not worth it. A good option is to stay back momentarily, regain your strength, and then return with more vigor and momentum.

Bacteria ■ If bacteria is present in your dreams it is synonymous with some kind of alteration, as these microscopic organisms cause changes in the human body. Bacteria usually announce that romantic relationships are altered and it is not the best time to make important decisions.

Bag ■ The bag represents the secrets and the most intimate psychological qualities that you have in life. For example, if it is full of junk it will manifest that you carry concerns. In this case, the problems are created by yourself. Instead, if it is full of food and valuables it will mean that you are incubating new ideas and knowledge.

❖ Depending on what you do with the bag the dream's meaning will vary. So, opening the bag and beginning to take out its content indicates the need to express your experiences or to reveal intimate secrets. But if you lose it, then it means that someone already knows about those secrets; and if someone steals it from you, then someone is trying to manipulate you. Similarly, the bag represents your responsibilities. Perhaps, you have taken on too many you had the chance to share them.

❖ Oneiric superstition says that paper bags in dreams portend bad luck in business. Fabric bags, however, the heavier they are the greater the success that will come to you.

Baking ■ This dream can represent the plans that you are going to begin and which are gradually developing. If you bake bread, soon you will obtain great profits, since this symbolizes nourishment and health.

❖ According to ancient superstitions, this dream has good omens. However, to dream that you burn the bread predicts a miscarriage.

Balcony ■ This dream indicates the enormous possibilities that life can offer. You just have to lean out the balcony of your illusions because you have everything necessary to achieve your intended objectives. Conversely, if you dream of falling from a balcony you must be careful in the future because you could lose a great opportunity due to precipitation or lack of foresight. Finally, if you are on a balcony with another person it indicates you will manage to improve the current situation but you must beware of envy.

Bald ■ Both your baldness or someone else's is always a negative omen. If you dream that you lose hair, you may be too concerned about your appearance or what others think of you. Perhaps, you feel anxious and insecure and do not trust your ability to cope with certain situations. On the other hand, to see a bald man points to the need to watch out for a possible scam, as well as the arrival of bad news about a lawsuit with little chance of success. If the dreamer is a young woman she should be wary of a suitor. When a man dreams of a bald woman it shows a strained relationship with his wife. If it is you who goes bald, it expresses concern about your virility. Finally, baldness on the forehead means that you could be mocked in your group of friends; and baldness on the back of your head, imminent poverty if you are not careful enough in business.

❖ Both European and American cultures believe that going bald in a dream is synonym with economic losses. In some African peoples, however, it is considered a really promising omen.

Ball ■ To dream that you play with a ball reveals the desire to escape present responsibilities and take refuge in the past. However, the dream can also have sexual connotations, especially in men. The dreamer should ask himself how he felt in the dream: Was he the star of the game, or did they always score against him? Did he skillfully handle the ball or was he always chasing after it? The answers will be key to interpreting his situation in the game of life.

Balloon ■ Dreaming of a balloon promotes reflection on the ideas of wholeness, freedom, and lightness. So you must meditate and contemplate calmly what concerns you from a broader view. In the case of a childish balloon that escapes from the dreamer's hands, perhaps in real life you are letting good ideas escape. However, if you let it escape while admiring its flight it indicates intellectual progress. Now, if the balloon bursts it denotes superfluous thoughts. The vision of the balloon predicts short trips, but can also reveal an excessive lust for power. Dreaming of getting up in the air in a balloon, on the other hand, indicates that you are going through a good time but you must not lose sight of everyday reality.

❖ Dreaming of a balloon cruise promises an unfortunate trip. Moreover, it can also mean that you see everything from a higher perspective. The condition of the landscape below the balloon can tell you a lot about your life and your circumstances.

Bamboo ▪ It is an important symbolic plant in Japan as well as in some primitive cultures in Africa and America. Throughout history, bamboo has been used to ward off evil spirits, to make sacred musical instruments, and to serve as a weapon in religious ceremonies in which sacrifice is practiced. Its presence in dreams is a sign of well-being and good wishes. It is related to success in business and to harmony of the context.

Banana ▪ One of the most well known phallic symbols, as much for its texture as for its shape.

Bandage ▪ The bandage symbolizes pain and blindness. In dreams, this element could indicate that someone is trying to capitalize on your suffering. At the same time, it could suggest that we are not seeing a situation clearly in what you find, which could cause economic and damaging shortfallings.

Bandit ▪ From a symbolic point of view a bandit is not like a thief. The latter is characterized by stealing the property of others, while the figure of the bandit (mythologized as the legendary character who lives in the woods) has a positive reading since it embodies the vigilante who steals from the rich to give to the poor. Thus, the bandit often represents a hidden force trying to restore justice within the subject who is normally forced to comply with excessive rules and dispositions. The oneiric aggression of bandits reveals, to the female dreamer, an unconscious fear about her sexuality, warning her it is too inhibited, suppressed, or—on the contrary—burgeoning or insatiable.
❖ It is a typical reversed dream that portends the opposite of what you dream, that is, safety and security.

Bank ▪ The bank represents your pool of resources, wealth, and accumulated energy. Therefore, dreaming that you save money or store jewelry or valuables in a bank reflects a clear need for safety and security to address the problems of life. On the contrary, if you withdraw money it means you will have enough strength and confidence to face such problems. Banks, especially the safes, represent your inner warehouse, your source of psychological potential. The unconscious is telling you to use your skill and energy reserves: your talent. Also, the dream can have a more literal meaning: you do not need to worry about the safety of your assets, as they are well kept. If you dream of robbing a bank maybe you are making too

much effort in something; there is risk of failure due to lack of resources.
❖ If in the dream you deposit money in the bank you will soon receive financial support. If, however, you see empty boxes, it predicts financial doom.

Bannister ▪ It is a symbol of safety, help, and protection. If it appears broken it indicates instability and lack of poise when making important decisions.

Banquet ▪ If the person who has this dream is religious, the banquet symbolizes the need to share spiritual pleasure with others. Conversely, if the dreamer is not particularly devout, it predicts the start of new relationships, meeting relatives, or finding new contacts in the job market.
❖ To participate in a banquet predicts an economic loss. Instead, the wedding feast is a promise of prosperity.

Baptism ▪ The presence of a baptism in a dream augurs the beginning of a love or total transformation of a relationship. The protagonist of the event will tell you the nature of the new birth. On the other hand, the person or the baby being baptized can also represent yourself. Your higher self is blessing the next step of your life: your hopes and purposes. It is ultimately the rebirth of your attitudes and the approach of others. The old and negative, in this respect, dies. So, you will soon get fortune and satisfaction. Likewise, the dream has a spiritual interpretation when referring to the renewal of your faith in God.
❖ If in the dream you drink the holy water of baptism you will become a great and famous singer.

Bark ▪ Just like howls, growls, and grunts, barks are an alarm signal, especially if you don't see where they are coming from. They indicate a feeling of insecurity and fear of the possible influence of negative external factors.

Barn owl ▪ Represents the night, fear, cold, and passivity. The barn owl symbolizes wisdom because it is a keen, nocturnal raptor. This is an animal that knows to wait before acting. Both the owl and the barn owl warn that you should be alert and keep your eyes open, since someone may try to trick you or make promise they will not keep.

Barrel ▪ Its meaning is associated with that of the BOTTLE. They represent the state of material and spiritual goods. Barrels full of wine indicate richness and well-being. Barrels precede the roar of a bull. This animal is associated with the creative power of spring. Empty or broken barrels signal the fear of ruin, or an economic or spiritual state that leaves much to be desired.

Barrier ■ Like walls and fences, it is symbolizing the inaccessibility of something. The repetition of this image points to the inability to move forward on the path undertaken. The area you cannot reach because of the barrier is the higher reality you want to achieve. Something is interfering with your path, preventing you from getting what you really want in life.

Basement ■ Buildings represent the personality of the dreamer, and the basement, equally as with other underground spaces, is a symbol of the interior of the body, the deepest levels of the mind. Because of this, it is associated with the hidden part of your being, that which is guarded closely from strangers. It is the place of your fears, problems, and feelings of guilt or regret. Once you manage to bring light to this place, there will be nothing that can resist you. In terms of dreams, dreaming of a basement full of food or treasures means that you have the sufficient resources to resolve your problems. You will not need to ask for external help. In contrast, if you glimpse a basement full of pottery, you may be mistakenly judging your situation, you should abstain from participating in unclear issues.
❖ Popular superstition says that dreaming of a basement full of wine signifies that you will get great benefits in an unreliable manner.

Basket ■ As a symbol of the womb, if a woman dreams of a basket in which there is a baby, this points to a possible pregnancy. If it is seen by a man, it is a sign that he should carry out projects he had in mind. A basket with flowers indicates joys for the couple; with bread, economic problems; and with spoiled fruit, long-term litigation.

Bat ■ Their presence often elicits fear, because it is an animal that lives in the dark. But in China, it is a symbol of happiness and long life. However, we usually associate it with fear and midnight. Bats share the symbolism of sexual desire with the devil. In oneiric terms, however, often they represent someone who wearing down the dreamer and causing him to lose self-confidence. There is also a claustrophobic element (bats live in caves and in the dark). Perhaps you are

afraid of confronting something related to your emotional life.
❖ This dream portends disaster. Bats predict injury and death. Because of their blindness, these animals are also considered oracles warning against eye problems. Other superstitions say that carrying a bat bone is the best antidote for bad luck. And in some parts of Europe, people believe that carrying the right eye of a bat inside a vest pocket grants invisibility.

Bath ■ Immersion in water takes its symbolism from this element (see WATER), although the action of bathing is not only associated with purification. It also represents the concept of regeneration. Consequently, if you dream of taking a bath you should let your feelings flow freely in order to live more harmoniously. If the bath is nice it indicates that such harmony is near. On the other hand, if the water is too hot or too cold is a sign that sometimes you are not honest enough. If you are not comfortable with your feelings, taking a bath is like a psychological cleansing. The water represents your emotional nature and the action symbolizes the desire of get rid of old attitudes, negativity, guilt . . . Some suggest that in this dream the bath water is like the mother's womb. The subject's desire is to return to such safety and warmth.
❖ Formerly, it was believed that washing with water eradicated not only dirt from the body but also sins from the soul. Conversely, bathing and cleaning oneself means expelling the subject's good fortune. To prepare a bath, however, is an omen of a battle won.

Battle ■ In an oneiric situation this image is always a sign of conflict. Its interpretation depends on the place the dreamer is placed within the scene: whether she is an observer, a participant, whether she wins or loses, or walks alone over the battlefield. The stage where the fight takes place is associated with the environment of the dreamer in real life. Moreover, you must address the feelings of triumph or defeat to understand the message of the unconscious.

Bay ■ It represents a cozy and safe place. It can be a relief at a stormy time, but it can also be interpreted as a situation of stagnation, immobility, cessation of activity and growth.

Bazaar ■ It indicates bewilderment and confusion regarding your values and your orientation in life.

Beach ■ In general, the unconscious associates the beach with two very different elements: the place you reach when you save yourself from a shipwreck, and a space to pass free time. In the fIrst case, the beach symbolizes the support that you count on to overcome your problems, while the second represents the need to take a break. (See SAND, ISLAND, SEA, and SEASHORE)

Beak ▪ Its symbolism is complex because it is related to the ability to communicate, with feeding, and with aggressiveness. To see a beak instead of your mouth signifies a conflict of your own image. To see it on another person could indicate the exaltation of a certain characteristic that you find annoying or exaggerated. The other symbols and surroundings of the oneiric scent will help with the interpretation of this dream.

Beans ▪ Beans symbolize prosperity; they announce an increase in material goods and conjugal happiness.
❖ Beans were the food that the Greeks sent to the dead and offered to Demeter; but, above all, that which they dedicated to Persephone, wife of Pluto and queen of the underworld for six months. As a consequence of this Greek tradition, beans have a negative meaning of discord and familial arguments.

Bear ▪ Symbolizes all instinctive things. It is considered the representation of the dangerous aspect of the unconscious. The bear is the example of the cruel and primitive man. In any case, if the dream is pleasant, it could represent maternal protection. Beneath its imposing figure, a generous soul may be hidden. In this last case, the unconscious is communicating the need to express your qualities. You have to externalize these noble thoughts that, sometimes, you hide behind a proud front.

Beard ▪ Shaving the beard in dreams may mean that you find yourself in a situation that requires direct and forceful action. You should therefore be more expeditious with your decisions. On the contrary, dreaming of a long and copious beard symbolizes wisdom and creativity. If you get carried away by creative intuition you will attain your goals. The longer the beard, the greater your chances of success. The beard also symbolizes the primitive and wild man present in subject's interior: the most indomitable sexual side. According to Freud, men who dream of shaving their beard are afraid of losing their confidence in sexual matters. On the other hand when a woman dreams that she grows a beard, it shows her desire for a more masculine role: for example at the workplace. In the case that an elder with a gray and long beard is portrayed, it is a sign that

your unconscious wants to convey its advice for greater knowledge and understanding of things.
❖ A long and strong beard denotes honor and eloquence; but a too long one indicates lawsuits and losses. A short one predicts litigation and family disagreements. As for color: a brown beard denotes evils; red, false friends; blonde, success; black, pain; and gold or silver, wealth.

Beautification ▪ It deals with aspects of personality that may need a review. According to the context of the dream and the elements present, it may represent anxiety about personal appearance or a misleading attitude toward others.

Beauty ▪ If you dream of reaching perfect beauty you are trying to create a chimera, a utopia. Beauty is a temporary attribute, something ephemeral.

Becoming deaf ▪ It may be a manifestation of a physical ear ailment. Otherwise, it is a warning from the unconscious that indicates a negative attitude toward people around you. It is also interpreted as a symbol of isolation. It portrays the inability to communicate in a healthy way with others.

Bed ▪ In dreams, a bed can represent both a resting place and intimate relationships. To be lying in bed means that you have an excess of activity in real life and, therefore, you really need a break. You should devote more time to yourself and your loved ones. But if the dream is unpleasant, it may indicate that you are incubating a disease. The bed also reflects intimate relationships. Thus, a larger than usual bed shows an obsession with sex; a small bed, however, signals a rather low libido.

Beer ▪ It represents reward after hard work. Such dreams invite to strive in your activities.
❖ For the ancient Egyptians drinking beer was a sign of joy. In dreams it portends success, celebrations, and profits.

Bees ▪ Due to their work producing honey, bees have symbolized values such as laboriousness and wealth since ancient Egypt. Bees in dreams are often a sign of prosperity. If dreaming they are making honey or collecting pollen, chances are you will have material success in the short term. Networking and teamwork will be beneficial and profitable to you. Laborious bees in dreams could also be a reference to your current working pace; perhaps you are not getting satisfactory outcome for the time and energy invested.On the other hand, to see bees in a flower announces a new love will come into your life.

❖ Dreaming of bees is considered a positive omen of health, strength, wealth, and prosperity. Usually, one single bee promises engagements and children; many, favorable business; if they are working, good hopes, and if they are swarming, abundant profits. However, not all dreams related to bees are positive. If you dream that they sting you, you could be subject to libel; whereas, if you dream of killing a bee, you will be unable to avoid ruin. A widespread popular superstition recommends you never chase away the bees but rather leave the windows open so they come inside. This way, you will be safe from enemies.

Beetle ■ To see beetles in your oneiric thoughts is a good sign: promises happiness and good luck at all levels. Thus, it is a good time to start businesses and to strengthen relationships. To kill one of these insects alerts of a misfortune that could fall on you.

Beggar ■ The unconscious is warning you, through this dream, that you are neglecting some important aspect of your personality. It may also indicate the beginning of a period of economic hardship.

❖ According to the esoteric interpretation, dreams of poverty are generally precursors to prosperity, well-being, love, and happiness, or at least ensure that the dreamer has no cause for concern. Popular superstition adds this advice: if you wake up with your hand itching, you should rub it on wood. This will bring good luck.

Beheading ■ Dreaming of your own beheading indicates that you never get to implement the ideas that come to your mind. This dream shows that you do not act too consistently due to your tendency of getting carried away by the first impulse. (See HEAD)

Bell ■ It is an announcement or calling the spirit because of some extraordinary occasion (which can be happy or sad). Due to its suspended position, it entails the mystical sense of all objects suspended between heaven and earth.

❖ According to some beliefs, hearing bells in dreams announces a happy life, a serene old age, or a quick marriage.

Belt ■ Symbol of bodily protection it is an allegory of virginity. Additionally, like any round and closed figure, the belt represents continuity and wholeness. Therefore, it serves as a symbol of marriage and it also represents the tie that binds you to a given affiliation, group, or society. It also provides security and power due to the support it symbolizes. However, this dream can also be a warning of abdominal discomfort due to inadequate night position.

❖ A beautiful and rich belt is, according to ancient oracles, a sign of good luck. If it is jeweled it announces the birth of a child. A broken belt is a bad omen for your children's life.

Bet ■ Betting in dreams means you are willing to take risks. The cause may come from a situation in real life. Maybe you are willing to bet blindly for a path in the future. In this case, you should weigh the items involved in this circumstance and calmly choose the choice you deem best. As for recreational gambling, there are people who believe in the premonitory power of dreams and have acted—in real life—as those dreams suggested. This does not mean you must depend solely on oneiric chance; no doubt you may suffer big economic losses.

❖ The meaning of this image must be reversed. If you dream of winning a bet, you will lose and vice versa.

Beverage ■ Sometimes dreaming of being thirsty lacks any symbolic meaning. Simply, it can be that you have such a physical demand and it is directly reflected in oneiric episodes. Nonetheless, if you discard this option, being thirsty and drinking water often means you have satisfied a pressing need. If instead of water you drink wine or spirits, it is a sign of joy, enthusiasm, and creativity.

❖ To drink from a cup made of glass announces disclosed secrets; from a beautiful container, releasing a weight and tranquility. A sweet drink promises happiness, while bitter, mild discomfort. Drinking fresh water indicates happiness, but warm water announces an emerging disease.

Bicycle ■ Bicycles reveal the need to relate to people who are far from you. However, unlike other modes of transportation, the energy that propels the bike requires your personal effort. Therefore, this dream advises that you only have your own resources and that, consequently, you should not expect help from anyone.

❖ Biking promises joy, happiness, and self-confidence.

Bill ▪ A bill is not a good sign, since it predicts unexpected economic problems and even bankrupt in business. On the other hand, it also points to the possibility of being stuck in lawsuits in order to keep certain properties.

Billiards ▪ Dreaming of this game has negative connotations because it is announcing the arrival of problems of material nature and even the failure of business affairs. If the table is ready but nobody plays, a friend might want to betray you; and if it is a woman who is playing, there will be critical tensions for the couple.

Binding ▪ See TYING
❖ Some tribal societies deem it possible to ward off evil spirits by a change in routine. So, walking backwards is a way to confuse them. In oneiric terms, therefore, it denotes that fortune is on the way.

Birch ▪ The birch is considered a sacred tree in eastern Europe and central Asia. In ancient times, it was believed to ward off malign spirits. Furthermore, it was used as a channel of communication between gods and humans. When it appears in dreams, the birch represents the beginning of important projects. The shape of its trunk—straight or twisted—could indicate whether or not those impending deals are on the right track.

Bird ▪ With the ability to fly, birds have always referred to freedom and spirituality. The flight across the boundless sky means that some aspect of your psyche provides fullness, restoration, and balance. It is the soul's desire to go beyond, to surpass. It may also symbolize that you want to get rid of everything you find banal. The unconscious may be providing solutions for your existence. If you dream of releasing a bird, the same will apply to your emotions. On the other hand, birds indicate the status of your relationships. The thieves, like magpies, denote adultery or any other threat. Territorial ones, like blackbirds, can express envy. Finally, a flock of birds represents your desire to be part of a group that you admire. (See WINGS)
❖ For centuries, dreaming of birds has been a positive omen. Albatrosses bring fortune; vultures warn against gossip; crowing roosters announce good news; pigeons signify a peaceful solution to your problems; an eagle predicts success in business; geese express that you will have improvements soon; hawks portend a bright future; owls prevent some disappointments; storks predict problems in the family; and turkeys, finally, are bearers of bad luck, unless you kill them or eat them in the dream.

Birds ▪ Birds are a symbol of spirituality since the time of ancient Egypt, not only in the West. The Hindu tradition also says that birds represent higher states of being. In oneiric terms, we can say that in general, dreaming of birds reveals the desire for freedom. Each bird, however, has its own symbolism. The eagle, for example, is associated with the ambitions of conquest and power. On the other hand, if you dream of a flock of birds flying high in the sky, it means that, quite possibly, you will achieve your goals.
❖ The dream itself advises you to focus on the goals you set, because you may be taking on too many things at once. If the bird is caged, you must ask yourself if this is how you feel in real life. Perhaps the bird is the dreamer himself and it reflects their desire for freedom and independence. According to the Freudian school, he who dreams of birds is the victim of unsatisfied erotic desires. Jung, however, links it to the soul. The bird represents thoughts and ideas that fly freely. (See BIRD and WINGS)
❖ To see birds in a dream is a harbinger of prosperity and health; if you heard them singing it is the most favorable omen. To catch one promises happiness; but caging them is a harbinger of misfortune. Talking birds denote success and good business.

Birth ▪ To dream of a birth predicts the beginning of something new, be it a friend, a job, a project, or a business. It is the beginning of an evolution, something that can satisfy your deepest longings. These images suggest a period of greater happiness will begin, in which you can direct your actions at will. If you are a woman who dreams of a birth, it could reflect your desires and feelings about motherhood. For Jung, this type of dream represented a very important stage in the process of individualization. Birth, in this case, is essential for maturation and completeness of the human psyche. Thus, it is essential for psychological development.
❖ For married people, this dream is an omen of good luck. For single women, it predicts problems.

Bison ▪ It symbolizes prosperity and abundance. It is interpreted as the triumph for having achieved a goal that required a long struggle. Hunting a bison represents acquiring—at the same time—food, shelter, and social recognition.

Biting ▪ This dream is a symbol of aggressiveness. Through the act of biting, you destroy an element apart from you to make it part of yourself or simply to eliminate it. Often, this is provoked because you harbor some anger or bitterness that you need to express. If you are the victim of a bite, you may be burdened by a problem or going through a difficult time. If an animal bites you, you should ask yourself what aspect of your personality that animal represents. (See MOUTH, TEETH, and JAW)
❖ To dream of bite marks means you will suffer a loss because of your enemy. To receive a bite foretells jealousy and annoyance.

Black ▪ The color black represents fear, the absence of light, and ignorance. It is also associated with death, pain, and sadness. When this color predominates in a dream, it means you are being brought down by pessimism and confusion. (See DESERT, MIDNIGHT, and DEATH)

Blackberry ▪ Thanks to its wild character and peculiar flavor, the blackberry is a symbol of seduction. In this manner, it could give us happiness, but could also occasionally bring us hardships.

Blackberry bush ▪ Its symbolism is somewhat complex. It refers to virginal purity, to pleasure, and to pain. The thorns of the bush express torment; the sweet fruits are joy, fertility, and abundance. They can be interpreted as a reward for effort and suffering. However, you should analyze all the elements of the dream and oneiric image as a whole to decipher the message from the unconscious.

Blackbird ▪ This talkative bird symbolizes gossip.
❖ To hear a blackbird whistling is a sign of slander.

Blackboard ▪ To see yourself obligated to stand up at the blackboard and explain something generally indicates a feeling of insecurity about your own proposals. On the contrary, it refers to the fear of being held accountable by others for those proposals.

Blacksmith ▪ In some cultures, the job of the blacksmith is sacred, given that it was considered the privilege of the king. There has always been a close relation between metallurgy and alchemy. In Western society, the figure of the blacksmith is usually associated with the action of shaping the hardest materials, whether for one's own benefit or that of the community. The dream suggests that you can transform many facets of your life to become what you really long to be. The blacksmith also symbolizes the passion that forges your personality. (See IRON)
❖ In Persia, the blacksmith appearing in dreams is a sign of violent fever.

Blasphemy ▪ It indicates rebellion against authoritarian impositions whose origin may be in others or in yourself.

Blind ▪ Dreaming that you go blind indicates you are unable to assess or consider a particular event, refusing to see the accurate side. Maybe you are rejecting something of your own personality. Always keep in mind that the truth takes you away from the painful slavery of ignorance, so keep your eyes open. Helping a blind person, on the other hand, expresses the willingness to serve others.
❖ In ancient Greece, the seer Tiresias was blind. In this sense, the oneiric blindness represents preference for insight discovery over external perception. Therefore, it symbolizes wisdom and self-knowledge.

Blinds ▪ Blinds symbolize the relationship you have the the exterior. To open them indicates willingness and good intentions to communicate. To close them, a state of isolation or confinement. To let light in through the slats manifests a certain precaution or fear of your privacy being invaded.

Blood ▪ Bloodshed symbolizes the sacrifice. All liquid materials that ancients offered to the dead, spirits, and to the gods (milk, honey, wine) were images or allegories of blood. This was the most precious gift, and was presented in classical cultures through the sacrifice of lamb, pig, and bull. Further, it is a symbol of life. If you dream that you are bleeding out, you may experience physical tiredness or you may feel emotionally drained. On the other hand, it could also indicate a profound change in your personality. In either case, blood can represent a range from passion and love to fury and violence. It is an admonition that you reflect on your actions, as you may be forgetting one of your values. (See RED)

In antiquity, one was supposed to drink the blood of sacrificed animals during rituals. It manifested the union of the force and power of man with that of the gods. In this sense, dreaming that you are drinking blood could foretell that you will receive energy and renovated vitality.

Blouse ■ This garment symbolizes the image that the dreamer projects socially; therefore, its style or condition will say a lot about how the dreamer looks to others. If it is stained or broken, the dreamer looks unconfident and misunderstood; if it is elegant, the dreamer looks happy in the family environment; and if it is one to be used at work, the dreamer will seem laborious and will have expectations of being promoted in the short term. For women, a blouse always has a negative meaning because it announces gossiping against her by very close people.

Blowing ■ For the primitive, blowing is a creating act that increase the force of something or changes its path. A priori, you have difficulty associating this interpretation with blowing (creative action). But, in reality, dreaming that you are blowing an ember to revive a fire signifies that you want to keep activity, enthusiasm, love, and friendship alive. This meaning is not very different from what your ancestors would have said.

❖ Blowing over a fire presages slander; doing it loudly with the mouth, evil-speaking.

Blows ■ If you receive blows from someone's hand this dream symbolizes the contradictions you have to bear; but if you do not see your opponent it announces the end of the problems. In the event that you are the one beating someone, it represents the setbacks that you will cause to others. Beating someone, in addition, portends disputes. Hitting against something and receiving a hard blow indicates that your actions and ideas are inconsistent. Anyway, your chances of success are based on your ability to roll with the punches. (See SLAP)

Blue ■ It is the color that represents the spiritual ideals, virtue, truth, and beauty. It symbolizes your emotions and feelings. Therefore, dreams where this color predominates will probably focus on your emotional life. According to Freud, blue denotes a good mental balance.

❖ Light blue is a sign of friendship, pure and sweet feelings, platonic. Dark blue indicates good health.

Boar ■ Like most animals, its symbolic meaning is versatile. On one side, it represent intrepidity and irrational bravery; on the other, it is a symbol of a lack of restraint. Given that it is difficult to fight the boar (he never gives up), the dream is indicating that if you repress your desires, your instincts will make your life impossible. Using the strength of the boar, you will be able to attain all that you wish. It represents free sexual impulse, not controlled by the conscious; that is, the libido, which is like the boar, is uncontrollable, violent, and irrational.

❖ As a negative symbol, the boar represents the oneiric personification of cruel and ruthless enemies. If in the dream the boar is captured or conquered, it portends joy and triumph.

Boarding ■ In any case, it means the desire to start something new; whether it is a journey, a relationship, or a project. It represents the intentions and expectations. The dreamer's life acquires different possibilities. (See BOAT)

Boat ■ In ancient times, boats were worshiped in Mesopotamia, Crete, and Egypt, as they were associated with certain deities. In oneiric terms, boats symbolize the ability to communicate with people who, by the way they think, feel, or live, are far from you. So, dreaming that you take a boat trip heralds the beginning of a new phase of your life or a new relationship. By contrast, a sinking ship warns against a breakup. Boats can also represent a journey through your emotions. Depending on the condition and status of the water, the meaning changes. If it is agitated it means that you feel tense about your feelings. If it is calm you are working calmly. And in the case you lose the boat you may have lost an exceptional opportunity. (See WATER, SHIP, and SHIPWRECK)

❖ In mythology it is said that boats are the means to go from one world to another. Given its symbolism, this dream shows the passage between personal stages. You may be conducting a decisive change in your life.

Body ■ The right side represents integrity and rationality; the left side, instincts. However, the body as a whole refers to the ego. Dreaming that your own body is stained indicates ethical and financial problems. If it is swollen it announces an increase of wealth; if it is too thin, illness or economic loss. Seeing your body in two places at once may mean that you are maintaining romantic relationships with two partners simultaneously. According to the Freudian school, pointy organs and all appendices are an image of the penis; cavities and holes represent the vagina and the anus; secretions, sperm.

❖ In China, the upper body is compared to the sky, and the lower to the ground; In India, the subject's bloody body is an omen of longevity, because blood is a symbol of strength.

Boiling ▪ In general, this is a symbol of positive transformation. It signals a favorable state for the healing of an illness that is beginning to diminish. It also can be indicative of the return of a relationship that had cooled off.

Bolt ▪ It symbolizes the will to impose your criteria at all costs, whether successful or not.

Bolt (lightning) ▪ The ray is a celestial fire in its activity, a symbol of creative power. This divine connotation provokes, generally, that the ray represents those circumstances that are imposed upon you and radically change your life. The ray is also a symbol of speed (fast as light), of wise insights and emotional explosions.

❖ To dream that you are struck by lightning is a favorable omen of achieved goals. Lightning over your house, on the contrary, indicates danger and unexpected events.

Bomb ▪ Being a victim of a bomb in a dream is a clear warning that a situation out of your control could explode if necessary measures are not taken. Therefore, you must rectify some aspects of your behavior. If the one who places the bomb is you it means you are losing control and refuse to accept responsibility. On the other hand, this dream also indicates your internal condition. Perhaps, something is affecting you that you may want to explode in rage. The same goes for all those feelings and emotions that you repress. If you avoid expressing them, they will end up exploding sooner or later.

❖ The oneiric superstition says that a discussion that besets you will end happily.

Bones ▪ Bones tend to be associated with death and the distant past. They predict problems, loss of excitement, and generally, indicate that we are going through a period of pessimism and dejection. If you dream of a broken bone, the foundations of your real life and personal power could be teetering.

❖ Goddesses that wear a necklace of bones around their necks or on their hip refer to the pressure of the passing and swiftness of time.

Books ▪ Books symbolize knowledge and experience, so you must pay attention to how they appear in dreams. If it deals with schoolbooks, reminiscent of the past, the dream expresses your nostalgia for that which no longer exists. In short, books symbolize yesterday and tomorrow, especially in the emotional realm. Thus, if many books appear, it means review your life, thoroughly analyze your past and present, and move forward with enthusiasm to your. A single book can symbolize the Book of Life: wisdom, learning, and revelation. This type of oneiric image also suggests that the solution to problems lies within us Finally, a closed dream means you may want to keep something secret.

❖ If you dream about books, you will have to avoid all sorts of evil that stalks you.

Booth ▪ A booth is synonymous with isolation, although this sense may differ depending on the type of booth you dream about. So, if it is a telephone booth, it predicts an unexpected call or visit; a photography booth, recognition in at the workplace; erotic, an unsatisfying sexual facet; and aesthetic, underestimation by the environment. The more uncomfortable the sleeper feels in the booth, the worse the situation in her circle of friends will be.

Boots ▪ Dreaming of boots is a sign of power or possession. Military boots denote domain by means of force and violence. Likewise, mountain boots suggest risk and effort. Luxurious boots indicate material goods. Boots for sports, however, comfort and lightness.

Bouquet ▪ A bouquet of flowers is a tribute to friendship, sincerity, courtesy, and emotion. (See FLOWERS)

Border ▪ It is a clear sign that you have concluded a process or activity and are about to start a new company. It is, therefore, time to review past experiences and start drawing conclusions—without leaving pending matters—so the new stage will be fruitful and happy.

Boss ▪ The figure of the boss has various connotations. On one side, it represents a lack of confidence in yourself and the fear of taking initiative. It is a symbol of a feeling of oppression and inferiority. The presence of the boss can be interpreted as an internal guide that neutralizes your instinctive impulses and makes you act more prudently.

❖ The first books on dream interpretation were written by upper-class people. So, they said that this dream as a sign of incompetence. But if the dreamer was the boss himself, it augured a rapid rise of social prestige.

Bottle ■ Inadvertently, sometimes you bottle up your emotions, preventing them from being freely expressed. This dream can be an invitation to be more spontaneous and to avoid repressing your feelings. However, the bottle's contents will illustrate your situation. Dreaming of bottles filled with water is a symbol of prosperity and joy; if they contain liquor it indicates that your feelings are not sincere: unpleasant incidents with the beloved are likely to occur; if it is champagne, you need to be more social; if it is poison, it represents evil thoughts on your part; if it is red wine, it will express your passions; and milk demonstrates your need for new ideas. Empty bottles indicate amorous disappointments, illness, or setbacks in your projects. You may be out of your internal resources and feel hollow. Despite the disappointments, you must try to recover and move on, and dreams may point out the way to do it.

Bottom ■ The interpretation of this dream is related to DESCEND. Getting to the bottom of something implies having fallen to lower levels, but also having reached the hidden truth of things, and being ready for ascension. Its meaning is related WATER if to get to the bottom you have to dive into it. Whether the water is murky or clear the interpretation will be different.

Box ■ When a box is opened, previously hidden items are unveiled. So, this dream can be a symbol of intellectual exploration because you are discovering the contents of your psyche. If what you find in the box displeases you it may refer to your fears or aspects of yourself that you want to hide. In case of a safe, what you keep in there will be your most precious intimacy, possibly, your best qualities. In the Greek myth of Pandora's box, the malignant part of the woman who wants to have everything is represented. The oneiric-psychological analysis of this story establishes it represents man's fear for the dark and feminine side of his nature. It can also refer to the way the unconscious projects the complex and negative attitudes in real life.

❖ If you force a safe in order to open it, the omens say you will not marry the person you currently love.

If it is empty, you will get married soon; and if it is full, late.

Boy ■ Seeing a boy in a dream means that you are happy and alive, with many possibilities and the desire to create. It is a way of preparing the ground for future changes in your personality. However, it may also indicate a desire to return to the basics and discover your true personality. Moreover, dreaming that you return to childhood reflects a need for love and protection. It can reveal, therefore, certain immaturity to life. In this sense, according to Carl Jung, dreaming of children is a metaphor for the things of childhood that we have forgotten. Maybe the dream image is warning you that you should learn to play again or have a more innocent attitude. (See GAME, YOUTH, and BIRTH)

❖ In history and mythology, divine children often appear, who eventually become heroes or wise men. This is the case of Hercules, who strangles two serpents when he is very small; or Jesus, who then becomes Christ who saves humanity. These children symbolize the true Self of man: vulnerable, but with a great capacity for transformation. In the dream, perhaps this relates to our spiritual potential.

Bracelet ■ See RING

Braid ■ Equal to knots, braids symbolize intimate relations and mutual dependency. For this reason, dreaming that you have long braids could announce that you will soon be implicated in a confusing situation. It is probable that it will be due to your behavior, which foments discord between the people in your environment.

Branch ■ Symbolizes the day to day. Dreaming of branches in bloom foretells the arrival of a positive period; if they are green, it is a warning not to be hasty with your decisions; if they are dry, it indicates a loss of physical energy, and if they are cut, it signals that you have forgotten one of your principal objectives. (See TREE)

Bread ■ Bread represents food in general, as well as effort; as the Bible teaches: "You earn your bread by the sweat of your brow." Therefore, when it appears in dreams, it always represents essential aspects of us. Giving bread to someone reveals your capacity for forgiveness and your desire to share. If you dream of having only bread to eat, it means that you feel poor inside. Similarly you must pay attention to the form in which it appears in your dreams, because sometimes it takes on sexual connotations, especially among teenagers. The Freudian school identifies it with the body of the loved one or the penis. Jung, however, recognizes in it an allusion to spiritual food.

Breakdowns ■ Depending on the item that fails it will be possible to identify the problem you have in real life. So, dreaming of a broken TV may denote a strong need to escape from home. A failure of a phone, on the other hand, is a sign you need isolation.

Breastfeeding ■ Breastfeeding a baby or to see someone else doing so predicts material prosperity. In the case such images are produced by a woman, it may reveal pregnancy.

Breastplate ■ See ARMOR

Breasts ■ Breasts represent maternity, sweetness, and safety. The dream reveals the emotional need and desire to return to the safety of childhood. For a woman, the image could signify pregnancy; for a child, protection; for a man, satisfactory sexual relations. Due to their nutritive purpose, breasts can also reference ideas and plans that will nourish your interior. According to Freud's vision, this dream alerts to the possibility that the dreamer depends too much on a maternal figure. (See BABY, MOTHER, WOMAN, and CHEST)
❖ To see breasts full of milk or to suckle from them reflects a desire to return to infancy. This dream could have various origins. Probably it is due to a feeling of insecurity or loneliness, or the need for affection and cover. It could be that the problems is an excessive load of responsibilities or a state of high stress or anxiety.
❖ If a woman dreams that her breasts are droopy and look bad, it means that she will experience heartbreak. If they are white and big, she will be rich.

Breath ■ Breath is the most precise indication of your emotional and physical state. It could reflect a situation in which the dreamer, in real life, has trouble breathing. The cause could be a bad sleeping position or a diagnosed illness. If it is not these, the dream of breathing with difficulty signals a moment of fatigue in which you find yourself surrounded by adverse circumstances that drown you. On the contrary, if you dream that you breathe deeply and intensely, the dream reveals a state of well-being in a positive

environment that stimulates the development of your personality and your projects.

Brick ■ To dream of bricks could indicate the desire to create your own space, safe and stable. In and of itself, it could suggest the need to restructure some personal aspect. In case of work problems, the dream urges you to build your projects without rushing. The best thing is to construct your purposes on solid ground. (See CONSTRUCTION)

Bridge ■ The bridge is something that mediates between two separate points. So, the pontiff, as the title's etymology indicates, represents a bridge between God and humanity. In many cultures, the bridge is the element that symbolically links the sensitive and the supersensitive (in China, for example, it is considered the symbol of union between heaven and earth). Without this mystical meaning, the bridge symbolizes a transition. Dreaming of this symbol is a sign that you are evolving or undergoing a change. Perhaps it is a job, a move, or a relationship that will soon begin. In this case it will critical whether the oneiric bridge was firm and if you crossed it safely. It may also refer to something more spiritual: the reception of new values and the burial of the past. Another possibility is that you are trying to join two pieces of your life or to fill an empty space of your life.
❖ According to the guru Sathya Sai Baba, life is a bridge that crosses a sea full of changes. We must cross it but never build our house on it. The dream may represent your life journey.

Bringing together ■ The action of bringing parts together reflects a situation in which the dreamer sees himself as a mediator or conciliator between people or groups in conflict. It is an indication of stable relationships and firm commitments.

Bronze ■ This metal—including articles made from it—announces a stable and profitable future, although after doing a lot of work. When a woman dreams of a bronze statue it reveals she will not get to marry the man she loves; however, if the statue comes to life she will live a short, though very passionate adventure. Bronze snakes bode plots around you that will result in betrayal; and bronze-plated metals, the false appearance of someone close.

Broom ■ Dreaming that you are sweeping with a broom may indicate the need to eliminate everything that disturbs you, whether at work, in relationships with others, or inside yourself. The message of the dream is clear: hiding the "mess" under the carpet is no solution. You must reflect on this in order to address your own problems. (See SWEEPING)

Broth ▪ In almost all aspects, broth is a positive sign. So, drinking it portends a long and happy relationship for lovers, unconditional support from friends and, harmony at home. A good broth announces healing for sick ones; but one of bad taste means that you will go through a bad time. Finally, to cook broth is synonymous with self-confidence and independence.

Brush ▪ The usefulness of a brush is clear: it serves to remove dust. Therefore, this element in dreams reflects the need to recover your values, because the unconscious is reminding you that some superficial feelings are changing your principles. (See TO SWEEP)
❖ Brushes and brooms have plenty of superstitions. It is bad luck to step on them and they can "sweep" away your good luck. Usually, omens are not very advantageous. Anyway, if you dream that you brush your hair, a new and exciting companion in adventure will show up in your life.

Brushing/styling hair ▪ To dream that you are styling your hair indicates that you are concerned with your physical appearance. This type of image should put you on alert: dressing up in an exaggerated manner is a sign of falseness in human relationships. Not in vain, when we modify our image, we can momentarily avoid facing our faults. Soon or later, however, the mask must fall and your costume can no longer hide reality.
❖ To find yourself in danger is an indication of success; to escape it has an inverted symbolism, it predicts misfortune.

Bubble ▪ Symbol of the ephemeral, bubbles and soap bubbles make it clear that the sleeper is immersed in a fantasy or living beyond her means, which would entail major problems. She must therefore be wiser and enjoy reality at the level of her potential.

Building up ▪ It involves construction and progress. If in the dream you are dedicated to building a house it means that you are rebuilding your life, so you have new projects. Buildings and houses present in dreams are symbols of the Self. The higher floors are your conscious. The lower levels, your unconscious mind. If going down to the basement produces an unpleasant feeling or frightens you it means that there are aspects that make you frustrated. A good solution is to develop activities and new knowledge. The building's condition also expresses how you value yourself emotionally. If it is in ruins it indicates suffering because of your image. You need to do things that make you feel better. On the other hand, it could also refer to your physical condition. The different parts of the building, finally, can represent life's time periods. Modern rooms are your present and conscious side. The oldest, your unconscious past. (See CONSTRUCTION)
❖ Small buildings presage bad luck; large ones, advantageous changes in the future.

Bull ▪ The bull symbolizes the more powerful and primitive forces of your basic instincts. Dreaming of a wild bull signals that you have a great capacity for creativity. If it pursues you, if means that you can no longer contain your impulses. You should find a way to free them, as they could lead to an internal disequilibrium. You should not forget that the bull is a frequently used symbol to refer to procreation and sexual wantonness. In this sense, if a man dreams of a bull, it represents his virility. If it is a woman, it refers to someone of the opposite sex. If the bull is wild and unbroken, then your passions are out of control. If you dream of a bullfight, it expresses the power that you have over your lustful and negative feelings.
❖ In mythology, the bull is considered a symbol of fertility. On the other hand, in antiquity there existed the belief that the roar of the bull produced in storms. Further, this animal is associated with the creative power of spring. Dreaming of a bull is generally a sign of fertility and sexual power.

Bullet ▪ Dreaming of a lead bullet reveals that the subject is going through a delicate moment in real life. If she does not meditate well on decisions she may suddenly be part of shady business.

Bundle ▪ Carrying a bundle reminds the sleeper of the large responsibilities or tensions she bears in real life. When the bundle is yours it demonstrates an excessive attachment to material goods. Instead, looking at others carrying bundles reflects selfishness and carelessness.

BURIAL

Joseph dreamed: "I was sitting in front of a black coffin, surrounded by strangers who were weeping and mourning the death of . . . I did not know who it was. I felt no sorrow, no pain, but the fact of not knowing who we were burying made me anxious, and still I did not dare to ask. Suddenly, I noticed that the coffin was open and I just had to get up from my chair to see inside. My surprise was great when I saw myself dressed as a clown with a stupid grin on my face."

Dreams about death **announce changes** or the end of a phase. Before this dream Joseph was a joker . . . too much! His friends and coworkers were always berating his heavy and tasteless jokes; however, he did not seem willing to change. Joseph took a few days to understand the message of his dream; a few months before, a friend of his had had a really hard time because of his jokes. The dream was announcing to Joseph a change of attitude, it was warning that: "If you do not want to lose all your friends and end up surrounded by strangers—like in the dream—you better bury your joker side." After this, he knew he had to give way to a more staid Joseph and, of course, it was not fair that others will have a hard time because of his inappropriate attitude.

Burial ■ Although dreaming of your own funeral is really unpleasant, the meaning that lies behind this image is positive. It indicates that you must move away from the past and look to the future. In contrast, dreaming of someone else's burial announces that, probably, a radical change is about to happen in your life. Something has come to an end and you have to forget about it; or in other words you need to bury it. When it comes to the funeral of a loved one, it shows that you should not cling to your possessions. Dreaming that you are buried alive warns you against a mistake you are about to make; your opponents will use it to harm you. If you are saved from this situation your efforts will correct the mishap over time. (See CEMETERY and DEATH)

Burn ■ Burns reflect internal damage that you have caused yourself through carelessness. They tend to indicate poor health and feelings of guilt and deception. You should purify your body and mind. In parallel, burns also indicate the existence of many resources that you are wasting. (See FIRE)

❖ Burning yourself with hot water foretells a positive emotional relationship.

Bus ■ As means of public transportation, the bus symbolizes the need to share projects, ideas, or thoughts. Dreaming of this vehicle shows that you should have to relate more often with loved ones, fleeing from negative isolation. On the contrary, if you see yourself as the only occupant of a bus, it means you have a great shyness or selfishness. Missing the bus denotes a frustrated hope of change or a desire to get out of the current situation, but without being clear on the new direction.

Business ■ This dream may be advising you to adopt a more "business-like" attitude in your circumstances. Perhaps you should be more astute, challenging, or cautious. The key is to take the experience you have and use it in your favor. If, in the dream, business is good, you are comfortable with your current situation. If, however, there are problems, it means that you feel insecure.

❖ In olden days, if you had this dream, the wise men recommended precaution against dishonest people.

Butter ■ Due to its texture, it is a symbol of softness and ease. Butter is something that melts. This could indicate that a distressing situation is coming to an end.

Butterfly ■ Although, among ancient cultures, it was the emblem of the soul and the unconscious attraction to the luminous, the butterfly is currently associated with lightness, fickleness, and imprudence. However, if you dream of the transformation of a caterpillar into a butterfly, it becomes a sign of metamorphosis, change, and regeneration. The meaning changes since this means you should trust your ability to the end, without allowing fear or despair to defeat you. In short, everything will eventually be solved. So, what at first seems negative may end up being positive. Other interpretations associate butterflies with romance, joy, freedom, and success. (See WORM, METAMORPHOSIS, and CATERPILLAR)

❖ Chuang Chou, a Chinese thinker, raises an interesting philosophical question about a dream similar to this one. One night he dreamed he was a butterfly and the oneiric scene seemed so real that when he awoke he did not know if he was a man who had dreamed he was a butterfly or a butterfly dreaming he was a man. The Turks believe that the dead may return in the form of a butterfly and, therefore, are careful not to kill them.

Buttocks ▪ This part of the body is typically a bad sign. Whether they are beautiful or deformed and drooping, they augur all kinds of nasty remarks and humiliations.

In the first case, it warns of a possible cheating partner; in the second, of an embarrassing action.

Buttoning ▪ This is an action of closing yourself; it denotes self protection. It could indicate that the external environment is hostile and the dreamer needs shelter. Notwithstanding, it can also be interpreted as rejection of new opportunities around you.

Buttons ▪ If you dream you are missing buttons on clothing it means that you tend to neglect personal issues and friendships. On the other hand, if in a dream you are dedicated to sewing them, it denotes efforts to overcome your mistakes.

C

Cabin ■ To see a cabin in dreams reflects a desire to live in contact with nature. It augurs a period of peace and tranquility. But if the person in question is a teenager, it indicates fear of accepting responsibilities. Dreaming that you take refuge in a cabin promises serenity and joy after pain.

❖ Esoterically the cabin is associated with loneliness, insecurity, or poverty. In the forest, it means fatigue and work leading to a modest happiness.

Cactus ■ The cactus is a negative sign because, like its spines, it reflects the painful moments that the subject is going through. This may be because someone constantly pricks you with her comments or because you need to protect yourself somehow. Dreaming of a cactus also evidences hardship in the professional setting. If it is in bloom, however, it announces that finally the value of the sleeper will be recognized at the workplace.

❖ For Mexicans, the cactus is an aphrodisiac, therefore it portends good times in the sentimental field.

Cage ■ The cage has different meanings depending on what it inside of it. So, if it contains a bird, this dream predicts friendship and love, and shows you know how to enjoy life. On the other hand, if the cage is empty, the image expressed a clear feeling of disillusion and and disappointment. If you see yourself caged, it is a sign that the unconscious wants to express its complaints, since you are subjected to heavy repression by the

Eva dreamed: "I was in a beautiful golden cage, on the edge of a terrace. I had a pretty landscape before my eyes: a green valley full of flowers of every color and very tall mountains on the horizon. The sky was intensely blue and bright. I feld good, safe, and happy in my cage and I sang constantly. From my mouth came beautiful melodies in strange languages."

To see yourself caged in a dream is a sign that the unconscious feels repressed and wants more freedom and freedom of expression. Eva is a very timid person who has a hard time with social interaction. Her dream is reflecting—with the golden cage—her comfortable world closed up in herself, in which she feels safe and sound. This is a calming dream that encouraged her to let her emotions flow freely, like a gentle melody. The idyllic landscape she contemplated through the bars represented the desires Eva could not reach due to her own inhibition. The fact that she sang in unknown languages reveal her inability to communicate with others, and to understand herself.

conscious. You have become a very strict judge of yourself and limit your acts and thoughts too much, which prevents you from expressing yourself freely. However, if wild beasts are caged, you have to interpret this dream as the retention of inner conflicts that torment you, in which case this oneiric image has some similarity to the previous (in which you are locked in a cage).

❖ If you are put in a cage with wild animals, the dream is warning you that you are in danger of an accident.

Cake ■ The meaning of this dream is, in general, the arrival of unexpected profits. To bake a cake shows the willingness of the dreamer to improve the quality of her friendships; and to eat it, the reunion with a loved one not seen in a while.

❖ Sweet cakes predict success in business; and those made with raisins, good times in social relations.

Calculation ■ To perform calculations in a dream is a sign of great concern for economic issues. When the final result is positive and you do not feel overwhelmed by the effort, it reflects your mastery of the situation. Otherwise, it will be a warning to be more cautious.

Calendar ■ This is a recurring dream for the terminally ill. The calendar allows you to place yourself

CALENDAR

Lidia dreamed: "I was sitting in a class of my old college listening to a lesson. I did not understand what I was doing there; It had been years since I graduated; however, I took notes and tried to be very attentive to the professor's explanations. Suddenly, I noticed a calendar hanging on the board. It marked the current date but its pages were detached by a gust of air and then they flew out the window, one by one, until the calendar was left with no pages. I had vertigo and felt lost."

Lidia's dream intrigued her for some time until she realized that it was warning her not **to waste time**; She needed to take full care of her responsibilities because the years pass quickly. Dreams in which time flies—and in this case happens literally: the calendar pages fly out the window—can refer to a hope for the time to stop and the current moment to become eternal. In the case of Lydia, it also revealed a **nostalgia** for the past and the desire to return to her student years, when her only responsibility was to be attentive in class.

precisely in the course of your temporality, which will allow you to gain some control over the vertigo that is produced seeing the time going by.

❖ Dreaming of a calendar is promise of love, loyalty, and perseverance.

Calf ■ See BABY and LAMB

Call ■ This can be interpreted in several ways, depending on what happens and who appears in the dream. If it is the dreamer who calls, it represents the need for external support at that time. Hearing a call and not paying attention, or being able to answer, alludes to a feeling of guilt about a lazy or careless attitude. To answer the call, however, indicates willingness to offer help to the people around you. On the other hand, it may be a matter of your unconscious trying to get your attention. Something important may be happening without you being aware of it.

❖ If you dream that someone knocks at the door, soon fortune will smile on you.

Callus ■ They represent hard work and effort. Often, they may indicate a loss of sensitivity. Perhaps, it is time to pay more attention to your emotional life.

Camel ■ This animal is a symbol of perseverance, frugality, and endurance, as well as fanaticism and heroic slavery. It is not a common dream, although it is a great omen that signals achieving goals and taking endeavors with determination and good work. (See ANIMALS)

❖ It predicts significant achievements for the dreamer.

Camera ■ In dreams, cameras usually represent yourself. The vision obtained through the lens is probably more impartial than the vision obtained through the eye. So dreaming that you photograph something or someone probably indicates a desire to see that thing or person in a more objective and less emotional way than you would in real life. It represents your desire to better focus on a particular person or situation. If the camera does not work well or when developing the picture the image is not clear maybe you are avoiding an issue in real life. It can also refer to your desire to revive the past and keep it forever.

Camping ■ Camping means your plans are provisional, so you must deeply analyze them, so you know how to guide them toward the intended goal.

Cancer ▪ To dream that you have this disease does not have to be a prediction (although if you have symptoms of discomfort, it is worth a check). Cancer is a tumor, and the dream could mean that an undesired element is becoming part of yourself or is growing in excess; for example a growing obsession that can affect your personality, and even your health. Having cancer in dreams also indicates that you do not properly deal with your emotions which end up being destructive; the dream is a warning against that.

Candle ▪ A lit candle indicates that you are trying to establish a connection with the essence of your being. If the candle is doused, the dream is suggesting that you utilize your energy in positive things, in activities that will directly benefit you. Possible, you are wasting your potential in affairs that will not bring you satisfaction.

Candlestick ▪ It is a symbol of spiritual light. Dreams that portray candlesticks are an invitation to potentialize all your sensibility as means of personal development.

Candy ▪ Eating candies or looking at someone eating them announces pleasant surprises, such as unexpected profit or a new love. Giving them away predicts help from friends during a period of difficulties. Receiving tampered candy predicts the existence of a false friend that will try to ruin you by slandering.

Cane ▪ It is an element of double meaning: support or an instrument of punishment. In the first case, if the dream in which it appears is pleasant, the image represents a solid and competent friend. If, on the contrary, you have an unpleasant perception of the dream (you are weak or limp), it is a sign that you lack confidence to address certain situations. When the cane functions as a weapon it means that in real life you are behaving tyrannically and are using your power arbitrarily. If you punish an animal with a cane you may be having problems with your own nature. If it is a person, it usually represents some part of yourself you dislike. For the Freudian school, the cane is identified with physical virility. For the Jungian, it refers to psychic masculinity.
❖ According to the old masters in the oneiric field this dream omen is negative.

Cane (plant) ▪ Reeds are fragile and flexible at the same time. They can point to a situation of insecurity or instability. Cutting cane is interpreted as a symbol of longevity. A sugar cane indicates a high degree of sensuality and serenity. A fishing cane (rod) is a means to a livelihood. It is important to analyze the other oneiric symbols for a correct interpretation.

Cannibal ▪ Although in our society it is not practiced we still maintain primitive traits when seeking divine values beyond our limits. Not surprisingly, the fact that some peoples devour foreigners derives from the belief that those foreigners are regarded as gods, and that through this practice it is possible to attain divinity. Consequently, this dream means that you pay too much attention to external references rather than to your own guidelines.

Cannon ▪ It is a symbol of impending battle. If the dreamer is armed with a cannon, the dream may have two different interpretations. On one hand, she is sufficiently prepared to solve a particular problem. On the other hand, she wants to violently finish a situation she is unable to control. If the barrel points toward the dreamer, it indicates excessive fear of a threat that cannot be avoided.
❖ The oneiric meaning of the cannon is, of course, war, broken balances, and associations. Instead, to hear it is a sign of ruin.

Canoe ▪ Its symbolism has a lot to do with BOAT. However, it can also be interpreted as an unstable situation that presents dangers difficult to overcome. Moreover, it is a symbol of interim conditions that do not offer enough support to the dreamer.

Cape ▪ Its image is related to the dome (circular shape with an opening at the top); in this sense, it indicates ascension, improvement, and spiritual growth. It also represents the action of covering yourself, denoting insecurity and a need for love. If you cover someone else it indicates desire to overprotect someone. Losing the cape is interpreted as a sign of insecurity. Wearing a too short cape, fear of embarrassment or lack of affection. Finally, it expresses dissimulation and secrecy. You may be hiding something from the outside world.
❖ If you dream that you wear a cape, a period of uncertainty is upcoming. And if it has hood, you must be alert because someone you trust can betray you.

Capsule ▪ It may be indicative of a desire to escape a desperate situation. The dreamer lacks tools to solve her own problems and needs external help.

Car ▪ Driving it represents taking the initiative, giving a new direction to your life. If someone else drives it you likely tend to let third parties lead you. The car also symbolizes the human body (like the CARRIAGE), so you can draw a parallel between the condition of both: a car in poor condition is a warning that you must take care of your health. The way of driving it is also the way you control yourself: if you do not drive it carefully or you suffer an accident the dream warns you about your mistakes. According to Freud, the car represented evolution of psychoanalysis.

❖ Formerly, it was said that driving a vehicle in a dream predicted changes at home or in business. If the vehicle breaks down, a friend will give you troubling news.

Caravan ▪ Dreaming that you are part of a caravan is a sign of a physical or spiritual change. It indicates a temporary situation, a process of change that needs to take place in a long time. Looking at a caravan, without being in it, can be interpreted as a situation of inaction while a desire for change is repressed.

Card ▪ If you are betting your money on cards, it means you want to rely on chance to solve your problems. The unconscious is warning you of this error and invites you to *discard* the possibility that the problems will solve themselves. If you are playing a game of cards and demonstrate ability and skill, these will be the qualities that you have in real life. Maybe the dream is telling you to adopt the same courage, strategy, and good timing required in card games. Games such as Twenty-one (or Blackjack) show that we should not let opportunities slip away. Others refer to the need for patience when it comes to making deals. Keep in mind another important detail: the symbolic origin of cards. The deck of fifty-six cards consists of fourteen figures for each of the four suits: coins (circles, discs, wheels), clubs (maces, scepters), swords, and cups. The coin symbolizes material forces; the club, power and control; the cup, love; and the sword action. This symbolism must be taken into account if you remember such details. (See GAME, LOTTERY, BETTING POOL, and ROULETTE)

❖ In a deck of cards, each figure has a meaning. In oneiric terms, diamonds represent wealth; clubs indicate work; hearts predict happiness in love; and spades, finally, portend future problems.

Carelessness ▪ Dreaming that you have not taken care of or have lost something can be interpreted in two ways. On one hand, it can be a warning that you are really not taking care of something important; but it can also be a sign of excessive concern that you feel for a particular object, work, or person. By making a detailed analysis of the dream and certain circumstances in the dreamer's life, she will know how to interpret the message from her unconscious.

Caressing ▪ Dreaming that you caress somebody shows you may not be treating the people around you well, as they deserve. If you are the one receiving caresses by others then it means you do not have all the affection you need in real life.

Carnation ▪ This flower symbolizes love and passion. If it is red such love will be fiery; if it is white it will be a faithful and disinterested relationship; if it is yellow it indicates jealousy.

Carnival ▪ This word is associated with the idea of orgy and a temporary return of the primeval chaos in order to release tensions. Therefore, if the dream provokes happiness, it is a sign that you should have more fun. Carnival also suggests the need to compensate and balance a life that is too tidy.

Carpenter ▪ To exercise a carpenter's job, good manual skills as well as some artistic sensitivity are needed. The dream is telling you to enhance these qualities in order to progress.

Carpet ▪ This element is much more important for the eastern culture than for the western. It represents happiness and tranquility, as it symbolizes the warmth of home. It predicts well-being in emotional and romantic relationships. The unconscious is seeking comfort and happiness. If in dreams you sell carpets, it means that you intend to deviate from the routine in order to jump into unknown adventures.

Carriage ▪ A major symbolic analogy of mankind is the carriage in relation to humans. The driver is the Self in Jungian psychology; the carriage, the body and mind; horses are the vital forces; and the reins, intelligence and will. In this sense, the overall meaning of the dream is the same as in CAR. On the other hand, a carriage represents slow but safe progress. If you are surrounded by pioneers it may suggest the desire to explore your unconscious or to adopt a more exciting lifestyle.

❖ If you drive someone else's car, it portends poverty. But if it is yours, you will be rich.

Case ■ A case—no matter the kind it is—stands for insulation; therefore, this dream reflects the sleeper's desire to avoid real-world problems.

Castle ■ Usually, a castle is the symbol of spiritual strength and vigilance. Its analysis is complex because it also derives from HOUSE; and the fact of being located on the top of a hill adds additional information. Furthermore, its shape, appearance, and color, as well as its darkness or luminous appearance, provide the final details for its interpretation. Therefore, the meaning of this dream is usually protection and transcendence. The condition of the castle as a solid fortress allows introspection, creativity, and spiritual contemplation. While the house represents the body, the castle symbolizes the soul. Dreaming of a castle can also demonstrate a need for isolation that depending on the castle's aspect, it may be positive or negative. To see the castle from the outside means that you still have some way to go but at the end of it, you will reach your goal. Conversely, if you dream that you live in the castle you will soon get spiritual wealth. If the castle is impenetrable it will be equally difficult to get to know yourself.

❖ To see a fortified castle means protection and virtue; and if it is closed, resistance. To enter it, uncertain hope or unexpected adversity. To live in it portends wealth. To besiege them is a sign of victory over enemies, both physical and spiritual.

Castration ■ In a man, it denotes fear of losing virility or of feeling sexually forced.

❖ The myth in which Saturn castrated his father represents the fear of maturity and the desire to supplant the father's figure.

Cat ■ Symbol of the feminine. To dream that a cat wants you to pet it indicates that someone is trying to seduce you. If it scratches you, you should expect professional jealousy. The color of the animal carries its secondary symbolism. So, black cats are usually associated with darkness and death, but this kind of analogy only works on superstitious people.

❖ In mythology, the figure of the cat was associated with the pagan fertility gods who represented the power and wisdom of nature. Similarly, for the Egyptians, cats were sacred and they guarded the souls of the dead. It was not until the arrival of the Christians when they began to be

CAT

Marta dreamed: "I was petting Gea [her precious Persian kitten] when she turned to me and said: 'pretty, more than pretty.' I was delighted that my cat could talk, I knew she was very clever . . . but this was too much! Suddenly, her feline face transformed into John's, but now she did not speak. He rather emitted terrible barking sounds and foam was coming out his mouth. I tried to hold him and calm him but he slipped out of my hands like a lizard."

One of the most magical and intense forces of our oneiric world is transformation: animals that become people; individuals who transform into trees, monsters, or other persons; buildings that disappear . . . These **transformations** are almost always a sign of psychological changes in our lives. When Martha had this dream she had just had a little argument with her boyfriend. This dream was warning her that she should be more considerate and attentive to him. To dream that a cat is seeking you to pet her indicates that **someone is trying to seduce** or feels strongly attracted to **you**. In the case of Marta it reflected her boyfriend's devotion and love for her. However, the fact that he first transformed into a fierce dog and then an elusive lizard denotes that such affection could also vanish or turn into resentment if she did not contribute to keep it up. The fact that she was gently petting her kitten and that the latter talked to praise Marta indicates Marta's ability to transmit affection and the certainty that all would be fixed with dialogue.

considered evil relatives of witches. For this reason, many books on dreams affirm that cats presage disadvantages.

Catastrophe ■ To dream of a catastrophe may signal the start of a psychic transformation. A transformation that, like other transformations, is born from the destruction of a previous process. Its dominant element (air, fire, water, etc.) can refine the symbol that the unconscious wants to convey. The more intense the catastrophe of the dream the greater the change will be.

Caterpillar ■ Caterpillars are the emblem of what has been corrupted. To dream of them is usually quite unpleasant and distressing. However, as you know, caterpillars turn into butterflies. This reminds us not to beat ourselves up because of our shortcomings. Not surprisingly, all creatures, including people, can eventually change and become beautiful and wonderful beings. (See WORM, BUTTERFLY, and METAMORPHOSIS)

Cathedral ■ See ABBEY and CASTLE

Cattle ■ Dreaming of any kind of cattle augurs wealth and abundance. The larger the cattle the greater this heritage. (See HERD)
❖ Grazing cattle promises fortune. Thin animals foresee hard times; fat ones, prosperous future; a large herd, agitation.

Cave ■ It provides the basis for certain identifications, such as the medieval one: the cave referred to the human heart as the spiritual "center." The cave, in this case, represents the unconscious, your subjective world, the experiences and knowledge accumulated over the years. All this allows you to reach maturity. It is very common dream during adolescence. The events happening inside the cave will reveal which aspects of the Self you are working on. In other interpretations, the cave represents the womb or female sexuality. What you find in it will be those elements the unconscious wants to cultivate in your: virtues, ideas, attitudes, etc.
❖ Many dragons and monsters from mythology lived in caves guarding a great treasure. This symbolizes that before winning the spiritual reward, you must fight the unconscious' fears. The cavern may also represent memories about a traumatic childhood that have been banished from conscious memory.

Cave ■ See CAVERN

Celebrity ■ Persons present in dreams may be aspects of yourself that you have not noticed yet. Everything you want to become is often present in this famous character. In this case, you must ask what traits this character symbolizes. Usually, those are traits that you need to incorporate in your behavior and in your life. If you dream that you are a celebrity perhaps you are demanding recognition for your achievements or you need admiration from people around you.

Cemetery ❖ This type of dream invites us to reflect on a terminal condition. If it is recurring, it could reveal unjustified fears. (See HANGED and CORPSE)

Chains ■ Chains symbolize the logical order of events. In this sense, the dream invites you to look at the past in order to solve present and future problems. If you dream that you are chained, however, it means that an internal aspect of yourself is being retained. You must set it free so it can express itself. If it is someone else who is chained, then you have to find out what aspect of the character that person represents. Similarly, if it is an animal, you have to ask yourself what aspect of your nature you are repressing. If it is a bull it might be your sexuality; if a dog, it may be your fury; and if it is an elephant it shows your inability to use your strength and wisdom.
❖ Dreaming that you are chained predicts you will be victim of injustice.

Chair ■ Indicates a stop along the way. It could be the response of the subconscious to physical tiredness, or the need of the dreamer to take a pause and reflect over the path that he has taken in his life. In either case, the circumstances that surround this state of vigil, together with the interpretation of other symbols that appear in the dream scene, will serve to understand the message and make a more appropriate decision.

Chameleon ■ For its ability to change color or camouflage, a chameleon points to betrayals from very close friends. For example, if a man dreams that there is a chameleon on top of his partner it alerts him about her infidelity. In general, it advises caution with those in whom you have trusted.

Chamois ■ To see chamois leather or other items made of it promises wealth acquired through personal effort. Dreaming of the animal indicates you should be more patient with the achievement of your goals.

Champagne ■ A newly opened bottle of champagne is a sexual symbol that is usually identified with ejaculation. It can also refer to a celebration or a personal achievement. The effervescence of this drink demonstrates creativity of your inner self.
❖ This dream portends difficulties in business. However, if the dream takes place in difficulties it announces a happy romance.

Check ■ Dreaming about the giving a check to a third person is a bad sign, since it predicts economic problems and debts. Receiving a check, however, involves the arrival of an unexpected sum of money that will improve your economy. Spending it expresses possible wastage in daily life.

Checkers ■ Black and white combo boxes symbolize the confrontation of forces in the life's battlefield. Therefore, depending on how you play checkers that is the way you will behave in real life. Usually, this struggle of antagonisms announces that there will not be great changes in your personal affairs. Winning the game, however, is always a good sign because it suggests the successful end of a risky operation.

Cheeks ■ They symbolize the dreamer's state of health: full and red suggests happiness and good health; pale and gaunt, grief and mourning. (See FACE)

Cheese ■ As it is aged, cheese is a food that is made through the fermentation of milk—it starts as a liquid and changes into a solid product. Therefore, the symbolism is clear: cheese represents the possibility that each feeling has to change into something stronger through constancy and fidelity.
❖ Dreaming that you are eating cheese predicts great deception and pain. In particular, fresh cheese will result in disgruntlement, betrayal, and loss of love.

Cherries ■ Its image is associated with the desires and innermost feelings of the individual. Although they have a high burden of sensuality, they are also tied to strong material and spiritual yearnings.
❖ They are, almost always, signs of physical and emotional well-being. Both picking and eating cherries are harbingers of joy, good news, and birth. To see them fall indicates a close love. The tree is also a good omen, it ensures happiness.

Cherry ■ Seeing a cherry or putting it on the top of a cake indicates satisfaction with the fulfillment of hopes and objectives that the dreamer intended.

Cherub ■ Cherubs are one of the new categories of angels that appear in the Sacred Texts.
❖ Given that their function consists of forming love and wisdom in the hearts of men, dreaming of them is interpreted as an invitation to altruism and to live the emotions in disinterested manner. Cherubs announce the happy circumstances related to higher values of the personality. You have the necessary elements to take a big step and grow.

Chess ■ Chess represents the analysis and strategies used in life: risks, defense, attack, and those small sacrifices necessary to achieve a high-impact goal. Keeping all that in mind, dreaming of this game is sign that you must be patient. Success is assured if you do not succumb to impatience.

Chest (body part) ■ If the person who dreams of the chest of a woman is a man, the image could indicate his need for tenderness and understanding. However, if a woman has this dream, it could be a symptom of early pregnancy. On the other hand, keeping in mind that we breathe through the chest, the dream could be referencing the central point of our lives. (See BREASTS)
❖ A beautiful, healthy chest is a sign of happiness; of great dimensions, economic debts.

Chestnut ■ It is a fruit related to winter and scarcity, suggesting the idea of foresight. ❖ Formerly considered suitable food for the dead, the chestnut is representative of long life, health, and protection. Some Nordic traditions advise to always carry one in your pocket, renewing it each year as a talisman of good luck and a charm against diseases.

Chickpeas ■ Chickpeas are both a symbol of simplicity and abundance. Almost always they reflect a state of comfortable calmness without unnecessary waste. Overall it is a positive dream. In any case, its meaning is related to EATING. The context of the oneiric sequence will be key to its interpretation.

Chicks ■ They express the feeling of affection or tenderness that someone awakens in the dreamer. They also allude to close family relationships, motherhood, and an excessive sense of protection.

Child ■ In dreams, a child can represent your most juvenile part, and your potential. Maybe, you recognize in him the hopes and ideals you had in the past. Arguing with him indicates that something in you is rebelling. If, in the dream, you get along with them or there is a reconciliation, it indicates that you are giving up due to certain demands or conditions. It may also deal with your own child and the meaning would be literal.
❖ To dream of a beautiful daughter denotes interesting friends; an ugly one, strange devotion. A son, on the other hand, denotes work.

Childhood ■ To return to childhood in dreams normally indicates a need for protection. It is the desire to return to the times when your mother cared for you and you didn't have to worry. This type of image is usually produced when you are afraid to face the unknown. The future causes insecurity. If you visit the neighborhood of your childhood, it may be able to help you recover an aspect of your past that remained unresolved, which you must now face in order to be at peace. In any case, childhood allows one to rediscover oneself.

Chimera ■ A chimera is a ghost, something unreachable. Its symbol—a mythological animal with the head of a lion, the body of a goat, and the tail of a dragon—represents perversion, as it invites you to trust in your delusions to the detriment of reality. Taken to the extreme, the chimera could bring you loss of contact with the real world. However, dreaming of chimeras cannot be considered totally negative: simply put, it reflects the need to live distinctly, to fight against the monotony that grips you. The subconscious urges you to start your imagination.

Chimney ■ To see a fireplace without a fire heralds an uncomfortable time in your lives: you may be involved in lawsuits and disputes over economic assets. However, if it is lit, it is synonymous with peace at home. If you dream of a crumbling chimney a misfortune could fall over your family; whereas if it is you who ruins it there is a danger of losing material things. If it is covered with ivy you will live happy but ephemeral moments; and if the ashes are the protagonists, then sadness will come for sure. Going down a chimney predicts tensions with friends; and climbing it makes clear your ability to escape gossiping.

Chinese ■ Dreaming of a Chinese person portends a difficult but necessary journey that will determine the successful completion of your projects. If you make a deal with that person your prestige will be increased. The presence of several Chinese individuals, however, is an indication that the business could end in failure.

Chocolate ■ Dreaming of chocolate augurs prosperity and serenity, both for yourself and for your close relatives. However, if it is stale it predicts disease or any other type of setback.

Choking ■ A situation in real life is crushing you emotionally and you are not able to overcome it on your own. Similarly, perhaps it is caused by a possessive partner or an overprotective father. All this hinders your psychological growth. It is very important that you restore the sense of identity in order to regain freedom of action. (See DROWNING)
❖ Superstition believes this dream announces sadness and poor health.

Chop ■ Dreaming of a raw chop indicates difficulties in achieving the objectives; but if it is cooked you will help others to attain those. To see someone else eating a roast chop is an omen of misfortune and betrayal. (See MEAT)

Christ ■ Each person has unique associations with this figure, depending on her religious influence. The symbol of Christ, as himself, represents perfection, martyrdom, universal suffering, and resurrection.
❖ There are many ways to reach spiritual truth, as there are many religions to reach your own God. Dreams of this type show those ways.

Christmas ■ A dream in which a fond Christmas party takes place may signal your desire to reaffirm traditional values such as: family togetherness, friendship, generosity, and optimism. However, the dream can also refer to feelings involving lack of affection and loneliness, especially if you do not like the holidays. Christmas symbolizes a spiritual birth which can manifest as the decision to change certain aspects of your life. It is also a way to embrace tradition and have loving moments with the family. Many people, meanwhile, associate Christmas with children. Dreaming repeatedly of the holidays may be due to emotional deprivation.

Church ■ Churches put us in contact with our inner harmony, since as it is known, they are places of seclusion and meditation. To dream that you find yourself in an empty, solitary church suggest a need for solitude and introspection. If the church is large and full of people, the dream encourages you to trust more in others, in what society offers you.
The dream is very positive if the protagonist becomes aware of his potential and decides to seek new projects to change his future. The purpose of the architecture of sacred buildings is to symbolize the unity of the soul with God. In psychological terms, these buildings represent the human mind at it's peak. (See ABBEY)
❖ Praying in a church promises joy.

Cinnamon ▪ This aromatic plant is associated with sensuality. Its presence in dreams indicates that the dreamer is in a period in which her sexuality is especially relevant in her life.

Circle ▪ The circle or disc is often a solar emblem. It also symbolizes, in many cases, heaven, perfection, and eternity. According to Jung, the square represents the pluralistic state of the subject that has not reached internal harmony (perfection); while the circle corresponded precisely to such final phase. The relationship of circle and square is very common in the universal spiritual morphology, especially in the mandalas of India and Tibet, as well as in the Chinese emblems (Yin and Yang). The circle also represents the idea of protection, especially when you dream that you are inside it.
❖ For Chinese people, circles have good feng shui. The omens of this dream, therefore, are always advantageous. Symbol of victory, a golden circle predicts inheritance; an iron circle, defeating enemies.

City ▪ The city symbolizes the human psyche. Depending on how it is represented in the dream it indicates how things are in your mind. If the city offers a beautiful spectacle it means that harmony reigns inside you. In case it is noisy and polluted, it is a clear indication that your ideas are altered by the internal chaos you are experiencing. On the other hand, the city can represent everything around you, including family and friends. If you feel alone as you enter it in the dream, you can feel that way with your social role in reality. If you dream that it is fortified with walls it will express your need for self-defense against outside threats; and a ruined city warns against neglected relationships. Finally, to get lost in the city shows your own existential loss.
❖ Mythological cities usually have eight gates, one of which is sealed. Each door represents a change in your life; the eighth is the end of the trip, in other words, death.

Clam ▪ Clams are a feminine symbol closely related to sexuality and fertility. When a woman frequently dreams of clams it means that she has difficulty living her sexuality as an adult is supposed to experience it. If she eats them next to the beloved one it means she will enjoy that person's success and trust; if she eats them alone, prosperity will be for someone else. Dreaming of clams signals that soon you will have to deal with a stubborn but honest person.

Clarification ▪ It is a symbol of physical and spiritual cleansing. It is associated with the desire to leave the darkness and seek the light. In oneiric images it may be represented in many ways: turning on the light of a dark room, cleaning the house, the car's windows, etc. In any case, it is a sign of the dreamer's need to clear the horizon, to see clearly and hit the road again. It shows a clear intention of spiritual growth.

Class ▪ This dream can be a continuation of the intellectual activity that you perform during the day; you struggle to get your thoughts away from it. While the individual sleeps, he or she continues to assimilate the information they have learned. However, the dream may also be telling you that you bore others because when you address them, it seems you are indoctrinating them. In this case, you should change your way of relating to others.
❖ A rare and ancient British superstition says that if you dream that you give a class of poetry, all our dreams will come true.

Claw ▪ As in other dreams, this one has not a single one interpretation: if it is a bird's claw, you will have serious difficulties carrying out your projects; if it is a feline's claw you will suffer a little upset with family; and if it is a dog's or wolf's one someone close to you will spread gossip about you.

Cleaning ▪ This dream almost always reflects the need to purify the body and soul, getting rid of superfluous things and keeping only that which you really need.

Cliff ▪ See ABYSS

Cliff ▪ Dreaming of precipices usually means that you suffer from vertigo. This vertigo can be physical, if you are lying on the edge of the bed; emotional, pointing to a lack of control over emotions; existential, the lack of goals that give meaning to your life; or it can also be provoked by the need to make a decision without being sure about the best option. In the latter case, it is advisable that you take your time so you can choose correctly and thus avoid any rush. On the other hand, if you dream you are climbing a cliff it means that you are striving to solve a problem of great concern. Once up on top, you will find that the path is smooth and even.
❖ If you dream that you get to climb a cliff it is an omen of good fortune for all projects you want to start.

Climb ▪ This dream indicated that you are trying to achieve a very high goal in real life or you are trying to escape something that frightens you. It is possible that you are about to achieve the success that you have been searching for a long time. Ambition will accompany you, but you may not be very sure of yourself. You should continue being humble and modest. In the event that you are too egotistic and climb too much, you run the risk that someone will make you fall. Arrogance will not serve you well. The walls or mountains that you should overcome symbolize obstacles of real life. If you conquer them quickly, the dream foretells victories. On the contrary, it denotes that it will be a difficult task that will require all of your efforts. That which is not achieved at first will need a gradual ascent, and quickly will produce more satisfaction. According to Freud, dreams in which you climb are a reflection of what it costs you to please your sexual desires.
❖ Oneiric oracles say that climbing up steps and reaching the final stretch in dreams foretells success in business.

Cloak ▪ All dreams in which cloaks are protagonists have different interpretations. So on one hand, to shed the cloak symbolizes the need to shake off everything superfluous. To put on a cloak means you are moving away from your essence and are not true to your authentic Self (the cloak, in this case, performs the functions of disguise). (See COAT and DISGUISE)

Clock ▪ As a machine, it is linked with ideas of perpetual motion, automatism, mechanism, etc. The clock can represent human destiny, as it is the measurement of your time. Its sound, further, reminds one of the beating of the heart, which identifies it with the emotional side of your personality. It could manifest that your life is governed by artificial routine that has created organized society. In this sense, you should live more casually and think less about time and dates. If you see a clock that is behind, it is a sign that you have the tendency to leave issues hanging. If it is fast, it means that you suffer stress and it would be best to relax some. If the clock shows the exact time, it indicates that you are losing time and that the moment to decide to act has already come; although it could also be a warning to be more punctual. If it shows that there is one minute to midnight, it denotes your desire to advance a situation that affects you. If it is stopped, it manifests the status of your emotions. Dreaming of various clocks with different times is synonymous with disorder and confusion. Lastly, dreaming of a chronometer evidences that you

do not have your emotions under control. (See HANDS (of a clock) and TIME)
❖ The regular movement of the clock indicates that everything is going well. Losing it in dreams indicates changes in your life or the possibility of starting a new stage of growth. Listening to the ticks of the clock presages the arrival of bad news.

Closet ▪ A closet represents the individual's place for keeping true feelings. This dream shows the need to hide something. Possibly you are not addressing issues as you should. If it is hidden, its location reflects difficulties when dealing with others. And if it's messy it means the subject suffers emotional problems. On the contrary, if it is clean, organized, and full of beautiful items, it certifies the health of spirit and possession of a great inner wealth.
❖ The oneiric superstition says that dreaming of a full closet portends good luck; the opposite if it is empty.

Clothing ▪ Clothing reflects the importance of appearance. It could show your true personality or hide your imperfections. It also reveals desire for elegance, notoriety, and success in love. The color and type of garment will supply more information about the meaning of this dream. So, clothing with bright colors evidences the need to call the attention of others, and generally, a lack in security. Warm colors denote happiness and optimism. Dark and cold colors indicate secrets and depression. If your clothing is worn, you should rethink some of your habits and attitudes. In this sense, you may need to improve yourself. When you dream that you are changing clothes, it means that you will soon experience developments in your life. And, if it is tight on you, maybe you are restricting some issue too much: it could be an emotional relationship or a position at work. (See SHIRT, TORN, NUDITY, RAGS, MAKEUP, and PANTS)
❖ The earliest oneiric interpretations found say that dreaming of a nude woman predicts good luck, as you will be provided with unexpected satisfactions. In contrast, dreaming that you are wearing too much clothing means that your vital needs are not covered. Dreaming of new clothing, lastly, foretells a domestic argument.

Clouds ▪ Clouds are a clear indication of difficulties. However, contrary to what it seems at first glance, this can be considered a good omen. The dream is telling us that, despite setbacks, we can succeed in our projects through effort and perseverance. It also augurs fertility after a long period of barrenness. According to other interpretations, clouds represent our mood. If they are very white and look like cotton, then they denote joy and spirituality. If they are black and sinister, they indicate depression or anger. Clouds also predict rain and, with it, the opportunity to release tension.

❖ Many traditions warn that you must clear your "clouds of ignorance" to make way for spiritual enlightenment. Similarly, clouds protected the Greek gods of Olympus. Only your intuition can cross that barrier and reach the higher knowledge.

Clover ▪ The clover is an emblem of the Trinity due to its ever beneficial presence. In dreams, clover foretells a period of good luck and prosperity.

Clown ▪ Just like the fool, the clown represents the opposite of authority. It symbolizes the instinct, the uninhibited, and childishness. If you dream of an anonymous clown, the image alerts you of the false camaraderie of others. If the clown has the traits of someone you know, this is the individual that the dream is warning you against. But if it is you who is dressed as a clown, you must watch out, because your attitude will cause people to not take you seriously. Maybe they think you're always pretending and hiding your feelings. However, if the dream is enjoyable there is nothing to object to: the unconscious suggests that you laugh at your concerns because their gravity is relative.

❖ In the Tarot, the Fool is depicted as the Joker from other cards. It reveals the unconscious side of the personality with all its potential for transformation.

Coal ▪ Coal symbolizes the hidden energy that is released only in contact with fire. This dream is an invitation to continue fighting because despite the odds, you can unleash energy, heat, or light that already existed in you.

❖ To see coal is sign of wealth; to eat it, negative events. A burning coal is a harbinger of love, but also of shame and reproofs linked to erotic aspects.

Coat ▪ Dreams which feature coats have various interpretations. For example, taking off the coat symbolizes the need to get rid of superfluous matters, to be sincere, and to eliminate behavioral norms that limit you. Putting on a coat, on the other hand, means you are straying from the essential, from your authentic Self (the coat, in that case, would play the same role of a costume). Given this last assumption, it is important to note that if wearing the coat produces a positive feeling, it implies self-confidence and the ability to successfully face any obstacle. Lastly, wearing someone else's coat can warn you against your excessive dependence on its owner (in a lot of cases, your mother).

Cobweb ▪ Cobwebs spun by spiders could symbolize the trap in which you find yourself in real life. It also represents loneliness, lack of communication, and disputes. On the other hand, if the spider in your dream has woven a beautiful web that you admire upon contemplation, it is a sign that the forces of the universe are in your favor to help you in your projects. Lastly, dreaming that the cobwebs are invading your home reveals that the nostalgia frequently takes over your mind, which impedes you from enjoying the present. You are too worried about events of the past and your energy is dispersed in things that cannot be changed.

Cockroach ▪ They are, almost always, negative dreams. There is something in your house, or inside you that disgusts or frightens you. They also indicate mistrust for people really close to you. On the other hand, they can be the announcement of a disease that has not yet been diagnosed.

Cocoa ▪ Dreaming of cocoa has usually, in all its variations, positive connotations: if you drink it, a rapid and intense infatuation is announced; if you eat it in a bar, happiness; and if you see it in beans, unexpected income.

Coconut ▪ This tropical fruit is a very positive sign for lovers as it announces quick and happy marriages. If the image is an empty shell it warns you against the bad ending of your projects due to betrayal from people you considered allies. And the dried fruit on the tree, mourning a loved one's death.

Coffee ▪ Dreaming that you drink coffee is a positive sign that is usually generated when the unconscious perceives that there is a circumstance that demands a lot of attention.

❖ Coffee in dreams is promise of happiness, luck, and success in love. To toast is an omen of a pleasant surprise or an unexpected visit; to drink it heralds longevity.

Coffin ▪ Although at first sight it indicates the contrary, dreaming of a coffin is a good omen because it represents the end of a cycle and the beginning of another, as well as liberation from an oppressive situation. Looking at a coffin holding a person that you do not know or cannot see indicates you are getting rid of useless items. If you know the person, this episode may be revealing your concern for their health.

❖ The interpretation of this dream varies depending on the character that is occupying it. So, if it is your partner it predicts eternal fidelity; an infant announces pain without hope; your own mother, enemies willing to forgive offenses.

Coins ■ Coins symbolize that which we desire intimately, but repress so deeply that the mind dare not mention its name. Therefore, it is common for these dreams to reference illicit love. To dream that you won many coins indicates that the thing they represent has a higher value than you thought, but also that you are experiencing a very creative period. By contrast, to imagine that someone you know steals your money means that you have exaggerated your feelings toward this person. To lose coins, if the dream is accompanied by a distressing feeling, reveals the fear of misplacing something very important to you.

❖ Gold coins promise great profits; silver ones, setbacks; copper, poverty; fake ones are an indication of dishonor and shame.

Colander ■ To use a colander in a dream reveals the arrival of lawsuits and legal problems because of material issues. If the holes are tight these issues will be favorable to you; but if, on the contrary, they are wide you will end up losing everything you had won. Seeing other people using a strainer means that, in real life, they do not accept you as you are and that this attitude will make you suffer.

Cold ■ If your dream is not simply a physical reflection (perhaps you are not snug and feel cold during sleep), this oneiric feeling expresses the dreamer's need for love and warmth. If you do not dislike this coldness, and on the contrary, it stimulates and refreshes you, it expresses your desire to be alone and disconnected.

❖ Promises happiness and near affection.

Collision ■ A collision with another person warns against the possibility of becoming hated because of your desire for advancement at any cost. If, however, someone collides with you, tensions will occur around you and you will be involved in many altercations. If

you dream of two vehicles crashing this points to a foreseeable period of bad luck.

Colors ■ Colors that appear in dreams express your inner impulses and that is why they complement the meaning. Psychologists often conduct a test of colors on their patients in order to determine their emotional status. An expert in feng shui also makes sure to have, at home, the color that attracts good fortune. However, depending on each individual the interpretation of each color varies, because every person has particular chromatic associations. The basic colors are YELLOW, BLUE, and RED. All other colors are the result of the combination of these three. Every color, as discussed below, has its own duality. Depending on the situation of the dreamer, the meaning is either. Red is the color of vital force, it represents passion and sexuality, but can also denote fury and blood. Orange is the refinement of passions, and is often associated with balance and healing. Yellow is associated with artistic inspiration, but there are cases in which it symbolizes cowardice. Green is the color of nature that brings hope and new life, although sometimes it expresses jealousy and envy. Blue is all the spiritual matters, it implies harmony and (like the sky) liberty; however, sometimes, it represents sadness. Purple is the color of royalty and spiritual knowledge. Black denotes depression and unconsciousness. Finally, white symbolizes purity.

❖ For a medium, every living thing has an aura (an energy field around the body) of a particular color. In this sense, the oneiric meaning of colors is related to the spiritual value they are traditionally associated. So, red is sensuality; orange, purity; yellow, inspiration; green, recovery; blue, healing; purple, clairvoyance; black, disease; brown, stability; and white spirituality.

Column ■ A column symbolizes support and firmness. The image of the two columns, however, represents vital and balanced opposites: the couple, marriage, emotion and action, the father and the mother, etc. In oneiric terms, two columns are the eternal stability and the hole through which you access the eternal matters. If one of them breaks down it means that you are losing balance, either because of a disease or because you have abandoned your convictions.

❖ The vision of a column promises prestige and influential friends; many (all aligned), honors and power. A column breaking down indicates loss of friends, misfortunes. Climbing it ensures popularity and renewal; falling off it, losing friends.

Comet/kite ■ The oneiric vision of a comet or a shooting star expresses fleeting and brief situations. Applied to relationships with people the message is clear: your friendships or love ties are unstable. In the case of a children's kite, flying it means that you have idealistic hopes. This association is very logical keeping in mind the difficulties of successfully handle a kite when we were kids. On the other hand, it symbolizes you want to have a relief from the problems and enjoy life with fewer responsibilities. Also, the fact that you are holding it by a rope manifests your desire to control your life or to start a business.
❖ The dream of a kid's kite promises health. If it crashes or the rope breaks it portends financial trouble.

Compass ■ Your unconscious may be showing you the way, either because you are not satisfied with the direction your life is going or because you need time to reorient. This dream manifests that the haze you feel will end soon. If the compass deviates in the dream and guidance is uncertain, you may have to change route. Other elements may appear in the dream suggesting alternatives for the future.
❖ According to feng shui, the eight directions of the compass symbolize eight different qualities. The south is fame, fortune, and recognition; southwest, marriage, and happiness in love and relationships; west, children and creativity; northwest, charitable people, mentors, and network connections; north, career success; northeast, knowledge, academy, and introspection; east, family, the elderly, people with authority, and health; and southeast, finally, wealth and prosperity.

Competition ■ To participate in a competition with strangers signals small expenses because of an unexpected trip; with coworkers, trouble getting a job promotion; and with family, heated discussions that could end violently. Earning money by betting on a competition is a positive sign: you will survive any problem; however, losing that money means you have to abide by the dictates of others.

Complaint ■ Complaining in dreams is a sign that you are having emotional or economic problems in real life, and you are unable to ask for help. The dream, usually, is an expression of your pain and is a warning to go to others in difficult moments. However, this dream could also warn of your tendency to complain and is suggesting that you stop lamenting over a certain event in the past.

Conjurer ■ It manifests the ability to provoke the fascination of people around you. It is a dream that reveals your way of relating to others. The conjurer may be a representation of a part of your own personality, or the image of someone you know. In any case, its figure refers to the attraction, manipulation, and deceit.

Construction ■ It is an image that has implications to all humanity. To build something in a dream indicates the intention to undertake something. The dreamer has the ability and the proper conditions to begin new projects. To see an unfinished construction or one in ruins may be the reflection of an undesirable situation for the dreamer in real life.
❖ Dreaming that you build something with your hands is generally an omen of abundance and rapid change. However, according to the type of construction, the meaning will be different. Building great buildings reveals grandiose projects; small houses, inconvenience, discomfort, losses, and illness for friends or relatives. Building a tomb promises a true and eternal love; Instead, a church or an altar indicates serious danger to the dreamer.

Container ■ The meaning of this dream will depend on the characteristics of the container: if it is big, it is a synonym of avarice; small, of conformism; full, of success; empty, of bad luck; and broken, of disagreements with your partner.

Convent ■ The convent represents the need to escape the conflicts of life. This type of dream reveals immaturity on the protagonist's part.
❖ Dreaming of a convent promises a secret love. To see a convent means peace; and to reside there, serene old age.

Cookies ■ Dreaming of sweet cookies suggests you give too much importance to frivolous and trivial matters: too much pleasure and little effort in life.
❖ To bake cookies predicts a period of family disputes over trivial matters. It also predicts poor health. For a young woman, baking them signals that she is too worried about not finding the right partner. Eating them, however, suggests that bad times will soften with the

support of family and friends. Taking them out from the oven invites the sleeper to have hopes.

Cooking ▪ To dream of a kitchen will reveal, first, the means currently available to you. Everything depends on whether the kitchen is well or poorly equipped. What happens in it will have a correspondence with your life at this moment. If food is burned it means that despite your good will, you still have a lot to learn. Cooking also symbolizes the desire to transform the harsh reality into something more "edible." On the other hand, if you dream of cooking for others, it can denote your intention to influence them. Maybe you want people to think something in particular or make them dependants from your care.

❖ It is said that this dream portends multiple visits of your friends in the future.

Coral ▪ In its symbolism the meaning of the tree, blood, and water are combined. It is a sign of a hidden treasure and many difficulties and risks to find it. Diving among coral is a warning sign. In Persia it was a sign of prosperity and wealth.

Corn ▪ Corn is a symbol of prosperity and fertility. To dream that you eat this grain can also manifest a need to nourish yourself spiritually.

Corner ▪ Sometimes you feel frustrated by things that do not have a solution. You feel cornered and impotent. The force to emerge is double, as as well as being forced to make a decision, you should be able to control the situation.

❖ Corners tend to be considered places where negative energy accumulates.

Corpse ▪ If a body is found in your dreams, it means that a situation is corrupting; there is something that smells bad and threatens to destabilize you. The corpse symbolizes the corrupt, those bad thoughts, hatred, and resentment that should be buried. That is why the dreams in which you become a corpse symbolize the desire of being done with a situation that concerns you.

Costume ▪ Dreaming that you wear a costume means that you do not feel comfortable with your personality and, therefore, you need to play a role or to pretend in order to succeed. This attitude can hide your authentic identity.

❖ Many myths and kids' stories portray characters wearing masks that cannot be removed. This shows that sometimes it is possible to become whoever you want to be by paying a high price: neglecting your true self.

Cotton ▪ Psychologically, cotton represents protection—often excessive—that you receive from people who love you.

❖ According to the way it appears, it's meaning varies. So, cotton in the form of thread predicts career success; in bales, problems in family or business; and in branches, hypocritical behavior or even betrayals around you. If you eat cotton candy a leisure trip is expected at short notice. Cotton fields indicate good times for business. It's collection will bring richness and abundance to those who are engaged in these agricultural activities.

Cow ▪ Although it is infrequent that it appears in dreams, the cow is related to maternity, goodness, patience, and fertility. So, fat cows signify richness, whereas skinny cows signify the benefits that you will await. It could equally denote a tolerant attitude. Maybe the dream is warning you that you should slow down and reflect more on your decisions. Cows, on the other hand, are also associated with dignity, strength, and passive resistance. For a man it symbolizes his feminine side; for a woman, it could be a reflection of her maternal instincts.

❖ For the hindus, cows are sacred and represent the protection and care of their gods. Krisna, for example, was the one who taught the shepherds that they should not worship the divinities that they could not see with their own eyes, but rather the cows. In them resides God.

Crab ▪ These animals are a symbol of indecision and doubt because of the backwards motion that characterizes them. When they star in your oneiric thoughts, they must be interpreted as a warning: you must not get carried away by prejudice because this would prevent you from moving forward.

❖ It is the astrological sign of Cancer, armored but with a tender heart, romantic and in love with the past (in fact, he walks backwards). Its presence in dreams portends disputes and separations, especially if it is red; black indicates delays in business.

Crack ▪ Dreaming of a crack announces economic losses and some internal imbalance. You should review your purposes, principles, and feelings, because you are not being too consistent with yourself. (See HOUSE, DISEASE)

Cradle ▪ An empty cradle is a sign of nostalgia, low self-confidence, and self-dissatisfaction. In contrast, rocking a child is, without a doubt, conjugal happiness.
❖ Symbol of the womb, the cradle in dreams promises an imminent marriage. If a baby is lying in it, it means fertility.

Crane (bird) ▪ From China to the Mediterranean cultures, the crane is an allegory of justice, longevity, and loyalty.
❖ Emblem of periodic regeneration and health, the crane announces, by inversion of the oneiric content, the illness of a friend. According to some keys, it also means argument and betrayal.

Crane (machine) ▪ Its interpretation is related to BUILDING. It is indicative of a favorable status; the dreamer has the necessary tools to carry out the projects that she has set for herself.

Cream ▪ Cream is the symbol of sweetness and inconsistency. To dream of eating it announces pleasant moments that do not last long. If you whip cream, it is clear that you have control over your own life; but if you just see it, you expect others to do things for you. If the cream is served at the table, on the other hand, you live in times of prosperous business.

Creditor ▪ Imagining that they demand you pay a debt denotes a misuse of your material and intellectual goods as well as the feeling of being overwhelmed by economic problems in real life. You must be more moderate in using those assets in order to avoid future complications.

Cricket ▪ Dreaming of crickets' sound reveals that you are going through a period of peace and tranquility. When you are worried, this sound can become really annoying, so you should relax and stop over-thinking problems.
❖ According to the oracles, the next day after the dream will be particularly difficult, especially if the sleeper is ill. It also indicates a poor harvest.

Crime ▪ See STABBING

Crocodile ▪ Because of their aggressiveness and destructive power, crocodiles meant, according to the inhabitants of ancient Egypt, anger and evil. This idea has survived to this day. Dreaming of a crocodile, then, represents the dark and aggressive inclinations of your unconscious: betrayal, jealousy, resentment, etc.
❖ It predicts a strong disappointment of your best friends.

Crops ▪ They represent fecundity and immortality. They are indicative of a good spiritual, economic, or emotional moment. They are also symbols that reflect the relationship of the dreamer with their sexuality, whether they are a man or a woman. The image of crops represents masculine and feminine genitals.
❖ According to some superstitions, crops that have the shape of male genitalia are aphrodisiacal.

Cross ▪ The cross is a symbol present in all cultures, therefore, it has multiple references. There are many types and each of them refers to its own meaning. For example, the Greek cross (with four arms of equal length) expressed wholeness; Native Americans used to draw crosses to represent the partition of the universe. For Christians, it means suffering, martyrdom, death, and sacrifice. In general, you can see, in its most simple representation, the four cardinal points and the image of the human body with arms outstretched. In the first case, you should interpret this dream as the need to make a decision on an issue makes you worried. However, if you link the cross to the human body this symbol suggests that you need to restore balance, as well as being consistent with yourself.
❖ From a mystical point of view, the cross symbolizes the division nature in four sets: four seasons, four directions, four elements . . . Formerly, the cross contained the ideal human body. It is also associated with the power of arboreal life.

Crossing ▪ This dream alerts you of any obstacles you must still overcome to achieve success in projects. If crossing a street, the obstacle is a social one. But if it is a natural barrier, the problem will likely be internal.

Crossroads ▪ This dream can be interpreted literally. That is, it reminds you that you must choose between several paths and possibilities to move forward in life. The unconscious advises you to stop postponing decisions. (See FORK)

Crow ■ Because of its black color, it is tied to the ideas of beginning (mother night, primeval darkness, etc.); for its flight, the chosen messenger. Formerly, it was believed that the crow was the "messenger" of the gods, which gave it a great cosmic significance. Over time, most people associate this bird to the ideas of misfortune and death. In oneiric terms, and taking into account the latter, the crow can be the messenger of your unconscious. First it frightens you, but then it reveals its spiritual wealth.
❖ Associated with witchcraft and oneiric prophecy, some superstitions believe that dreams in which crows appear foretell the future. If it flies above the dreamer, it predicts hazards and bad news. Dreaming that a loved one transforms into a crow predicts strong pains.

Crowd ■ To dream that you are in the middle of a huge crown and that it prevents you from advancing or moving easily, suggests that you feel unable to direct your life. Equally, the dream may be telling you that you need some space. On the other hand, the crowd could represent problems and worries that never stop pressuring you in reality.
❖ If the majority of the people in the crowd are well dressed or wear bright colored clothes, soon you will meet many new friends.

Crown ■ To be crowned symbolizes triumph and self-improvement. If the crown in your dream is made of flowers it announces future pleasures; if made of orange blossom, marriage; of ivy, friendship; of gold, dignity; of olive, wisdom; of thorns, sacrifice.

Crutches ■ In many cases, they represent a solid and true friendship, since crutches symbolize the outside support (moral or economic). This is why crutches so often appear in the paintings of Salvador Dali. Perhaps the dream is questioning the support you receive from the people around you in real life, or that which you offer to others.

Crying ■ Dreams make us face situations that we tend to avoid in reality. In this case, theres is something that makes you very sad, so it is very important you take note of the other symbols in the dream to discover what is causing you such grief. (See WEEPING and TEARS)
❖ According to oracles, the meaning of this dream is the opposite. So, crying will bring happiness and laughter.

Crystal ■ Like gemstones, crystals are a symbol of the spirit and intellect. It also represents, because of its transparency, sincerity. In the dream, a crystal can be your purest and eternal Self. If you look at it carefully it means that you are seeing within yourself to discover your true fate.
❖ Crystals are related to peace, harmony, and healing powers of the spirit. Dreaming of them means that there lies your hidden potential.

Cuddle ■ This symbolizes communication without words. The dreamer may feel the need to know or understand something that, at the moment, escapes her. However, it is not a negative dream. Although it is nonverbal communication, the intention to communicate beyond words it is very valuable and should be heeded.

Cudgel ■ It is a symbol of brutality and aggression that alerts the dreamer of her personal relationships. It may be time to revise them and to try solving problems or changing attitude.

Cup ■ To dream of a cup is generally a sign that you will participate in a pleasant project that could bring you a lot of satisfaction. However, the interpretations vary based on the type of cup. If it is a porcelain cup, you will enjoy peace and tranquility; but a plastic cup will bring economic difficulties, and the conflicts will torment you. A full cup is a sign of unexpected earnings; empty, of bad luck, and broken, of familial disagreements.

Curtain ■ If you dream that you open the curtain then you are ready to disclose what has been kept secret. If you close it you are trying to hide or suppress your feelings.
❖ This dream portends that you will have guests that will displease you. Disputes will take place soon.

Customs ■ It is a clear sign that you have concluded a process or activity and are about to start a new endeavor. It is time to review the experiences of the past and to begin drawing conclusions, so the new stage is enjoyable and successful.

Cutting ■ To cut is to break and to separate. This dream can be the allegorical representation of your circumstances in real life: it is perhaps a broken relationship or the end of a pattern of behavior. (See KNIFE)
❖ If someone else cuts you, a friend will betray you.

Cyclone ■ A cyclone always indicates an external force that drags you without any chance to control it.

Its interpretation can be positive if it is an energy that pushes you to make a move or a task that you find too difficult. However, it can also be a force that takes you closer to a danger, against your will. To understand the message of this dream you must be very attentive to the feeling of well-being or anxiety that it provokes on you.

Cypress ■ Although it has a long life, it is the tree of cemeteries. Its image has to do with death, but also with eternity. It symbolizes the passage of time, death, and the beginning of perpetual existence. It represents the transition from the physical life (perishable) to the spiritual life that lasts forever. In the Middle Ages, it was considered a sign of welcome. A pilgrim who felt well taken care of in a monastery would plant a cypress at the entrance, so other pilgrims could tell that in that place they would be welcome. Thus, we can say that its symbolism is very complex.

Cyst ■ Dreaming of a cyst on the chest could mean a lack in sensibility towards someone who is suffering. You are behaving coldly with someone who needs your support. Cysts in other parts of the body reflect upset and unattended situations that could come back against you.

D

Daffodil ▪ A symbol of a self-contemplative, introverted, and self-centered attitude. The warning from the unconscious is obvious: if we rest on our laurels (that is, if we let ourselves be tempted by vanity) we will lose everything. Other more positive interpretations associate daffodils with springtime and rebirth. In this case, the dream indicates that a time of growth, optimism, and hope will arrive. The latter is based on the yellow color and the beautiful symmetry of these flowers, whose symbolism refers to the light of inspiration and psychological wholeness, respectively.

❖ Celtic tradition of the city of Wales believes that a bouquet or field of daffodils means that, in future, you will receive more gold than silver. A single daffodil, however, portends misfortune.

Dagger ▪ It represents a cut, wound, or a violent break, probably betrayal. It can cause moral pain. (See KNIFE)

❖ The dagger symbolizes desire for aggression, tacit and unconscious threat, because it can be concealed. Unlike swords, a dagger's short size demonstrates its lack of nobility and its offensive power constraints. In oneiric terms, dreaming that they hurt us with a dagger could sometimes be related to some violent break-up, probably by betrayal. It can lead to emotional pain.(See KNIFE)

Daisy ▪ They symbolize simplicity and ingenuity.

Dam ▪ Dreaming of a water dam may mean that you have retained some emotions inside that need to get out. If you see a dam burst, then it means that you have lost control and perhaps you have unleashed your fury too much. Emotions run over you. A good solution is to be kind and express your feelings in a gentle and controlled manner.

❖ Victorian books about dreams interpret obstructions, hindrances, and obstacles as harbingers of problems that will occur soon. Dams, therefore, fall into this category.

Dance ▪ Dancing in dreams reflects how you move in your inner circle. Through dance you can harmonize internal opposing sides, so this kind of dream often has a strong emotional sense. Depending on how it develops it is possible to draw conclusions applicable to sexual, emotional, familial, social, or professional relations. So, if you see a group of people dancing, it means that you should be more generous and live each moment intensely, without staying on the sidelines of the world. On the contrary, dancing merrily indicates that you are happy with how things are going and you feel free from any influence. It also denotes the possibility that your current situation improves. Dancing with your beloved indicates that your love is requited. However if it is a costume dance, the dream is a warning that you must avoid being hypocritical to your partner. If you see a man and a woman dancing it can show the harmonious union of the masculine and feminine sides of your personality.

❖ In a dream, dancing can be a spiritual symbol that expresses, for example, the dance of Shiva, the Hindu god of eternal flow of time, the power of creation and destruction. To see old people dancing ensures success in business; dancing at a wedding, disease; with family, luck. It also augurs well for the prisoner, who will be released shortly.

Danger ■ Sometimes, during a dream, an alarming sense of danger invades you, though it is not based on anything tangible. It is possible that the unconscious is warning you that you suffer unknown physical problems. In other occasions, this danger materializes in a concrete situation (an accident, an attack, etc.), in which case you have to see what that particular threat suggests in order to interpret it.

Darkness ■ Traditionally, it is identified with the principle of evil and the occult forces, though dreaming of darkness possibly reflects your mood, perhaps somewhat depressed or pessimistic. If the darkness frightens you, perhaps you are afraid to investigate the unknown parts of youself. If you get lost in it, the dream is representing your feelings of insecurity, despair, or depression. If it is, instead, "the darkness before dawn," your unconscious is optimistic that your prospects are more promising than you think. A light at the end of a tunnel or the stars and the moon shining in the sky is an indication that your aspirations and desires are positive and urgently seek a light to guide you in life and tell you where to go. During the darkness, that's when the unconscious lives more intensely. For this reason, the night is the symbolic moment in which characters from horror novels such as witches, ghosts, etc. meet These frightening figures are only representing our hidden aspects, or the lower forces mentioned earlier.
❖ The Chinese oracle I Ching, used by Carl Jung to help with dream interpretations, says that when the darkness is so great that you can see absolutely nothing, it is to get darker. So, things can only get better.

Dart ■ See ARROW

Date ■ When a date appears in your dreams it is important you mark it down. It may be related to an important event in your life.

Dates ■ Dreaming of dates on the palm predicts happiness in the affective dimension; and eating them, upcoming pregnancy or maternity.

❖ In ancient Greece, wives ate dates at the wedding feast because its symbol of sexuality and fertility makes it an omen of wealth and luck. An Arab belief promises the birth of a child to whoever dreams of dates.

Day ■ A sunny day is synonymous with optimism, improvement of living conditions; however, a cloudy sky involves bad luck and economic losses. Dreaming of the day's first hours predicts successful businesses and prosperity in social and emotional relationships; The afternoon promises deep and lasting friendships; and dusk, unfulfilled hopes.

Daycare ■ It is a dream that brings back childhood memories. If the environment is nice the dream can be interpreted as a need for warmth and shelter. If, however, the feeling is of being overwhelmed the dream indicates overprotection from someone very close in the dreamer's life.

Death ■ Such dreams do not have to be premonitory or have any relation to physical death, but rather should be interpreted as a sign of the end of an era. It is the beginning of something new, because every death implies a change, a transformation, or rebirth. Thus, dreams in which you die indicate radical changes in your life or in your personality. To see other people or animals die may reflect those parts of yourself that are transformed. For example, if it is your mother who dies, you may be rejecting your maternal instinct. And dreaming of death is primarily a signal change, perhaps a deep-seated psychological change your unconscious has noticed before you did. To dream that a loved one dies means you will lend valuable support at a crucial and difficult moment in that person's life, while also reflecting your fear of losing them. (See ACCIDENT, DROWNING, MURDER, SCYTHE, and MOON)
❖ To encounter someone who has died in real life in your dream is part of the painful process of healing. Sometimes, this loss is also represented oneirically through a divorce, an attack, or a rejection by the person you so loved. All this comes from the overcoming and acceptance of the death. Other cases cannot be explained by metaphors or allegories, but rather depend on the beliefs of each individual. These are those in which the dreamer claims have communicated with deceased persons.

Debts ■ Being in debt alerts you of the need to rely more on your own opinions, because other people's opinions will only bring you concerns. Acquiring debts in dreams announces a troubled time when you might endure the betrayal of a friend. To settle them, however, is a clear sign of a positive turn of events.

Decay ■ Psychologically, putrefaction is the destruction of mental debris that obstruct spiritual evolution. Putrefaction, then, transmits the idea of new life that comes after the decay. Do not forget that in order for something new to rise, a breakdown of the old is required. This dream may seem harrowing but it actually transmits high hopes to the protagonist.

Deciding ■ Making a decision in dreams is evidence of your inability to do so in real life. It reflects the stress that this situation provokes on you. If it is a different person who makes those decisions it shows that you tend to let others decide for you, and that this will eventually harm you.

Decomposition ■ To see something breaking down or rotting can be a sign that the dreamer has lost her interest or motivation in real life. It indicates an environment conducive to leaving behind a project that is not promising or that has been spoiled for any reason. It is very important to look at the dream's breakup, because it can allude to work, business, project, or personal relationship.

Decorate ■ Decorating your house indicates the desire for reconciliation with yourself or with people that have been away. It reveals the intention of looking inward in order to recover lost affections and feel comfortable with what you are and what you have.

Deer ■ Because of the similarity of its antler to tree branches, it is often linked symbolically to the Tree of Life. By virtue of its large antlers it also represents the elevation. For these reasons, it is identified with the idea of nobility. Its presence in dreams may be related to a job promotion.
❖ The oneiric image of this animal in the forest announces benefits. A deer running bodes well for business. Deer fighting one another denote obtained powers; to see them die, well-being; to have one in the garden, misfortune. However, a herd of deer predicts good and numerous friendships.

Defecation ■ The act of defecating in a dream—strange to say—has, in general, a very positive

meaning. This oneiric vision expresses the need for an internal cleaning.

Defoliate ■ It is a dream indicating a ideal time for change and renewal. The mind needs to leave behind old attachments and to take a new path. It can be interpreted as a desire to learn new things, to travel, and to broaden the horizons.

Deformity ■ Deformity reflects that you reject some aspects of yourself. If any limb of your body grows uncontrollably it means that this limb is relevant, so you have to analyze its specific meaning.

Dejection ■ When it is associated with a passive or pessimist attitude, dejection indicates a type of frustration or fatigue. On the contrary, when this feeling is linked to optimism, it denotes the possibility to achieve important goals. In this case, the dream is reminding you of the need for perseverance.

Delay ■ Dreaming that you arrive late to a train station or bus stop is a very recurrent dream. This image symbolizes that, due to your laziness and inhibition, you are missing opportunities. Arriving late or delayed to a place also indicates that there is a gap between your interior work rhythm and the course of events.

Deluge ■ Science has confirmed the historical events of the Great Flood; a catastrophe that destroys the forms but not the forces, enabling the emergence of new life. The flood symbolizes the end of a period because, like any rain, it brings purification and regeneration. Ultimately, this involves the idea of rebirth. In the oneiric field, a deluge announces the shipwreck of your emotions. If you are experiencing serious emotional problems, this dream suggest you need to end the relationship that is causing you trouble.

Demon ■ The image of the devil in a dream (whether he has horns and tail) indicates that you should not be tempted to use illegal means in order to achieve your goals. It means that you are in an obscure, hidden situation, or that you have a double intention. In addition, the devil can impersonate your fears, desires that you repress, or some misconduct in real life. The best weapon against the latter is to make use of love and honesty.
❖ The figure of Satan appears in the Jewish, Islamic, and Christian traditions. Originally, it represented fertility

and the powers of nature. Maybe your unconscious is giving you the keys (compost) for your inner growth.

Dentist ▪ The image of the dentist is associated with the idea of achievement with suffering. You feel the need for a third party to help you and save a difficult situation, although you know that this intervention will be painful.

Depilate ▪ When a woman dreams of depilating after a long period of neglecting her image, it shows the need to take care of unfinished business. To a man, however, it is a clear sign of pain and sexual ambiguity. If another person shaves you, it marks a trend to comfort and even the abuse of other subjects.

Descending ▪ Descending may have a negative interpretation. It can be a symbol of failure, disappointment, or frustration. However, it may also represent that you want to get into an unknown world. In oneiric terms, descending to a basement marks the desire to find hidden aspects of yourself. And get to the bottom of a well also allows you to find a secret truth and be ready to go back to the surface. In general, this decline is usually toward your unconscious, especially when it is into caves, wells, tombs, and cellars.
❖ There are legends claiming that the ancient civilization of Crete built temples in underground caves. There, they performed their dances, ceremonies, and rituals. Since the beginning of time, descending to underground places symbolized the divine and spiritual quest of the human being.

Desert ▪ It represents death, aridity, and nonexistence. If you dream of being in the desert, without water and suffering from the heat of the sun, it means that you feel lonely, unloved, and unmotivated. Therefore, you must start giving to others in order to receive later. But if the dream involves a pleasant feeling it announces that you expect significant possibilities and creative projects. On the other hand, the desert has always been seen as a favorable place for divine revelation and meditation. This is because the desert can also be defined as "pure abstraction." (See AIR, YELLOW and SAND)
❖ This dream could signify a time of spiritual settling and beginning. Great historical figures, like Jesus, the Tibetan Lamas, and the Hindu Wise Men, stayed for long periods of time secluded in desert lands to get closer to their true nature. Distanced from mundane distractions, they recognized their divine interior. Your dream expresses the same sentiments

Detective ▪ In real life, detectives seek hidden truths. While you sleep, you act in the same way: trying to solve a problem and to approach it sincerely. Perhaps, you perceive that something is wrong or that someone has not been completely honest with you.
❖ If you are falsely accused by a detective, the dream portends that fortune and honor will soon be on your side.

Devil ▪ See DEMON

Devouring ▪ It indicates a high degree of anxiety about getting something. When someone else devours greedily it indicates that you have a negative concept about that person. Being devoured by a wild beast is interpreted as the excessive fear of a situation or a particular problem that you are unable to solve.

Dew ▪ Synonymous with purity, virginity, and divine blessing. Its meaning is associated with that of Water, Dawn, and Rain.
❖ According to mythology, dew is the tears of Alba (Eos) for his lost children; a sign of pain that, in reverse, predicts felicity, inheritance and fortune.

Dialect ▪ If you are among people who speak a strange dialect, this dream indicates the need to feel accepted in a group that you do not belong to. Indicates isolation and loneliness. If, however, you are able to speak a language other than your native, it is interpreted as a sense of security. You are prepared to face new situations.

Diamond ▪ Emblem of light and splendor. Like all gemstones, it participates in the general meaning of treasures and wealth, symbols of moral and intellectual knowledge. Modern psychology attributes to diamonds the meaning of complete personality and mental balance. The person who dreams of a diamond is on the road to spiritual and moral perfection. Diamonds represent the fulfilled Tao.
❖ In oneiric terms, diamonds indicate sovereignty, greatness, eternity, and great courage in adversity. Therefore, these images portend prosperity and success achieved through effort.

Dice ▪ They represent chance, which may involve a fatalistic feeling or powerlessness in life. However, if the presence of the dice, in your dream, is pleasant, the unconscious is recommending you to trust fate.

❖ Playing dice in dreams is, generally, an omen of change of fortune and deceit. A win predicts debts, loss of property, and litigation. However, the number you get in the game (may be the combination of two dice) will be crucial to interpret the dream. So, number one denotes betrayal; two, wealth; three, pleasant surprises; four, complaints; five, adventure with a stranger; six, loss; seven, scandal; eight, deserved punishment; nine, marriage; ten, baptism; eleven, death of a relative; twelve announces a letter.

Dictionary ■ To dream that you use a dictionary denotes interest in research, desire to learn, and to make a greater spiritual growth. It can also be interpreted as the fear of not being sufficiently prepared to perform a given task. (See LIBRARY)

Difficulties ■ Dreaming of difficulties is a good omen because it means that you can succeed in your projects through effort and self-improvement.

Dinosaur ■ It is a symbol of archaic things, stagnation, and immobility. Maybe it's time to change attitudes, to renew yourself and to better adapt to the circumstances around you in real.

Diploma ■ It is the symbol of reward for a work done with care. Getting a degree in dreams can be interpreted either as the satisfaction of duty done or as the need for recognition and approval.

Disability ■ To see yourself disabled in a dream probably means that you feel as if something or someone was stealing your self confidence. However, this dream can also be due to the fact that you can't act as you wish in real life. The feelings of negativity themselves may be the cause of not being able to move or advance.

❖ With patience, you will have success.

Disappearance ■ Dreaming of a missing person or object denotes repression, shyness, feelings of inferiority, and shame. In short: fear. Especially when the disappeared object has a sexual connotation.

Discovery ■ Announces unexpected events, frequently of a very positive nature. A sudden encounter could resolve some of your stress.

Disease ■ Dreaming of a disease indicates that, despite not being aware of it, you suffer emotional or health problems. In this case, the episode not only freely expresses your emotional reaction to this situation but also contains important messages that may contribute to your healing. Keep in mind, however, that each condition generates its own recurring dreams. For example, people who have been diagnosed with a terminal illness often dream of clocks and other time references, which means that they have a keen sense of the time left in their lifespan. In contrast, for those with cancer is not surprising to dream of scenes in which cars suddenly lose control and crash. These images usually represent the fast growth of cancer cells. Likewise, cancer patient often dream of issues related to contamination or poisoning. However, it is noted that dreaming of a disease is common, and the protagonist does not have to suffer any condition. In these cases, the oneiric perceptions may simply reflect a need for affection.

❖ If you have this kind of dream, the African belief recommends you visit the healer. In general, superstitious people consider the meaning of this dream opposite. Therefore, it portends a long period of good health.

Dispute ■ This dream often occurs when an internal conflict is taking place or when you have to make a difficult emotional decision. As with real-life disputes, reaching a happy medium means the best solution. Nothing is black or white. On the other hand, this dream is trying to express those emotions that you do not normally show. If you know the person you are arguing with, it may represent aspects of your nature that you do not accept. Its meaning can also be literal and you are truly resentful of that person.

❖ Superstition says that this dream portends unhappy relationships in love and business.

Ditch ■ If you dream of a ditch in the ground caused by water, it signifies that the feelings that you harbor are creating a hole inside you.

Diving ■ In general, water represents the subconscious. Diving into it symbolizes our insertion into the most hidden parts of our mind. On the other hand, the dream could be encouraging us to be opportunists, and that you dive in regarding a particular issue.

❖ In many myths, the hero dives into the depths of the sea, and returns to the surface with a great treasure. In the case of dreams, this represents the self that ventures to explore the subconscious and finds the valuable and true self.

Divorce ▪ Dreaming of a divorce is evidence of complicated love affairs and urges you to reflect calmly before making important decisions. This oneiric thought may also reflect an internal division between mind and heart. If they are not reconciled, you can end up suffering psychological problems. On the other hand, dreams that are generated after a marital separation tend to be distressing. Often, one spouse (particularly the one that has been abandoned) dreams of scenes involving sexual rejection or direct infidelity. Therefore, during the first stages of a divorce, dreams and nightmares are a measure of your disorientation and intense feelings of pain.
❖ According to oneiric oracles, this dream is a warning. It advises you to improve the atmosphere of your domestic environment.

Dizziness ▪ To experience the feeling of dizziness in a dream is usually the product of low blood pressure or a physiological craving. You should be attentive to this type of warning and care for your health.

Doctor ▪ This dream is a warning that your current attitude hurts you, because you are not sufficiently valuing your health. It can also mean that you will soon receive aid and protection from someone.

Dog ▪ Throughout history, the dogs have helped man to hunt and drive their herds. They are the emblem of fidelity, friendship, and companionship. In addition, they show a good understanding of our nature. To dream of a dog may reflect the desire to feel loved and protected, to have someone to share life with. Depending on how the dog appears in the dream, however, changes the interpretation of its meaning. Do not forget that this is an animal that behaves aggressively if it does not know you or believes you are threatening the property it defends. In this case, you may be developing an internal conflict with your more instinctive side. If dog pulls at the leash that ties it, it denotes that your emotions cannot take any more. Maybe you need to act out your anger about something that saddens you.
❖ According to a dream oracle, this dream predicts ruin. In particular, tradition affirms that a gentle, happy, and well behaved dog is an omen of deception. If the animal barks and bites, the dream is a sign of injuries, betrayals, and adversity.

Doll ▪ This dream (especially if a woman experiences it) represents childhood nostalgia, the desire to feel protected and cared for, and above all, the urge to avoid present responsibilities. Sometimes the dreams featuring dolls suggest that the dreamer faces overwhelming situations. If the dreamer is a man, the dream may indicate in very scathing way that his attitude toward women is old-fashioned and immature. The dream could also refer to dreamer's maternal instincts. If you have your own children, maybe you should ask yourself if you behave maturely enough with them.
❖ Dolls have played an important role in history. From Voodoo, in which they represent the enemy and are stuck with needles, to the image of a girl telling a doll about her problems. This dream expresses the same concept, our needs, fears, desires, and hopes to seek a way to be expressed.
❖ During childhood, you have much more trust in a doll than in any adult. Perhaps, in the dream, you are telling your doll a big secret.

Dolphin ▪ It symbolizes joy, sincerity, and selfless love. Dreaming of these animals indicates the need to interact more often with your relatives. If you have children you should spend more time with them. If the dolphin gets in and out of the water continuously it means that communication between your conscious and the unconscious is being established.
❖ A regime change is predicted.

Donkey ▪ This animal predicts, in general, difficulties and delays of all sorts; however, depending on its appearance, the dream's meaning will vary. So, if it is fat and carrying a pack it predicts success and material gain, while if it is weak, the opposite will occur. To see a dead donkey is a bad sign because it predicts not only the failure of companies but also bankruptcy and misery. If it is chasing you, it means that in real life you are afraid of something; you will likely be victim of a ruse or a scandal. Finally, to ride this animal means you are on track to reach the projected goals, though it will take a while to get there. If you ride the donkey against your own will, you may have arguments with those close to you.

Door ▪ It is a beautiful symbol full of meaning, especially if it is opening. In that case, it generally represents personal development and desire to explore your inner world, or it suggests that you are about to cross the threshold of a new life stage or to begin an important new

D O O R

Mireia dreamed: "I dreamed I was in a dark hallway surrounded by rooms on either side. Hanging on the walls there were old portraits of people who seemed to follow me with their eyes. I was terrified. I knew it was a test and needed to choose a door and walk through it, but I was afraid to be wrong; I was afraid that if I chose wrong I could fall into the void. Suddenly, one of the doors opened. I decided to go in. I found myself on a light and airy corridor; at the end I could see another golden door. I walked toward it, this time without fear and with confidence that something wonderful was waiting for me inside. I opened it, confident, and realized it was in my own room. I felt safe and calm but very tired. I laid on my cozy bed and gave myself up to a peaceful sleep. Then I woke up."

Mireia's dream reflects a very specific time in her life when she had to make **important decisions** that would affect her future. Her company had offered her a promotion that involved a transfer across the world: Australia. The dark and gloomy corridor reflects the situation at the moment of her dream, full of doubts and fears. The ancient portraits of people who seemed to be looking at her signal the **pressure she was under**. However, the door opening represented the opportunity that fate was offering to her; suggesting that she was about to cross the threshold of a new phase of her life.

The golden gate was the confirmation that her decision to leave would be the right one. Her unconscious was encouraging her to accept it. The fact that the door led her to her own room is a message that she did **not have be afraid of changes,** because home was also waiting for her over there.

project. If in the dream they shut the door in your face, you may have the feeling of being excluded or ignored by others. If you are not able to open it, it is a reminder that, right now, you should not try to alter the situation in which you are. If the door is too narrow you may have to give up some of your demands in order to succeed. For Freud, this dream has a clear sexual reading: door represents the vagina. Consequently, if it is narrow it is a symbol of sexual difficulties, and the act of opening and closing it continuously is a clear allusion to intercourse.

❖ The doorknob predicts unexpected good luck; its hinges, family problems. A closed door predicts lost opportunities; an open one, fortune; a revolving one, the arrival of a monotonous period; and a trapdoor, shocking news.

Dove ▪ As is well known, the dove is a symbol of peace, as well as tenderness, love, fidelity, and hope. It symbolizes spirituality, platonic love, and the free soul.
❖ Its presence in dreams predicts happiness in romantic relationships. If you see the dove in flight, you may receive new from a loved one.

Down ▪ Down is a symbol of energy and sexual potency; Therefore, if a man is seen with it, it makes evident his insecurity in the unexpected and his fear of rejection. When a woman is seen with an excess of down, it is a sign that she is approaching a time of dispute and adversity.

Dowry ▪ To see a dowry in dreams announces a wedding in the immediate future as well as fulfillment of sleeper's secret desires. Furthermore, to buy a dowry denotes that you can completely trust your partner and that economic matters will not suffer major changes.

Dragging ▪ This dream reveals something that attracts you and that is greater than your will. It can be either a passion or a negative feeling, perhaps as a result of a loss. It is urgent that you recover your center, because otherwise you are at risk.

Dragon ▪ It is a universal symbolic figure that is present in most traditions of the world. We can say that is a combination of all dangerous animals, both real and fantastic. For this reason, the dragon represents the enemy par excellence. Consequently, fighting it symbolizes your effort to excel and achieve your vital projects. This dream is very common in childhood. If you manage to defeat your oneiric dragon you should interpret this victory as evidence that you are sufficiently prepared to play any position involving responsibility. On the other hand, sometimes dragons guard the entrance of a cave containing a treasure. This refers to fears that must be overcome in order to meet with your true Self. The dragon also could be guarding your spirituality. According to Freud, this figure is the devouring aspect of the mother. It is the resistance that prevents men from developing their natural feminine side.

❖ In China, the dragon represents wisdom of mind and has an extraordinary power, in addition to superior spirituality. So, dreaming of dragons is highly promising.

Dragonfly ■ This is a symbol of lightness, frivolity, and fickleness.

Drawer ■ Its image is that of a closed place where treasures are stored. To open a drawer and to find it empty indicates disappointment. To see an open drawer is a sign that the mind is open and ready. To fill it with objects and to close it indicates foresight. To empty its content is signal of moving and changes (both physical and mental).

Drawing ■ The dream may be telling you that you have latent artistic abilities to be expressed. It also reflects your approach to solutions of some pending concerns and problems.

❖ It represents your plans. The higher the degree of beauty and precision the greater the chances of success in your projects.

❖ A strange superstition says that if a woman makes a pencil drawing and then erases it her lover is unfaithful.

Dressing up/styling yourself ■ Makeup usually symbolizes falsehood in human relations. Consequently, when the characters of our dreams groom themselves, these images are related to cheating and lying.

❖ The same happens when you use makeup yourself. Distorting your image can prevent you, momentarily, from seeing your own shortcomings. But sooner or later the mask will disappear and your disguise will not hide the truth any longer.

Driver ■ If the person that drives the car is the sleeper herself it is a sign of sorrow and disappointments. If, in contrast, someone else drives it, there is the possibility to live an intense love affair.

Drowning ■ Drowning expresses nothing other than a feeling of anxiety that has been extended for quite a long time. Generally, suffocation indicates that you are burdened by excessive responsibilities. Therefore, it can be interpreted as advice: you should rest or take a short break, as you have reached the limits of your strength. If you drown in dangerous waters, you may be afraid to be absorbed by the hidden power of your unconscious, as if you were giving yourself to it too quickly. In these cases, it is helpful to discuss these fears with a friend so

they can restore your sense of reality. From the emotional point of view, you may also be afraid to sink into your problems. You should make sure you are on firm ground before making any decision.

❖ If, while you are drowning, someone rescues you, it is considered a good omen for business. The contrary applies if nobody comes to help.

Drugs ■ Dreaming that you use drugs or you look at drugs evidences you want to escape using dangerous means that will eventually pull you away from family and friends. Dreaming it too often alerts of the possibility of falling into this world.

Drum ■ Hearing a drum warns that a friend or family member will find themselves in trouble and will urgently need your help. Playing a drum, in contrast, shows your capacity to communicate yourself and to establish relationships with more disparate people.

Drunk ■ Being under the influence of alcohol is a clear sign of repression and desire for escape: not wanting to see reality. Although it also portends wealth and health, the type of beverage leads to different interpretations: if it is wine drunkenness, there will be successes in business and love; water drunkenness, excessive fantasy and bad luck; and strong liquor drunkenness, licentiousness. Feeling drunk when you had no alcohol at all is a warning of unreliable companies around you; and to see others in that situation, sad events in the near future.

❖ For the gypsies, seeing a drunk person means that soon you will receive a small but pleasant surprise.

Drunkenness ■ It can be interpreted as a negative dream, since it involves the loss of precise control over actions and circumstances. However, it can also have a positive interpretation when it represents a release of schemes and limits (social, moral, economic, etc.) governing the conscious rational world. (See DRUNK)

Duel ■ Duels are fairly common in the dream world. These are verbal clashes against a rival. In many cases, these dialectical fights indicate the existence of emotional conflicts with your partner or a close relative who intends to limit your liberty. They can also express an internal conflict, probably between your conscious thoughts and your unconscious instincts. In this sense, you have to find a happy medium. These matters always have nuances, so you are not supposed to lean toward either extreme. You will not be calm until you solve it.

❖ Many stories for kids are full of oneiric symbology and illustrate psychologic processes. An example of this is present on Lewis Carroll's characters: Tweedledum and Tweedledee. They represent internal facets of a subject's childhood.

Dunes ■ They predict obstacles on the way to achieve intended goals, so it is advisable to be patient and smart in order to avoid them. Lying in between dunes evidences withdrawal during difficult moments, as well as outright emotional or economic losses.

Dust ■ It is the sign of maximum destruction of matter. Therefore, dust has a negative meaning related to death. Dreaming of dusty objects is also a symbol of abandonment and neglect. It is evidence of the rejection of that which you haven't even touched in a while. This may include aspects of yourself you are not aware of or have forgotten. Similarly, these aspects may be positive and refer to talent: the dream makes you aware of the artistic, musical, or creative skills that you do not use. The objects that are covered by this dust will give you a hint of the final oneiric meaning. (See ABANDONMENT and ASH)

❖ According to gypsy tradition, the more dust in the dream, the less the annoyance you have to face.

Dwarf ■ Dwarves tend to symbolize values like thoroughness, careful work, perseverance, etc. However, if in the dream you are the dwarf the meaning changes completely. The latter signals a very stark view of things; you might be limiting your potential. Your creativity, therefore is underutilized.

❖ Gold symbolizes our true self and, as in Snow White's story, the dwarfs extract it from the mine. So, this image can also represent the search for self-knowledge. To see your friends dwarfed predicts good health for them and a great joy from living with them. If in your dream dwarfs appear ugly and malformed, the outcome is disaster.

E

Eagle ■ The eagle is one of the most universal symbols in the world. It is a strong animal that portrays
our strength on the intellectual or spiritual field. This
bird indicates that we have high aspirations, usually
of conquest, power, and command. The dream will be
positive if you identify with the animal, and negative
if it transmits fear or pain. If you have the impression
of being an eagle and contemplating everything from
above, your oneiric thoughts are denoting feelings of
liberation. If you see an eagle's solemn flight high on
the sky, it means that in real life you are about to give
everything up for the sake of a goal or an ideal. Now,
if you imagine an eagle flying while holding its prey, it
is warning you that a relationship is about to turn to
enmity. If the eagle attacks you, there is a chance you
will suffer a misfortune. The altitude of the bird's flight
is proportional to the importance of the events that are
being planned. Similarly, the speed of such flight indicates the pace of those same events. Finally, if an eagle
appears before a teenager attacking her in a dream, it
could symbolize the emotional problems she is facing,
as well as her inability to take on the responsibilities of
mature love.

❖ Formerly, it was believed that eagles were the messenger of the sun god. In this sense, your oneiric eagle
may be the messenger of your unconscious. On the
other hand, many mythological stories refer to this animal (the eagle and the lion, the eagle and the snake).
It regards opposing psychologies: the spiritual against
the animal; masculine against feminine; the conscious
against the unconscious; reasoning against instinct . . .
It is also said that dreaming of an eagle portends fame
and fortune. To see a calm eagle and to hear it speak
is a favorable dream. A dead one is a sign of difficulty.
Shooting it always signals loss. To lock it up in a cage:
a great family shame. To take it off the nest: danger
or threat. A white eagle promises a sizable inheritance.

Ear ■ It represents hearing and therefore, communication. The presence of one ear in a dream means that
you must pay more attention to the instructions of your
inner voice. This image should also make you reflect
on the need to be more open and listen, especially the
advice of older people. According to the theory on
which auriculotherapy (ear acupuncture) is based, this
organ symbolizes the whole individual, because of its
resemblance to a fetus. Freudian psychoanalysis associates ears with the vagina and the act of piercing them,
the symbol of deflowering. Thus, if a woman dreams
that she does not have ears or suffers from otitis, it
signifies the unconscious refusal to support the sexual
desires of her partner.

❖ Soon you will receive news. But if you ears hurt in
the dream, you should not rely on the person who gives
you the news.

Earrings ■ According to the culture you come from,
earrings could be indicative of certain social rank.

But, this is also a dream that reflects the dreamer's relationship with the image he projects of himself. It's meaning is associated with that of ADORNMENT. On the other hand, they allude to frivolity and flippancy.

❖ Although ancestral tradition says that all the bad humors and negative energies of the body exited through holes in the ear lobe, modern tradition attributes this oneiric image to an omen of death.

Earthquake ■ The earthquake is part of a general sense of total catastrophe: it is a sudden mutation that can cause havoc, but it can also—in the symbolical plane—be beneficial. Given that an earthquake represents a strong disequilibrium in vital circumstances (it generates insecurity and fear), dreaming of this phenomenon should animate you to make a radical turn in your projects. In the same manner, the latent possibility of the earthquake could be something that is from your consciousness and which brings you fear. It surely deals with those repressed feelings in real life and have relegated to a subconscious level.Lastly, this image could also warn you that you are putting your health in danger, so you should try to relax yourself. (See ABYSS, CATASTROPHE, and RESCUE)

❖ Dream superstition interprets this dream as a change in circumstances.

East ■ The sun rises in the east. This direction represents a new dawn or rebirth. It can also mean your interest in philosophy and spiritual wisdom from Eastern cultures.

❖ If you have this dream, old superstitions predict that your plans will be canceled.

Eating ■ The dreams in which you ingest food have often a purely physiological origin (simply, you are hungry). However, these images can also be representing your "hunger" in intellectual, emotional, and professional matters. So, if you eat something you dislike it means your current situation displeases you in any of the stated elements. You only remain on it, solely and exclusively, because you are unable to propose new alternatives. If you dream you swallow something you dislike without chewing it first, it indicates you do not want to face an unpleasant issue. In contrast, a food binge warns you against a saturation (physical or mental) so you should enhance communication with others. To Freud, the mouth was a primary erogenous zone. The dreams in which you eat, therefore, are

EARTHQUAKE

analysis of a dream

Guillermo dreamed: "I was bicycling when the world began to shake beneath my feet. I soon understood that it was an earthquake, and I began to panic. People ran quickly with panic in every direction and I did not know which course to take. The buildings crumbled around me, filling the street with debris. Suddenly, the ground opened under my feet and before I could react, the ground swallowed me in its abyss. I awoke screaming with cold sweats."

Dreams of disasters are usually nightmares in which you awaken startled, bathed in sweat and with difficulty going back to sleep. They are dreams that **try to agitate you internally**, and they send you a message in a convincing and effective way. However, you do not always understand what they are trying to say. In general, they allude to an internal change, a **psychic transformation** that brings about the destruction of a previous process. Guillermo had this dream a few days before he came out publicly with his homosexuality. His fall into the abyss represented the difficult situation in which he found himself and his fear of making such a decisive move in his life.

closely related to sexuality. A food binge, in this regard, denotes that you are too lenient in the sexual arena. Starving, however, denotes the denial of your sexual needs. If the dream's atmosphere is pleasant it reflects intimacy with others and good relations. Otherwise, it relates to the frigidity and the poor condition of your social contacts.

❖ Usually, it warns against a dispute or economic loss. Eating salt or lard means you will be the subject of a heated argument.

Ebony ■ It is a valuable wood with magical and divine connotations. To use it in your works is a sign of nobility, dedication, and hard work. To cut it down indicates rebellion, feelings of isolation, and loneliness.

❖ Dreaming of furniture or other ebony objects is a warning of misfortunes and fights at home.

Echo ■ If, in dreams, you hear your own voice echo everything, it indicates that you should try not to preach, if not by example. Otherwise, all your actions, for better or worse, will end up impacting you in some way.

❖ To dream that you hear an echo means foreign news. But if the dreamer herself produces it the dream is an omen of slander.

Eclipse ■ An eclipse points to obstacles that prevent you from envisioning things correctly. If the eclipse is solar the dream may indicate that your reason is blinded by difficulties; however, if it is a moon eclipse, your reason is blocked by emotions.

❖ According oneiromancy, dreaming of an eclipse indicates bad omens of illness, death, and loss.

Eggs ■ They symbolize fecundity, the periodic renewal of nature. After a waiting period, a new horizon opens to us. This dream indicates wealth and prosperity, except when the eggs are broken; in this case, the represent the fear that projects or emotional relationships will not end well. Eggs symbolize, in the Jungian school of thought, caution for the future, the economy; the Freudians compare eggs to life in the seed, with rebirth. To dream of finding them in the nest denote a strong desire for parenthood.

❖ There is a superstition that says this dream predicts insults.

Elder ■ See GRANDPARENTS

Electricity ■ It indicates a significant flow of energy that must be used properly to be out of danger. It is a positive dream when it comes to the dynamism and potential energy it symbolizes. However, it can also be an unconscious alert of a risk that you have not yet detected during wakefulness.

❖ Dreaming of electricity indicates, generally, sudden changes that will not cause progress or pleasure. If a shock is received you will have to deal with a deplorable danger. Seeing a flux of electricity through a wire predicts that your rivals will sabotage your plans.

Elegance ■ Dreaming of wearing elegant dresses can be a sign that, in real life, you have neglected your physical appearance or your intellectual growth. Seeing other people dressed elegantly expresses the social or cultural distance that separates you from them. The feelings that these people provoke in you will be key to the correct interpretation.

Element ■ The elements symbolize the total sum of the universe, including humanity. It is divided in solid (earth), liquid (water), and gaseous (air). Each part can transform into the other two by using energy (fire). Psychological traits of the dreamer may be represented in each of these elements. Its balance denotes completeness and integrity. (See WATER, EARTH, AIR, and FIRE)

❖ In astrology, the four elements are the essential qualities of human beings. The earth is fertility and loyalty; water, imagination; air, intelligence; and fire, ambition and will. The mystics believed in a fifth element that permeated everything. It was a fluid state of existence called ether. Today, many mediums believe that, thanks to it, astral travels are possible.

Elephant ■ In the broadest and most universal sense, the elephant is a symbol of strength and power. In the Middle Ages, this animal was the emblem of wisdom, temperance, eternity, and even piety. Anyway, if you dream of an elephant it is likely that the oneiric scenes are positive. According to Jung, the elephant represents the Self. If it behaves defensively it denotes the introverted part of yourself.

❖ Hindu people have an elephant-headed god called Ganesha: a divine strength that removes obstacles. Similarly, the western oneiric interpretation has always believed in the elephant as a sign of good luck.

Elevation ■ Indicates the action of climbing to reach a higher material or spiritual level. If the rise is smooth and pleasant, the dreamer will know she is in the right circumstances to achieve her goals. If, on the contrary, it is painful and difficult it marks the difficulties you should overcome.

❖ Formerly dreaming of rising without obstacles or setbacks had the best omens.

Elevator ■ Elevators represent the rise and fall of social or professional rank. An empty elevator signals a missed opportunity; whereas if it is full, there are many people who aspire to be at the same level where you are. If you are locked inside it possibly means that you refuse to evolve. In the event that the elevator comes from the basement it means that there are certain ideas in the dream that come from your unconscious. The act of ascending indicates a higher and more objective point of view. You will be more rational but do not forget your instinct and intention at any time.

❖ Modern superstitions consider the omen to be good if the elevator goes up, and bad if it goes down.

Email ▪ To receive an email marks changes in personal affairs as well as the arrival of a friend who has stayed away. Sending one alerts of the need for closer relations with others, even at the risk that some of them may fail. Finally, when you are unable to read your emails the dream reflects serious difficulties regarding communication with the people around you.

Emerald ▪ As oneiric signs, emeralds symbolize supreme knowledge, acquired by contemplating the cycles of nature and life itself. It suggests careful observation of natural phenomena and lessons to be drawn from them.
❖ Mercury's stone (emblem of communication with the afterlife) but especially Venus's (Love and art), the emerald is a powerful talisman of love that increases libido, accelerates delivery, and protects sight. In ancient times, this gemstone predicted a great joy; according to the latest esoteric tradition, the emerald is a harbinger of a long wait.

Emotions ▪ According to some psychologists, we dream to relieve and stabilize our emotions.
Otherwise, we would ultimately explode. Sometimes when we dream, we feel very strong emotions impossible to experience in real life. According to Jung, they come from the less developed part (the shadow) of our psyche.
❖ Some superstitions recommend interpreting dreams by reversing the emotions provoked. If, for example, you dream that you are angry, it means that soon you will receive good news.

Emperor ▪ It symbolizes power, justice, and rigor; the Emperor marks a social and career advancement. However, if he's in a bad mood the meaning of the dream will be the opposite. Freudians identify him with the father figure, severe and rigorous. If the emperor is from a foreign country, there will be possibilities of a trip that will not bring you great benefits. Finally, pleading with such authority indicates a concern in the romantic ground.

Employment ▪ Job hunting in a dream predicts favorable changes in the professional field. Helping someone find one shows that you are solidary with others, though perhaps you are ignoring your own progress. Having a steady and well paid job suggests you should have a closer relationship with the environment and even think of a joint project with your partner.

When you work hard in dreams it predicts that you will get rightly rewarded for your efforts. If you are unemployed in the dream it means that you will soon receive a good contract offer.

End ▪ This dream is literal. Therefore, to see the end of a situation reveals the dreamer's desire to formalize a relationship or to finalize something that has been hurting her for a while. Everything will depend on whether the dream reflects your everyday life. In case it does not make any sense it dictates you to open yourself to the world and communicate more with others.

Enemy ▪ Fighting enemies in oneiric thoughts literally reflects your problems. Thus, if you win, it means that you have taken the decision to actively intervene in real life. However, if you only talk to them, the unconscious is suggesting you to solve things peacefully. If the enemy attacks you and you do not fight back, it means that you not only accept defeat but also do not strive to change the situation. (See CROSSROADS)
❖ Dreaming that you have enemies means your friends are helpful and attentive.

Entanglement ▪ If the entanglement of your dream is physical—you are tangled up in bushes or in underbrush—the dream tells you about a problem that could get worse and give you a headache. The way the dreamer approaches the situation and tries to break free from the entanglement summarizes her attitude toward the events that occur in life.
❖ When the nature of the entanglement is personal and you are involved in a situation of misunderstanding with people around you, the dream augurs good relationships and good environment for communication and understanding.

Entrails ▪ To see human entrails announces great adversity. If they are yours, you will have problems you do not know how to solve and, the resulting anguish will make decisions even more difficult. If they are eaten by wild animals, conflictive family relationships will eventually break apart. An acquaintance's entrails denote that you will be able to use any means to achieve your goals; and relative's entrails predict her death shortly. Dreaming of animal entrails marks the defeat of enemies; and if they are a bird's entrails the dream announces pleasure and happiness in all areas.

Epilepsy ▪ This condition expresses that the sleeper will face a time of great stress in her life, so she is advised to do so with the utmost calm and rationality: only in this way she would achieve her goals.

Epitaph ▪ Dreaming of an epitaph announces the arrival of bad news about a loved one; it is probably a death or a serious illness. It can also show sorrow for delays in the payment of a prize or inheritance.

Equation ▪ In mathematical terms, an equation is a mathematical equivalency containing unknown variables. Therefore, in dreams it can mean confrontation between equal forces. Also it points out a situation that is unclear and indicates difficult problems.

Erasing ▪ It indicates the need to make a stop along the way and start again with renewed energy: intention to rectify. The path is wrong, projects have gone wrong. It is interpreted as a moment of exhaustion and defeat.

Escape ▪ The act of fleeing in dreams indicates that you find refuge in appearances and that, when things don't go as you would like, you flee. Fleeing implies, basically, fear of accepting yourself as you are. The message of the dream gives evidence that you should face reality if you want others to trust you.

Escaping ▪ This dream, which typically occurs quite frequently, relates to leaving something behind and opening new horizons. In many cases, it indicates that you do not dare to face particular situation in which you have to take care of problems. However, if this flight gives you a feeling of joy it is a sign that there is hope for the future and for your psychological growth.
❖ According to the oracles, an individual that dreams of escaping danger will soon have to face a major problem.

Evasion ▪ When you dream that you avoid an imposed responsibility it is a sign that, in real life, you have responsibilities that are too heavy. If circumstances have become so overwhelming, you may need this release or break that the subconscious gives you while you sleep.

Evil ▪ Everyone has a dark side to their personality. The wicked thoughts and actions that appear in dreams, therefore, come from within you. Normally, they represent the most destructive psychological forces we harbor, such as jealousy, rage, vengeance, and hate. If you

recognize yourself as the owner of these tendencies, you should accept them and practice the opposite in real life. That is, if you hate someone in a dream, love more; if you avenge yourself, forgive; if you are jealous, be good and generous.
❖ According to an old teaching of I Ching, the perseverance of good is the only way to ward off evil.

Exam ▪ It reveals mistrust and fear of failure regarding the situation that you are experiencing. Awareness of this uncertainty indicates that you should trust your own skills more. Exams are quite stressful experiences that require you to deal with them in the short term. If you dream that you fail an examination, or arrived late, or did not study enough, it means that you are not yet ready for the challenges of real life. You are advised to make the greatest effort and to forget your fears.
❖ The two esoteric interpretations that exist about this dream are opposite. The first states that passing an exam portends success in life; canceling it, failure. The second interpretation, however, predicts the opposite.

Excrement ▪ Despite what it may seem, excrement in dreams are associated with money and wealth. Handling it indicates the desire to improve and excel. The act of defecating also symbolizes elimination of all waste and excess, except when it is difficult to do so (constipation). In the latter case, the dream reflects greed and stubbornness. (See MANURE and DEFECATION)
❖ Stepping on dog poop in a dream promises windfall in business.

Execution ▪ This dream's interpretations vary according to whether you are the victim, the executioner, or a simple witness. If you see an execution it is a sign of a great misfortune caused by others; if you are the victim you will suffer not only losses of any kind but also diseases; and if you are the executor it indicates rebellion against social conventions. Dreaming that you are about to be executed but that a miraculous salvation occurs means that you will defeat your enemies and succeed in your projects.

Exercise ▪ It notes the desire to get moving, to exercise the body and mind, and to train yourself on what you want. Perhaps, in real life, you are going through a time of apathy and the unconscious reminds you of the need to get going immediately.

EYES

Angela dreamed: "I was sitting in a park reading a book, when I noticed dozens of eyes flitting around. They were the size of a pea and had small wings on their backs—like flies. At first, it made me laugh; they were of all different colors and kept blinking, closing and opening their small, long-lashed eyelids. But soon I began to feel harassed. They kept watching me intently, they would slip between the pages of my book. I decided to go home, but the eyes began flying after me, determined not to leave me be."

Angela's dream is closely related to her profession as an actress. When she had this dream she had to shoot her first nude scene and felt very insecure. She knew that during the shoot there would be **many people watching**: director, cameraman, makeup artist . . . and she worried she was not up to the task. The book reflected her desire to prepare well for the moment, to study and rehearse well all the techniques for a convincing, professional performance. However, the eyes stalking her at all times, preventing her from reading, was a message warning that her unconscious fear could stop her.

    At the time of the scene, Angela remembered the dream and understood it perfectly. The thought made her smile and immediately relax. She forgot about the eyes all around and concentrated on her role. The scene went well in the first take, and when the director shouted: 'Cut!,' everyone applauded.

Eyes ■ Dreams in which one eye appears indicate the desire to know and to find the truth. Two eyes suggest that you are probably about to have a major revelation. Losing your sight is a sign that you fear being cheated. This dream denotes insecurity and helplessness in the face of all that happens. The eye also represents the masculine sphere, thereby identifying blindness with impotence; have something driven into the eye corresponds symbolically with intercourse. The story of Oedipus going blind after realizing that he unknowingly married his mother, as predicted by the oracle, seems to confirm this correlation of eye-sexuality. However, according to other interpretations, the eyes are "the windows to the soul," a symbol of wisdom that offers clues about our spiritual state. The condition of the eye will give you plenty of information. For example, if the eyes are shining, there is a healthy inner life; it may also indicate psychic awareness and insight. If they are green, however, it is likely that you harbor feelings of envy. (See GLASSES)

❖ In the mystical tradition, the eyes are a symbol of higher consciousness. It is believed that people have a third eye located above the eyebrows, in the center of the forehead. It perceives other dimensions and spiritual realities. In fact, it coincides in its placement with the gland of the brain that produces the chemicals to control consciousness. Many say that, centuries ago, this eye was real but, eventually, ended up being buried in the forehead. In fact, a species of lizard from New Zealand still has this third ocular member on its head.

F

Fable ■ If you are the protagonist of a fable it can symbolize a desire for adventure in order to put a twist on your daily routine. This dream suggests you to let your imagination fly without losing the sense of reality.

❖ Dreaming of reading or telling fables announces pleasant tasks and a literary bent. In dreams, a fable promises joy. For young people it means romantic unions; for the elderly, placid old age.

Fabrics ■ Generally these represent richness. The state, the material, and the colors of the fabrics signal the relationship between the dreamer and material goods. If a loom appears it indicates that you have at your disposition the means necessary to obtain economic benefits.

Façade (building) ■ If the house is a reflection of the soul, the façade represents the image we project and the way we relate to people around. A façade in good condition is an indication that you are satisfied with your relationships. Likewise, if in ruins it indicates that your external image is poor and does not satisfy you. If the façade does not match the interior of the house, the dream indicates a mismatch between what you are and what you project.

Face ■ If you dream of your face, the dream could represent that part of yourself that you show to others, but that is totally opposite to the true you. This is increased if, in the dream, you are putting on makeup. On the other hand, dreaming of an attractive face foretells a period of peace and happiness with your loved ones. In contrast, if it is unpleasant, you should expect the unexpected arrival of something that will harm you economically.

❖ According to oneiric oracles, dreaming of your face announces that a secret will be brought to light. If it is swollen, you will receive money; if it is pale, in contrast, it foretells that you feel disappointed.

Factory ■ In dreams, a factory is like a thermometer of employment. Therefore, if you dream that you work in a factory, your position at work may improve. But if the factory is empty or abandoned, there's a good chance you will face employment problems and could even lose your job.

Failure ■ Fear of failure can derive from your childhood, when you used to get scared of punishment or of being unloved by someone. In general, failure is a recurring theme in dreams and has different oneiric expressions. Sometimes we get stuck in what we do wrong instead of directing our life towards what we are capable of doing.

❖ In the past, this dream had opposite meaning: it predicted success. Similarly, success in dreams predicted failure.

Fainting ■ No matter who faints in the dream, it predicts serious problems for family and bad news about absent friends. For a young woman to dream of fainting is a warning that her disorganized life would bring her big trouble in the long run. The oneiric fainting denotes, for men, lack of appetite and motivation.

Fairy ■ Fairies represent the extraordinary powers of the human soul. Concretely, the prodigious capacity for imagination. They invite us to use all our qualities, announcing projects that up until now seemed undoable. However, if you have too much fun in the fairy world—looking to flee from your frustrations this way—you run the risk of losing sense of reality. For a man, dreaming of a fairy represents the feminine side of his personality. For a woman, it symbolizes her maternal instinct.

❖ Some traditions believe that fairies are real beings that direct the powers of nature. There is a culture that, when a land is infertile, invokes the help of fairies to make it bloom. In fact, there are those that claim it's possible to communicate with them through dreams.

Falcon ■ The falcon and the sparrow hawk symbolize spiritual, moral, or intellectual elevation. In Ancient Egypt, this bird was the emblem of the human soul. However, in the Middle Ages, the falcon became an allegory of the sinner's guilty conscience. Not in vain, images have been found from this time period of falcons tearing up hares, that is to say, attacking animals that symbolized fecundity but also lechery. In the improbable case that you dream of this image (of a falcon attacking a rabbit), you can interpret the scene as a symbol of the victory of self-control over lewd desires. If, on the contrary, the falcon is flying, it means that you could receive an assignment for a project of great importance that you should not let escape. In this case, your ambition will be put to the test. Given that the falcon represents moral elevation, you should go above certain interests in the assumption that you fervently desire power. Success is not at odds with elevated values.

Falling ■ Normally, dreams in which you fall are the result of "falling while sleeping," provoked by physiological causes. However, in symbolic terms they express a loss of emotional balance or self-control. Maybe you are afraid, in real life, of letting yourself get carried away. Anxiety is closely linked to this dream. It reflects insecurity, low self-confidence, fear of failure, or inability to take care of a situation. (See ABYSS)

❖ According to oneiric sources consulted, dreaming that you fall into mud means that someone has lied about you. Other dreams of this type predict economic losses.

Family ■ Dreaming of your family indicates the need for a return to basics, to a part of yourself from where you have been running away. If you fight with family it means you are dragging internal conflicts that affect your life. But if the relationship is good it means that you seek harmony.

Fan ■ Dreaming of fanning yourself to get air signifies a desire to begin new activities. Conversely, if you use it to cover your face, the fan indicates that your relationships are not precisely sincere; it can even denote you are lying to yourself. In many cases, dreaming of fans is a sign of infidelity, intrigue, or even frivolity. On the other hand, it is important to keep in mind that the character handling the fan in the dream is often the one who takes initiative in the real world.

Farewell ■ It always indicates the desire to make a major change in the dreamer's life. Attention must be paid to the feeling that it produces. It may be nice to release old moorings and take a new direction; or it may be a painful farewell. When you say goodbye to yourself in dreams, the unconscious is reminding you of the need to move away from something or someone that hurts you, when you are reluctant to leave.

Farm ■ A farm symbolizes your heritage, in general, as long as you dream you live on it. If you manage it and turn it into a productive enterprise you will likely be able to do solid businesses in real life. However, if you see it wasted and abandoned it is a advising you to change the course of your career.

Farmer ■ This profession has special significance because, on one hand, the job consists of extracting the fruits of the earth (with the symbolism that it represents), while on the other, farming adapts to the four seasons of the year—the cosmic order reflected by the calendar. In strict oneiric terms, to dream of issues related to agriculture reflects growth of personality and attitude towards life. Dreaming of a well-kept and fertile field indicates bliss and joy. Nevertheless, if the field is dry and abandoned, your bliss hangs in the balance because of your carelessness.

❖ In prehistoric agricultural mystique, this figure is anchored to one of the main human rituals: to bury the dead. So, like the seed buried in the ground, they expect the deceased will be back to life in a new form.

Fasting ■ If you are fasting in the dream it means that you should abstain from certain things for your own good. Perhaps, earthly pleasures are endangering your physical, emotional, or spiritual health. Moreover, a dream of these features can also represent internal peace and the desire to meditate, to hear the deep voice of the conscience.

Father ■ The interpretation of a dream whose central image is your father depends largely on the relationship that you have with him in real life. At a simple level, maybe the dream is offering you a bit of "fatherly" advice that you should consider. Or perhaps it refers to the masculine aspect of your personality, encouraging you to be more energetic. If the father of the dreamer was ineffective as such, the dream may refer to an unconscious search for the father figure. However, if he was too strict, perhaps the dream is warning you not to repeat this behavior with yourself or with your own children. To dream of the death of your father may reflect your desire to break family ties and start being more independent. The father represents command, laws, and rules. In dreams, usually he appears through figures like a king, an emperor, a wise old man, the sun, or a weapon. Therefore, it symbolizes the world of moral precepts and prohibitions that restrain instincts. Thus, in dreams, the father often embodies traditional morality and the principle of authority. It is no wonder, then, that in adolescence (formative period) it is very common for dreams of the father to appear, often as a hostile, tyrannical figure. According to Jung, this symbol played a crucial psychological role in the development of the individual. In contrast to the mother, which is the protection, security, and tenderness, the father symbolizes values closely linked to the masculine: risk, adventure, struggle, effort, rational inquiry, calculation, etc. In this respect, Freud emphasized the importance of the ancient Greek myth of Oedipus. If the subject could not be separated properly from parental influence, it triggered a complex. According to his theories, in childhood (especially four to seven years) children experience a stage of incestuous desire for the mother. The complex arises when they do not overcome this stage and begin to harbor feelings of resentment, seeing the father figure as a rival to defeat. However, the Oedipus complex usually resolves itself during

puberty. (See EAGLE, AUTHORITY, SWORD, FIRE, LIGHT, and TEACHER)

Fear ■ Fear in dreams reflects a latent state of anxiety. Insecurity, fears, and concerns are taking a worrying toll on you. First, to interpret such dreams properly, you must analyze the events of recent days, without ruling out the possibility that you recently watched a horror movie or read a scary story that has affected you unconsciously, and filtered into your dreams. Often these grisly scenes resurrect dark parts of your past, repressed in the unconscious. The purpose of these dreams is to remind you what you are afraid of. They are the ideal opportunity to discover and resolve what frightens you. To be afraid in a dream reveals, according to the Freudian school, an intense guilty complex. (See ABYSS, ACCIDENT, and DEMON)
❖ Popular superstition about this dream is very similar to the opinions of modern psychology. If in dreams you conquer that which you fear, the same will happen with the things that scare you in real life.

Feast ■ It reflects your emotional need to give yourself a banquet. Your appetite can be both sexual and nutrition-related. You must find such vital imbalance that seeks to be satisfied. On the other hand, you may be too lenient with yourself, or you just want to gobble all material goods. It is important to be aware of your own desires' limits.
❖ If you enjoy it during the dream, all is good. If, however, you feel sick or you reject the feast you will experience disappointment.

Feathers ■ Like wings, feathers symbolize, since immemorial times, spirituality, imagination, and thought. They also express our desire to show warmth and tenderness to someone. In oneiric terms, feathers predict success, achieving goals, and overcoming difficulties. Therefore, such images should encourage the person to jump into action. If the feather is floating in the air it denotes your desire to ascend in spiritual knowledge or increase your intellectual ambition. Its lightness also represents the good condition of your heart and pleasures that you enjoy in life. The message is clear: you should get carried away, like the feather, by the fortunate air stream that you currently enjoy. (See BIRD)
❖ Many cultures such as the Incas or Native Americans wore feathered headdresses to represent spiritual authority and the wisdom they possessed.

Feces ■ See EXCREMENT

Fence ■ It is possible that you feel that there are barriers obstructing your path. In this sense, your capactiy for action or expression is fenced. The cause could be an unsatisfactory relationship in which you cannot act your true self. In a similar manner, your work or circumstances could be restricting your personal growth. It is your duty to try to topple such fences and barriers to bring out your sincere self.

❖ A fence is an obstacle and, in many places, ancient dream tradition says that this dream predicts future difficulties.

Fennel ■ Fennel is a symbol of sight and rejuvenation, so dreaming of this herb can be a symptom of clear improvement, if you were suffering an illness. It can also reveal a desire to appear younger.

Fern ■ This dream indicates the feeling of protection, coming from an external factor. The dreamer feels supported and safe in their environment and the people around them.

Fertilizer ■ To fertilize a field indicates that the person is using their best resources to achieve their intended goals. It points to a situation which, in the long run, ends up benefiting the dreamer.

Fever ■ Dreaming that you have fever indicates that, even though you are not aware of it, you are suffering emotional or health problems. In the latter case, the dream may contain important messages that will contribute to your own healing.

Field ■ The width of a field can express your desire for freedom. It is a fertile place, so it also symbolizes the possibility of personal growth. The land, in this case, is the figure of the mother whose job is to represent your instincts, where growth should come from. On the other hand, it denotes that you want to be in touch with nature. When you are seized by everyday difficulties, taking a break in the countryside has great therapeutic powers. Nature is able to feed you and make your inner self recover.

❖ According to gypsy tradition, this dream portends that you will have a lot of work. If the field is full of weeds the reward will be small. If it is full of clover, you will soon have rich new friends.

Fig ■ Historically, figs have represented abundance and fertility, as well as sensuality and sexual desires. They can be considered an oasis in your journey across the desert, an oasis that should be taken advantage of with maximum enjoyment.

❖ Fresh and ripe, they indicate happiness; dry, luck that is diminishing. To eat them picked directly from the tree promises amorous pleasures.

Fight ■ A fight is the result of a situation that has reached its limit and cannot be resolved peacefully. In this case, its meaning is the same as DISPUTE or WAR. But it can also be associated with VENTING. The dreamer feels uncomfortable or attacked by someone around him, but in waking life cannot, or will not, express his unconformity. So, the unconscious releases an inner battle and represents it in an oneiric scene.

❖ This dream could represent your most intimate frustrations and feelings about the circumstances around you. Deep down, you fight because the situation you are living does not meet your expectations.

❖ According to the guru Sathya Sai Baba, the inner struggle does not exist: everything is provoked by the mark left by the past on our lives. Reminiscence for yesterday creates apparent problems in the present and future. It is a matter of letting love flow and worrying less. So, the fight that your heart carries out will diminish. Often, this guru says, it is all the product of an illusion.

Filming ■ If the dream unfolds like a film that stars yourself, different conclusions may be drawn according to its genre: if it is drama, an unfortunate matter will depress you; if it is a comedy, however, you will experience pleasant surprises. To direct a film involves excessive zeal to control everything that goes on around you.

Filth ■ Dreaming that you are dirty tends to indicate that you are guilty of something and that you need to cleanse yourself to the depths of your life. Filth could be related to turbulent issues in which you participate or in which you intend to take part. On the other hand, it is also associated with sexual instincts. You may be disgusted by this facet of your life. It is possible that this feelings of guilt precedes birth. Some parents refer to early sexual activity for their children as a dirty thing, and this idea could affect the subconscious of the child. If the dreamer feels repulsion towards filth, it could mean that they do not want to explore certain areas of their own sexuality.

Fingers ▪ They symbolize the loved ones to whom you feel united. According to their condition, you may guess the health of those people. Fingers also relate to gestures and how you express yourself. Therefore, seeing a threatening finger indicates that your words and opinions are too aggressive and may hurt others. However, if the fingers are used affectionately the arguments you state will seduce and convince even your adversaries. If they point to you the dream involves self-blame. If they point to a particular direction maybe they are showing the way forward within your own existential confusion.

❖ If you cut your finger and it bleeds the dream augurs good fortune. If you dream that you have an additional finger you will receive an inheritance.

Fir ▪ Seeing a fir tree in our oneiric thoughts is a good sign. This tree is identified with peace and happiness, so its presence predicts positive moments in personal and social relationships. If you also see a sun or a moon over the spruce then love and fortune are sure to come.

❖ This tree, which—according to Nordic tradition—comes into our homes every Christmas loaded with balls and colored ribbons, promises certain success, and honest and loyal friends.

Fire ▪ Dreaming of fire indicates that your enthusiasm and energy reserves are in crisis. Maybe in real life you are facing a situation that puts you to the test; if the fire warms you and is well received, maybe it is encouraging you to be more optimistic about your problems. The presence of fire in dreams may well be an incentive to continue along the path taken. If you are lighting a fire it may be an indication that you must begin a project. To move in flames without burning denotes strength and ability to overcome obstacles, a burning desire to reach the goal. Finally, if you dream that a forest or a house burns down your situation is reaching a dangerous limit. (See FIREPLACE, BURNS, RED, and BLOWING) Jung said that fire represents the process of psychological change. Alchemists used fire to transform the simple metal into gold, so it is a symbol of inner transformation. This element can purge corruption from the past, provide light, and reveal spiritual truth. It is the eternal flame in the temple of the soul.

❖ In dreams, fire reflects your feelings of love and hate, the forces of creation and destruction. Thus, a small well lit fire indicates desire for a lasting love or friendship. In addition, it predicts success, health, and happiness. A fire that produces too much smoke, however,

F I R E

analysis of the dream

Laura dreamed: "I was on my bed surrounded by flames. The fire was all over my bedroom devastating everything, burning all of my belongings . . . but I was not able to move, I was paralyzed by fear. Suddenly, I noticed that the fire was not hurting me, the flames caressed my skin without burning me. That made me smile and I thought: 'My skin is like an asbestos suit. I am fireproof.' I left my bedroom by walking through the flames, whistling, convinced of being endowed with a magical power against fire."

Dreaming of fire may indicate that your reserves of both energy and enthusiasm are in crisis. You might be facing a **situation that puts you to the test** in real life. If the dream's fire is well received, it is encouraging you to be more optimistic about your difficulties. When Laura had this dream she was going through a difficult domestic situation: her daughter had just been born, she had to take care of her mother who had a broken femur, and she was about to get seriously depressed. Fire was encouraging her to be **more optimistic and energetic.** The uncontrollable fire was telling Laura to act with precaution and a more relaxed attitude.

A dream in which you end up being safe and sound after an encounter with fire, like the phoenix, indicates growth in the face of difficulties. The unconscious was trying to calm Laura by reminding her of her courage and ability to overcome life's setbacks. She managed to get her mother—who was in wheelchair—to help with the baby's care. This new responsibility made Laura's mother feel useful, despite her injury, forgetting her incipient depression.

announces betrayals and conflicts. If the flames are threatening you, it represents fear of facing a problem or project; if it swelters you are wasting or misusing your energy and efforts.

Fire (in the sense of a house fire or forest fire) ▪ To dream of a fire is evidence that your current situation is reaching a dangerous limit. The image of a house or forest burning indicates that you should destroy memories, prejudices, and all that is a hindrance to your progress and renewal. If the flames threaten you, you will have to face a problem or project; but if they burn you, you are wasting or using your energy and effort in vain. To enter the flames without burning manifests resolve and the ability to overcome obstacles, such as a burning desire to reach a goal. (See FIRE)

Firecracker ■ The noise of the firecrackers is an alarm warning of the unexpected events that could cause you great harm, as much in the professional sphere as the emotional one. You should be alert to any suspicious evidence that appears in your surroundings.

Firefighters ■ To see them putting out a fire is a negative sign because it portends a bad end for your projects; but, on the contrary, if they show up when the fire has been suppressed already, then it is clear that all your troubles are over and a beneficial period is starting.
❖ When a woman dreams of a wounded firefighter, chances are that her partner will have a misfortune.

Firefly ■ Its image alludes to a discrete light that helps you find your way in the darkness. If the dream is pleasant, it indicates that the dreamer feels safe, although the conditions may be adverse. If the dream causes stress, it could be a cry for help from the unconscious.

Fireplace ■ Dreaming of a fireplace reveals the need to burn memories, prejudices, and all that is a hindrance to your renewal and progress. (See FIRE)

Firewood ■ Just like fire, firewood is associated with concepts such as ardor, willpower, and bravery. Seeing mountains of firewood means that you will receive providential help, a fortuitous circumstance that allows you to move forward with plans. If it is wet and cannot be lit on fire, you should be careful: your emotions could interfere with your goals to the point of ruining them.

Fish ■ By proximity to the sea, many cultures have considered fish to be sacred. In fact, in Asian rites, fish were worshiped; and priests, for this reason, were forbidden from eating fish. Given that fish inhabit the depths, they are also located at the unconscious level and their interpretation is associated with WATER. Therefore, when they emerge at the surface, they come to consciousness as a warning sign or to remind you of hidden emotions or past experiences. To dream that you try to catch a fish with your hands and it escapes expresses frustration and disappointment. Fish represent everything

you want to hold on to, that turns out to be slippery. In addition, they are indicative of states of loneliness and isolation. To see fish inside of a fishbowl denotes a longing for freedom. The dreamer may feel emotionally withdrawn and their dream reveals a repressed desire for release. The Freudian school links fish exclusively to sexuality and associates it with the phallus. However, the cold blood that characterizes the fish seems to contradict this symbolism, attributing connotations of frigidity or impotence. Finally, we must not forget the connection between fish and fertility. This dream may announce that you are experiencing a period of personal growth. Fish oppose the material and mundane point of view of everyday life.
❖ The fish symbolizes Christ. In many other religions, the fish has also served to represent their gods. They are the spiritual abundance that feeds everyone. The dream may be highlighting all these qualities in you.

Fish hook ■ It is a clear symbol of disappointment, betrayal, and deception.

Fisherman ■ The figure of the fisherman is associated with preaching and ministry. But, the fisherman is also one who draws elements from the deep, that is to say, the unconscious. In this sense, the figure of the fisherman can be a great help on the road to self knowledge. You should pay attention to the elements that he pulls from the bottom of yourself and what they symbolize.

Fist ■ Symbol of threat and stubbornness.

Flag ■ An important feature of flags is they are placed on top of a pole or mast. This elevation symbolizes the exaltation of victory and self-assertion of a community. For these reasons, in dreams, a waving flag suggests you need encouragement to move forward, a backup that provides safety. If you are carrying this flag to the top of a mountain it means that you will soon attain your goals. But if you lose it or it is stolen from you, you could lose the position you hold. It also has a sexual interpretation due to phallic connotation of the mast; If the flag hangs loose from the top of the mast, it may be a strong symbol of sexual unconfidence, impotence, or frigidity.

Flagellation ■ Some people are very strict with themselves, so they tend to dream of flagellation. This represents their reproaches against themselves. Through flogging you punish yourself for what your "internal judge" considers wrongdoing. Moreover, this mechanism also diverts attention from any other pain or uncertainty you may have. In short, the dream reveals that there is a negative aspect you should change in your life.

Flame ▪ The flame is, in general, a symbol of purification; therefore, to see it lit denotes the arrival of peace and sincerity in your life. If it goes out, it announces obstacles to achieving that serenity.

Fleas ▪ They symbolize little annoyances, real or imagined. (See INSECTS)
❖ Dreamed of being invaded by fleas indicates guilt, envy, losses, and obstacles. In particular, to see them reveals gossip; to catch them, a need to rearrange your life; to be bitten by them, earnings; and to kill them, several problems and anxiety.

Flies ▪ These insects embody resentment, fear, and disdain toward others. If you dream that they invade the house, it means that you dread rumors. Flies also may symbolize repressed impulses and desires. Because of the association of flies with filth and disease, you may also interpret this dream as a message from the unconscious telling you to take care of your health and clean more. In the same way, an annoying buzzing fly could indicate the existence of a restless, irritating person in your life. If you are the fly, you should ask yourself if you are butting into other people's business too much.
❖ According to popular tradition, to see flies in a dream is a sign of success. However, to see them in food is a sign of danger.

Flight (escape) ▪ Fleeing signals a desire to evade, if the dreamer herself is the one escaping. It is possible that, in real life, you are carrying a really heavy responsibility or do not feel capable of solving a particular problem. In addition, if the dreamer witnesses someone else's flight, the dream reflects a tricky situation: the protagonist knows of a secret truth and fears the consequences that may entail its disclosure.

Floating ▪ In order to float you have to relax and accept the water's support. In psychological terms, this dream means you have accepted your feminine side and are being led by it. Floating implies acceptance; It is time to stop worrying about problems, concerns, and restrictions and to enjoy your true self.
❖ This dream bodes well. But if you struggle to stay afloat success will be delayed.

Flood ▪ Water symbolizes the emotional part of our unconscious. So to dream of a flood indicates that an emotion that is too intense has become too much for you, especially if the current takes you and you are unable to stop it. You must try to dominate this feeling or find a means of expression or relief, such as art or relaxation, that allows you to bring it out without emotional explosions. In this way, the flood will become illumination and inspiration. If you don't watch them, your emotions could ruin more than one project. You must not forget of course the nourishing effect of water (such as what happens in a baptism). In this way, the dream could represent the start of a new stage of life. (See WATER or DROWNING)
❖ The story of Noah's ark and other similar ones represent the purge to obtain something better. After a flood, all the old has been destroyed. It is the moment to start anew.

Floor ▪ The floors of a building represent the levels of the dreamer's consciousness. The attic is spiritually, and the lowest floor, the unconscious. The floors that are in between manifest the different mental stages that you experience. (See HOUSE)
❖ If you dream that you are on the highest floor, you will have success.

Flour ▪ Symbol of wealth. Dreaming of this product means that you will not lack the means to live comfortably. But, on the other hand, given that flour is a food that cannot be eaten raw, its meaning also indicates that you will still have to wait a little. Consequently, what the unconscious is trying to tell you is that you should wait the necessary amount of time to complete your projects. Only the wise let everything flow naturally.
❖ According to popular superstition, flour is a sign of death in the neighborhood. To grind it makes one fear for financial loss; but seeing someone else grind it is an omen of happiness and wealth. To be covered in flour denotes prosperous business. To knead it assures the dreamer will be a good parent.

Flowers ▪ Each flower has its own meaning but you can say that, in general, they symbolize joy, fleeting beauty, love, and happiness. Therefore, contemplating flowers in dreams may portend the beginning of a new relationship. If you pick one, this relationship is likely to be reciprocated; however, if during the dream you just smell them you will probably be the one who ends up quitting such a relationship. If you can tell the color of the flower that appears in the dream the interpretation will vary according to the meaning of each color.

❖ Buddha's teachings say that every person goes through the same phases a flower does. You may be in the dirt of desire or you may rise up and gradually open up to the light.

Flute ■ Listening to its music indicates you have taken the right path. The sound of the flute has the ability to enchant us and make us forget our desires. If in the dream you play this instrument it means that your persuasive skills will help you carry out projects. Therefore, this is a good time to launch collective initiatives in which you have a prominent role. However, if the dreamer is the one who follows the music this points to excessive credulity and lack of critical spirit.

Flying ■ Imagining that you are flying signals the arrival of change that will be very beneficial for you. The action of flying, however, implies the desire to evolve, to connect with the essence of yourself to progress spiritually. Further, it denotes that you have undone something that was worrying you. It is a dream from which you leave with optimism and renewed strength, with a stimulating sensation of liberty. It also indicated the need to discover, to invent, and to do new things. This type of image foretells success, the completion of objections and overcoming difficulties, and encourages the dreamer to action (it is the time to fly by one's self). However, you should not forget the Greek myth from Icarus; he who tried to go too high, his ambition brought him to a fatal destination. Further, if the protagonist is a young woman, it announces the break from relations in her couple.

❖ In antiquity, if a person dreamt of flying, it was considered that he had entered into the sphere of the immortal gods. The Native Americans, the Babylonians, the Hindus, the Tibetan Buddhists, and many other peoples believed that the world had the ability to abandon the physical body during sleep. During these astral voyages, the psychic body could fly to other dimensions, communicate with people of a certain spiritual belief or learn of the souls that once were angels and divinities. Some scientists believe that these voyages are factual and that there exists the possibility to verify them empirically.

Foam ■ The foam goes up as fast as it fades. In case you have started an emotional relationship, this dream may indicate that you distrust its solidity.

Food ■ Food represents the traits you want to internalize or model. The different types of food, therefore, have different meanings. Fruit, for example, is sensuality, the received reward, or abundance. In case that it is a bitter fruit, it could represent an unfavorable influence on your lives. Milk, on the other hand, is kindness; sugar, sweet words; and frozen food, emotions you need to awaken. Depending on the feeling that every kind of food produces in you, it will be possible to find out the correct meaning of the dream.

FLYING

Montse dreamed: "I discovered with astonishment that I could fly. I just had to move three steps ahead and push myself a little forward; I didn't even have to swing my arms. The wind marked my direction and I was able to feel the incredible sensation, I felt happy, free, powerful . . . Around me there were no birds, nor sounds; I was on my own in the immensity of the blue sky, flying over a sea in calm blue, yet brighter. Suddenly, I saw a group of dolphins jumping joyfully over silver waves. I awoke smiling, with a very pleasant sensation."

Dreaming that you are flying is associated with liberty, the desire to elevate yourself from the earthly bindings and conquer the heaviness of reality. It is a dream of evolution, which reveals you **need to freely express yourself**, to create . . . Montse, by profession a designer, had this dream a few days before completing a design for an important magazine, very artistic and vanguardist, renowned with many awards . . . A few days before she had felt very pressured and tired; however, her dream calmed her and revealed her **creative capacity** and **her strength of expression**. Dolphins are a symbol of intelligence that s related to clarity and purity of thought. The face that there were jumping through the water (entering and leaving) indicated the level of connection Montse had established between her conscious and subconscious.

Dreams of flights also match an **interest in spiritual evolution**. Curiously, through this period, Montse had given some tries in this direction, with courses on growth and personal overcoming, in which she learned much about herself.

❖ Since the Greeks, dreaming of food has had sexual connotations. Throughout history, juicy peaches and other fruits have been linked to lewd and lascivious behavior; pomegranates, with fertility; apple, with the expulsion of Adam and Eve from paradise; and bread, with restrained and reproduction-oriented sexuality. On the other hand, many cultures still believe that dreaming of eating meat involves acquiring the spiritual features of that animal.

Foot ▪ They are the fundamental support of the people, which holds us upright. Therefore, their good condition represents security and stability. To dream that you see some footprints in front of you is an invitation to move in the direction they point. If see that your foot has been amputated, it could be that you are losing your balance, either physically or mentally. The dream may warn you that you should be more practical and realistic, and your feet on the ground. On the other hand, it could indicate that you are reconsidering the direction in which your life is going or questioning on which your existence is based. For

a Christian, to dream of washing your feet denotes forgiveness. In India, the feet of gurus are considered the most sacred and divine part of their body. (See AMPUTATION, CROSS, SHOES, and ORIENTATION)
❖ In China it is said that all great journeys begin with a single step. The dream recommends that you move cautiously, taking one step at a time.

Footprints ▪ Your own footprints, when they are clear, signal rapid success and well-being. In the opposite case, they are synonymous with wavering before making decisions. If the footprints belong to someone else, you should distrust those who seem excessively interested in your job: they could be looking for information in order to get a promotion at your cost.

Footsteps ▪ To hear footsteps that draw closer or farther away, without being able to see who is walking, indicates the fear that some external agent out of your control invades, or negatively affects, your vital space. It denotes insecurity in your environment. Perhaps the dream is advising you to take a step forward in some area of your life.

Forehead ▪ The forehead symbolizes the character and value of an individual. The appearance of the individual's forehead in the dream can give you clues about her personality. For example, a wide forehead is a sign of intelligence and also indicates that this is a serious person you can trust.

Foreign ▪ Dreaming of a foreign country reflects changes in your work or social life. If the dream is unpleasant and you feel anxious it means you are not prepared for these changes. If, on the contrary, you feel excited to discover something new, the dream reflects your pleasure of tackling various opportunities other than the ones you already have. Related to travel and projects, places abroad also symbolize the different choices you have in life. If the dream is about a foreign person it may represent an aspect of you that has not been integrated into your identify. Perhaps, you are neglecting important feelings or hidden talents.
❖ If you dream of a foreign country, the dream shows that with patience, your wishes will come true. On the other hand, an affable foreigner portends good luck.

Forest ▪ The forest symbolizes the unconscious, anxieties, instincts, and secret passions. If it is accompanied

F O R E S T

Ana dreamed: "I was on my way to the office, on the same streets as always, but the smoke of the city would not let me breathe and I could barely see the path I was walking over. I suddenly found myself surrounded by a lush forest. I knew that if I followed the trail I would reach my destination, so I decided to enjoy the scenery while walking confident and happy, at a medium pace. In the dream I could identify the different species of trees and flowers. Birds were coming to me with their joyous trills. I felt full of vitality. I woke up with a very nice feeling of peace, as if I had enjoyed a comfortable vacation."

Ana had this dream two days before she was diagnosed with a chronic respiratory condition. Besides being prophetic—the smoke of the city would not let her breathe—Ana's dream was warning her against a need for her body: healthy and fresh air. The confident and safe walk passage reflects the Ana's strength and the fact that the problem would be easily solved. Months later she was granted a transfer to a mountain village with a very suitable climate for her health.

by a sense of peace, completeness, or exuberance, it indicates that you are self-confident and proud of your personality. But if you feel fear and anxiety, or if you get lost in the forest, it is a sign of fear, repression, and complexes. On the other hand, birds and animals found in the forest represent your instincts and emotions. Finally, if you dream of being in a dark forest and try to find the way back, it denotes that you want to take a decisive step in life.

❖ The plot of many fairy tales like *Hansel and Gretel* and *Snow White* takes place in the forest. Like dreams, these stories symbolize the exploration of the unconscious. According to an esoteric interpretation, to get lost in a forest is an omen of alterations; to hide in it, of impending disasters; to cross it, promise of inheritance; to go for a walk in the forest, joy. A felled forest, however, is a sign of wealth.

Forgery ▪ Dreaming that you carry out forgery brings serious problems; you will not get rid of them easily. Also, you will be slighted by your friends who will refuse to help you.

Fork ▪ A road divided, a crossroads, is a clear message: you have to choose, to take a direction and guide your actions toward it. The unconscious is telling you that you cannot postpone making decisions any longer. This can be hard and painful but you must act soon.

❖ Formerly, criminals were hanged at the crossroads so many people could observe the dire consequences of committing a crime. In an oneiric sense, the fork represents crime, punishment, and death. However, many books about dreams also say that it alludes to an important decision to be made.

Fortress ▪ See CASTLE

Fortune ▪ Dreaming of owning a fortune has a positive meaning but expresses ambition and pride. These feelings, if not unconscionable, can favor your plans; but if they are excessive they can harm you.

❖ If someone offers you a fortune you may have a windfall. However, this prosperity will be capricious and arbitrary, with no guarantee of continuity.

Fountain ▪ In the earthly paradise, four rivers start from the center—from the foot of the Tree of Life—and are separated according to the four directions marked by the cardinal points. Consequently, they spring from the same source, which symbolizes the center and origin of any activity. Jung associated the fountain to the source of inner life and spiritual energy. Also, he related it to the "country of childhood" in the unconscious directions are received, and stated that the need of the fountain mainly arises when vital impulses are inhibited. In oneiric terms, dreams in which fountains are present highlight a desire for regeneration and purification. Additionally, its waters' quality reveal the status of your emotional relationships. So, if you drink from clear water fountain it indicates that you will satisfy physical, spiritual, or emotional needs; you will also achieve success. But if the fountain is dry or its waters are murky your love is withering. (See WATER)

❖ This dream foretells an upcoming happy and satisfactory period. If the fountain is dry, however, it predicts problems.

Fox ▪ Owing to its reputation as a clever animal, this dream could be associated with a type of scheme in the life of the dreamer.

❖ Frequently a symbol of the devil in the middle Ages, it expresses the inferior impulses and the difficulties of the opponent.

Fraud ▪ Perhaps, you feel disappointed because you have not been given the recognition you deserved. On the other hand, it may be you who have committed fraud, especially if you have not been honest regarding your feelings or you have taken advantage of someone in real life.

❖ If you dream that you expose fraud or catch a thief, luck will be favorable to you.

Freedom ▪ To dream of freedom is evidence of too many responsibilities in real life. It also denotes insecurity about important decisions you have to make in the future. The desire for freedom reflects the spirit's need for new experiences. This dream may also indicate that there is a good chance that you will be involved in unforeseen, strange, and possibly incomprehensible circumstances.

Fridge ▪ See SHELF and COLD

Friend ▪ Dreaming of a friend tends to be favorable to your interests. It usually indicates confidence and support, as well as hope and comfort. The appearance of the friend will reveal the state of your relationship. So, if she looks good it indicates that the friendship is solid. On the contrary, if your friend appears to be in bad shape, it means that the friendship is declining. It never hurts to visit whoever you have seen in dreams. || This dream also warns you to be alert, because it is possible that the oneiric friend represents an aspect of your personality that you do not accept or that you fear. You must do everything possible to integrate it into your character and make the best of it.

❖ Dreaming of a true friend portends good news. If our friend is in trouble, that news will be disadvantageous.

Frigidity ▪ It not only represents an actual sexual problem but also reflects a sense of fear, failure, or disappointment that do not have to be related to sexuality. The set of elements of the oneiric scene will provide important clues as to what is creating such unfortunate sensation.

Frog ▪ The frog symbolizes the transition between earth and water, and the reverse. Therefore, dreaming of this animal expresses your capacity to adapt to whatever change or circumstance. Possibly, your instincts are demanding adventure, you desire a different situation or job. On the other hand, frogs are also associate with some unpleasant due to their texture, the monotony of their croaking, and their lives in green and mostly stagnated water. The dream could be a reaction to certain unwanted company that you are obligated to attend.

Frost ▪ A frost impedes the growth of plants and even symbolizes destruction. Most likely the dream references the emotions of the dreamer: she may behave coldly, or someone may show this attitude toward her. The beauty of a frost can represent a person who is beautiful but unattainable. The dream may also announce an illness related to cold, such as a cold or flu. (See COLD)

❖ May be a warning that your relationship is going cold; foretells emotional solitude.

Fruit ▪ Fruits often reveal a desire or appetite, whether emotional, sensual, economic, or spiritual. In dreams, they predict abundance, prosperity, and earthly pleasures. If the fruit was too green or too sour it will take you a while to enjoy such prosperity; if it has worms or is rotten, it seems that you are on the wrong path because the dream announces that those pleasures will be reached when you can no longer enjoy them.

❖ Like flowers, each fruit has its specific oneiric interpretation. For example, grapes indicate prosperity; watermelon, fertility; plums, immortality, etc. Picking ripe fruit is a happy omen of wealth and goods of all kinds.

Fruit salad ▪ As a mix of different fruits, fruit salad expresses the arrival of a variety of events or people in your life. This will be positive or negative depending on the context in which the dream occurs. As each fruit has its interpretation, you should pay attention to the types of fruit that make up the salad. (See FRUIT)

Frustration ▪ Some dreams reflect great frustrations. For example: missing a train, not being able to read a message, searching for something without finding it, failing to convince somebody . . . Maybe you think that your life is not going the way you want or feel angry at others' stubbornness. It is very important to find out what frustrates you so much in real life in order to deal with issues in a more effective manner.

❖ The oneiric superstition says that frustrations mean the opposite: they predict great success in your plans.

Funeral ▪ Dreaming of a funeral symbolizes rebirth because every ending ultimately leads to a new beginning. It indicates pain relief and urges you to trust in the future. Therefore, although it apparently concerns a bleak picture, the truth is that dreaming of a funeral is associated with a positive message. Not surprisingly, it suggests that, from now on, you can bury everything about the past and look to the future. (See CEMETERY and DEATH)

❖ Occasionally, these dreams are premonitory. For example, Abraham Lincoln predicted his own death days before being killed. He saw in dreams his own corpse in one of the White House's rooms. However, most of the time, funerals in dreams represent the state of your mind.

Fungus ▪ The fungus as a complex symbology. It represents the tenacity of life to be born, grow, and endure in time. Additionally, it as curative, aphrodisiacal, and hallucinogenic properties. Its interpretation is complex and subject to the context in which the dream develops, and other elements that appear in it.

Funnel ▪ Funnels can highlight the feeling that someone tries to take advantage of you. This dream usually occurs when your personal relationships are going through a period of difficulties, particularly when these problems have to do your superiors.

Furniture ▪ The furnishings of a house can symbolize the elements of the dreamer's character. Therefore, if you buy something new or are renovating something, surely the same process is happening in your life; perhaps your personality and mind are developing, making room for new actions and attitudes. To buy furniture that is too heavy and difficult to move could represent that you are carrying unnecessary responsibility. Furniture also reflects a specific part of your home. Each one has a function and meaning, so you should interpret them separately.

Fury ▪ Dreams give us the opportunity to express those feelings and emotions that we repress in real life. Perhaps, you are not aware that you harbor some aggressiveness. In this sense, the dream may be advising you to stop being a passive person and to take action. Likewise, you may be secretly underestimating or being jealous of someone close to you. When you dream that a person is really mad at you, the dream might symbolize everything you dislike about your personality.

❖ Fury in dreams predicts you will have to face a life challenge. Besides, it announces disappointments and attacks against the dreamer's character. Additionally, if you get mad at a stranger it means you will receive good but unexpected news. Chances are it is an invitation.

Future ▪ A dream based on the future is quite complex. It reflects the dreamer's hopes and expectations, as well as her fears and doubts. The experience can be either positive or negative. If the dream is pleasant it signals the dreamer's agreeability for the direction of her future. If it is uncomfortable it indicates fear and guilt for the way the dreamer is carrying out her life in the present. Some dreams come to us in the form of prophecies and it seems that they reveal future events to us. Other times, we have the impression that we had already dreamed of an actual event. However, it is hard to tell whether we dreamed of that particular event for sure.

❖ It is advisable not to take these dreams as premonitions because, usually, the unconscious significantly distorts the information.

G

Gag ■ If you are gagged in the mouth, the dream manifests your inability to express yourself as you wish about a particular subject. Similarly, there may be something important that you want to say but do not know how. However, the meaning of this dream may be the opposite. Your unconscious could be alerting you to remain silent. (See MOUTH)

❖ The dreams in which an obstacle that hinders communication appears often presage misunderstandings. You must be wary of rumors.

Gallows ■ Dreaming of the gallows is not a good omen, since it announces all kinds of problems. So, if the hanged person is the sleeper, they will suffer the betrayal of a friend; if it is a loved one, they should make a quick decision to avoid misfortune. If it is an enemy thought, the dreamer's triumph in all fields is certain. For a young woman, seeing her boyfriend hanged means she will end up marrying a cruel man.

Game ■ If you take part in a children's game in dreams, the interpretation is clear: you take refuge in the past to escape from present responsibilities. On the other hand, if you dream you are playing a board game it reveals that your social relationships are superficial. If you dream you are betting your wealth on some game of chance, it means you hope chance will solve your problems. Finally, if you are just the spectator of a game—without participating—the image is a symptom that you are behaving indifferently to certain problems that concern you directly. (See LOTTERY, CARD, BETTING POOL, and ROULETTE)

❖ According to the saying of an Indian guru, life is a dream and we should realize this. But it is also a game and it's essential that we play our part.

Garage ■ Using a garage for your car heralds a stage where you must choose between several options. The concern for this dilemma is mitigated if the garage is outdoors or you do not own the vehicle. On the other hand, getting into a garage predicts a long period of tension and nervousness; to leave it indicates that a conflict has come to an end.

Garbage ■ Garbage is generally synonymous of shady affairs and scandals; however, it can also prove to be a good omen. If you do not feel disgust toward it you will have economic gains; but if it is stinking, you will experience negative moments with people around you. If a woman dreams of garbage it is a warning against a humiliating breakup with her partner. On other occasions, garbage symbolizes all the things that you want to eliminate because it prevents you from progress: your character traits, attitudes, fears, memories . . . On the other hand, it represents that you have been appointed to a position that has nothing to do with you.

❖ Some beliefs say that this dream portends that your wildest dreams will come true.

Garden ▪ The garden is the field in which nature is submitted, ordered, and rationalized. For this reason, it is a symbol of dominion of the conscious over the chaotic unconscious (that is, the jungle). Also, it represents caution over spontaneity. At the same time, the characteristic intimacy of gardens (favorable place for lovers) makes them considered to be an archetype of the inner world, subjectivity, and feelings. So, dreaming of a well-kept garden can indicate peace and harmony, while seeing one abandoned means that you are not taking care of yourself. Water, ponds, and fountains that you find in the garden are the spiritual energy that makes up your nature. Finally, after a period of difficulties, this dream can manifest inner healing (See FLOWERS)
❖ This dream predicts that the sleeper will marry a beautiful woman or a good looking man.

Garland ▪ In ancient cultures they used to hang garlands in the doors of the temples when a party was being held. These objects have always been a sign of welcome and tribute. Dreaming of garlands, however, suggests that you should not rest on your laurels because joy is brief. (See NECKLACE)

Garlic ▪ As an oneiric symbol, garlic suggests the need to dispense with appearances so you can focus on what is considered the most appropriate. Not surprisingly, despite its unpleasant odor, garlic is a food with great healing properties.
❖ It is indicative of arguing, adventures, and erotic relationships. Touching it promises good business, and strongly smelling of garlic resembles a feeling of disclosed secrets.

Gas ▪ It is a symbol of transformative energy. To light or to cook with gas is an indication of satisfaction with the flow of everyday life's events. However, dreaming of a gas explosion is interpreted as a warning against an impending danger. The dreamer may need to look around and determine what attitudes or circumstances are dangerous.

Gasoline ▪ Gasoline is usually a good omen: it evidences the strength and energy acquired after some difficulties. However, it may have a pessimistic tone if you see an empty tank because it indicates that you do not feel motivated to continue the daily struggle. The gas station is a sign that you need a break to reflect on your future.

Gaze ▪ The gaze is another means of communication without words. It can be a weapon of seduction or repression, and a means of expressing love, understanding, complicity, anger, hate, joy, sadness, or disapproval. The important thing in interpretation of this dream are the feelings and sensations awakened in you by the gaze you are subject to.

Gazelle ▪ From the earliest times, the gazelle has appeared in the collective unconscious as an animal fleeing a lion or other beast. Therefore, it symbolizes the pursuit of pleasure and the aggressive aspect of the unconscious. Meanwhile, the gazelle's qualities are beauty, speed, agility, and visual acuity. Thus, in oneiric terms it symbolizes the soul or, more often, women. Therefore, you should interpret this dream literally: the attitude that you have toward the gazelle will reflect your attitude in your emotional relationship.

Gear ▪ Gears in a mechanical system usually represent the dreamer's conditions to solve her own issues in real life. The interpretation depends on the condition of those gears and the ease or difficulty of their engaging and rotation.

Gemstone ▪ Gemstones are almost always symbols of well-being and wealth, whether material or spiritual. Its image is full of magical meanings. The other elements of the dream will help in the interpretation process.
❖ A gem is considered a piece of colored light made stone: a drop of solidified cosmic energy full of magic and protective virtues. Therefore, esoterically, it has been used as a talisman and amulet for millennia. || The gem's oneiric image promises, in general, fortune, wealth, and high social position.

Genie ▪ If a genie grants you a wish you will receive providential assistance. Because of it you will achieve your goals.

Germinate ▪ To see a plant germinating in dreams is a good omen because it indicates that your projects could materialize soon. (See AGRICULTURE)

Getting fat ▪ Although apparently this dream has negative connotations, dreaming of getting disproportionately fat can mean that you feel strong enough to undertake major projects. Dreams of this type may also reflect a misdirected intimate impulse or an attraction or repulsion unconsciously accepted. On the other hand, it can also reflect the dreamer's fear of gaining weight.

Getting up ▪ This is a very positive dream that manifests dynamism and activity. It reveals your desire to get moving after a state of rest. The intention of activity, the start of projects with renewed vigor. To get up after a fall signifies the strength to want to move forward despite difficulties.

Ghost ▪ Ghosts swarming the house indicate that you tend to alter reality at will. Dreams of this type point to a lack of practicality about the situation you are currently experiencing. According to other interpretations, ghosts represent what you fear of yourself and refuse to accept. It is advisable to face these fears because, often, no one but yourself is provoking that they have such terrifying image, evocative of anxiety states. In many cases, ghosts represent inner world forces that you reject.
❖ Dreaming of a white beautiful-faced ghost provides comfort and love for the dreamer. In contrast, a black and dirty one predicts pain and betrayal. Being chased by ghost expresses grief and sorrow.

Giant ▪ We can say that in the most profound and ancestral aspect, the myth of the giant refers to the existence of an enormous living being, primordial, whose sacrifice originated creation. The giant's figure—prevalent in ancient cosmological cultures—is neither benevolent nor malevolent, it is simply a quantitative magnification of the ordinary reality; therefore, as appropriate, there are legendary protective and aggressive giants. In Jungian psychology, their presence seems to correspond with the symbol of the father, representing the spirit that places obstacles to the instinctive impulses. Other interpretations assign a sexual nature to the giant. This dream can mean that the subject's sexual needs are disproportionate.
❖ The oneiric giants portend commercial successes.

Gift ▪ The exchange of gifts reflects the relationship you have with the environment. Dreaming that someone makes you a gift could mean that others take you into consideration and offer you help or that there will be an unexpected or unasked for event in your life. In either case, it is an omen of good luck, as much as in material

issues as in love. In contrast, if you give someone a gift, there are two opposing interpretations. On the one hand, it indicates that you are generous. On the other, it is synonymous with tensions and disputes of any kind. The way in which the present is wrapped and what it is made of supplies valuable additional information.
❖ Receiving a gift in dreams could foretell disadvantages. But, if you give it, it means that you will soon start a new project.

Glass ▪ A glass, especially chalice-shaped, is traditionally identified with the human heart, which can also be associated with other symbols such as love, revelation, and immortality. Sometimes it is seen as a feminist sexual symbol. If the glass is filled with wine, the dream will have a spiritual meaning. If you toast with someone else it reflects your desire to share your love and happiness with that person. (See DRINKING)
❖ The dream may be referring to the Holy Grail and the search for spiritual nourishment. A glass can also reprsesent love and sincerity. In the Tarot, glasses symbolize emotional life. Omens are usually pretty good in this regard.

Glasses ▪ The dream should be interpreted according to personal connotations attributed to this object in the dream. Someone shy about wearing them will surely recognize in this dream a source of sadness and shame. If the dreamer losses or breaks her glasses it refers to the loss of self-esteem or reputation. But there could also be a comment on how well she sees events and problems of daily life. If you wear corrective lenses, you do not see things as they are and, therefore, need to increase your perception of reality. Sunglasses indicate that you hide from the truth and try to escape from everyday reality, and the experiences it provides.
❖ Glasses denote, for the dreamer, a conflict in the way she perceives life events. They also symbolize clairvoyance.

Glory ▪ When we dream of glory is because we are not satisfied with our situation in real life. Such episodes evidence immaturity. (See TRIUMPH)

Gloves ▪ Gloves may be considered the outfit of the hands. Therefore, its meaning depends on the condition of those hands. If you use gloves in the dream to decorate and highlight your hands it will be a sign of satisfaction with the completed works; if, instead, you use them to hide your hands, then it is a sign of timidity, the result of past mistakes; Finally, if you are performing a delicate activity with rough and uncomfortable gloves it means that you have an evident inferiority complex. (See HANDS)

Gluttony ■ The interpretation of this dream is related to EATING and DEVOURING. In any case, it is not a positive dream. Whether the gluttonous person is the dreamer or the dreamer sees a gluttonous persona, the dream denotes either an excessive anxiety or a hoarder attitude.

Gnome ■ The encounter with a group of gnomes in a forest symbolizes the search for very different values and principles than those conforming your current reality. At this time, you are pursuing a utopia. The latter could be materialized if you are willing to get carried away by imagination.

Goal ■ The meaning of this dream is related to that of RACE. The goal of the dream may be a literal representation of the objectives you have set in real life. Whether you overcome obstacles and reach it, or lose strength and give it up, will be indicative of your enthusiasm for current projects.

Goat ■ The wild goat conveys an idea of freedom and agility. The male goat represents sexual potency. Some people associate this animal to the devil. The latter, of course, has negative connotations; it states that you are judging and condemning yourself.
❖ This animal has a negative esoteric interpretation in either case. Thus, owning a goat is announcement of discomfort; milking it indicates family illness; slitting its throat, misery. The only exceptions to this negative aspect are represented by the white goat, which promises luck, and by owning a large herd, an indicator of wealth.

God ■ Dreaming of God is rare. It expresses your hope for relating to the most basic part of yourself and for bringing out your strengths. The nature of this dream can be very spiritual. Sometimes the unconscious uses symbols of ancient traditions to express your feelings about divinity. According to psychoanalysis, dreaming of God means finding solace or answers to questions that are beyond our understanding. It also represents the need for protection, the search for the father's figure, and a desire to return to childhood.

❖ Although they are currently quite unusual, dreams in which gods are present were very common in ancient times, because gods then were similar to humans in terms of vices, passions, disputes, loves … To Artemidorus, a divinity that smiles ensures wealth; and an angry one, disaster and economic or health losses. According to the latest keys, praying in dreams portends the solution to your problems.

Gold ■ Gold is the image of sunlight and, therefore, of divine intelligence and life. Consequently, this material symbolizes all things superior, plus the hidden treasure of our true Self (i.e., the spiritual goods and supreme enlightenment). However, its mercantilist connotations can alter all these meanings, so it is also associated with money and jewelry. (See COINS and JEWELS)
❖ For alchemists, gold represented the treasure that is the result of the transformation of the spirit. In mythology, it appears as the spiritual prize for defeating dragons and monsters of ignorance.

Goodbye ■ If someone says goodbye to you it is a sign that you have quite a negative attitude or habit in your life. This dream indicates that you have released something that hindered your progress. If the sensation associated with this goodbye is unpleasant, it may indicate you are too relaxed in your habits. If, however, you are saying goodbye to another, it is likely that soon you will meet this individual again. The farewell can also be a sign of peace, when you say goodbye to annoying aspects of your life; and a sign of great relief when obstacles that kept you back fall behind you.
❖ According to most traditions, to say goodbye is a sad omen of marital separation and death of a loved one.

Goose ■ The goose is related to destiny, as is demonstrated in the Game of the Goose, which is no more than a playful representation of the symbol this animal embodies. In both the said game and the dream, the participant-dreamer has to overcome danger and fortunes of life to return to the mother's bosom. Some psychologists associate the goose with the figure of a tactless friend.
❖ To dream of a goose in the house predicts power, honors, and profits in business. To behead it assures satisfaction and happiness.

Gorge ■ It suggests a narrow and risky crossing. It may enclose a feeling of insecurity when facing difficulties that, at first glance, seem insurmountable.

Gorilla ■ This animal represents our instincts, especially our sexual impulses. If you are able to master them in dreams it is a sign of good psychological health. Now, if you fight against it you will be expressing the mental block caused by you repressions.

Government ■ This dream can represent our most powerful psychological force. It invites us to reflect on what qualities govern us in real life. It is important that you identify each of them, whether honest or greedy. Similarly, this dream can also get an idea of what we think about society and how we organize our daily lives. If you see yourself as part of the government it means that you control your life perfectly. However, you should pay attention to opposing parties, which may be somewhat directly represented in the dream.
❖ Dreaming that you occupy a powerful position in the government predicts an uncertain season.

Grandparents ■ Grandparents represent experience, the past, wisdom learned with time. Therefore, they symbolize social norms that are learned. When they are in dreams that cause pleasant feelings, it suggests you have to seek serenity and calm before getting carried away, paying attention to past events. If these images, on the contrary, are not very comforting, the interpretation is the opposite. You are too anchored in the past and that limits your possibilities for personal development.
❖ All traditions agree that elders are a symbol of certainty and wisdom.

Granite ■ It reflects strength and poise. It is a dream indicating a high degree of security and self-confidence when performing work or pursuing your intended goals.

Grape ■ In clusters, grapes symbolize fertility (due to its fruity character) and sacrifice (due to wine, especial if it is the color of blood). All of the symbolism related to grapes and the vine is positive. For this reason, dreaming that you are pressing grapes to make wine foretells a period of abundance and economic well-being.

Grate ■ Dreaming of a grid most often implies difficulties. To a certain point, it is a good omen, as it means that you can achieve success in your projects with strength and perseverance. (See PRISON and CAGE)

Grate/railing ■ Dreaming that you jump a railing is a sign that you will reach all objectives; to climb over it a sign that illegal methods may be used to get there. Falling from a railing announces an upcoming setback, as much as economic as health; to stay seated on it that you are hoping for the resolution of the problems. Finally, when a woman dreams that she is building a railing, she will have a stable and happy home.

Gravel ■ It indicates a slow road, full of small difficulties that delay and hinder the path to achieve desired objectives.

Gray ■ It is the symbol of indifference and lack of determination. Dreaming of this color may be a warning against a crisis of values that threatens to make you lose your way. No wonder, therefore, that the gray also represents symbolic elements like fog or ash. In oneiric terms, fog symbolizes the fears and anxieties stored in the depths of the unconscious.

Gray hair ■ Gray hairs are symbols of worries and difficult times. They can reveal fear of aging and solitude. They also indicate that the dreamer faces a problem whose solution is beyond her means.

Grazing ■ To see animals grazing on a field indicates a period of calm and restorative rest. It appears that things will get back on track after a tumultuous time.

Greedy ■ Oneiric thoughts in which a greedy person is portrayed are very negative, because it announces not only the abandonment of the protagonist by their loved ones but also poverty and disease. It is advisable to pay attention to the attitude you have with your surroundings in order to avoid misfortune.

Green ■ It is the color of vegetation, calmness, relaxation, and toning. It symbolizes life, hope, and immortality, although it also can indicate poison or unexpected dangers when associated with the jungle. Green represents irrational instinct. If you dream that this color appears in the middle of a desert scenery, it signifies that you are going through a period of unproductivity, but that you will soon leave this period. However, an excess of green evidences that you get carried away by your instincts. If you are in the middle of some sort of resolution, the presence of this color advises you to wait until things mellow.

Green vegetables ▪ Healthy and simple, green vegetables allude to a simple style of life, without complications (usually they are fresh or cooked).

❖ The vegetable in dreams has a positive meaning, since it announces success in negotiations and satisfaction in love. It also provides the accomplishment of the most hidden desires, in general, the end of some type of badness.

Greeting ▪ Greetings to a friend or acquaintances reveals the desire to maintain good relations with the people around you. If the greeter is an adversary, there exists the evident desire to reconcile; meanwhile, if it is a woman, it ensures that difficult projects will achieve success.

Grotto ▪ See BODEGA and CAVE

Group ▪ The presence in the dreams of well-characterized groups—whether ethnic, racial, national, or cultural—represents the qualities, attributes, or prejudices that you usually associate with these groups.

Growing ▪ If you dream that one object, plant, animal, or person grows disproportionately, its symbolic value will increase in proportion to its size. Instead, if it is you who grows, your situation could improve soon.

Growl ▪ Hearing a growl is almost always an alarm. The dreamer should be attentive of the real-life environment in order to discover something that is not going well.

Guardian ▪ Psychologically, guardians symbolize the forces that concentrate on the thresholds that separate the different stages of a person's evolution. Hence it follows that, for many dream analysts, this figure represents the father who forces you to abide by the standards, but at the same time, watches over you, protecting you from the dangers. Dreaming of a guardian, therefore, reveals immaturity because you still need an authority to feel safe.

Guide ▪ See SHORTCUT, PATH, and AVENUE

Guillotine ▪ A guillotine highlights the many difficulties that the dreamer will find in real life because of their enemies. However, if you manage to escape, you will be able to solve all the problems and succeed in life. (See HEAD and DECAPITATION)

Guitar ▪ Traditionally, the guitar has enabled people to express their feelings, facilitating bonding between individuals. Dreaming of this instrument means that you need to rely a little more on yourself because large technical resources are not required to transform the world. Skills, enthusiasm, passion, and love are enough. The guitar is also a symbol of the female body because of its shape and sensuality of its sound. The dream of a man playing the guitar—or simply listening—can lead to a sexual fantasy or expresses the desire to improve her sexual relations. A woman that has this same type of dream is, perhaps, canceling her most feminine side in real life.

Gum ▪ Gum is an erotic symbol, so dreaming of it signals repressed desires that need to be satisfied. Stepping on someone else's gum evidences your dependence on that person; and if someone else steps on yours, you will not likely receive help from others because you continually bother them with your demands.

Gunshot ▪ Gunshots in dreams indicate that you must remain alert. You have to be cautious because unforeseen circumstances can alter your current life.

❖ If in the dream you enjoy shooting, you will have good luck. If, however, you are frightened, the dream portend difficulties. Shooting up at the stars is, universally, an advantageous and promising dream.

Guru ▪ The guru can represent our higher self and our innate wisdom. In dreams, she often takes a religious form—like Buddha, Shiva, or a saint—or appears in a long-bearded old man body, a priest, a prophet, a magician, or a king. She can also take a female figure (Mother Earth or a goddess). For example, the Virgin Mary is the oneiric symbol of supreme compassion and love for fellow beings. Dreams of this type announce your life opens up to a great spiritual opportunity.

❖ Traditions such as the ones of Tibetan Buddhists, Hindus, or Native Americans believe that our inner guide is someone who communicates with us through dreams. This guide may come from our own being or some areas of our spirit.

Gymnastics ■ Physical activity provides an opportunity for body development. This training may be necessary, but if you dream that you exercise, the unconscious may be suggesting that you should also train your mind in order to deploy its full potential. The dream might also be questioning the dreamer's fitness, and suggesting the need to exercise the body.

Gypsies ■ Gypsies sometimes represent prejudices that people have about this ethnic group. Thus, if you think you cannot trust them, those are the emotions evoked in the dream. But if you simply consider them a nomadic people with different customs, the dream will reveal your desire for freedom and rebellion. In addition, this mysterious people, full of old legends and secret stories, can represent that part of yourself that you have not yet discovered. On the other hand, maybe the dream suggests that you have to consider the future.

❖ Because the prophecies surrounding the gypsy tradition, it is possible that the dream is giving you clues about future events. And since this people is associated with good luck, fate will come to you soon.

H

Hail ■ Hail indicates anxiety and fear of external factors that negatively affect the dreamer's life. The latter is unable to cope with them. Possibly, you feel the need to seek help from others overcome a disadvantageous situation.

❖ To see hail is a harbinger of sorrow and pain; eating hail grains, disguised lies.

Hair ■ If you dream of an excess of body hair, the image alludes do you primitivism. You are a slave to sensuality and your instincts always overcome reason. However, if you totally lack hair, the dream reveals you sentimentality and weakness of character.

❖ According to popular tradition, to dream you are entirely covered in hair is an omen of good health.

Hairspray ■ To dream that you apply hairspray to your hair indicates a rigid attitude toward your own criterium and also when it comes to judging others around you.

Hall ■ The hall is the center of a house. If you go through one in a dream, it represents the start of an exploration of the self.

❖ Dreaming of a large and long hall foretells a period of preoccupation.

Hallway ■ It indicates a state of transition. The dream may be pleasant or terrifying, depending on how fluid or winding the way is and the existence or lack of light at the end of the hall. It is important to analyze all the elements that appear throughout the corridor because they reflect the dreamer's emotional state at the time of transit. However, the final key is the feeling that you have as you follow the path into the unknown. Running along a corridor without ever seeing the end may show the need to escape from a distressing situation that is repeated too often in reality. Also, it may refer to the attitudes that you must leave behind to pass from one life stage to another.

❖ Corridors and passages are places where energy is moving rapidly but never accumulates. This dream, therefore, may denote that we are in danger of losing all our energy and vitality.

Ham ■ To dream that you eat ham can be interpreted as the need to feed your primal instincts. This dream, on the other hand, could also advise you to be careful with superfluous spending.

Hammer ■ The hammer is the tool of the blacksmith and is equipped with a mystical power of creation. To dream of this tool means that, although it is a great sacrifice, you are working enough to achieve your goals. The hammer, then, can be interpreted as a symbol of constancy in work. In addition, it is related to virility, authority, and strength. For Freud, the act of hammering a nail symbolized the sexual act.

❖ The Teutonic god Thor, controller of time and crops, carried a hammer that, after throwing it, returned to his hand. In this sense, the hammer represents power and spiritual strength.

Hammock ▪ Symbolizes rest after an extenuating effort or experience outside of the norm. (See BED)

Hand ▪ Hands reflect the way we use resources. The right hand symbolizes the rational, logical, and analytical side, while the left represents the irrational, impulsive, and emotional (for left-handed people, the meaning is reversed). When you dream that your hands are large and strong, it is a sign of security, success, and progress. If, however, you see small and weak hands, it expresses helplessness, insecurity, resentment, and dissatisfaction. White, smooth, and clean hands suggest a comfortable and easy life. If they are rough and dirty, they embody effort, suffering, and work. Hairy hands reveal primitivism and an uncontrollable sex drive. We also use our hands to express ourselves. At heart, they are extensions of our personality. If you discover the meaning of every gesture you make in the dream, you will know the nature of the feelings that you must understand. For example: a clenched fist indicates aggressiveness, selfishness, or passion; holding hands expresses affection; a hand held high represents forgiveness. (See FINGERS and GLOVES)

❖ If you dream of the palm, you may be worried about the future. According to palmistry, its shapes and lines contain data about our destiny. The dream, therefore, may be giving you clues about your future potential. Fortunately, you have the option to act voluntarily. What you do now will improve what is to come.

Handicap ▪ To dream of an impediment indicates that the path you've chosen to complete a project is the wrong one. If you see yourself in a wheelchair, this could mean that you are experiencing a period of immobility, so you must work to attain your goals. If you dream you cannot move from where you are because of some incomprehensible handicap, it means that your life is not working and not progressing as it should. It is best to seek balance.

Handkerchief ▪ If you use it to dry your tears, the handkerchief plays a role of comfort; maybe your unconscious is claiming the need for someone to comfort you and be a "shoulder to cry on."

❖ Seeing a handkerchief indicates, in general, the desire to live in a relationship, although this interpretation may be qualified. If the handkerchief is red, the love affair will be shocking and cause all kinds of gossip; but if it is white, it will be honest and will end in marriage. To lose it announces the couple will break up; and to tear it, a serious argument. If the handkerchief is silk, you will enjoy the company of friends at any time; and if it is cotton, family bliss will be certain. When it is a young woman who dreams of a handkerchief, she runs the risk of being deceived by a man who tries to conquer her.

Hands (of a clock) ▪ Seeing the hands of a clock in detail or hearing the sound they make almost always produces a feeling of distress. The dreamer is obsessed with the passage of time. Perhaps you lack enough time to finish a job; or you feel guilty about having wasted precious hours on superfluous things. (See CLOCK)

Hanging ▪ This type of dream may indicate the peak of a depression from which things will start to change. The individual that is being hanged begins to appreciate what they possess instead of being sorry for what they lack.

❖ Divination interprets this oneiric image as loss of property, unfair trials, being unable to claim an inheritance, or infidelity.

Harassment ▪ Feeling haunted by something or someone is a sign of severe restlessness, the cause of which has not yet been discovered by the dreamer. It is possible that feelings of guilt are affecting your sleeping. However, it is also possible you need to face a problem that, so far, you have consciously refused to see.

Hardware store ▪ Being at a hardware store announces the arrival of means to achieve your goals. Therefore, the better equipped it is the sooner you shall reach your goals. If in the dream you see an ironmonger it means that you seek advice from someone more experienced and mature.

Hare ▪ Because of its great fertility, the hare is associated with sex and, by extension, the female genitals. On the other hand, it is also considered a messenger of the unconscious and the weak but astute part of your personality, that which is found on the edge between conscious and unconscious.

❖ Hares have always been considered figures of misfortune because of the popular belief that they were witches in disguise. Similarly, if a pregnant woman has this dream it meant that her child would have a cleft lip. Nevertheless, there are dream oracles that insist that a hare approaching you portends good luck.

Harem ■ This dream tends to be related to sexual appetites, since it reflects repressed desires, as well as your emotional relationships in general. In a man, this dream may warn him about the presence of external circumstances that distract him from his true objectives. In a woman, it can represent the desire to have her wishes for social status and luxury fulfilled, although for that she must give up her independence and dignity.

Harlequin ■ An harlequin may represent the grotesque dimension of your personality. If the dream is pleasant, the unconscious is suggesting you to laugh at concerns because their impact is relative. But if the oneiric images are unpleasant, it is indicating that your attitude is not the most appropriate.

Harvest ■ It represents wealth and joy from collecting the fruits cultivated with effort over some time. (See FARMER)

Hat ■ As they serve to cover the head, hats are a symbol of what is harbored (or thought). In the same fashion, it references the role that you play in life. And, if you change it, it indicates a change in attitude or direction in your existence. It is possible that you are turning towards the assumption of more responsibilities at work, or be searching for a new work position. According to Freud, hats (and gloves) represent the female genitals due to its ability to surround the body. In contrast, Jung thought that the hat, relative to the crown, gives people a determined expression. So, the type of hat changes the meaning of the dream. A tophat manifests that you want health or that you are too pretentious; a baseball hat that you want to be younger or more athletic; a straw hat, that you hope to adopt a more natural and unworried attitude; a military cap indicates an excess in authoritarianism; lastly, if you wear a ridiculous hat, it is a warning of the grotesque posture that you maintain in the situation represented in the dream. In general, imagining that you are wearing a hat shows a lack of security in what you do and a fear of being judged by others.

❖ The predecessors of Freud believed that if a woman wears a man's hat, she wants to maintain relations with the owner of the hat. And, if you dream that you lose the hat, you will soon be married.

Hate ■ If in the dream you harbor a lot of hatred, perhaps it refers to a negative feeling that is part of your personality. The hated person or thing is, logically, important but other factors must be analyzed in depth in order to correctly interpret the dream and get to the root of this emotion. Once the real object of your hatred identified, you will have already partially solved the problem.

❖ To feel hatred towards a stranger is a bad sign for everything related to material concerns: there is every chance that you will ruin yourself in business. To hate a loved one, however, denotes emotional and family quarrels; and yourself, dissatisfaction and uncertainty about your self-worth.

Hay ■ This is a symbol of prosperity and material well-being. To reap it, transport it, or lie down in it are all signs of a good economic situation. To watch it burn indicates the fear of an unfavorable period, and may be a warning to be prudent and not take on unnecessary expenses.

Haze ■ Seeing yourself enveloped in haze indicates that perhaps your life is not as perfect as you think: they could be deceiving you while you remain clueless. If the mist, however, fades, certain problems would be coming to an end. To see mist in a landscape, or sea, advises caution; and if it covers other people, a feeling of guilt for wanting to take advantage of them.

Head ■ The head embodies the soul and intelligence. It is your conscious. If your head is separated from the body and the feeling is nice, the image indicates changes in your personal situation, resulting in an increase of creative power. When the feeling that it produces is unpleasant the dream can manifest split personality. The Jungian psychoanalysis maps the head with the highest part of the subject; instead, the Freudian one assimilates it to the penis and recognizes in the beheading an analogy with castration.

❖ If in your dream you have an oversized head it is a sign that you will receive good news. Conversely, if it is smaller and lighter it indicates servility and dishonor. To have someone else's head foresees a change of mind; and to have it turned backward, a change of house.

Headache ■ To suffer a headache in dreams announces mild but reccurring sorrows.

Healing ■ Usually, they are positive dreams. They indicate that, after passing hardship, things are back to normal. The person who is healing you will have a special significance, because with her help she demonstrates her unconditional support.
❖ A feeling of comfort will soon pervade the dreamer's life.

Heart ■ In the vertical scheme of the human body there are three basic marks: brain, heart, and genitalia. Heart is thus the central point. It is no coincidence, therefore, that it was the only organ that the Egyptians left inside mummies. Symbolically, in this organ, life, emotion, and wisdom are concentrated. Furthermore, it is an ancient archetype of love. The dream is probably describing your emotional side and how you approach it with your feelings. If the heart is damaged, has been operated on, or has a bullet wound, it means that you are going through a bad time. In these cases, the other elements of the dream usually contain advice and recommendations you should to follow. Finally, if the heart is in perfect condition, it reflects you feel very good in emotional matters.
❖ In India, the heart is the symbol of divine love. It also represents your most intimate motivations.

Heat ■ Dreaming of a stifling heat suggests that you have a lot of energy but you are not using it properly. This dream may indicate a tendency toward aggression and conflict. You despise yourself and tend to externalize your own dissatisfactions against others. If you burn and have a burning sensation in the dream, it is a sign of lawlessness in your instincts.

Hedge ■ This dream could represent the restrictions and physical or psychological obstacles that make your vital progress difficult. If you dream that you are pruning a hedge, it could suggest that you have accepted that a given obstacle is immovable, and you will have to overcome it no matter how bad the situation.
❖ Dreaming that you are pruning a hedge signifies that you will soon have good luck.

Hedgehog ■ It is a warning that you can run into problems or prickly issues. This dream often suggests you not to make decisions in haste.
❖ The hedgehog's oneiric image alerts of judgments resolved wrongly and deception in relationships.

Heel ■ Twisting your heel in dreams signifies that you are about to commit an important error in some issue in which you are involved. The image also reflects that it costs you to make decisions due to your insecurity.

Hell ■ The idea of hell has a mythical and constant value in human culture. It is conceived, in the first place, as a form of "sublife" (hidden life of the dead in the bosom of the earth). Then, it is situated as a place of torment. With this panorama, it is evident that—simply by analogy—it can be associated with all negative aspects of existence. Representations of hell appear in all religions, from that of ancient Egypt to Christianity. Fire, instruments of torture, and demons are its iconographic expressions. Don't forget that hell symbolizes the subterranean world of the unconscious, where we have condemned the impulses we don't want to admit for moral or cultural reasons, or ignorance. When dreaming of hell you may feel fear or guilt, which indicates that you are repressing one of your acts or thoughts. The message of this type of dream is that you should stop being ashamed and cleanse your soul of negativity.
❖ Ancient dream dictionaries say that this dream comes from inner conflicts. However, they add that it also predicts gains in business.

Helmet ■ The helmet is the part of the armor that soldiers used to protect the face. To dream of this element, therefore, is related to our desire to hide ourselves to feel protected. You probably want to pass unnoticed before others, be it due to humility or due to repression. (See ARMOR and MASK)

Hemorrhage ■ This is a clear symbol of the loss of vital energy. (See ILLNESS)

Hen ■ Since immemorial times, the hen is a symbol of superficiality because of its clucking and passivity. It is no coincidence that the hen is associated with rumors, whispers, and slander. Therefore, the presence of a hen in your dreams may suggest that someone is making malicious comments about you behind your back. A totally different sense arises if you dream of a hen laying an egg. In these cases, the dream images portend a profit in short time. This dream can also be attributed to excessive concern for your partner, children, or friends to the point of becoming a "mother hen."

Herb ▪ Herbs, whether for their medicinal power or their venom, appear frequently in legends and folktales. ‖ To dream that you are lying on grass reveals the need to reestablish contact with yourself. You are wasting life by following some rules that are, by all indications, unnatural. The dream invites you to not lose hope for a major transformative change. However, if your oneiric images show dry, wilted grass, it is an unfavorable sign: it means you feel defeated and you've given up on harboring new ideas. Weeds also represent your worst habits and attitudes. These may come from your interior or from others. Most likely, the dream is showing you the way to regain harmony.
❖ If in your dream you are pulling out weeds and they do not contain nettles or thistles, the signs are good. Soon you will be very lucky.

Herd ▪ The herd is an image that denotes, without place for doubts, insecurity and lack of personality, the reason that you are searching insistently for integration with a group. The dream may be censuring you for going along with the herd, without thinking and acting for yourself. This dream also means that you desire to leave the protective environment that you usually inhabit, despite the possibility that if gives you the fear that it may result in loneliness. However, you have to learn to trust in yourself.
▪ A herd of animals is generally a good omen.If they are buffalo, it is evidence of your great potential; elephants, that you should act sensibly when facing new challenges; and felines, that a time of strong emotions is near. In the case that the sight of the herd frightens you, you must be careful with people around you: an unfavorable alliance could emerge between them.
❖ To overflow: a container that overflows could be interpreted in various ways. On one hand, it is a sign of abundance; on the other, it reflects overwhelming emotions and lack of control. In this case, the meaning of the dream is related with that of CRYING and RELIEF. It is possible that the dreamer has reached the limit of their emotional resistance.

Hermaphrodite ▪ Seeing yourself as a hermaphrodite may indicate that your sexual tendency is not entirely defined. However, it may also reflect the need to strengthen the feminine side, if the dreamer is a man, or the masculine side, if she is a woman.

Hermit ▪ Dreaming of a hermit predicts study, patient work, and acquisition of knowledge, if, of course, it is on a clear and sunny atmosphere. In contrast, the vision of a hermit in a dark and gloomy place represents a laborious and tedious work.
❖ Dreaming that a hermit gives you shelter denotes generosity toward friends and enemies.

Hero ▪ To dream of a hero or heroine is an alert sign about the need to ask others for help in solving certain problems. However, if the dreamer is the hero, it makes clear the image of strength he has before others. Many times, in this dream, the hero represents your conscious part. This goes on an unconscious journey to challenge its powers. Equally, numberless myths and stories tell about how heroes venture to strange lands to find a treasure or rescue a beautiful damsel. These are symbols of the reward you will receive by investigating your most hidden side. For a woman, dreaming of the figure of a man made a hero could be evidence of her masculine side. For a man, finding the princess he was looking for could manifest that, finally, he has found the feminine aspect of his nature.
❖ Some oneiric beliefs consider this dream to portend that someone who spurns the dreamer in real life will soon fall in love with them.

Hieroglyph ▪ Dreaming of a hieroglyph is a way for your unconscious to remind you that, in order to achieve your goals, you have to overcome many complications. These problems, however, can be simplified if you clarify your ideas and get right to the heart of the matter.

Highway ▪ Traveling on a highway during a dream should be interpreted as a positive sign. This image indicates that you have all the means to solve the problems. However, no matter where you go you still have to pay the price for mistakes. You must, therefore, respond to commitments without giving up.

Hill ▪ Elevation allows you to see your surroundings more clearly. If you are climbing a hill with enthusiasm it means you are improving your professional or social situation. In contrast, it can also be an obstacle to be overcome in real life. Depending on what it takes to climb the hill, it means abundance or scarcity of resources that you have to attain your purposes.
❖ In this case, popular superstitions are in agreement with the psychological interpretation.

Hilltop ▪ It indicates the goals the dreamer has set for herself. Getting to the hilltop is a sign of feeling confident and satisfied with your achievements. To see it from the bottom represents the effort you need to do in order to get to the top. Falling from a hilltop may be warning against the dreamer's unpreparedness to begin the course; or, the dreamer's fear of both the failure and success of her company.

Hippopotamus ▪ In the Egyptian hieroglyphic system, this animal represents strength and vigor. It is also associated with the idea of fertility. If you see it submerged in dirty water or mud, the dream points to your lower passions and depraved impulses. These impulses do not give you any pleasure if you are ruled by them.
❖ Announces strength, animal vigor, and fertility.

Hive ▪ Because of its well-organized social structure, a hive symbolizes community and order. If your dream visions are pleasant, it means that you have the support of family and friends. However, if the bees are threatening it indicates that the organization to which you belong is making you lose your identity. These images should prompt you to reflect on the need to find a time for solitude and meditation.
❖ Superstitions of the people who live in the country claim that bees are very wise creatures with special knowledge of the future. The dreams that include bees or hives, therefore, may contain prophetic clues about events that will take place soon.

Hoarding ▪ It refers to a situation of non-conformism and dissatisfaction regarding our own goods, our context, or the people around us.

Hoarseness ▪ When you are voiceless in dreams or talk so quietly that others are unable to hear you, it means that you are losing your ability to decide, and your confidence in yourself.

Hole ▪ By analogy, a hole is related to the vagina and fertility. Dreaming that you are falling into a hole indicates your attitude is not so positive. A feeling of emptiness may be invading you and bringing complete sadness. This could mean a period of regression and decline in your values. The message that this dream tries to convey is that you might plunge into a depression if you get carried away by these negative approaches. It is recommended to seek new interests in order to recover with confidence. If the holes appear on clothing, maybe you are too worried about your external image.
❖ The omens of this dream are disadvantageous. You will establish friendship with seedy and unreliable people. Additionally, holes in the clothes denote debts.

Holm Oak ▪ This sturdy tree symbolizes wisdom and strength, both physical and moral. It is the favorite sacred tree of the gods because, more than others, it attracts Zeus's lightning. The Celts, who got mistletoe from it, attributed great powers to it. God appeared to Abraham in an holm oak branch, thus symbolizing stability, protection, and strength.
❖ A lush and sturdy holm oak casts longevity, prosperity, and happy old age. Climbing it portends great energy. The branches represent the strength and courage of the dreamer. If it does not have leaves it predicts loss of property. A downcast holm oak endangers the sleeper's finances; pruned, portends marital infidelity.

Home ▪ See HOUSE

Homicide ▪ See MURDER

Honey ▪ It can represent two things: first, sweetness, well-being, wealth, and happiness; secondly, honey is also the product of a complex process of production that bees follow in order to make it. Its meaning, therefore, is associated with personal growth, with effort in work. Finally, in the Far East, lies are called "poisoned honey."
❖ Honey is the food of the gods. This dream may indicate your desire to possess divine consciousness.

Hood ▪ The hood that hides the face provides invisibility. It represents the desire to hide, to evade responsibility, or a negative judgment of the people around you. It indicates guilt and shame. If you see someone wearing a hood, it is a sign of distrust against that person.

Hook ▪ A hook expresses the need to deal with neglected issues before it is too late. Getting hurt by a hook indicates that these matters are very unpleasant to you. In addition, your relationships could turn a bit complicated when you begin to tackle those matters.

Horns ▪ They symbolize strength, fertility, and patience if they are a bull's or cow's. The ram's horns represent aggressiveness. As it is well known, they are also associated with adultery.

Horse ■ The horse has always been a mythical animal. Centuries ago, especially in England and Germany, dreaming of a white horse was considered a harbinger of war. According to Jung, the horse expresses the magical side of man, unconscious intuition. Indeed, from this magical character comes the belief that horseshoes bring good luck. Because of their speed, horses can also embody the wind, the fire, and the light. Dreaming of horses means you can tame your passions and, therefore, your will has control of your actions. If the horse runs wild it means you have lost control and let yourself get carried away by your passions. If you are afraid in the dream it also indicates that you fear your most natural instincts. The horses are also sex symbols and, according to Freud, they represent the terrible aspects of the father figure. In short, horses are the wild forces of the subject's psyche, whose primary need is that you master them without repressing them.

❖ In some myths and fairy tales, horses have the ability to speak like humans. If this happens in the dream, it is the voice of your unconscious contacting you. In Greek myths, horses were linked to Hades, god of the underground and death. However, the most common oneiric prophecy says that horses announce news from a far-away place. If in your dream someone is putting shoes on a horse, you will soon have the best of fortunes.

Hose ■ Because of its long cylindrical shape, and function, the hose is clearly a sexual image. To dream of one predicts virility and sexual potency for a man, and fecundity for a woman. However, to interpret the dream better you should analyze the rest of the elements of the dream such as the water or the element that you watered (plant, object, etc.).

Hospital ■ To dream of a hospital can be, to a certain point, alarming, since it manifests the fear of being sick. If in the dream you visit someone who is sick, you should take special care of your health, since your body is crying for help.

❖ In Ancient Greece, it was believed that dreams not only diagnosed the dreamer's state of health, but also had a curative ability. This was claimed by Hippocrates, considered the father of medicine. Tibetan medicine also takes note of patients' dreams to discover the spiritual cause of the physical illness.

Hotel ■ If you dream that you live in a hotel, you definitely have a longing for a better, less worrisome life, without having to struggle to cover basic necessities. You probably desire a much different existence than your real one. If you are the owner or administrator of the hotel establishment, it is saying that you aspire to have power over others. According to other interpretations, the hotel is related to a change of residence and lack of permanence. So, it could represent the transition from some circumstances to others, or the loss of your own identity.

❖ If the hotel is luxurious, it predicts failure. But if it is old and dirty, soon you will have the help of good luck.

House ■ The house symbolizes the personality, the current situation, and the emotional or professional relationships. Therefore, to find out the meaning of this dream you must analyze all aspects. The interior of the house is your body; the dining room and the kitchen represent the digestive system; the bedroom, rest and sexual activity; bathroom, kidneys and cleanliness, both physical and spiritual; the upper floors, the mind; and the cellar or basement, the unconscious. (See HUT, CAVE, BALCONY, CELLAR)

❖ Nomadic gypsies believe that dreams in which you are forced to leave your home indicate that you expect a favorable opportunity.

Hug ■ To dream that someone embraces you can indicate a need for affection and understanding. If the hug is pleasant, it means you must express your feelings to somebody. If the hug comes from your father, it signifies that you accept yourself just as you are and have achieved the recognition you wanted. Conversely, if you seek the embrace, it generally means you are in want of love and protection. For that matter, a mother or grandmother is more likely to be the ones present on the oneiric images. Dreams that portray hugs do not always have a positive reading. So, if an unpleasant feeling goes along with them it could suggest insecurity or lack of sincerity towards the person with whom you share your body. It is important to keep in mind that in western Christian tradition the famous embrace from Judas to Jesus is associated with high betrayal.

❖ An embrace from someone unknown is a sign of prosperous businesses. From foreign subjects it announces imminent travel; from a friend it indicates low morale; from a relative, cheating and scams; from a deceased person, bad news.

Humidity ▪ In general, this is a negative dream that reflects discomfort and fear invading our vital space. It is also related to painful emotions and feelings of sadness and abandonment.

Humiliation ▪ To humiliate yourself in front of someone else denotes that, in real life, you are acting foolishly. It will only bring us unpleasantness. If the humiliated one is an adversary, it means you will receive unexpected winnings and old flaws will be pardoned.

Hunchback ▪ The back symbolizes physical strength and resistance. If it is curved—as happens with hunchbacked people—it reflects a weakness of character and emotional dissatisfaction. For this reason, if you see a hunchback in a dream, it could indicate you are hiding something and feel insecure.

Hunger ▪ If it is confimed that the dream does not have a physiological origin (sometimes we have the urge to eat when we are asleep), hunger can indicate the presence of some dissatisfaction, in most cases intellectual. This image, therefore, represents the soul's desire to find the answer to deep questions. When the dream repeats often and the hunger is never satiated, it may reflect sexual problems or problems with communication with a partner. If the hunger is satisfied, it is important to pay attention to what calmed it, since that may be necessary in your waking life. (See EATING and APPETITE)
❖ Popular superstition says that the hungrier you are in dreams, the more destiny smiles on you.

Hunter ▪ Some cultures associate hunting with the subject's insatiable obsession to pursue her wishes. In turn, hunting dreams reveal a desire to escape from the problems and at the same time, a willingness to revolt against them. On many occasions, you should read this image as, instead of being aggressive against it, an attempt to get used to it, because with an aggressive attitude you are not going to solve much. If you kill an animal while hunting, perhaps you are trying to destroy an instinctive part of your personality.
❖ According to popular oneiric tradition, hunting a hare indicates that you will have problems. If it is a fox, a friend will let you down. Whereas if it is a deer you will conquer the person you are in love with.

Hurricane ▪ A hurricane could indicate an emotional conflict or confusion building in your interior. Further, it references the fury and frustration that you cannot find relief.
❖ Superstition says that this dream symbolizes an obstacle that keeps you from something you desire. If your house is damaged by the hurricane, you have people near you who have bad intentions.

Hydrangea ▪ This flower is a symbol that tends to denote frigidity.

Hyena ▪ The hyena represents cowardice and lower passions. Not in vain, it is a scavenger and a nocturnal

---

analysis of a dream

HUNGER

Felipe dreamed: "I often dream that I am very hungry and I can't find food anywhere: my fridge is empty or full of inedible objects—like a watch, a ball, a sock.... I decide to go out and buy something, but the grocery stores are closed or close just as I am about to go in. So I get really mad. Other times I dream of a table full of exotic fruits (figs, grapes, papayas, strawberries) but when I bring something to my mouth, it turns to smoke or disappears. Then I wake up in a very bad mood, but curiously, I'm not hungry."

Dreams about food sometimes have a merely physiological trigger. However, in Felipe's case—since he wakes up not hungry—they are warning him about another type of necessity, concretely **hunger for affection and safety**. When Felipe began to have this type of dream, he had broken up with a partner several months earlier. Even though it was his girlfriend who make the decision, he felt strong and optimistic and bragged about having gotten over it easily. However, his unconscious was reminding him, through dreams, that he was **emotionally dry** and more vulnerable than he thought. Gluttony sometimes has a sexual connotations: the fruit especially reveals a **unsatisfied sensual desire**. The fact that he couldn't find food or stores open reflected his inability to understand his emotions and express them.

creature with powerful jaws. Symbolically, it is the opposite of the falcon.

❖ The oneiric image of the hyena announces illness and domestic sorrows.

Hypocrisy ▪ To dream that you are surrounded by hypocritical people warns you that someone, under the guise of a friend, seeks your downfall. If you are the hypocrite, you should reconsider the type of relationships you establish with others.

I

Ice ■ While water can show the creative flow of feelings, the presence of ice indicates little enthusiasm and emotional rigidness. You should try to live more intensely and give warmth to loved ones. Ice warns us of the risk we run if we harden too much to the detriment of our feelings. It is the petrification of water, which signifies a lack of life force and love.

❖ Skating on ice predicts disasters.

Ice cream ■ The coldness of ice cream evokes a certain sensuality and sweetness; the dream may suggest you should savor the expression of your emotions more. The uninhibited enjoyment of ice cream also makes your erotic and sensual side blossom.

Iceberg ■ An enormous block of ice represents the obstacles that impede your path. These barriers can appear in the work or family plane. It is a dream of warning and, at the same time, of encouragement to fight these impediments to your happiness. (See FROZEN and ICE)

Idea ■ In general this is a positive dream related to creativity. The unconscious has been accumulating and processing data and the oneiric scene presents the fruit of this work. It may be a very useful dream in real life to resolve a certain problem or to the development of artistic, intellectual, or scientific activity.

Idol ■ If you are acclaimed as an idol but don't see the faces of those who congratulate you, it means you are in danger (vanity is harming you). However, if the acclaim is scant and you see the faces of those who praise you, success will be fleeting and will only serve to inflate your ego. (See ACROBAT)

Image ■ A religious image denotes insecurity in your own resources; one of parents, family dependence; and of your partner, tension in the relationship.

Imitation ■ The act of imitating someone has two opposite meanings: on one side, the inability to make your own decisions, and on the other, a high degree of originality. It can also be interpreted as a great ability to adapt to your surroundings.

Immobility ■ In general, this is an anxious dream in which the dreamer tries to move and is unable to. This nightmare could originate from a physiological problem or an uncomfortable position of some body part. If this is not the case, the dream reflects a real situation in which immobility—whether spiritual or intellectual—is the fruit of an inferiority complex or low self esteem. In this case, you must study the causes to get to the bottom of the problem and find an adequate solution. When the dream does not generate anxiety, but rather tranquility, then it is interpreted as a sign of physical or mental exhaustion. In this case, it warns of the immediate need for a break.

Immune ▪ To see yourself as immune to some kind of sickness that affects others indicates that you have a great deal of security and confidence in yourself. it is a favorable moment to face daily problems of all sizes.

Impotence ▪ To dream that you cannot complete the sexual act is a sign of a feeling of impotence; the basic problem is that you feel a lack of enthusiasm and energy to face a situation. It is a symptom of laziness, of a negligence that will end up affecting your work and personal relationships. This episode is evidence that your ideals are very high, but you let yourself fall into comfort and easy options. The impossibility of connecting to your essence is detrimental to your creativity.

In love ▪ Its interpretation is often literal. This dream recreates exactly the same situation as in real life. It is very common during adolescence. Almost always it reflects joy, awakening of new sensations, insecurity, need for approval, and fear of abandonment or fear of a change of the loved partner's attitude. (See LOVE)

Incense ▪ This dream tends to have religious or spiritual connotations. It represents elevation and subtlety, as well as the desire for immaterial beauty and seclusion in oneself. (See SMOKE)

Incest ▪ According to Carl Gustav Jung, incest symbolizes the desire for union with the essence of oneself. This is why some gods of ancient mythologies were conceived in this way. In any case, this dream is very uncommon. In oneiric terms, incest can indicate various things. The most normal is that it reminds you of the dependence you have on your mother, as well as the fear you have at the idea of separating from her. All this reveals immaturity and an inability to make decisions. It may also remind us, as Jung claimed, of our origin and the strong desire to return to it, recover our identity, and be reborn. Incest with a brother or sister represents the union of your feminine and masculine sides. (See SEX)
❖ In ancient times, this was so taboo that no books about dreams make any reference to it.

Indigestion ▪ This dream may be a reflection of a real situation. A large dinner shortly before going to bed can cause some of these nightmares. If this is not the case, indigestion is a symbol of excess. It is possible that the dreamer feels guilty for wasting spiritual, emotional, or material resources.

Infidelity ▪ Being unfaithful to a partner in dreams does not necessarily mean that the situation will happen or is happening, but rather that you are being unfaithful to yourself, betraying your own principles. You are not fulfilling your promises, or the goals you set. Your partner is nothing more than the reflection of your interior, the darkest part of your person. In general, an act of infidelity demonstrates the disconformity you feel with some kind of rule. If it refers to your sentimental relationship, the dream denotes deception and unsatisfied needs. If your partner is the one who is unfaithful, it may mean that you are denying their emotional desires.
❖ Oneiric superstition says that this dream expresses the opposite. It promises a happy relationship, full of fidelity.

Inflation ▪ To dream that you blow up balloons means that you tend to feed utopian illusions in order to avoid facing urgent questions. You dedicate yourself to wasting time and daydreaming, fleeing from daily reality. Therefore, you should center yourself to help your life find a concrete goal, without wasting time on impossible ideas.

Infusion ▪ It's curative properties indicate that the dreamer should be cautious, discreet, and patient when it comes to resolving personal matters. This may be the opportune moment to reconsider a pressured or aggressive attitude toward someone around you.

Ingredients ▪ To see a series of ingredients ready can indicate the need to put a certain aspect of your life in order, whether it is in your work or domestic or family setting. It is possible that your personal relationships require review. If you see the ingredients in bad shape, it could be that you harbor guilty feelings about missing an opportune moment to begin a certain task.

Inheritance ▪ To dream of an inheritance augurs that you will receive something, but this type of image does not usually give hints about whether what arrives will be positive or negative. So, it could be the case that the reward for your sacrifices will finally arrive, or, on the contrary, that you inherit debts or illness.

Initiation ■ These dreams often represent the transition from one psychological stage to a higher one. For example, the passage from childhood to adolescence, from youth to middle age, or from middle age to old age. On the other hand, initiation hides the dreamer's desires to change her earthly aspirations to more spiritual ones.

❖ In ancient times, initiation rituals were very common. They were used as a dramatized representation of the structure of the psyche or life.

Injection ■ This is an indicator of the relationship that you have with people around you. Generally, it represents the positive or negative influence that someone has over you. If the dream generates a feeling of anxiety, it reveals fear of this external influence or the excess value you place on the opinions of others.

INSECTS

Silvia dreamed: "I was laying in my bed when I discovered an enormous cockroach on the ceiling of my bedroom, just above my head. It was dark green, it emitted a faint buzz, and it moved its long antennae quickly, brushing my face. I felt panicked, but I didn't dare move or shout for fear of startling it or that it would jump on me. I stayed immobile, with eyes closed, wishing it would disappear."

Insects tend to reflect our fears or insecurities. If they are gigantic, often it indicates the oppression we suffer from an authoritative figure, toward which we feel a series of emotions such as repulsion, fear, respect . . . It took Silvia several days to understand the meaning of her dream. It happened one day when she was meeting with her boss. He was pointing out a careless error and reproaching her for incompetence. The dark green suit he wore made her remember the dream. Then, she saw it clearly. Although Silvia worked a lot, she felt that it was never enough for her boss, who took every opportunity to criticize her work. The tentacles of the enormous insect brushing her reflected the sharp gaze of her boss, always waiting for the smallest mistake to tell her off. Although it was unfair, Silvia did not dare protest, she just nodded her head, hoping it would be over as soon as possible. She was afraid that her boss would get angry or, even worse, fire her.

However, the dream can be telling you to inject more entertainment and determination into your life. The syringe is also considered a phallic symbol. What you need may be more enthusiasm on the sexual plane. Finally, injections symbolize healing and protection. In this case, you should think about the current state of your spiritual side.

❖ An oneiric interpretation from the thirties considered that dreaming of receiving an injection meant that you would be free of those enemies that plot against you.

Injustice ■ Committing an injustice in dreams is evidence of certain tendency toward abuse that, in the long term, could result in grave consequences for the dreamer. To suffer one, on the other hand, signals a delay in the completion of plans, as well as all types of losses.

Ink ■ Ink symbolizes prosperity, as it allows you to write and enrich your intellect. But, if it is smudged, it foretells unexpected difficulties. (See DIFFICULTIES, SMUDGES, and PAPER)

Inn ■ The inn is a positive image, especially if it is full of people. This prompts the sleeper to move forward with their projects with the most energy possible: even in the worst moments, they will have the support necessary to achieve their goal. To see an empty inn is, however, a sign of unhappiness and bad business. Seeing yourself looking for one, on the other hand, means that you need time to reflect on your issues.

Inquisition ■ Generally this is a negative dream, related to feelings of guilt and impotence. It is possible that you feel unfairly punished or that you have carelessly judged someone around you.

Insects ■ Insects embody resentment, fear, and disdain for others. Because of this, dreaming that insects invade your house signals that you fear rumors. A giant insect indicates that someone oppresses you, perhaps a parent or strict boss. Also, they can symbolize all those repressed desires and impulses. On the other side, insects represent all the little problems in daily life. In Kafka's *Metamorphosis* (1912) the protagonist wakes up one day as an insect. Kafka spent a lot of time doing office jobs that he hated. This dream could represent how the work sphere transforms you into something insignificant, eradicating your personality. In this sense, ants represent social conformism, manifesting that you are too obedient. Flies are crises, rot, and guilt; lady-bugs, happiness in your job; locusts, lack of psychological nourishment, destruction of creativity; and finally, wasps are angry emotions and thoughts.

❖ In Ancient Egypt they worshiped the beetle, which symbolized creation. In dreams, this insect can represent the soul. In some stories, insects appear when the resolution of the plot seems impossible and their help is the only option (for example, asking them to separate grains of sand or some similar task). In oneiric terms, they symbolize precision and meticulous thought.

Inspection ▪ To imagine that an inspector wants to review your work or accounts expresses the fear of having some secret or weakness discovered. If you try to look deeper at the symbols that accompany the inspection, it can be very useful to get to know yourself better.

Insulation ▪ The dreams in which the individual sees himself insulating something or those that show insulating materials represent a strong need for protection. The dreamer feels attacked by the environment and seeks a way to defend himself.

Insult ▪ The dream could refer to some insult you have received lately and the reaction you had, whether it was disproportionate or, on the contrary, ineffective. In the case that someone is rude to you, perhaps you should reconsider how you think of this person. To receive an insult in a dream may also be a sign you do not have a very clear conscience. The message is easy to interpret: you must correct your attitude or life will end up taking its toll.

Internet ▪ To dream that you connect to the Internet shows a desire to widen your circle of friendships and live new emotions. However, it also makes plain your fear of not being accepted and an attempt to fix it by hiding behind a computer. Not being able to access the Internet denotes a failure to strengthen relationships with others.

❖ Physicists believe that all that has life is connected by an extremely fine layer of energy. What happens in one place affects the rest. By comparing this to the universal network, it is possible to perceive events in any part of the world. Dreams sometimes offer you the opportunity to connect to this ethereal, conscious internet.

Interruption ▪ This dream is related to some type of frustration or deception that you suffer in real life. You must analyze the context and elements that appear in the dream to interpret it correctly.

Intertwining ▪ The message highlights the need for a closer union with a person or activity. (See TYING)

Intestines ▪ These are related to everything visceral. Through the intestines we absorb food and discard non nourishing substances, converting them to excrement. So in oneiric terms, the represent the filtering of daily experiences to extract knowledge. (See EATING and EXCREMENT)

Invention ▪ If you design an invention if a dream, it reflects the need to escape from previously set guidelines. The unconscious is trying to tell you that you should inquire about, seek out, other forms of expression, of creativity, and go beyond the conventional. It also expresses your anxieties about being different and leaving behind routine.

Inventory ▪ This dream indicates the need to take a careful, detailed internal inventory of the circumstances that have shaped your personality.

Invisible ▪ This type of dream usually carries two distinct but coupled interpretations: it indicates your need to go unnoticed, or that people do not value what you do. In general, if you don't want to be seen, it means that you are afraid of society and feel insecure. (See DISAPPEARANCE and SMOKE)

❖ In ancient Greek mythology, Perseus used a blanket that gave him the power of invisibility. Oneirically speaking, this can represent the hidden spiritual strength needed to explore the unconscious.

Invitation ▪ To receive an invitation reveals a desire to start new friendships. At the same time, it also indicates that you like to follow social norms of courtesy and diplomacy. It is important to pay attention to this dream. It could be the announcement of an important commitment, either emotional or professional. On the other side, having a guest manifests the hidden part of your personality that you want to integrate into your conscious life. In the same way, a guest can represent new challenges and interests. Or, on the contrary, the dream may be calling your attention to certain circumstances that are temporary, like guests. These come, are entertaining, and then they go.

❖ According to a saying by I Ching, when one is a stranger, one cannot be brusque or tyrannical. One should, however, be careful and reserved. This way, one protects oneself from evil. This may be the advice your dream is giving you.

Iris ■ The iris represents innocence and virginity, as long as the flower is white. If it is not, it symbolizes desires.

Iron ■ While gold and mercury are associated with spirituality, this metal relates to the earth and the inferior. It symbolizes fortitude, lack of flexibility, and excessive rigor. These ideas are usually linked to violent images, in which power is acquired through physical force. (See BLACKSMITH)
❖ This dream has unfavorable omens, since iron portends stress and pain. Among the Persians, however, iron was very esteemed and, seen in dreams, promised goods and happiness.

Island ■ The island is associated with ideas of salvation and refuge, in the case that it is a pleasant dream. On the other hand, an island can become a prison because of the isolation it produces. In general, the island demonstrates a desire to flee from reality, as well as the individualism of everyone. If you are isolated on the island, you should try to analyze your feelings from other perspectives, since everything indicates that you don't count on others when making decisions. Keeping in mind that the ocean symbolizes the unconscious mind, the island can signify the desire to stay safe in the conscious Self rather than wanting to investigate your interior. The sea, according to Freud's studies, also symbolizes the mother figure. This dream, therefore, could be showing your maternal-filial relationship. If the island is swallowed by water, it may mean that you feel pressured by an overly strict mother or by the lack of control of your unconscious forces. (See ARMOR, CASTILLE, ABANDONMENT, WATER and HERMIT)
❖ In respect to this dream, oracles predict comfort and favorable circumstances.

Ivory ■ Its images is associated with a sense of strength and power, but also with the magic abilities of the amulets made from this material. It alludes to good health, requited love, and longevity. It also has sexual connotations.
❖ The esoteric interpretation of this dream also derives from its use as a talisman, according to tradition, to promise long life, health, and love.

Ivy ■ Symbol of friendship, sincere and lasting love. It is also a good omen for a change of residence or new professional position.
❖ According to popular superstition, it foretells lasting happiness and eternal love.

J

Jacket ■ This garment, symbol of the subject's personality, leads to multiple interpretations. If it is new it announces intellectual creativity; if torn, the loss of a good friend; someone else's jacket, the call for help to a friend in order to solve a problem. Wearing a military jacket denounces the tendency of the dreamer to be authoritarian and even intransigent; and if it is a physician's jacket, the need to rely more on yourself. Finally, losing them announces economic losses: business were left to chance.

Jade ■ Like all precious stones, it carries magical and spiritual symbolism. For the taoists, it represents immortality of the soul and the highest degree of perfection the spirit can attain. To see it in dreams is a sign of loyal, healthy, stable, and lasting relationships.

Jaguar ■ It is an animal with sacred and magical connotations in some native cultures of Latin America. For them, it represents power and wisdom. In general, however, seeing a jaguar in dreams indicates a dangerous situation that is difficult to escape. The dreamer is going though a moment of uncertainty and anxiety and doesn't have the means necessary to solve the problems that afflict him.

Jail ■ The dreams in which a prison appears or in which you are imprisoned allude to a limitation of your energy and creativity. They denote the need to transform your routine. They are also related to the changes that occur on the outside and cannot be reached from your prison. Therefore, images such as this one advise you to reflect on the causes of your imprisonment. Finally, these dreams express those attitudes and emotions imprisoned within yourself and that must be freed. When you see someone behind bars, it likely symbolizes that part of you that you repress.

❖ The most common superstitions say that if you have this dream one of your greatest wishes will come true. Others, surprisingly, predict marriage.

Jam ■ The jam is one of the sweet things in life. On the other hand, according to the English saying: "Jam yesterday, jam tomorrow, but never jam today," this dream may refer to the fact that you did not receive a reward for hard work and live at the expense of promises that are never going to be kept.

❖ If a woman dreams that she is making jam, she will be surrounded by friends who appreciate her.

Jar ■ Like all containers, it is a symbol of the feminine and conservation. In general, dreaming of a jar or jug can be interpreted as a call to attention for the dreamer, since the message, in this case, will deal with the need to attend to your feelings (you have "dried up" from too much activity). Depending on the liquid the jar contains, the message may vary some. (See DRINKING and CUP)

Jasmine ■ Symbolizes virtues such as friendliness and delicateness. (See FLOWERS)

Jasper ■ The image of jasper is related to fertility and, above all, the moment of giving birth. It is an important symbol of well-being for pregnant women and those who wish to be mothers.

Jaw ■ The jaw or chin are symbols of willpower. To dream you have a large jaw indicates that your determination has perhaps devolved into stubbornness. On the contrary, if the chin is abnormally small, the unconscious is reminding you of the weakness of your character.

Jealousy ■ It is likely you will experience this feeling in real life. The dream manifests all the greed that you unknowingly keep inside you. Likewise, through the unconscious, you have just recognized that you are jealous of your family and friends. These dreams are usually warnings.
❖ Oneiric oracles, in this case, warn against people wanting to argue and hidden influence from some enemies.

Jew ■ It may be that you feel attacked by prejudices around you. On the contrary, it may be you yourself who needs to learn tolerance.
❖ Jewish people are usually related with themes of loans and debts, so in this sense it could mean you must be more careful with money. If the dreamer is Jewish, this dream could refer to their faith and relationship with the rest of the community.
❖ Dreaming of a Jewish person predicts that you will prosper or win legal disputes. The Jewish proverbs themselves contain a lot of wisdom. One of them says: "Do not worry about tomorrow. You don't even know what will happen today."

Jewels ■ In many cultures, jewels represent spiritual truths. So precious stones, necklaces, or bracelets are symbols of higher wisdom. But careful! Do not fool yourself: in dreams positive attributes are inverted due to the vanity of the person who flaunts the jewels. In oneiric terms, these elements are a warning that we should not trust appearances. Behind an attractive image may lurk a deceitful or even dangerous situation. Dreaming of broken jewels expresses a clear feeling of frustration. Other interpretations believe in the sincerity of jewels. So, they represent patience, creativity,

understanding, peace, and love. Traditionally, in this sense, gold and diamonds were the incorruptible part of the being; rubies denoted passion; emeralds, fertility; and finally, sapphires, the truth.
❖ This dream augurs good luck.

Joke ■ Dreaming of teasing others is evidence of excessive seriousness of the dreamer's life and her need for fun; the funnier the joke, the more extreme her condition will be. However, if it becomes annoying, it might hide in the background a desire to hurt others with mean jokes.
❖ If the joke explained in the dream is funny, business will go full speed ahead. If it is not funny at all, business will fail.

Judge ■ The judge represents the blame and reproaches you inflict on yourself. Maybe you are afraid of being found out, or that others will realize your secret plans. The dream could be helping you make a decision, by judging the circumstances you find yourself in. Other times, judges represent society and the way it evaluates us. According to Freud, conventional morality, learned from our environment and our parents, is what judges and censures our instincts and desires.
❖ Thanks to your sharp tongue, you will make a new friend.

Jug ■ It is a container where a liquid that represents material or spiritual goods is stored. The jug's condition: full, empty, broken, or spilled, will reflect the particular situation of the dreamer in real life. (See BOTTLE)

Juggling ■ This dream tells you that you try to keep all matters in your life active and in order. Without a doubt, sometimes this means too much work. In this sense, it would be more advantageous to do things little by little.
❖ Your indecision will result in failure.

Juice ■ To dream of juice expresses the possibility of gaining leverage in the initiatives in which you participate. Everything indicates that we are at an optimal moment, although it does not signify that the things will happen without an effort. You should express your resources.

Jumping ■ If you jump up, the image symbolizes your desire to rise up and reach a better social or professional position. So, you should be more energetic and not act according to the will of others. In contrast, dreaming that you are jumping into nothing indicates that you should meditate more consciously before taking on a certain initiative, as although you dare a lot, sometimes you complicate your life by lacking of prudence. (See DIFFICULTIES and CLIMBING)

❖ According to superstition, if you stumble as you jump, you will overcome difficulties, and will eventually reach success.

Jungle ■ A jungle symbolizes the subconscious. Its animals, your most primitive and indomitable instincts. You should pay attention to the elements that appear in the oneiric scene to obtain the correct interpretation.

❖ If you are lost in the jungle, the dream foretells problems. In case you encounter the way to exit the jungle, the problems will vanish.

Junk ■ Metal waste symbolizes the failure of the material projects; therefore, to dream that you walk through a junkyard denotes conformity because you do not dare to carry out plans that would allow you to progress.

Justice ■ Its presence in your dreams signifies anxiety and worry about a situation you are experiencing. The appearance of this idea can derive from the fact that you feel treated unjustly in your waking life. You may also have the feeling that you are the one being unjust to others.

K

Karaoke ■ Being at a karaoke bar and not singing means the dreamer wants to establish more open and spontaneous relationships with others, but is too timid. On the contrary, to see yourself singing is a sign that you desire such an exaggerated starring role that you run the risk of alienating those around you from imposing your opinions. (See SINGING)

Key ■ The key symbolizes the solution to a problem. The dream may be giving you the right clue to get rid of obstacles that prevent you from progressing On the other hand, to dream that you open a door with a key implies the arrival of major changes in the your life; to use it to close a door instead reveals a fear of renewal. Breaking a key shows a breakdown of a relationship with a partner; to lose it announces delays and even failure in attaining goals. Throwing the keys away predicts that you will be involved in gossip. And finally, to have a lot of keys predicts acquiring a lot of varied knowledge.
❖ To find a key in dreams is a symbol of good luck. If you find a whole set, then business dealings will be very advantageous.

Kidneys ■ An emblem of strength, power, and physical resistance.

Kill ■ If you dream that you kill someone, it means that you are facing a serious conflict between your desires

KARAOKE

analysis of a dream

Rosa dreamed: "We were celebrating my birthday in a karaoke bar. At first I didn't want to go up to sing. I know that I'm bad at it, so I was very embarrassed to go off key and that everyone would laugh at me. But my friends insisted so much that finally I felt I had to. After all, everyone was there for me. By luck, I could chose my favorite song and I began to sing the first lines and I did it really well! People clapped enthusiastically, while I followed the lyrics on the screen. I surprised myself with my voice. I was signing a really tough Mariah Carey song and I did it better than her!"

When Rosa had this dream she was very worried about an important business meeting she had scheduled the following week. She hadn't worked at the company very long and she was worried what her bosses and colleagues would think of her. The fact that she didn't want to sing in karaoke reveals her fear of public speaking and being judged; however, her unconscious was calming her and encouraging her to do her best.

and the moral principles that you are forced to follow. This dream also reveals the unconscious attempt to suppress part of your mind you do not accept; so you may be killing some aspect of your nature you dislike. A good example of this is the case of a man who dreams of killing a woman. The real reason is probably that he wants to reject his feminine side at all cost. Such dreams must be analyzed very carefully, as they reveal the need to deepen within ourselves and find some acceptable outlet in order to avoid a violent situation. The dream could also be motivated by a feeling negative toward someone, which leads you to let off steam in a dream.

❖ There will be disputes and you will have to make sacrifices.

Kilos ■ Seeing yourself weigh something in dreams to determine its weight in kilos suggests you evaluate a situation to determine if it is really serious (heavy) or insignificant (light). To gain kilos in a dream is evidence of immaturity; especially, fear of having to face obligations when you feel unprepared for them. If you lose the weight, it means that you don't know how to defend your opinions and you find yourself subject to others' desires. (See LOSING WEIGHT or GAINING WEIGHT)

Kimono ■ Seeing yourself dressed in this garment foretells the defeat of your adversaries through hard, constant work. It also shows that it is the ideal moment to start an emotional relationship. If it is someone else that wears the kimono, you should be alerted to someone in your environment who, under the appearance of seduction, wants to trick you.

King ■ The king symbolizes, in an abstract sense, the universal and archetypal man. As such, it has magical and supernatural powers. It also expresses the guiding principle, supreme conscience, the virtue of a judge, and self-control. On the other hand, the coronation means accomplishment, victory, and culmination. From here man can be named kind in the culminating instants of his existence. If the dreamer is young, the king could represent his father or another similar figure; on the contrary, for an adult, it corresponds to the dreamer. In this case, the dream could announce that you are reaching maturity, or professional success. Carl Jung used the strange and symbolic language of the alchemists for many of his interpretations. In this sense, the king is the personification of work. Its appearance in dreams, on the other hand, could have diverse meanings. If he is sick, it represents out of place attitudes and sometimes conflicts between reason and instinct; if he is decrepit, it signifies a limited conscience; and if he

fades or comes with his mother, it is the return to the subconscious.

Kiosk ■ To be able to interpret this dream it is essential to remember if you were buying or selling at the kiosk and what type of wares were for sale. Was it a conventional kiosk of newspapers and magazines? Or was it one of those kiosks that sells candies and sweets? If you focused your attention on the titles of the papers, the dream could be signaling your need to know more about something that worries you. On the contrary, if you bought comics or candies, the dream reflects nostalgia for your childhood.

❖ Dreaming of a kiosk announces the arrival of events that will obligate you to make serious decisions that will radically change your life.

Kissing ■ Kissing symbolizes a reconciliation with the person receiving this affectionate gesture. The dream shows the attachment you feel for that person; perhaps it is a repressed attraction in real life. Likewise, this kind of dream may come from guilt caused by your minimal affection for someone. Although it might be a sexual dream, kisses, as we said, are identified more with love and how you offer it to others. However, they also have other negative connotations, such as the kiss of death or the kiss of betrayal. In this sense, the dream is showing your innermost feelings.

❖ For gypsy tradition, kissing predicts that a dispute will soon come to an end.

Kitchen ■ The food prepared in the kitchen is the spiritual food you offer to your own body.

❖ If the kitchen is clean and tidy, this dream portends harmony and understanding within the family.

Knees ■ Dreaming that you are crawling in front of someone is a sign of submission. It also reflects a feeling of inferiority. Generally, knees symbolize the social position of the dreamer. (See LEGS)

❖ Dreaming of knees is an omen of misfortune. Further, if they hurt it foretells terrible calamity.

Knife ■ To fight with a knife portends a possible conflict related to your ideals. It represents a cut, wound, or violent break, probably by betrayal.

■ Symbol associated with the ideas of revenge and death, but also sacrifice. The blade's sharpness points to the primary character of the person who is holding the knife. Similarly, the length of the blade shows the

KNIFE

Veronica dreamed: "I was walking quietly down the street, confident and calm, when suddenly a mugger appeared in front of me with a knife in his hand. He told me to give him my bag if I didn't want him to use the weapon. I reacted immediately grabbing his hand, but his fingers became sharp knives. Although I was very scared, I grabbed his other hand and shouted: 'No!' The robber disappeared."

When Veronica had this dream she was going through a **difficult time at work**; they had just transferred her to another department. She felt insecure and thought she would not be able to perform her new role. In addition, her new boss did not seem very happy with her. The knife, or any sharp tool, indicates a possible conflict related to our **self-worth**. The dream was warning Veronica of the difficulties she would have to face to defend her territory. However, her attitude in the dream was telling her that she had the ability and strength to overcome it. Far from giving in, Veronica worked hard to earn everyone's trust. Months later, her boss recognized her worth with a promotion.

spiritual stature of its possessor. If you use it against something or someone you should inquire within yourself what makes you too worried or upset that you resort to violence. Knives are also considered masculine sexual symbols. (See DAGGER).

❖ It is said that dreaming of a kitchen knife reports good luck. Any other type of knife warns against possible dangers ahead.

Knight ■ The man on the horse is symbol of the virtues that have mastered instincts and passions. It is interpreted as a sense of accomplishment and pride. The dreamer has made progress on the path of spiritual growth.

Knot ■ Knots in a dream means you are subjected to some form of tether, i.e., any impairment that is delaying or limiting your projects. You are tied to the circumstances, prisoners of the environment. You feel coerced and lack enthusiasm, which limits your creativity. According to other interpretations, the knots represent the problems we are trying to solve. Furthermore, they can also symbolize the union of two people or the feminine and masculine aspects of our personality.

❖ The popular superstition has always associated knots with problems. For example, at a wedding, the bride should wear a shoe lace loose to scare off witches who want to "untie" her virginity. Similarly, in Scotland, it is believed that the body of a deceased person may not be placed in the coffin if there are any lumps in their clothes. This would prevent their spirit from resting in peace. In oneiric terms, this dream portends that you will run into issues that will trigger anxiety.

❖ To help the knight into the saddle is a promise of happiness. But if he is getting off the horse it predicts you will lose a friend. The medieval knight is a symbol of love affairs.

L

Labor ▪ If you rebuild the house you live in with your own hands, it means you need to undergo a deep reconstruction. This dream is revealing the need for a change of environment, of reality. (See CONSTRUCTION)

Labor (giving birth) ▪ To dream of labor indicates, in most cases, that you have a great desire to be a parent. But, at the same time, it could also suggest the "deliver" of a project or business that has been gestating for some time. The common denominator in these dreams is the effort and suffering that precedes any birth.
❖ A fast and easy birth is indicative of prosperity and happiness. If it is complicated, this is a warning that difficult times draw near.

Laboratory ▪ Being in one signals a lack of initiative to seek solutions and the consequent need to ask others for help. If you are an alchemist, you will find yourself involved in ambitious projects that will not bring economic gain. In this sense, the image of the laboratory could also refer to the transformation of being. Additionally, in many cases, it is related to psychological experimentation and new forms of facing the world. Perhaps you need to try new ideas and attitudes. The type of experiment you do in a dream is obviously important and can offer other symbols to interpret.
❖ Superstition says that this dream foretells an episode of ill health.

Labyrinth ▪ The labyrinth represents obsessions without solution and vicious circles that often weigh us down. If you dream of this figure, it means that you have doubts and indecision. It could be a reference to lack of experience or immaturity. If you manage to escape the labyrinth, maybe you will resolve your problems. In the case that someone accompanies you in searching for the exit, the dream warns that you must be careful of your alliances. If you rescue others from the labyrinth, the dream is positive and means you are in control of your life.
❖ In mythology the labyrinth is a place of transformation where destructive tendencies of nature are overcome. A classic example of this is the myth in which Theseus and Ariadne emerge victorious from the labyrinth of the minotaur.

Lace ▪ Given that this is a labor of care and attention, it can be interpreted as a desire to reward patience. Overall it is a positive dream. However, it can also be a warning that you focus too much on minor details. As symbol of beauty and transparency it is associated with certain sexually provocative clothing; this dream may also be reminding the dreamer of her desire to be more sexy or her concern for attracting her partner's attention in some way.

Lake ▪ The water of a lake symbolizes life, because its calm flow and natural movement links to our future. In contrast, the waters of a reservoir represent diseases since their violent movements are the result of artificial construction. In oneiric terms, the lake is a manifestation of the state that is our unconscious: if its waters are calm, it is a sign of inner peace; if, however, they are agitated, it indicates emotional disorders If vegetation covers its shore, the dream manifests inner wealth, creativity, and emotional satisfaction; however, if the banks are dry and rocky, an emotional disorder is evident. Finally, to fish in the lake demonstrates a desire to find companionship or a partner. If we see ourselves reflected in its waters, the meaning of the dream changes completely, perhaps reflecting a narcissistic attitude. (See WATER, STREAM, MIRROR, and FOUNTAIN)

❖ In Japanese Zen Buddhism, the lake is a symbol of the mind. If the surface is moving, you cannot see the reflection of the moon. However, if the water is calm, the moon appears. Similarly, the mind must be calm to perceive spiritual enlightenment.

Lamb ■ The lamb expresses purity, innocence, and gentleness: your true self. All these attributes are positive but the lamb may also represent ignorance and blindness.

❖ The sacrifice of the Lamb of God takes away the sin of the world. In psychological terms, it represents the desire for forgiveness.

Lame ■ Dreaming that you are lame means that something is holding you back and is preventing you from achieving your purposes, or that your plans will suffer delays.

Lamentations ■ Hearing complaints and lamentations in your dreams can be a reflection of a real life situation. It is possible that the dreamer is going through a repressed period of profound sadness and mourning and the cries he hears are the ones he would like to utter. If this is not the case, the cause of the cries is a feeling of guilt that manifests in the dream.

Lamp ■ Symbol of knowledge and study. The appearance of a lamp in dreams indicates that you have a lot of inspiration and a wealth of good ideas. Depending on how much light the lamp gives off, it will show your degree of motivation to learn and grow personally. Thus, if the light is dim, it shows that your performance is minimum. You are not using your resources appropriately. You let yourself be dominated by the unwillingness and laziness. (See LIGHT)

❖ In Tarot, the Hermit card is represented by a wise old man carrying a lamp. As in dreams, he warns that everyone should carry their own spiritual light.

Lance ■ A symbol of war and a sexual icon. To dream that you attack others with a spear indicates that you use the force of your arguments to attack others. Your intransigence towards that which you dislike is causing problems. But if you dream that you are wounded with a spear, it means that you continually seek confrontation.

❖ The spear in a dream makes one fear its contents. To carry it indicates security; to break it, an unsuccessful job.

Land ■ Dreams associated with land, like those in which you find yourself lying on the ground, show that you should be more realistic. In this sense, it is preferable that you adhere to the issues that directly concern you and that you leave whims aside. On the other hand, land is a tangible manifestation of your will. So, dreaming that you are covered in dirt signifies that you have a mission to accomplish. On the contrary, cultivating the land indicates that you should work hard so as to finish a project. In the case that the land on which you are working is dry, it means that you lack strength and enthusiasm. If you dream of planet Earth, it could mean that your true self is not yet fully realized.

❖ Mother Earth represents the subconscious mind. She is the uterus that contains the potential for the development of the future. The myths about the descent into the inside of the earth are allegories that describe the exploration of you hidden and unknown side. If the appearance of mother earth is fearful, it is possible that you are afraid that the forces of the subconscious will put your life in disorder. Mother Earth, herself, was the antique symbol of fertility. Dreaming of a sterile land generally announces that you should plan some seeds if you want to preserve your future.

Landing ■ Dreaming that you land in a plane indicates that your conflicts or fantasies begin to appear in real life. If landing is not completed it is because you think too much about the problems that concern you. On the contrary, if the plane successfully lands after falling out of control, it means you are facing a huge conflict that you are capable of solving after all.

Landscape ■ The landscapes of dreams are symbolic scenarios in which each and every one of the elements that comprise it should be considered. For example, for a person overwhelmed by financial problems, a mountain ridge can mean a profit chart and economic losses. Now, to understand the symbolic meaning of a landscape you must distinguish the predominant features from the minor ones. So, when an element reigns above all others and unifies them (sea, desert, etc.), you must interpret the dream in terms of this main component. But if, instead, the landscape offers variety and balance of different elements, then it must be analyzed as if it were a painting, paying attention to the shapes of objects (flat, pointed, round, etc.) and the colors that stand out.

Lantern ▪ See LAMP and LIGHT

Lasso ▪ The meaning of the symbol varies depending on the type of lasso. If decorative ones appear in your dream, you are probably in a moment when you need others to show you affection and tenderness. Your emotions are going through a fragile stage and you are not very sure of what you feel. You also don't know how others feel about you. That is why you seek security in expressions of affection If a lasso is around your neck, preventing you from breathing normally, it means that you are immersed in a stressful process that may make you lose your nerve. You

L A U G H I N G

analysis of the dream

Joaquín dreamed: "It was a dream that I have very often. I explain a funny joke and begin to laugh alone without stopping. I am surprised by my ingenious and sense of humor and I take joy in it. Hahahaha . . . I am so funny! Then I wake up dying of laughter, wanting to share it with someone. Hours later when I think about it to tell it to a friend, it seems like senseless nonsense."

Dreams of humor rarely make sense in the light of day. However, waking up laughing is one of the most pleasurable sensations that the subconscious can give us. In Joaquín's case, these dreams served **to relax the daily tension** that he dealt with. As an air traffic controller, Joaquin worked under a lot of pressure, in which a sense of humor or distraction had no place. In the dream world, his subconscious displayed **his fun and humorous side** in compensation. When Joaquin has these dreams he wakes up happy and optimistic, facing his work day with less tension.

feel threatened by a danger that others don't seem to consider very serious.

Last ▪ Seeing yourself in the last spot of any kind of event denotes that in your working environment, your opinions are not listened to, and that you are not valued enough.

Laughing ▪ Waking up laughing from a dream, or remembering a dream image in which you laugh unworriedly, is one of the most pleasurable sensation that the subconscious gives. Almost always it is a mechanism of compensation for moments of stress and anxiety. It could also be a reflection of your god sense of humor and mood in real life. Without a doubt, this dream lets you start the day with more optimism and happiness. When another is laughing at you it is possible that a part of your personality reproves your behavior when you are awake. It is also a sign of the fear of making a fool of oneself.

Laurel ▪ Laurel is a beautiful, fragrant plant with therapeutic virtues, and mystically related to medicine, glory, and loneliness. In dreams it represent the possibility of finding something that orients you in your matters, given that laurel is the symbol of triumph. (See GLORY) ❖ To see it or to adorn yourself with laurel promises abundance and success. If the drams is a man, it is an omen of marriage.

Lava ▪ This dream reveals a state of great passion. If the lava is white hot, it denotes uncontrollable violence. If it is cooled, it indicates a moment of calm and serenity that comes after strong storms.

Lawn ▪ It is a symbol of hope. If it is a grass field, your purpose will have many chances to be reciprocated.

Lawyer ▪ Dreaming of trials in which lawyers are present or hiring one of these professionals to solve a problem is a sign of insecurity. The oneiric thoughts of this type indicate a lack of confidence in a situation, as there are aspects of it that you do not foresee clearly. It is a matter, therefore, of reconsidering your plans and the way you implement them. If the lawyer happily solves the problems there are great possibilities of finding help in order to achieve your goals.

Laying down ▪ The dreams in which you lay down in bed indicate a period of uncertainty or waiting regarding problems that you do not feel able to cope with without help. If you are lying down outdoors, something that is causing you suffering is nothing more than a passing concern, not as serious as you originally thought. If you are sharing your bed with a person of the same sex, in addition to the aforementioned uncertainty, this reflects a concern about what others might think of you. Conversely, if it is a person of the opposite sex, chances are the problems will be solved soon.

Leading ▪ To dream that you lead something shows that you are taking control of certain facets of your life. For example, if you walk a dog in the dream, it may be a reference to your sexual nature. If you are led by someone, you must ask yourself what psychological principles you are following, and if they are leading down a good path.
❖ The dream could represent your desires. In this sense, Eastern tradition says that a person controlled by his anxieties will never be happy. This saying comes from those who know how to direct themselves and limit their ambitions.

Leaf ▪ When they are green, they symbolize prosperity. When they are dry, however, they may announce problems and illnesses.
❖ Leaves that fall predict melancholy.

Leaks ▪ Dreaming of a leaky house is a clear indication that your emotions get out of control easily and that you do not take enough care of them. Conclusion: you should not put emergency "patches" on your relationship, but rather strive to build your feelings on more solid foundations. In short, leaks reveal lack of attention to our emotions.

Leather ▪ It is a noble material that symbolizes protection and welfare. They are, usually, positive dreams, unless the dreamer sees a torn and dirty leather, or if a prized piece of leather disappears.

Leeches ▪ This dream represents people or external agents that drain your vital resources. It tends to cause anguish, as the dreamer sees himself being drained. Being able to pull out or eliminate the leeches is indicative of a feeling of security and confidence in oneself, despite the adversity of the circumstances that are presented in life.

Left ▪ The right hemisphere of the brain controls the left side of the body. It represents our instinctive, artistic, and intuitive side.

❖ An ancient belief says that the Devil appears to the left of people to tempt them.

Legs ▪ Legs represent movement. In another, more metaphysical plane, they are also related to the ability to recover from misfortune. Legs symbolize, equally, the support of the body, that is, of your life: plans, goals, projects, etc. If in the dream you see yourself without your lower extremities, it is a sign that you have little confidence in your possibilities when it comes time to take on any venture. On the contrary, to see yourself with strong legs denotes confidence in yourself.
❖ According to the traditional interpretation, if in the dream you have a wooden leg, it predicts new concerns. Fortunately, this dream is very uncommon.

Legume ▪ As an image of the simplicity of homemade food, legumes show the dreamer a serene and uncomplicated life. This will only be clouded in some moments by minor problems. However, legumes have a negative meaning if they are sown, since this announces tension and arguments in the heart of the family.

Lemon ▪ This dream urges you to continue forward despite difficulties, since you can still learn from unpleasant and bitter events if you know how to juice them.
❖ The sour taste of its juice and the roughness of its peel make this a symbol of betrayal, deception, and bitterness. To drink a refreshing lemonade is an omen of success and unexpected earnings.

Leopard ▪ Although it's meaning is similar to beasts that signify immediate danger, the leopard is also a symbol of pride, skill, and strength. And, more than an external situation, it indicates aspects of the dreamer's personality that the dream manifests.
❖ In esoteric terms, the leopard is an omen of good luck followed by misfortune.

Lethargy ▪ To see yourself being lethargic can have two interpretations. If it causes you stress, it is a sign of anxiety. You feel the need to get moving, but you can't, whether it is because of external factors or your own inability. If the lethargy is pleasant, it could be an unconscious way to compensate for a stressful or exhausting state you are subject to in real life.

Letter (character) ▪ If you are writing letters in a dream, it indicates the need to clarify certain situations;

this images can suggest the need to give explanations. (See WRITING and READING)

Letter (communication) ▪ This dream shows the desire to hear from someone or to change your current situation. You need either a new opportunity or a new challenge. If by reading it a pleasant feeling comes up, then your future is protected; if it produces anxiety, it may indicate that you need to take things more positively. If the letter is from a friend, you need support; if it comes from a company or institution, you crave changing your job; however, if you dream that you do not receive letters, it should encourage you to get in touch with your loved ones. It could be that they are requiring your help. The letter could also come from your unconscious that tries to give you a message about your behavior or circumstances. It is important that you pay attention to it.
❖ For some superstitions, dreaming of a letter portends unexpected news. For others, it predicts a close marriage.

Lever ▪ In the masonic religion, the lever is a tool that symbolizes knowledge and technical mastery. It alludes to the need or ability to use a mechanism to solve a certain problem.

Library ▪ Symbol of knowledge and experience, so you must pay attention to the aspect offered in your dreams. Thus, an empty library means that you have to learn in order to attain your goals. If it is your own library, it suggests the need to rely on what you had already acquired. If it is someone else's, it is indicating the convenience of being informed or further studying the issue that concerns you today. The library of your dreams also represents the world of ideas created within the self. If people in the library are talking or if you have trouble finding a particular book, the dream suggests that you should concentrate more.
❖ According to some beliefs, this dream portends you will disappoint your friends.

Lice ▪ They represent everything that is unpleasant and that feels too close, as if it were an invasion of your space. They are associated with those people that you are tied to by strong family bonds against your will.

Licking ▪ Apart from the sexual and sensual connotations that this dream can have, being licked by an animal indicates a state of well-being, comfort, and satisfaction in your relationships with those closest to you. If the situation is extremely unpleasant, then the dream may reflect the fear of having your personal space invaded.

Lie ▪ This dream reveals a sense of mistrust and insecurity in real life. Whether it is you who is lying, or you are talking to someone you know is lying, this dream is not at all positive. You should carefully analyze the dream sequence in order to reach its correct interpretation. Moreover, to find a solution, you must also take into account the particular situation you are involved in in real life. It may be useful to remember that we never lie without reason.

Light ▪ Light has traditionally been identified with the spirit. It symbolizes knowledge, inspiration, and intuition. For this reason, if your dreams are luminous, it means you posses great self confidence. However, if they are dark, it reveals the presence of feelings of insecurity and low self esteem. To turn on a light in darkness augurs that you will discover a secret. Finally, you must pay attention to the different forms of light, since the reading depends on it. So, the rainbow represents hope; the sun, happiness; and the moon, the guide that comes from your most hidden unconscious self. (See YELLOW, CLARITY, and LAMP)
❖ The light you see in dreams can have a great spiritual importance. It may deal with a journey toward enlightenment, or an experience in the interior, similar to those the mystics had. In many cases, it has a religious meaning. Christ is often called "the light of the world" and, regarding the Buddha's nirvana, they say it is "unlimited light." Equally, the teachings of yoga describe "the light of ten thousand suns."

Lighthouse ▪ It announces aid, a guiding light, and the beginning of a new cycle in life. It saves you from the stormy journey through the unconscious. It is a positive dream because it symbolizes rebirth. It may be caused by someone who has given you hope and has revealed something important to you. Because of its phallic shape, Freudianism identifies it with masculine genitalia.
❖ To a sailor, seeing a lighthouse forecasts a peaceful sea and prosperous voyage. To an ill person, quick recovery and lasting health. Missing the lighthouse in a storm or bad conditions indicates setbacks at the time it seemed everything was finally improving.

Lightness ▪ To dream that you feel very light signifies that you want to elevate yourself spiritually, that you aspire to a better life. Although it may also indicate a lack of conviction in your relationships. (See DANCING, SMOKE, and INCENSE)

Lightning ▪ Symbolizes creative and destructive strength of the divine. It indicates a potent flux of energy that could be beneficial if linked to water, or devastating if it strikes someone in its path. The image of lightning is associated with that of the storm, the violent force of rain and wind that parallely destroy, impregnate, and purify. It manifests a difficult and turbulent moment that overcomes the calm. It is possible that you have been surprised by the circumstances. On the other hand, lightning can destroy, but it can also show its great brilliance and illumination. In this case, it could represent the ideas and inspiration that you have. Also, lightning suggests that that forces that control your life will be under your control.
❖ Even in the most ancient mythological stories gods of thunder and lightning appeared. It is believed that their origin is the divinities of the neolithic man. Like many other prominent symbols from archaic myths, lightning possesses sexual connotations. When lightning fills the sky, it represents Mother Earth being impregnated by the gods of the sky.

Lightning rod ▪ This dream warns you that you must be prudent to avoid disasters.

Linden tree ▪ Represents tranquility, serenity, friendship, and tenderness.

Line ▪ Waiting in a line has several interpretations. On one hand, it is a sign of impatience. On the other, it indicates the discomfort of being in a group of anonymous people without standing out in it. In that case, the dream reflects your desire to differentiate yourself from the rest. This can be interpreted as either an inferiority complex, or as a desire to excel.

Lintel ▪ It is the part that holds the wall over an opening (door or window), and thus prevents the weight of the building from falling upon you. If you see a strong and well established lintel, you feel safe from the environment. If the lintel presents danger of breaking it may mean you are afraid of problems you cannot solve on your own and that are caused by external factors.

Lion ▪ The lion is, as "king of beasts," the terrestrial opponent of the eagle in the sky. Because of its wildness, according to Jung, it represents the latent passions and may appear as a signal of the danger of being devoured by the unconscious. In oneiric terms, the lion embodies power, pride, and justice, but often appears as a tyrannical being, cruel and insatiable. It could stand in for a father, teacher, judge, or boss. Therefore, depending on their behavior, the dream will be positive or negative. We frequently dream about fighting this animal to his death. This scene represents triumph over the world; if the lion is threatening, you are victim of your own instincts and passions, whereas if you face it and conquer it, you will reach your goal. To dream of a family of lions promises joy and good family relationships (See AUTHORITY and TAMING)
❖ Pride, generosity, and ambition are the characteristics of the fifth sign of the zodiac: a sign of fire, solar, masculine, king by vocation and actor in each stage of life. According to astrology, the sign of Leo likes to be the center of attention; so perhaps your dream is warning you that you are too self-centered and narcissistic. In the Tarot, the Lion card symbolizes strength that can be controlled by the sweetness (the figure of a woman dressed in white).

Lips ▪ The meaning of this dream varies depending on the appearance of the lips. Badly shaped lips signal tense relationships with friends; big and beautiful ones, happiness and harmony with your partner; thin ones, bad temper and intolerance; thick ones, honor; and drooping ones, the failure of projects. (See MOUTH)

Liquor ▪ This expresses a desire for freedom and inhibition, such as the need to overcome shyness. It also represents a weakness of character and emotional dissatisfaction.

Liver ▪ The liver of a person symbolizes the two sides of the coin: joy and pain. What happens to the liver in the dream indicates the contingencies these two antagonistic concepts are subject to.
❖ If it belongs to a horned animal, the liver is an omen of success, employment, and dignity.

Living room ▪ When the entirety of the dream develops in your house, especially in the living room, it could point at the need to reunite more with your loved ones. As busy a you are, you will have to try not to lose sight of your family and friends, whose company is the basis for enjoying a balanced life.

Lizard ■ This is an animal whose image is loaded with symbolism. In ancient cultures it was considered sacred, since it was a representation of the soul that seeks the light. From the investigations of Freud, it is considered to have sexual connotations and is associated with the penis (because of its mobility and elongated form).

Load ■ Carrying a heavy load is a clear sign of fatigue. The dreamer feels physically, mentally, or emotionally overwhelmed. Your unconscious is warning that you need to rest.

Loan ■ The cause of this dream can be your economic worries in real life. However, it may also suggest that you rely too much on your emotional resources. Maybe you are in a time when your basic need is that your friends give you some help and support.
❖ According to a strange, old English superstition, dreaming that you pay a loan while laughing portends good luck.

Lock ■ This dream indicates the existence of a problem, a change of situation, or dilemma. If you are able to open the lock and move on, the response will be positive, but if not it will be negative. If you force the lock it means that you will try to achieve your goals using any strategy, whether lawful or not. (See DOOR and THRESHOLD)

Locks (of hair) ■ Although it usually refers to a vanity item, it symbolizes the superior force of will and knowledge. For this reason, when you have long and healthy hair in a dream, the image indicates that you are able to succeed. By contrast, if it falls or if it is cut, the image reflects fear and insecurity; it predicts loss of prestige and power. However, to get a haircut voluntarily indicates liberation, renunciation, and sacrifice. In the event that you shave your head, it means you reject all earthly matters in the pursuit of purity of spirit. And regarding the vanity aspect mentioned, dreaming that someone combs your hair expresses you are too concerned about your external image. If in your dream, you have your hair loose to the wind, it indicates that you need more freedom to express your feelings. Body hair, meanwhile, symbolizes the primitive and instinctive force.

❖ To get a haircut can show conformity. In the past, they used to cut the hair of prisoners, soldiers, and school boys. When the Beatles grew their hair long back in the sixties, they unconsciously expressed a generational revelation.

Losing ■ To dream of the loss of an object denotes repression, shyness, an inferiority complex, shame, and ultimately fear. The sense of loss is linked to guilt. Also, you should ask yourself what the misplaced object means to you. If it is you who is lost, it symbolizes the beginning of a new life phase and expresses your nervousness about leaving behind what has so far been familiar. However, this meaning may be the reverse: in reality you do not know which direction to take. In such moments of utter confusion, it is advisable to go along setting small goals and gradually achieving them.
❖ Losing something cautions that you may be cut with a sharp object by accident.

Losing weight ■ The symbolism is similar to CLARIFICATION, given its allusion to purification, discarding all that is waste or negative. Also, depending on the particular case, it represents the desire to lose weight. A dream in which you dramatically lose weight may signal some physical ailment.
❖ Seeing yourself too thin in dreams is a sad omen of legal scandals.

Lottery ■ Dreams in which the lottery appears, unfortunately, are not premonitory. That is, if you dream about it, it doesn't mean that you will guess the winning number. However, the dream is positive, because dreaming you win the jackpot shows great confidence in your life and in the goals you have set. If, however, you dream that you are betting your wealth on a game of chance, it means that you behave as if chance will solve your problems. Your unconscious is warning you that it is a mistake to wait for conflicts to be resolved by themselves. (See GAME, CARD, and ROULETTE)
❖ According to many superstitions, the omens in this dream are unfavorable.

Lotus ■ The lotus flower is full of spiritual and physical symbolism. For some ancient cultures, it meant spiritual purity that remained immaculate in stagnant waters. But it also has sensual and sexual connotations. It is related to harmony in life with a partner, and with fecundity.

Love ■ For a correct interpretation of the dream you must first consider who it was who loved you, and at the same time, who was the object of your love. Overall, love in dreams represents the desire to achieve an idealized relationship that is difficult to achieve. Although it can also be a reminder for you to pay more attention to your partner, thus avoiding neglect of that person's love.

❖ From the oneiric point of view, to dream that you are loved and blessed augurs hardship. Instead, to dream that you are often disgraced or rejected often implies happy days.

Luggage ■ Our symbolic baggage is nothing but the material we consider essential to "travel" through life. For this reason, losing your luggage is evidence of the inability to perform what you intend, because of lack of resources, or knowledge, or skills. If it is too heavy and you can hardly move it, the dream indicates that you need to make concessions and revise your values. If you give your luggage to someone the dream can express your desire to get rid of certain responsibilities.

❖ Sometimes you carry too many material possessions, desires, concerns, and needs. This weight is delaying your spiritual progress. The lighter this luggage the more pleasant your life journey will be.

Lust ■ Lustful dreams are, almost always, a reflection of repressed sexual desires. The unconscious generates a mechanism of compensation that is set off by a lack of real sexual relationships or unsatisfactory ones.

M

Machine ▪ From the earliest times, machines were compared with the human body; therefore, when one appears in dreams, it may be referring to your physical well-being, especially if the machine malfunctions, is broken, or needs some kind of maintenance or repair. Therefore, if you dream of machines, you can interpret these images as a report of the state of your body and mind. The way they work will let you know how your health is. The fuel of the machine can symbolize your sexual energy or power. If the dreamer is driving the machine, it probably alludes to their ability to function in life and deal with problems. The meaning of each machine depends on the elements that compose it and the pace at which it moves.

Machine gun ▪ If you are using a machine gun in dreams, it means you must respond quickly and with certainty to situations as they arise in real life. However, you must ensure that this aggressiveness not come back on you when dealing with others. If the weapon gets jammed or you lose control over it, your plans will fail despite the effort invested.

Madness ▪ Dreams that talk about the madness of the protagonist are not very frequent. If this occurs, it may be an unconscious warning about your inappropriate behavior. The cause is surely the desire to stand out or be different than others, tired of the daily grind. On the other hand, dreaming that someone else is not sane reveals a serious concern. It may manifest a dangerous situation related to your finances or your family that has you very worried. This dream also warns you to care for your health.

❖ If we dream that we chance upon a lunatic, good fortune is assured. According to some oracles, it predicts that we meet someone who will positively influence our lives and make us prosper.

Mafia ▪ This image reveals that you are restricted by one or more persons who prevent the spontaneous manifestation of your personality in real life. This dream is a warning sign not to end up a puppet to others' wishes.

Magic ▪ To visualize that you are performing a magic trick is a sign that you have reached the limit of rational possibilities and you don't know how to face the difficult circumstances around you. The "enhancement" of the magic makes you believe you can solve your problems easily.

Magnet ▪ Symbolizes a mysterious attraction that goes beyond the dreamer's willpower. It almost always refers to physical attraction between two people, which can be fascinating as well as dangerous. This dream sometimes is interpreted as a call for precaution.

Magpie ▪ This dream foretells theft, jealousy, and rumors, which are the results of this bad omen.

Makeup ■ Dreams in which you are applying makeup indicate that you do not feel comfortable with your personality and, therefore, you need to change your ways in order to become successful. Putting on mask can be useful to protect yourself from others, but this attitude often hides your true personality. If the makeup is very exaggerated (garish and artificial colors), the dream also indicates that you try to draw attention ostentatiously, and may be living beyond your means. (See MASK)

Man ■ If he is an acquaintance or family member, the dream is limited to revealing the feelings that join you with him. But if it is a stranger, the interpretation depends on his appearance. A young man augurs problems and disputes (regardless of the sex of the dreamer), while an old man suggests you will receive protection and advice from a friend. According to Jung, if a woman dreams that she is a man, this represents the rational, competitive, and aggressive side of her personality.
❖ If the man is handsome, everything will go well, you may even become rich. If he is very ugly, you should be cautious because you could have problems with your friendships.

Mandarin ■ Dreams in which sweet, juicy fruits appear almost always allude to sensuality and pleasure. The could be compensation mechanisms of the unconscious, or literal reflections of a situation of well-being in real life.

Maneuver ■ Manifests a compromising position in the life of the dreamer. He sees the need to change his approach or attitude unexpectedly in order to achieve what is proposed, or to get out of an adverse circumstance.

Mannequin ■ The vision of a mannequin points to the dissatisfaction felt by the sleeper with his social status. This position will soon be able to change if you take advantage of the opportunities that are presented.

Manure ■ Manure is a fertilizer that is used to enrich farmland. This dream, therefore, reminds you that you have a lot of creativity and must use it to the fullest. This does not mean absence of difficulties in the way (unpleasant odor) before getting the long-awaited triumph. As other feces, in general, manure indicates abundance because it is similar to wealth and gold. (See FECES)

❖ For the farmer dreaming of manure is a good omen. But if she dreams about sleeping on top of it that is an omen of dishonor and misery.

Map ■ The map means that you have lost sight of north. You want a change of scenery and circumstances; you have no direction, you are not satisfied with your current situation. This dream shows the need to meditate at length in order to redirect your life in a way that that better fits your personality.

Marble ■ The presence of marble in a dream predicts that all your efforts to progress will soon be rewarded. If the marble is in the quarry, you will succeed in the professional arena, but your emotional relationships will be brief and superficial. In contrast, if the marble appears polished, you will have a strong and deep romantic relationship, but you must fight the fear that it will fail.
❖ Some interpretations also consider the color, and considered black marble a symbol of pain; and white, of wealth and fortune.

Marjoram ■ As with most aromatic herbs, marjoram is a symbol of solace and slow but careful recovery. It may represent a state of convalescence. It is your path between a difficult situation you have just left and the complete recovery of your strengths and abilities.

Market ■ To dream that you shop in a market means that you have many resources that you do not take advantage of. You must value yourself more, since you enjoy great untapped potential. The dream can also have a deeper origin: the need to externalize your talent, your most elevated desires. But careful: the market offers the possibility of acquiring the essential and, very often, you leave with superfluous things that divert your interest and can increase your confusion. That which is sold in the market will clarify the theme of the dream. Antiques represent the past; fruits and vegetables show your ability to grow internally; cheap stuff tends to express that you underestimate your talents. (See LABYRINTH)
❖ According to popular superstition, this dream denotes frugality. For a young woman, it means changes.

Marmot ■ This animal symbolizes sleep, passivity, and laziness. However, it also is a sign of patience in the face of adversity.

Marriage ■ This not only symbolizes the emotional union of the protagonist with another person, but also internal balance between the masculine and feminine polarity. Additionally, the dream could represent the relationship you maintain between your brain hemispheres (that is, that which governs intuition and that which governs analytical reason). Despite all this, this type of image reveals inner conflicts that affect the personality. "Literal" dreams about conjugal life tend to evolve throughout your life: first they tend to reflect the desire to find a soulmate; then, when the wedding is approaching, elements linked to compromise appear; later, dreams refer to a common project based on mutual love and respect. (See WEDDING)

Mask ■ To dream that you disguise yourself with a mask reveals that you do not feel comfortable with your personality. Consequently, you hide behind an artificial element to become successful. Although the mask may protect you from others, this attitude leaves your true self on a lower plane. You must ask yourself why you put it on. It is necessary to gather your courage to be who you really are.
❖ According to Arab tradition, he who has a pure soul will never be disappointed by his dreams. Otherwise, it will means that we are fooling ourselves.

Mass ■ To listen to a mass in a dream reveals the arrival of a period of peace and harmony for the dreamer. To celebrate it indicates the ability of the protagonist to give moral and material support to the most needy.

Massage ■ Dreaming that you give or receive a massage can have sexual and emotional connotations. In general, it signifies shortcomings in the dreamer's life. Oneiric massage therefore develops within a system of self-compensation. However, it may also warn you of a disease that has not yet become evident. If the dream repeats frequently, you should be alert to possible health problems. The correct interpretation of this dream depends on the circumstances of the dreamer in real life and the analysis of all elements and events that occur in it.

Maw ■ It is a dream that denotes fear and aggression. Being in front of a beast's jaws indicates fear of a situation that is out of control. It can be interpreted as an alarm, a call from the unconscious to be cautious.

Meat ■ It is a symbol of passion and force that has different meanings depending on the culture or religion to which you belong. The condition of the meat and the action of eating or rejecting it will be crucial for the correct interpretation of the dream. It can be both positive and negative.

Mechanic ■ To dream that you take your car to the mechanic manifests the need for help to solve a practical problem. Although the dreamer is not able to solve the problem by their own means, the fact of having to ask for help does not generate stress or guilt. The image of the mechanic is sometimes associated with the doctor. There may be an undiagnosed illness.

Medal ■ Just like the DIPLOMA, the medal is a symbol of distinction and recognition. It's appearance in a dream can be interpreted as a feeling of satisfaction for having completed a task, or the need to receive a reward that was unfairly denied. The interpretation depends on the feelings awake in you and the circumstances developing in real life.
❖ To receive a medal as a reward announces love; to wear it is an omen of endeavors that end well.

Medicine ■ To see or take medications is usually a positive dream that manifests an adverse situation and, at the same time, the intention of using some mechanism to get out of it. If the dreamer gives medicine to another person, the dream indicates her desire to help someone around her or to give them knowledge.

Melon ■ This fruit announces, in general, illness and strained relationships with your surroundings. To eat it warns that acting foolishly creates problems in the long run; to see it planted advises that the current problems will eventually bring benefits.
❖ To dream of eating a melon portends healing if you are sick.

Melting ■ This dream sometimes refers to those bad habits and attitudes that will cease to be so after they fade. If snow is melting it shows that your insensitivity begins to warm up. Perhaps, you have behaved in a really cold manner (in terms of emotions) and the time is right to change this. Similarly, the circumstances that kept you paralyzed in real life may begin to be easier.
❖ According to popular superstition, dreaming of melting gold portends sadness; if silver, economic problems; and if it is ice, a situation that gets out of control.

Memory ■ To dream that you lose your memory reflects an evasive attitude or feeling of guilt. You forget things that are too shocking or made you uncomfortable or embarrassed you. It may be an opportune time to analyze aspects of your life that you are unable or unwilling to face.

Mercury ▪ Mercury (both the liquid metal and the Roman god) represents mobility, speed, and adaptability.

Metamorphosis ▪ Dreams in which living beings experience changes are symbols of evolution. If, for example, you see the transformation of a caterpillar into a butterfly, this means you should trust your ability to the end, without allowing fear or despair to defeat you, because all will work out eventually. At the same time, metamorphosis can also be a negative sign, if it is a transformation of degeneration or corruption. The context of each dream tell you how to interpret it. (See WORM, BUTTERFLY, and CATERPILLAR)

Meteorology ▪ The weather that appears in the dream may represent the state of your mind and your emotions. A stormy sky, for example, is evidence of disputes and anger; a sunny one, however, denotes happiness; if it rains, your stress may have found an outlet; if it snows, then your emotions are cold.
❖ Dreaming of a nice weather predicts happy events. But if it is unpleasant, your fortune will exude the same.

Microscope ▪ Looking through a microscope can indicate a desire to be meticulous when analyzing a given situation. But also denotes a tendency to place too much value on minor details, neglecting what is truly relevant.

Midnight ▪ Midnight represents the most intense moment that our unconscious can live. For this reason, throughout history, it has been a symbolic time when the characters in horror stories (witches, vampires, ghosts, etc.) meet. These frightening figures are merely representations of our darkest aspects, so, logically, they reach their peak in the central hour of the night. (See WITCH, DEMON, and FAIRY)

Milk ▪ Ths is a symbol of abundance and fertility. To dream of milk could reflect your maternal instincts. In the same sense, it manifests the love of a mother and the nourishment of ideas. Perhaps the dream is showing you the spiritual needs of your interior. If you dream that you give milk to others it represents the spiritual values or inspiration that you give to others around you.

❖ If you drink milk, especially mother's milk, this dream is an omen of good health.

Milking ▪ This dream indicates that you know how to take advantage of the spiritual or material goods you have. It is also a symbol of fertility and familial well-being.
❖ To see someone milking a cow signals a time of prosperity and a strong feeling of satisfaction.

Millionaire ▪ It is a typical dream of frustration. It is often experienced by people who are not satisfied with their material, intellectual, or emotional possessions. The message from these images is that you should discover and appreciate what you have and what you keep within yourself. You should not waste time on ephemeral things.

Mimosa ▪ This tree is a symbol of the melancholy states.

Mine ▪ Mines are a major source of hidden wealth. Therefore, if one appears in a dream it symbolizes that within you or your unconscious you will find the greatest treasure. In general, such a dream predicts achievements and improvement.

Mineral deposit ▪ The dreams in which mineral deposits appear are a reflection of the potential that you harbor. This type of image should comfort you in the times of trouble; you have many resources with which to solve the problems. You simply have to find the most appropriate way to use them.

Mirror ▪ Symbol of imagination and conscience. It reproduces the reflections of the visible world. Therefore, this instrument allows you to glimpse your true personality, or whatever you are hiding. Generally mirrors in the dreams demonstrate the individual's low communication with her inner world. If the mirror lets you see a positive image of yourself it suggests that you are satisfied with your character and current situation. Otherwise, it evidences fear of disclosing shameful desires. Finally, if you are in front of a mirror with your eyes closed it indicates that you are unwilling to face reality. Clearly alluding to narcissism, the mirror is, according to Freud, an emblem of conceit. According to the Jungian school, however, it is a symptom of introspection, a need to return to the true essence of the subject's unconscious saving the façade that tends to be the public face.

❖ A broken mirror is a harbinger of grief and pain. To break it with your own hands denotes inability to recognize your own mistakes.

Misfortune ▪ To imagine that you go through a misfortune announces a time of serious problems and suffering humiliations inflicted by people nearby. When others are the ones who fall into it, the subject will successfully overcome the difficulties and achieve success.

Missionary ▪ The presence of a missionary in dreams indicates the need to find selfless and sincere help. Its meaning can be similar to the ABBOT. If the dreamer sees himself as a missionary, the dream expresses his desire to serve and comfort to the people around him.

Mist ▪ Mist is a symbol of the indeterminate, of the fusion of the air and water elements, of each stage of evolution. In oneiric terms, fog symbolizes the fears and anxieties stored in the depths of the unconscious. It is therefore not the best time to undertake a new initiative, since you have an unclear understanding of the situation. Likewise, you must not forget that mist is usually associated with gray, i.e., the symbol of indifference and a lack of determination. To dream of this color may be a warning that a crisis of values lies ahead. You may not see see things clearly or as they really are. This disorientation can end if you try to be more energetic and decisive.

❖ If the fog is dense, the omens are disadvantageous. If it is clearing up, you will obtain success.

Mistletoe ▪ It is a parasitic plant associated with the holm oak, endowed with remarkable hypotensive virtues. The Celts considered it a symbol of strength from heaven, defined as the plant of immortality, because its upper branches are evergreen. Following Celtic design, this dream is a clear omen of regeneration, strength, health, and well-being.

Mix ▪ To dream that you mix chemicals, potions, or even drinks does not symbolize the entry of a new element in your life but rather that something different comes from the combination of what you already have. For example, it may reflect the union of your most opposed facets and that as a result, you adopt a more flexible and tolerant attitude. According to another interpretation, this dream indicates the mixing of the

right and left sides of the brain. Or, logic and intuition respectively.

❖ The Tarot card of Temperance shows an angel pouring water from one cup to another. The card of the Star illustrates a woman pouring water into a pond and, at the same time, onto the ground. The sign of Aquarius is also a water bearer. All this, as the dream of mixing, refers to the flow of life. It is the connection between the conscious and the unconscious, and the masculine and feminine elements.

Mockery ▪ To suffer the taunts of others in dreams highlights the sensation that you feel unappreciated, either in the professional field or by your partner. On the other hand, laughing at others is evidence of false confidence as well as hidden fears. So, if it comes from an old man it reflects being afraid of aging; from a disabled person, losing autonomy; and from a homosexual, being afraid that unaccepted inclinations will be made public.

Mole ▪ A mole evidences the tendency of the dreamer to hide themselves from their daily problems, and to relegate fixing them to other people. It is generally a dream that reflects immaturity and it encourages overcoming it.

Money ▪ It symbolizes everything you secretly want but repress so much that your mind does not dare to mention its name. Therefore, this type of dreams typically regard an illicit love. If you make money it indicates that it is more valuable than you thought, but also that you are in a period of high creativity. On the contrary, dreaming that someone steals some money from you means that you have exaggerated your feelings towards that particular person. Losing money, if it is accompanied by a distressing feeling, reveals the fear of misplacing something you consider very important. If money is not enough to cover your debts it means that you are wasting your energies. Finally, if you accumulate money it denotes selfishness; if you share it, generosity.

❖ Formerly, it was believed that to find or to receive money in a dream was a sign of good luck. For other superstitions, it means that soon there will be a birth.

Monkey ▪ This represents the worst of ourselves. It indicates that your instincts are about to run wild, since the monkey is considered a restless, mocking, and lascivious animal. Very often, this dream is related to sex: the unconscious struggles break free and unleash its most primal desires. The message associated with these images is that you must control your impulses, channeling them in the proper way (without, however, repressing them).

❖ In India, monkeys are associated with those human attitudes that surrender in the face of worries, doubts, and fears. The dream may be telling you to try to find inner peace.

Monster ■ In dreams, monsters take much more terrifying dimensions and shapes than any horror movie or novel. However, in spite of fear that they can provoke, if the figure reappears frequently in your dreams, you need to approach them and try to get to know them. Although they are frightening, it will give clear clues to your fears. Dreams are usually representations of ourselves, therefore, the dreaded monster can be a part of yourself that scares you. It could also represent people around you who are hard to relate to— parents, a boss, a partner— or aspects of life that scare you, like sex, old age, or death. Typically, monsters appear in children's dreams. In this case, they represent the dominant and powerful role of adults in the lives of children. It is recommended that you face whatever these monsters represent in your emotional life.

❖ According to old books on dreams, to vanquish a monster in a dream means that you will overcome our enemies and become more important. The ancient peoples of Tibet believed that the most terrible monsters were divine guardians. Therefore, they symbolized those inner powers of being that could deter and defeat ignorance.

Moon ■ Its symbolism is very broad and complex. In general, it represents feminine nature, but it is also related to the unconscious and human emotions. This complexity stems from the fact that its meaning depends on the lunar phase. When you dream of the new moon, it indicates that a new love is awakening in you; if the moon is waxing, is an ardent love; if it is full moon, culminated love; waning, the passion burns out. And if the moon is surrounded by a halo, the dream may portend pain and problems of all kinds, whose severity are greater if you see an eclipse. (See WHITE and ECLIPSE)

❖ According to palmistry, the lunar region of the hand (opposite the thumb) is the area where the travel lines are. Dreaming of a moon, therefore, portends that you will soon leave for somewhere, probably by water.

Morning ■ This symbolizes conscious activity, work and joy, as well as hope. To contemplate the morning boldly represents triumph of doubts, regrets, or disturbances. And to dream of a sunrise indicates that a period of greater happiness will begin, in which you may direct yourself at will.

Mortgage ■ To dream of a mortgage or any document or paperwork that implies a significant sum of money reflects the dreamer's fears about a difficult economic situation. The feeling of guilt and stress from not having achieved proposed objectives is also implicit.

Mothballs ■ This refers to things that have been stored for a long time. They need to air out. Possibly this is an opportune moment to air out old issues that were forgotten, but still have a place in your life.

Mother ■ The symbols of the mother have a remarkable versatility. On the one hand, the mother appears as an image of nature (i.e., life) and, conversely, as a representation of death (for the Egyptians, the vulture symbolized the mother). The mother relates to virtually all stages and circumstances of existence. It always represents our origin, our roots, security, shelter, warmth, tenderness, etc. At the same time, this symbol also appears when we die, that is, when we return to the bosom of Mother Earth. Dreaming of this figure is usually more common during childhood. In adults, however, the maternal figure appears through indirect references. Often, those who fail to reach maturity still have these dreams. Acts of rebellion against the mother are also frequent. These episodes manifest adolescent dissatisfaction, the need for independence, and the desire to break away from the maternal ties. A dream of this kind can occur at any age. On the other hand, Freud referred to the Greek myth of Oedipus, who killed his father to marry his mother. According to the psychoanalyst, Oedipus was driven to this crime by incestuous desire and envy of his father. As for women, Freud believed that their feelings of inferiority were based on the jealousy they felt toward men. (See COAT, WHITE, FOUNTAIN, INCEST, and MOON)

❖ Legends and myths of many traditions contain the symbol of the mother. She may appear as a figure of generosity or, on the contrary, be that bad guy in the story.

Moths ■ They indicate the dangerous fascination for a flash of light. The dream may be a warning against the dreamer's glibness. Probably, the dreamer has exaggerated admiration or affection for a person who is actually not trustworthy. Or, conversely, it may show a too nonchalant behavior in relation to material goods.

Motorcycle ■ The speed, the agility, the feeling of the wind on your face, all of this is associated with the motorcycle. So, in general, it can be said that this figure alludes to purest freedom, the desire to reaffirm your identity.

Mountain ■ High ground enables us to admire the surroundings more clearly. If, in dreams, you are climbing a mountain enthusiastically, it means that you are improving your professional, social, or spiritual situation. Reaching the summit of the mountain is a sign that you have achieved your goal. If you dream you are at the summit of a mountain, your dream is probably telling you that you don't have that many problems in life to worry about.

❖ If you strive to climb a mountain, all of your businesses will be successful. But if you gave up and did not get to the top, your plans will fail. In China, the mountain symbolizes the unshakable peace that comes after meditation.

Mourning ■ It is a manifestation of death. This does not necessarily mean that the dream is premonitory of such an event. More than anything, it alludes to the dreamer's desire to see the end of an undesirable situation they do not know how to bring to a close. To dream of death is not a negative dream. It almost always manifests the intention of rebirth, of renewal. (See BURIAL and DEATH)

Mouse ■ The mouse is occasionally associated with the devil. It represents your instincts. It could also be a symbol of timidity or little worries that "gnaw" at you psychologically.

❖ The plague of mice and rats from the story "The Pied Piper of Hamelin" could be interpreted as an allegory for the overcoming of instincts over rational thought.

Mouth ■ The mouth is related to the ability to communicate with others, but also with the ability to breathe, to eat, to drink, and to kiss—in other words, to establish any external relationship. When you speak, you have the power to either be affectionate or aggressive toward the interlocutor with your words. Therefore, perhaps the dream is reminding you that you should not have said something or you need to express certain feelings verbally. Similarly, if you dream that you wash your face or brush your teeth, it means that your words do not match your true feelings. If the mouth is fleshy it will indicate a repressed desire to maintain an emotional relationship. On the contrary, to shut up and to utter no word at all when someone speaks reflects a refusal to communicate and a profound rejection of that person. According to Freud, besides a sex symbol, the mouth represents an immature childish fixation on verbal assault.

❖ Dreaming of a big mouth portends wealth; of a small one, poverty. To see someone with a twisted or deformed mouth portends a family dispute.

Move (in the sense of moving house) ■ To dream that you are moving suggests that you want to change your way of thinking or modify your habits. The unconscious is telling you to undergo a major renovation. Of course, this implies abandoning certain aspects ofthe past. If you sit around waiting, you will never find what you're looking for.

Movie ■ The cause of this dream may simply be that we have watched television or have been to the cinema just before going to bed. Maybe you identified with something that you saw and it has surprised you unconsciously. In oneiric terms, the evocation of a movie can be a good opportunity to think about your own situation. In this case, the dream should be interpreted as any other. If you appear watching a movie, the scene may be showing you that your thoughts are disconnected from your person. You are able to observe yourself and your life without getting involved emotionally.

❖ Modern superstitions say that to undertake the direction of a film predicts the arrival of a rewarding gift.

Mud ■ Mud is a product of soil (i.e., the concrete and solid) mixed with water (feelings). Hence, it relates to all things biological and nascent. Therefore, mud is linked to physical or material appetites of the protagonist. So, dreaming that you wallow in mud reflects a desire to live positive romantic relationships. However, it can also symbolize the need to be more realistic and more mindful. Mud as raw material for artistic creativity suggests the ability to do projects. If you dream of a liquid mud that gets streets, objects, or yourself dirty it means that you should review your feelings and avoid being carried away by lust.

Mule ■ The mule represents the body as a living support for human activities. Therefore, if the animal appears weak, you have to look after your health. A dead mule can express the lack of foundation in your projects and the consequent impossibility of completing them.

❖ The oneiric image of the mule indicates evil enemies. If it is burdened, it announces problems; an unburdened mule bodes well for business.

Mummy ■ Based on the environment of modern life, the appearance of a mummy could seem terrifying, however, the interpretation of this dream is a little more complex. The unconscious brings back aspects of remote past that had been forgotten but, perhaps, were not entirely resolved at the time. Old feelings of guilt, fears, insecurities, and accusations against people who have been with you throughout life may come to light.

Murder ■ When you dream that you killed someone, you are demonstrating a serious conflict between your aspirations and moral standards with which you are forced to comply. Such dreams must be analyzed very carefully because they indicate the need for deeper knowledge of the self before you reach a situation of real violence. If in a dream you murder someone you know, you probably have a hidden resentment toward that person. On the other hand, the murdered person could also be a facet of yourself that you have been trying to suppress or destroy. If the victim is yourself, perhaps you live subdued by your own emotions. The very same instincts that you refuse may be seeking revenge.

❖ Some oracles believe this dream portends sadness. Notwithstanding, many others say that the act of killing someone in a dream surprisingly promises unexpected joy, recovery from of an illness, or a way out of an unfortunate period.

Murmurs ■ To listen to the murmurs of others is a clear indication that gossip will emerge you that may harm you. If it is you who murmurs, it becomes clear that you harbor ill intentions toward others.

Museum ■ Museums represent our past history. They exhibit the most important events in our lives. On the other hand, they are also a symbol of refinement and good taste. In this sense, they reflect a cultural concern and the possibility to enjoy profound things. Your oneiric museum can also reflect your personality with symbols of your psychological characteristics, which you may observe from an objective point of view. You should analyze your reaction to the content of the museum.

Music ■ In most cultures, music is synonymous with creation, because it seems to have accompanied this divine act. In India, in particular, Shiva created the world by dancing and playing the flute. The symbolism of music is very complex. In general terms, you could say that it is either an integrating element or a divisive one. Thus, if the music is melodic or harmonic it expresses placidity of spirit; however, if it's blaring music, it suggests a situation of chaos; finally if this music is an unsettling or unrecognizable background noise, it reveals anxiety and insecurity. The sound of music could reflect the overall atmosphere of your life. harmonious, discordant, rhythmic, unpredictable, or unduly shrill.

❖ Many melodies express the ambience of worlds beyond the grave, of the unconscious, and of death. Others try to symbolize the harmony of the universe. Music has great power for spiritual representation. Many claim to have heard the songs of angels in dreams.

Mustache ■ The presence of a person with a mustache in dreams suggest you should not trust him. If it is a stranger, the warning concerns the proposed work or projects that you will receive shortly. But if it is yourself who has a mustache (provided that in real life you do not) the dream indicates that you are fooling yourself.

❖ To see long whiskers announces upcoming luck; short ones, disease; gray ones, serenity.

Mustard ■ Mustard is associated with irritability and arousal. If this dream repeats to frequently, you may be living too intensely.

❖ To dream that you eat mustard and feel it burn your mouth denotes bitter regret for an action that caused someone harm.

Muteness ■ This is a dream that manifests difficulties, whether it is the dreamer who becomes mute or someone else. It signifies the inablitly to communicate and understand your surroundings. Sometimes, they are very stressful dreams in which the dreamer wants to shout as loud as she can but can't. In this case, it indicates a situation in which her desire to express herself is repressed. According to Carl Jung, silent people who appear in dreams represent an imbalance between the emotions and the intellect of the dreamer. One part is annulling the other, leaving him impotent and unable to speak.

❖ To dream that you are mute means it is hard for you to convince others of your opinions and plans.

Mutilation ▪ If you dream that you have a mutilated limb, whether it be an arm or a leg, or suddenly, you are missing one of these limbs, it means that you are wasting your talent. Behind all this, is a hidden fear you should try to overcome.

Muzzle ▪ Generally, it symbolizes the relationship between the dreamer and her surroundings. If it is the muzzle of a domesticated animal, the circumstances are favorable and offer a context in which you feel comfortable and at home. If it is the muzzle of a threatening beast, you feel distressed and unable to change that which is hostile to you. If you see yourself with a muzzle in place of a human mouth, the dream expresses discomfort with the image you project to the world.

Mythology ▪ If mythological characters appear in your dreams (a rare event), you should ascribe the same meaning they were given in their time period.

N

Nail (body part) ■ The external aspect of a person's nails says a lot about that person's physical and mental health. So, dreaming of dirty and bitten nails evidences poorly controlled anxiety. If, on the contrary, the nails are well taken care of, it indicates that you know how to control your nerves and that you have a strong enough will to succeed in your objectives.

Nail (object) ■ Nails announce little reward after a lot of work. However, if they are new and shiny, it means that the dreamer will have better means to carry out her task. If, on the contrary, they are old, broken, or corroded, then they indicate diseases and poor emotional relationships with others. Working with nails announces participation in a task that will give you great satisfaction; to find them, fulfillment of your desires; and to nail them, murmurings of someone who despises you.
❖ Since the Romans, iron has been considered a sacred metal. Dreaming of a rusty iron nail augurs good fortune.

Names ■ The names that appear in dreams can contain word play that leads you to their true meaning. It is important to pay attention to them and try to guess their hidden meaning.
❖ There are superstitions about different names. For example, if you dream your name is "Jorge" ("George") you will never be hung. If the name happens to be "Ines" (Agnes), you will go mad.

Nausea ■ Nausea during sleep warns of the arrival of great danger, so you must be alert to any worrying signs.

Navel ■ In addition to the sexual connotations it may have in a dream, the navel is a symbol of connection. It is the link between your own body and the maternal belly, and, by extension, contact with the earth, the darkness, and the unconscious. It can be interpreted as the desire to distance yourself from those who are not family, or with the aim to explore unknown lands. It also alludes to a desire to procreate.

Neck ■ It represents the union between body and soul. Dreaming that you have neck pain can be a sign that, in reality, you are experiencing such a physical condition. Otherwise, a sore neck symbolizes a spiritual malaise for having a lifestyle or job that does not correspond with the true desires and inclinations of the dreamer.
❖ The longer and healthier it is the greater the prosperity it augurs. Washing your neck promises good health.

Necklace ■ Symbol of the bond between giver and recipient, dreams in which a necklace appears predict passionate relationships in the erotic field, and family happiness. Having a necklace announces wealth, although the latter could be brief, especially if the subject leaves her business to chance.

❖ A golden necklace reveals material success; made of sapphire, slander; of diamond profusion of enemies; and of pearls, tensions in the couple.

Needles ■ Needles symbolize small pains (anxieties) that each person finds along life's path. When the needles are crocheting they refer to those intrigues plotted behind you. If you are portrayed sewing or knitting, it means you need to be more active or repair the damage you have caused someone. If in the dream, you are pricked with a needle, the pain will be the same you feel from little things that concern or frustrate you in real life. In short, a dream of this nature could remind you that you can take advantage of difficulties by transforming them into critical learning for your life.

❖ It is generally associated with deception. In many traditions it is believed that to utter the word "needle" when waking up in the morning portends bad luck.

Neighbors ■ To dream that you are fighting with neighbors reveals an interior conflict. It is possible that you are acting against your conscience. In contrast, if you maintain a good dream relation with them, it indicates that you are reconciling with your environment.

Nest ■ As is well known, the nest represents the family home and domestic life. The interpretation of the dream depends on the circumstances in which the nest is found. If it is empty, it expresses abandonment and loneliness; however, if it is full of vipers, it points to a betrayal. As a place where eggs hatch, the nest also represents the mother and the feminine in general. Similarly, it may be that you are developing new ideas and opportunities. (See HOUSE, MOTHER, and WOMAN)

❖ If in your dream the nest is full of eggs, it means that you will enjoy a prosperous time.

Net ■ A net serves to hunt, fish, or trap something. In dreams, it reflects the need to have power over other things, be they people, feelings, or objects. If you dream that you fall into a net, if means that you feel trapped or defenseless, in an emotional relationship or in a certain work situation. In case you dream of a fishing net full of fish, it means that you should have patience to collect the fruits of your labor. On the contrary, if it is empty, it implies that you find yourself in an adverse circumstance. (See HUNT, THIEF, FISH, and FISHING)

❖ According to popular tradition, the constellations are the net imposed by heaven so that no one can leave the universe.

Nettle ■ Nettles symbolize betrayal and cruelty. However, to notice the itching caused by contact with this plant indicates dissatisfaction with oneself and the inability to make others happy.

❖ According to popular tradition, to see nettles is a negative sign of falsehood, betrayal, and disappointment. Hives, however, by inversion, are a sign of prosperity and family happiness.

News ■ To receive news in dreams could be indicative of a situation of loneliness and isolaton, voluntary or involuntary. The dreamer in this case desires contact with the outside world, or is looking to change his circumstances.

Newspaper ■ The dream reveals your desire to be well informed and educated. It shows your fear of public ridicule for not keeping up with news.

❖ Reading several newspapers or magazines denotes a favorable business and portends success. Destroying it announces lies in your inner circle. However, a newspaper can also predict marriage with a wealthy person.

Night ■ According to the Greeks, the night was the mother of the gods because they believed that the darkness preceded the formation of all things. As a result, like water, the night also has a meaning of fertility, of seed. In our culture, tradition has linked night with the unconscious. Moreover, it is also often linked to the color black, death, ignorance, evil, and despair. To dream about it thus portends misleading, artificial, unclear, and sordid situations, especially as related to economic and sentimental matters. As with death, the night may say that something is coming to an end, or that some limitations will emerge that you should follow.

❖ An old superstition says that you can avoid nightmares by hanging your stockings or socks on the edge of the bed. According to gypsy tradition, unless the sky is starry, night dream announces despair.

Nightclub ■ Dreaming of being in a nightclub may signal a desire to escape and superficiality. (See DANCING and MUSIC)

Nightmare ■ If you suffer nightmares, it is evident that the insecurity, fears, and worries are having an effect on you. However, to interpret this type of dream correctly, you should try to remember if you have recently seen a horror movie or read a hair-raising story that could have affected you subconsciously. Not in vain, these mechanisms of a narrative type have the ability to awaken dark points of the past that are repressed in the unconscious. Their function is to remind you what types of situations frighten you.

Noise ▪ Noise could predict the interior dialogue that happens in your own thoughts. For this not to occur, practicing meditation before going to sleep helps increase mental calm and peace. The noise could on the other hand also be caused by the subconscious's need to call your attention so that you value a concrete issue to which you do not give importance in real life.
❖ Some oracles believe that dreaming of loud noises presages the obtaining of a new job.

N U D I T Y

Mary dreamed: "I was in the office when I realized I was not quite dressed. I had forgotten to put pants on and was not wearing underwear! I tried to get my jersey down so it would cover me but it was too short. I felt really bad, insecure, and helpless. However, my colleagues—all perfectly dressed—did not seem to notice anything. At that time my boss called me to come to his office and I could no longer resist; I burst into tears like a little girl. Seeing me so crushed, Ana (a partner) offered me a jacket so I could tie it around my waist, but she said, 'Girl, I do not know what's wrong with you lately, but you get too easily distracted . . .' and continued her work without caring much about my situation. Then I woke up."

Almost everyone has dreamed of being naked—or half-dressed—in a public place. This dream is often associated with **sexuality** (with a sexual inadequacy or guilt); but also with the fear of somehow "being exposed," regarding your private or professional life. However, depending on the circumstances of each person, the meaning varies. In Mary's case, it reflects her **vulnerability** at the workplace and a concern for revealing some deficiency or inability to others. In the dream, peers do not seem to notice—or do not pay attention to—her nudity, and that is a reassuring element indicating that perhaps Mary was worried for no reason. Failure to wear trousers and the fear that a figure of authority—such as her boss—would find out reveals her **concern for success** and professional skills; they could be questioned.

Nomad ▪ This is a dream that could be positive or negative, depending on the case. The nomad represents the traveller, the adventurer who is able to move through the world unburdened with baggage. He does not have any great needs and can carry all that he needs. In this sense, the figure of the nomad means freedom. On the other side, it manifests a provisional and precarious situation. It also expresses disregard toward familiar places and loved ones, and the inability to establish yourself and put down roots. The character and circumstances of the dreamer together will help the interpretation of this dream.

Noon ▪ Just as midnight is the peak of our darkest aspects, noon symbolizes the peak of our brightest part, that is, of our virtues. Therefore, the appearance of a bright midday in a dream indicates you are in a moment of great personal growth. (See ANGELS, GOD, LIGHT, TEACHER, and MARRIAGE)

North ▪ North symbolizes the way, orientation, that which gives our lives direction. Its presence in dreams should make you reflect on what you really want. However, this cardinal point also represents cold and darkness, since the sun never passes to the north. (See SHORTCUT, AVENUE, PATH, and COLD)

Nose ▪ It represents will and determination. If you dream of an overly large nose, it means you tend to stick your nose where it doesn't belong and talk too much, without knowing why. This reflects your lack of confidence. If the nose is very small, it denotes candor, insecurity, and passivity. If you have a broken or bloody nose, your plans will be frustrated. (See FACE)

Notary ▪ To dream of a notary predicts concerns about a lawsuit you are unlikely to win. If the notary issues a certificate, it may even announce misery.

Notebook ▪ School notebooks remind you of the past and make you feel nostalgia for what no longer exists. If you write something in it, the dream indicates an understanding of reality, intelligence, and fortune.

Nudity ▪ This dream has an ambivalent sense. On one hand, it is a symbol of physical beauty, purity, and divinity (in fact, goddesses like Venus or Diana have always been painted naked); and it reflects a desire for freedom, sincerity, and self-improvement. On the other hand, it represents lust or vain exhibitionism. If in the dream you feel distressed or embarrassed it means that you reject your own body. If you see other people naked it can reveal both a desire to know their secret thoughts or a mere sexual attraction. When you find yourself naked in public it denotes anxiety, fear of ridicule, emotional vulnerability, and low self-confidence. You are afraid that others may hurt you if you act spontaneously or make a mistake. Nudity, finally, also means that you feel nostalgia for lost childhood. It represents your true self, without norms or social constraints.

❖ Formerly, mothers used to warn her daughters that if they dreamed of being naked they would soon learn about a scandal. According to some oracles, it predicts that you will make serious mistakes in business affairs, unless you listen to the advice of others. For gypsies, however, this dream brings good luck, especially if the oneiric scene is developed under a starry sky. In general, this dream can also mean innocence.

Numbers ■ In the symbolic system, numbers are not purely quantitative terms, but "key ideas" with a specific characterization for each one. However, these representations are unknown to most people, so in oneiric terms, the numbers tend to symbolize simply calculation, accuracy, and order. Our dreams, in this sense, remind us that we live in a rather chaotic state. It is a call to find internal order. On the other hand, depending on the number shown, the dream manifests different stages of your spiritual growth and the various archetypal energies of the collective unconscious. Zero is the unmanifested void and the indescribable vastness of space, without time limits. Its symbol is the circle, the perfect whole. One initiates the action. It is the source of life or the unity of creation. It is associated with the figure of the point. Two is diversity. It is the number of duality and divine symmetry. Thanks to him, opposites meet, such as male and female, father and mother, yin and yang, or heaven and earth. In Ancient Greece, three was the perfect number. It is the combination of body, mind, and spirit. Its shape is the triangle, which represents creative force.

❖ It can also refer to the Holy Trinity. The symbol of the number four is the square. This is the number of stability and harmony. Furthermore, it connects the seasons, the four elements and the four mental functions that Jung described (thought, feeling, sense, and intuition). Five represents the link between heaven and earth. Its symbol is the pentagon. Six symbolizes inner harmony

and perfection. Its figure is the hexagon or the Star of David. Seven is the number that completes things. In the myth of creation, the world is formed in six days and on the seventh is completed. According to an old belief, the soul is renewed every seven years. Hence breaking a mirror brings seven years of bad luck, as the mirror represents the soul. Eight, for the Chinese, is a lucky number that brings good fortune. It represents rebirth and new beginnings. In India, nine is the number of God, of life, and of death. In the West, it represents eternity. Finally, ten is considered the number of law, due to the Ten Commandments.

❖ Sacred books, such as the Bible, contain many numerological references. Numerology is the study of the mystical meaning of numbers. Originally, it was based on the Hebrew and Greek alphabets: each number was assigned a letter. By adding numerical equivalents of the letters of names, or the numbers of birth dates, they obtained a lot of information. Through this practice, you can find the personality, qualities, and the fate of each. Sometimes Numerology has been applied for the interpretation of dreams. There are certain human traits associated with each number. One is the initiation; two, attractiveness; three, communication; four, the love of home; five, experience; six, calm; seven, philosophy; eight, business; and nine, freedom.

Nun ■ They represent devotion, piety, and feelings. The figure of the nun also expresses, above all, purity and chastity. Her presence in dreams reveals a strong need for communication with oneself. Often, it announces the need to spend time alone. If you are going through a difficult situation, the dream indicates that you should reflect at length before making decisions. When a man dreams of a monk, it may deal with the spiritual side of his personality.

❖ Dreaming of a monk announces unpleasant travel and disagreements in the family. If you dream that you are a nun, you will be disappointed in love. But to meet her predicts emotional happiness.

Nurse ■ If a nurse appears in your dreams the interpretation can have two different directions. On one hand, this could indicate that soon you will receive help from a friend, especially if you are depressed. But it can also be considered an announcement: you will have to provide your services to someone.

O

Oak ■ This tree represents power and strength. In dreams, it should be interpreted as the presence of a great interior energy that permits you to confront all sorts of difficulties. If the dream has a dry or dead oak, it is a sign that your character is ostensibly weakening.

Oasis ■ An oasis symbolizes abundance and creativity in the middle of the dryness of the desert, that is, your problems. For this reason, if you cross a desert in dreams and see an oasis in the distance, it means a difficult time that has been worrying you is coming to an end.

Oath ■ To dream of an oath about something that directly affects you indicates a significant level of insecurity. Not in vain, the oath denotes a lack of confidence in the completion of the agreement. In and of itself, it also reflects doubts about commitments acquired and the regret caused by a situation that can affect your future.

Obedience ■ This dream indicates an act of subordination. It could be positive or negative depending on the feeling that the action generates in you. If it denotes firmness and discipline, it is a positive sign from the unconscious. But if the dreamer feels humiliated or put down, the dream reflects a situation of inconformity or lack of self expression that should be remedied.

Obelisk ■ As an ascendent symbol of the sun's rays, the obelisk has the same oneiric meaning: honor, wealth, and clarity. Its figure is also associated with the phallus and alludes to everything that has to do with masculine sexuality: creative energy, strength, and power. Depending on the case, you can interpret it as repressed sexual desires, the need for recognition, or well-being in a situation. Studying the other symbols in the dream and the scene as a whole will be useful for its interpretation.

Obesity ■ To dream that you are obese, but are happy with your body, means that you are satisfied with yourself and your life. If you dream that many obese people surround you, it means that you have everything you need to achieve the success you long for.

Objective ■ This dream refers to the objectives or ambitions of the dreamer. To see yourself completing your goals in dreams announces that you will also achieve them in real life. On th contrary, not reaching them is a bad sign, since it means setbacks will delay your plans. However, if the dream highlights the word "objective" itself, it may be that the dream is indicating that you should be more objective when considering your problems.

Observatory ■ To be able to look at the universe from an observatory means you put yourself on a higher plane, from which you have a different perspective on things. It is a positive dream. It can be interpreted as the desire for elevation, or as a situation in which the dreamer has reached a superior level of spiritual growth and understanding in real life.

Obsession ▪ To dream that you are obsessed with something points to frustrated plans. Possibly, you are taking on more than you can handle, and also, you do not control your impulses.

Obstacle ▪ To dream of elements that block your progress indicates that you are not very certain you can achieve your goals in real life. You must leave this lack of self confidence behind and not worry so much about what others may think of you. Most likely, due to fear and indecision, you created these obstacles yourself.
❖ Often we imagine that obstacles are bigger than they really are. In this sense, it is likely that the impediments that appear in dreams are larger than those in real life.

Occultist ▪ To visit the occultist in dreams may be the reflection of a physical problem related to eyesight. If this is not the case, it manifests that you know you have certain limitations you understand what goes on around you. So, you have the intention to put yourself in the hands of someone who can help you see, open your eyes. (See GLASSES)

Octopus ▪ This dream is rather negative because the presence of an octopus in your unconscious indicates that you experience strong temptations that can harm you. This situation can lead to the absolute decline. (See ABYSS and HELL)

Offense (criminal) ▪ An offense you commit is a sign of nonconformity to the rules imposed by society. It shows the desire of rebellion but, at the same time, the guilt that it entails. If the offense is committed by someone else it indicates your disapproval of her attitudes or actions.

Office ▪ Dreams that take place in the workplace often describe our behavior and how we present ourselves to the world. Likewise, offices are organized places with everything classified and laid in order. Perhaps the dream warns you that you should take a look at the organization of your real life. A dream that takes place in the office where you work may well refer to your personality, or perhaps be reminding you of the way

you conduct your affairs. If you are in a strange office, it could be that in real life you compare your lifestyle, activities, and ideals to those of others.
❖ If you dream that you are in an office and you feel happy, it is an omen of prosperity. If you leave the office, soon you will be deceived.

Ogre ▪ The origin of this character (very common in folktales and legends) is found in Saturn, who devoured his children as Cibeles brought them into the world. If the oneiric ogres frighten you, it means you are hurting those around you and, possibly, yourself. The figure of the ogre also denotes ignorance and weakness of character.

Oil ▪ Oil can lead to different interpretations. For example, if it is in the middle of your path, it indicates an impediment. Consequently, you will have to be careful to avoid "slipping" in situations you are immersed in.
If, on the other hand, you are anointed with this substance it means that you have received exceptional knowledge that enables you to succeed in the particular circumstances in the dream. Oils are also used in perfumes and massages in order to care for and improve our skin, thus, it may refer to sensuality.
❖ In traditional wisdom, if a man dreams that he is an oil trader he will become very rich. However, he will never be lucky in love.

Ointment ▪ Dreaming of ointment predicts that you will overcome bad moments thanks to your strength of will and your hard work. If you prepare yourself, you will have to make a stand against the adversity without the help of others; if you see it being made, you will tell friends about it; it you are applying it to yourself, you will find yourself in the middle of the disputes of others. Ointments with a pleasing smell indicates that you will live a good period of time in the emotional sphere; but if it smells bad, you will not know how to communicate with the people in your environment. The properties of the ointment can also be healing. In this case, something may have entered your life that will bring you calm and relief from the injuries of the past.

Olive tree ▪ Symbol of peace. It maintains the same meaning in many cultures of the East and Europe. It is also associated with fortitude and fecundity.
❖ If you see this tree full of olives, you will soon have a reconciliation. (See OIL and OLIVES)

Olives ▪ To share this fruit with others is a symbol of peace and friendship. The presence of olives usually denotes a simple and friendly environment. Therefore, dreaming that you are eating this food with a group of friends predicts favorable results in businesses and in personal relationships.

One-handed ▪ To dream that one of your upper extremities is amputated is a sign of the inability to complete one of the activities you normally do with that arm. Behind it all is a fear that you must try to overcome. Don't forget, equally, arms symbolize your ability to relate with others. To see yourself without arms, therefore, denotes a serious emotional problem.

Onion ▪ This food symbolizes the human essence hidden under the layers that cover it up. Dreaming of onions, therefore, indicates that the path to self knowledge can be tough and make you cry. If you are able to take advantage of each stage (if you learn what each layer of the onion teaches you) you will successfully develop your personality.

Opening ▪ The act of opening something symbolizes the arrival of a new influence in your lives. Perhaps, you will feel very inspired or have new ideas. Depending on the context, it may symbolize an open door that offers the possibility of entering, leaving, or changing a given situation. It could express: leaving confinement, entering into a desired situation, or leaving behind pleasant things and people. In this sense, it is also good to ask yourself if you are truly influenced by the spiritual or, if you always opt for the easy way out.
❖ If it is a door opening, it tells you your enemies will slander you.

Operation ▪ If you dream that you are about to undergo a surgery, and suddenly, you get up from the operating table, convinced that you are cured, it means you have self confidence. You believe in the resolution of a problem that at first seemed incurable. So, you will find the correct answer without outside intervention. In addition to this, the image of the scalpel urges you to act with precision, decisiveness, and conviction to put an end to a situation that is worrying you.

Opposites ▪ In dreams, opposites that appear are metaphors for those contradictory aspects that our minds contain. It deals with the masculine and feminine, extroversion and introversion, activity and passivity . . . All this is represented through figures such as light and shadow, left and right, man and woman. The brain is divided in two hemispheres that have different functions. The best options is to make both work harmoniously in our favor.

Orange ▪ Fruit, in general, represents joy, well-being, and sexual relationships. The orange, in this sense, is no exception.
❖ The omens of this dream predict the meeting of new friends.

Orchestra ▪ The symbol of a group in action. Like many dreams, it should be taken in opposite sense. That is, if you direct an orchestra, it means that you are not a good teammate. The dream tells you that, though you are a great professional, you must learn to work in groups. You should delegate tasks to people around you. In this way, they will feel included in your affairs.

Orchid ▪ This exotic flower is a symbol of femininty. It is associated with vanity, but also fertility. In ancient China, it was considered to have magical abilities to get rid of evil related to sterility.

Orders ▪ To receive orders from a stranger suggests problems with integration; while, if they come from someone you know, it denotes a lack of security and lack of understanding. When you are the one who gives orders to a loved one, tension will emerge in your inner circle from an excess of intransigence. If the subject is a work mate, you will obtain a promotion and have bright future.

Orgy ▪ To dream you participate in an orgy reflects your desire to temporarily abandon your submission to rules. Perhaps the dream is also is reminding you that your sexual relationships are too conservative and you ought to relax a bit more in this aspect of your life. We "thirst" for chaos. This is common experience in humanity, as demonstrated by Carnival festivities, in which the social order does not matter. You must find a way to vent these repressed inhibitions that weigh on your unconscious before doing something that you can't take back.

Orientation ▪ In the event that you have to choose a path or geographic orientation in a dream, it is important to remember which you choses, since the direction could be vital to get things back on track in your real life.

Ornaments ■ They not only represent an excess of attributes but also—proportionally—taking care of your own image or home. You must pay close attention to the context of the dream because it can be indicative of either vanity or nobility, as well as austerity or loss.

Orphan ■ To see an orphaned person indicates compassion and the desire to protect them. To see yourself as an orphan indicates isolation and loneliness. It reflects a need for acceptance, affection, and protection.
❖ This dream predicts that you will gain benefit from wealthy friends, but be unlucky in matters of the heart.

Ostrich ■ The ostrich represents the denial of reality when it is unfavorable because this animal hides its head in a hole when it feels threatened. This type of dream warns you must be honest and face the circumstances of life even if they take a lot of work.

Oven ■ The oven can predict food in the future. At the moment, despite everything, you must wait patiently for the reward. For Freudian psychologists, the oven symbolizes the uterus and denotes pregnancy. So it may be that you are incubating new ideas or attitudes. (See ALCHEMY, COOKING, FIRE, and BLACKSMITH)
❖ To cook something in the oven is a sign of changes. If the oven is hot, the change will be good, but if it is cold, you must be prudent.

Owl ■ The owl embodies the wisdom that comes from the world of the night: the unconscious. It is a very precise bird of prey who can wait before acting. Both the owl and the barn owl advise you must be alert and open your eyes, it is possible that someone tries to deceive you or to promise something that she cannot fulfill.
❖ The most common belief is that this is a sad dream that predicts gloomy moments and poverty. Sometimes, it even predicts misfortunes.

Ox ■ For obvious reasons, the ox is a symbol of sacrifice, suffering, patience, and work. It also indicates sure but slow actions, which can have both positive and negative connotations.
❖ Symbol of physical strength—though docile and subjected to reason—the ox occupied in ancient Egyptian religion a key place: Apis, of bovine appearance, was the god of fertility. According to modern esoteric interpretation, dreaming of oxen signifies that the subject feels obedient; eating it, loss and suffering; letting them graze, happiness; to see them yoked to plow augurs success and profits; and to see them dragging a cart, emergence of influential friends and professional unions.

Oysters ■ They represent humbleness that is capable of producing the pearl of spiritual perfection inside. The shell symbolizes fecundity and eroticism. They are also the symbol of the maternal bosom that encloses the pearl: they indicate fertility, but also loneliness and distance in unknown seas. (See PEARL)

P

Pacifier ■ As a symbol of childhood, a pacifier is evidence of immaturity on the dreamer's part: he or she wants to return to the worry-free years, thus, avoid facing the trials of life.

Package ■ To dream that you receive a package predicts that you will find something unexpected. However, if you don't open it it means the doubts you have about some project are confirmed, so you should abandon it before it crashes and burns. The content that you take out of the package could represent some aspect of your mind that you begin to be aware of, or your hidden talents. In this sense, the package symbolizes self discovery itself.

❖ You will have a chance encounter with someone you have not seen in a while.

Pact ■ To make a pact with one or more people is a sign of maturity and responsibility. It will bring great satisfaction in the near future.

Padlock ■ It is an invitation to discretion, to be faithful and prudent with your words. Though dreaming of a padlock can also highlight confinement or isolation.

Pain ■ It is possible that pain in dreams reflects an actual physiological cause. Otherwise, pain is interpreted as atonement or purification. You have to go through hardships in order to grow physically or spiritually. Similarly, it worth taking a look at your diet, your rhythm of life, and your emotions.

❖ According to some oracles, this dream shows that a minor business can make you very unhappy. However, other superstitions ensure that you will receive an unexpected sum of money.

Painting ■ This dream has very different interpretations depending on whether it refers to painting as a task or as art. In the first case, painting a wall with a brush is evidence conformity in life; and to see some professionals doing so, the success of long-conceived projects. In the second case, we must pay attention to the way in which the painting in question is done, since what is represented could be describing your situation in reality. Thus, if the painting is realistic, sincerity will mark all your relationships; but, if it is abstract, tension and disputes undermine your surroundings. Based on whether the colors are bright or dark, you will learn a lot of information. For example, red denotes aggressiveness, while blue manifests melancholy. On the other hand, this dream may also indicate the need to express your creative potential.

❖ In general, it means that you love your work. If you spill paint on yourself instead, others will criticize you.

Palace ■ Sign of wealth, ostentation, and power. If a palace appears in your dreams, it is synonymous with ambitions, since it demonstrates that you think you deserve a higher destiny. The image of a palace also indicates the desire to advance on the social ladder to a desired position.

❖ All stories have their palace, their enchanted castle, the dark side of the heart where both monsters and treasures dwell.

Pallor ▪ To see yourself as much paler than usual in a dream could be a warning of an illness that has not yet been discovered. If this is not the case, paleness could indicate the disappearance and sapping of spiritual or mental strength. To see others go pale could reflect a fear of losing them, of them disappearing, or that they change their opinion of you.

Palm ▪ This is a symbol of ascension, regeneration, and immortality. Its presence in dreams indicates the satisfaction of triumph, or being very close to achieving it.

❖ Integrating the values of fecundity, victory, and the triumph of good, the palm promises satisfaction, happiness, and progeny for married women.

Panther ▪ The panther could symbolize for a woman that she is being stalked, and represents great danger (sexual assault, betrayal, vengeance, etc.).

❖ This is an oneiric symbol that alludes to the ingratitude of friends and family.

Pants ▪ Symbol of authority and prestige. To dream that someone puts on your pants implies a fear that this person will usurp your position or authority. If the pants are too short for you or look ridiculous on you, it means you fear not being up to speed on your circumstances. In the case that you buy pants, it manifests that you want to obtain more power; if they are torn, your projects may have serious holes; to lose them reveals your fear of the opinions of others.

Paper ▪ A sheet of paper may symbolize a new beginning in our lives. Or, also it indicates that you want to express yourself through writing or art. If the paper is a document, it may refer to a matter from your past. The presence of a paper in dreams also must relate to its written content. However, if you are unable to distinguish this, things change. Not surprisingly, a sheet of paper carried by the wind indicates that your hopes or your purposes are unsound and that you will probably miss the opportunities that arise. If you are behind a mountain of papers, it represents that you live overwhelmed by stress, excess liability, and major concerns.

Wet paper, finally, is a symbol of loss of prestige. (See LIBRARY and NOTEBOOK)

❖ According to the dream-oracles, a blank paper presages a period of pain. However, a paper with writing predicts much joy in love.

Parachute ▪ To dream of a parachute shows the subject's need to feel protected in a tough moment. You may urgently need help from your friends, but you're unable to ask for it. If the parachute falls slowly, it is a sign that you want to end an emotional relationship, but do not dare.

Paradise ▪ This is a wonderful, peaceful, quiet dream, and sometimes even romantic. This may be a sign that you may need more peace and quiet in your daily life. Or maybe the dream is telling you that you are very fortunate because in real life you are living in an earthly paradise. The idea of paradise is found in all cultures. We can define it as a spiritual state of absolute bliss and balance that we want to reach. Dreaming of paradise can denote a longing to enjoy a charmed life with little work and responsibilities. Just like the umbrella, it is a clear sign of immaturity, as you tend to get carried away by laziness and fantasy. If you dream that you are banished from paradise, it could refer to the end of something pleasant, or even a guilty conscience.

❖ If in your dream paradise palm trees appear, the good luck promised by this dream doubles. Among sailors, it was believed to predict a save and lucky journey.

Paralysis ▪ To dream of paralysis indicates an unwillingness to make certain commitments to society and yourself. A lack of confidence in your own potential leads to you stop acting and feel progressively paralyzed. Because of this state of mind, in your dreams you appear unable to move and, thus, decide for yourself. If you dream that it is others who are paralyzed, they can represent those aspects of yourself that you do not externalize. Similarly, if you dream of a paralyzed animal, it can refer to your instincts and inhibited sexual feelings.

❖ There is a belief that claims that nightmares are huge spirits that sit on top of us while we sleep. Thus the feeling of paralysis is explained. In olden days, in Europe, the solution for nightmares was to sleep with a knife beside the bed because the spirits feared iron and steel.

Parasol ▪ Given that shadows project the dark part of the mind (fear, insecurity, etc.), dreaming that you are using a parasol symbolizes the fear of not earning credibility with others. You should try not to make assumptions about what others think of you.

Park ■ Dreaming of walking through a park means you will enjoy free time after overcoming a spell of hard work and suffering. If the stroll is accompanied by a loved one, you will have a long happy marriage with this person. If the park is dirty and the vegetation unkempt, a series of sudden, unforeseen events will delay your plans. If you enter illegally into a park or private garden, the dream could be telling you that you are meddling too much in someone's life.

Parrot ■ This symbolizes criticisms, rumors, gossip, and slander that occurs behind your back.

Partition ■ Building a partition is usually a good sign, which shows the arrival of positive changes in the life of the protagonist. However, if the construction is a response to the desire to isolate yourself from the environment, there exists a problem with communication with others that could lead you to loneliness. If you take down the partition, it signifies that you yearn to open yourself to others and establish new social or emotional relationships.

Partner ■ This dream often expresses the need to unite the masculine and the feminine mind. This is a reference to your other Self. If the dreamer is a woman, the dream is an allusion to the masculine and rational part of her nature. If it is a man, his most intuitive and feminine side. The dream may also refer to the attitude you adopt towards your partner or to your own sexuality. The context and other elements that appear in the dream will be important to analyze it in depth.
❖ The alchemist tradition sought spiritual transformation of the psyche. The combination of your masculine and feminine aspects, in this respect, gives rise to a unique being who symbolizes the whole.

Party ■ Going to a party in a dream indicates that you are too frivolous at handling certain situations, which can have very harmful results. If you are the one organizing the party it could mean that you are in a position to find necessary tools in order to accomplish your projects. On the other hand, a party can represent pleasures of life and, especially, social interaction. Maybe enjoying the others' company will benefit you. The nature of the party is also likely to hide your desires and hidden fears.

A nice party indicates confidence. If it is disagreeable it express your lack of confidence at social events. A too formal party represents your work environment. Finally, if it is an orgy it denotes sexual frustrations.
❖ Unless the character of the celebration is exceptional, the traditional interpretation says that this dream indicates future disputes.

Passenger ■ Sometimes we devote so much effort to bear the parasitic attitudes of others. So, your friends and family become passengers on your own body, restricting your freedom. If you are the passenger, it may mean that you are not in control of your life and always accept the decisions of others.
❖ If, in the dream, passengers carrying baggage approach you, your situation will improve. If they move away, a deterioration of our living conditions is predicted.

Passport ■ Just like other documents, the passport reveals your identity, that is, your public persona. If you lose it the dream denotes a profound disorientation and a total lack of motivation to take initiative. The passport also leads to foreign lands and the unknown world of the unconscious. So, this dream can mean that you begin an analysis of your own personality. Perhaps, you are about to embark on the journey of self-knowledge. If you dream that they examine and stamp the passport, it could mean the approval of a new project or plan.
❖ According to the oracles, passports in dreams are not related to travel at all. In fact, they announce that our love life will improve.

Pastries ■ To eat pastries in dreams is synonymous with happiness. However, to eat sweets compulsively —that is, gluttonously—reveals a feeling of anxiety and frustration. Another characteristic dream, which is often accompanied by a strong feeling of guilt, is when you steal a cake and hide it to eat it. This image alludes to an excess of sentimentalism which causes conflict with more realistic people. If the cake appears divided in portions it means that there are things you should share. Perhaps you are being too selfish with certain people in your life. Finally, a pastry can refer to your emotional life, to the slice of affection and love that you need from others but do not receive.

Path ■ The path can be interpreted as an invitation to conduct your life in a positive direction. If you want changes you must take action. (See SHORTCUT and AVENUE)

❖ A wide and smooth path, surprisingly, denotes emotional problems. A rocky and rugged one, however, predicts a happy marriage.

Patient ▪ The dream could be a reflection of reality or a warning about an illness you are incubating. It also may be a call for you to be more patient and stay calm at all times.

❖ A pleasant surprise is on the way.

Patio ▪ It is a good sign when a patio appears in your oneiric thoughts, since it predict strong and lasting emotional unions. However, it is not so positive if the patio is empty, dirty, or full of abandoned junk. In this case, you could suffer considerable economic losses, or abundant gossip that harms you.

Paying ▪ This dream can indicate that you are taking charge of your situation, no matter how hard it is.

❖ The act of "paying" shows the work of karma, and that every cause has its effect. Everything has a cost. For example, gluttony brings health problems; selfishness generates loneliness; and covetousness, spiritual poverty. Happiness is in the middle ground between belongings and austerity. You must accept things are not yours, everything you have the world has only lent to you. Often, when one has nothing is when one has everything.

Peace ▪ To dream that you are at peace with yourself is a sign of maturity. You have reached a moment in which you are conscious of how your defects are compensated by your virtues. The personal balance is acceptable just as it is.

Peaches ▪ These fruits represent abundance and joy.

❖ Good omens for health and pleasure; to eat one promises reconciliation with a loved one; to pick them is indicative of wealth; to see one on the tree, temptation.

Peacock ▪ Represents vanity and the fragility of appearances.

Pear ▪ Pears, just like other fruits, represent abundance, fertility, and sensuality.

❖ An erotic symbol, the ripe pear predicts satisfying and happy relationships; a green one, however, expresses difficulties (because it is rough and hard).

Pearl ▪ The Chinese philosopher Lao Tzu once said: "The sage wears coarse garb, but in his chest hides a jewel." The situation can be extrapolated to the pearl hidden in an oyster, that is, to the spiritual perfection that is hidden under the shell. On the other hand, the pearl also represents the feminine, love, and beauty. When it is in jewelry or necklaces, indicates material grandeur and exhibitionism. And if, in the dream, a pearl necklace breaks and they are scattered it means that something has been dismantled in our waking lives. Possibly reveals your fear of not finally getting that for which you fought so much. (See SHELL)

❖ Threading pearls on a necklace is a harbinger of loneliness.

Peas ▪ This variant of legumes is a positive sign in the romantic field because it predicts long and lasting emotional unions. Dry peas, however, warn that you are not taking enough care of your health; and eating it predicts a reversal of fortune after a fruitful period. Planting peas signals that you have chosen the right way to achieve your intended goals; collecting them announces the arrival of benefits after hard work.

Peasant ▪ The figure of the peasant is associated with the job: to plow the soil, to sow, and then to collect the fruits represent those rewards that come after a hard work. The oneiric farmer's task indicates the circumstances of the dreamer at a given time. Planting represents a time of constant occupation for a profit in the future. If pruning, it indicates the need to eliminate the superfluous and focus only on what is relevant. If it is harvest, it is time to enjoy the fruits of a job well done.

Pedaling ▪ Its interpretation is associated with that of BICYCLE. It indicates a state in which dreamer depends solely on her own effort to start the projects she desires to complete.

Pelican ▪ Symbolizes authority, responsibility, and sacrifice for others; it is said that when a pelican can't find food for its young, it nourishes them with its own blood. Because of these connotations, it's related to paternal love. It indicates a feeling of generosity toward people close to you, but could also be a symbol of an excess of responsibilities that burden you. In this case, the dream is interpreted as the need for a well-deserved break.

Pencil ■ This is a dream that's of special interest for those who do creative activities, because it is a symbol of self-expression. To see yourself writing down or drawing something indicates the desire to collect scattered ideas, to order them and shape them into new projects. Sometimes what is written or drawn is a key to completing a real task.

❖ If in the dream, the pencil or pen you are using does not write, it means someone will accuse you of immorality.

Penis ■ It's not very frequent that the form of the penis itself appears in a dream. Normally it appears camouflaged under phallic objects. The clear appearance of this masculine organ is such a conclusive sexual affirmation that if it provokes fear or distress, the dreamer should reflect on their attitude toward sexuality. (See PHALLUS)

People ■ Dreams of being in a crowd that prevents you from moving easily suggest that you are unable to direct your life. If, in the dream, there are people you know your unconscious can be pointing at the attributes you admire and want to get. Feelings produced by the interaction with these people are allegorical of those feeling you are experiencing in the present. If, among the people, you do not know anyone, it may be a way to address some of your inner aspects. It is your duty to find out what they mean and how they adapt to your Self in real life.

❖ The dream books of ancient times say that as long as people in those dreams are gentle and well dressed, you will have good luck.

Perfume ■ Whether or not it is possible for a dream to bring you the real scent of a perfume, it is definitely possible for it to bring you memories associated with a perfume. The perfume is a symbol of spiritual presence, since it feeds memory and nostalgia. If it is gentle, it indicates delicacy; if it is strong, abruptness.

Periodical ■ As an instrument of communication of the press, the oneiric newspaper could indicate the desire to find more information before making a decision about some important matter that worries you. (See NEWSPAPER)

Persecution ■ Just as when you dream of falling, feeling persecuted comes from your own insecurity. Thus, it is one of the most common images produced during sleep. This dream mainly indicates the power that facts or feelings from the past have over you, since the conflicts arising from these past situations stay with you and prevent you from moving forward. It could be episodes of childhood or adolescence that are lodged in your memory and have taken the form of guilt or obsessions.

❖ Native Americans believe that if you have this dream, you should address your persecutor and fight him to unmask him. Following this advice, it is quite possible that you will discover your fears are not that threatening.

Petrification ■ In almost all the mythological stories, petrification is the gods' punishment for a gaze that has crossed the permissible limit. In this case, the dream is indicative of a guilty conscience. On the other hand, there are occasions when the dreamer tries to react to a violent situation, or simply tries to move, and can't. These dreams reflect a state of involuntary paralysis that could be physical, emotional, or intellectual. It is best to analyze the circumstances of your life to discover the cause of this immobility.

Phallus ■ In addition to masculine sexuality, the phallus represents life's creative force. It is a symbol of energy and power. A phallus in dreams indicates a time of high creativity. If a woman sees herself with a phallus, the dream indicates that she wants to develop her masculine side. Similarly, if a man dreams of an unknown woman with a phallus, he may feel like highlighting his feminine side.

❖ The phallus is the representation of all things masculine, bright, and Yang. Symbol of fertility, regeneration, power, and immortality, to many ethnic groups and tribes the phallus is the most commonly worshipped symbol. The ancient cave paintings found in Australia, Senegal, Niger, France, China, Japan, and India contain drawings of human reproductive systems. They prove the power of this symbol. Similarly, the Romans used phallic charms to ward off evil spirits. Furthermore, the god Priapus was represented as a large phallus with human face. Other Mexican peoples worshiped a winged serpent and the Hindus still pay homage to Shiva, a phallic emblem. On the other hand, the favorite deity in China is Shoulao, the god of longevity. This god has an enormous and elongated bald head like a phallus. For some traditions, dreaming of your own phallus predicts transient wealth, because it grows and shrinks. It can also denote secret projects, poverty, and captivity.

Pharmacy ■ A pharmacy is usually a sign of a bad time that will only end by making difficult decisions. If the pharmacist is the dreamer herself, she needs to be willing to accept help from people she trusts; if you own the pharmacy it evidences you are afraid of becoming ill; and if you are a customer of the pharmacy you will face unexpected events.

Pheasant ■ It is associated with the rooster, so both symbols are similar (the rooster more or less represents watchfulness). In China, the pheasant is an allegory of light and day. In oneiric terms, dreaming of a pheasant can be an invitation to carefully watch your environment. (See ROOSTER)

Photographs ■ Dreaming that you look at old photographs denotes a very strong link with the past and a pessimistic attitude on life. However, photographing a person evidences positive feelings toward her. If you are in a photo the dream can have the same interpretation as in MIRROR. The photograph, on the other hand, may represent your thoughts or ideas. Perhaps, it alerts you of something that requires your attention. The content of the photograph may tell you what it is.
❖ The oneiric superstition establishes that this dream warns against false hopes you may have about something. It can also mean heartbreak, especially if your image is photographed.

Picture ■ Dreaming that you paint or contemplate a picture highlights your need to escape from reality. Not surprisingly, a picture symbolizes the imagination. Therefore, its appearance and beauty reveal the way you are.

Pie ■ Seeing in a dream that someone gives you a pie foretells the possibility that a great job opportunity will soon appear. It could also signal that you will receive extraordinary profit with something that you do not expect.

Pig ■ It is a symbol of impure desires, passions, dirt, ignorance, stubbornness, gluttony, and rudeness. It can also have lewd sexual connotations. If a muddy pig appears in the dream it means that you get carried away by your most primary instincts. Conversely, if the pig is clean, it can be interpreted as a symbol of pragmatism and utility, since, as it is well known, all parts of this animal are used for human consumption.

❖ Pigs have been, for a long time, the main theme of disadvantageous superstitions. For example, among the fishermen it is believed that if someone utters the word "pig," before fishing begins, it means fisheries will be of low quality. However, in dreams they portend good news or a fluke.

Piggy bank ■ It's symbology has to do with the accumulation of material goods and the dreamer's relationship with money. To fill the bank indicates self discipline and precaution. To break it could be a warning that you will have an unexpected expense. To lose it, fear of squandering or of ruin.

Pilgrim ■ Symbolizes the search, atonement, purification, and homage. He sets forth on the journey in poverty, with humility, from which he participates in an initiation ritual that leads to enlightenment and saintliness. It is important to analyze the motive of the pilgrimage and know who accompanies you: if it is another person or an animal. Both cases will inform you about the aspects of your nature that carry you in your inner journey. (See CANE, CROSS, CROSSROADS, and ORIENTATION)

Pill ■ It could be that, in real life, you've found just the remedy to achieve inner harmony. If in the dream you are addicted to some sort of pills, it probably indicates that you behave too impulsively. This fact could be hurting you.
❖ Some people believe that, through hallucinogenic pills, the higher conscious is awakened. Evidently, this is not the best path to achieve this. Concentration and meditation are always much more innocuous and useful ways.

Pillow ■ Associated with softness and rest in real life, the pillow represents in oneiric terms the need for confidence and trust. When it is used to support the head, it signals a calm stage of life with blissful relations with the others. A dirty or torn pillow leaves it easy to tell the protagonist's unwillingness to face the problems of daily life.
❖ To a young woman, making pillows predicts good luck and happiness in the emotional field.

Pine ■ Represents longevity. The fir in particular symbolizes true friendship.

Pipe ■ To smoke a pipe in dreams is a symbol of comfort commonly associated with the act of suckling, which therefore denotes insecurity. It may also symbolize the longing that the dreamer has to escape. However, the effect that this act has on you in the dream is very significant. Do you enjoy the aroma of the lit pipe? Or was it disagreeable? It may be a warning that you are getting tired of your insecurity or dependence on something or someone.

Pirate ■ This dream indicates that the dreamer harbors some feeling of guilt or shame for having taken something that did not belong to him in real life. You should ask yourself if you have looted something, or maybe stolen someone's partner. The key word is "to pirate"; therefore the dream does not have a positive interpretation. Perhaps some unscrupulous person is taking advantage of you, or you of him.
❖ Pirates can be romantic, but they are also violent and dangerous. The dream is interpreted as a warning to work with caution.

Pistol ■ In addition to the relation that its meaning has with WEAPON, the image of the pistol is associated with the penis. Therefore, it indicates strength and virility. in general, it is a sign of a repressed desire, or the need to celebrate the masculine side, whether the dreamer is a man or a woman. If you kill someone with a pistol, the victim could represent all the aspects of your personality that you dislike or don't want to accept. If you kill an animal, it denotes that you repress your instincts, advocating for reason. If you are the victim, perhaps someone is making your life impossible in reality.

Pitcher ■ Pitcher image refers to female sexuality. Its content symbolizes everything that love can offer. A full pitcher indicates the willingness of a woman to give love and affection. To fill the pitcher indicates the desire to love a woman. To drink from it, the need for love. If the oneiric image is a known woman carrying a pitcher, it can be interpreted as a secret attraction to her.

Plane ■ All those dreams containing aircraft (airplanes, planes, spaceships, balloons, etc.) symbolize the desire for improvement, ambition, and the need to rise. So, to look at a plane reflects that you are greater than your problems or that you crave a fast rise in the professional, social, or spiritual realm. Conversely, if it crashes it means you are using an incorrect procedure to make progress. If you imagine that you fly in an airplane it is likely that your hopes are utopian and therefore are doomed to failure. On the other hand, it is likely that it is announcing a pending departure or imminent trip in life. This may include a new job, a new affair, or an adventure. Although, perhaps, it is simply a result of wanting to take a vacation. When you dream that the plane has an accident it means that you are very ambitious and have set goals too high. From a material or spiritual standpoint, you are having too high expectations compared to your capabilities so you may be unable to reach what you originally intended. (See LANDING)
❖ For modern superstitions, this dream means that soon you will receive money. If you are the pilot, then the business you are planning will be successful. If the plane crashes those plans will fail. The gypsy tradition believes that dreaming of a plane indicates you must share your projects with family and relatives.

Planet ■ To see planets in dreams reflects the relationship of the dreamer, no longer with a close inner circle, but rather with the universe that surrounds her.
❖ The spirit has reached an elevated position in dreams, from which it contemplates its situation from the cosmos. This may be an ideal moment to ask existential questions about the meaning of life. In any case, it denotes a high degree of spirituality.

Plank ■ Seeing a plank denotes that you will have methods to come to a good finish with your projects, given that the atmosphere of your environment be favorable for it. Cutting it is synonymous to the arrival of unexpected things that will delay your plans; and not being able to use the plank because it is not in good shape predicts discussions ending in great sorrow. Lastly, gathering planks indicates that it is a good time to associate yourself with others and go forward with a complex deal.

Planner ■ A planner symbolizes an extremely detailed personality. If the dreamer sees herself using it, then it is likely that some events will change her life. On the contrary, to lose or to tear it is a sign of frustrated plans and delays in business.

Plants ■ Image of the birth of life. A dream related to the growth of plants is probably related to your own growth and development. Plants express the evolution of the cosmos and the appearance of the first forms of existence. Another essential aspect of plans is their

PLANT

Monica dreamed: "I was a fearless biologist who had been entrusted with the task of analyzing some exotic plants, very difficult to find, that grew in the Amazon. To get them, I had to plunge into a deep swamp with dangerous murky waters, full of poisonous snakes. Still I did not hesitate for a moment; I jumped headfirst into the lake with a machete in my mouth, under the watchful eyes of a native, with white paint on his face, who from the bank held a rope attached to my foot. It did not take any time at all to emerge with a triumphant smile on my face and five samples of these curious plants in my hand. I sat down to examine them and discovered, astonished, that inside their buds, the plant contained tiny human skulls."

When Monica had this dream she was facing a very difficult situation: they had detected a malignant lump in her left breast, and she had to undergo treatment. Even then, she did not crumble, she trusted in the **strength of her body and spirit** and made every effort to fight the disease. The stagnant and muddy water of the dream reflected the difficulties she would have to face due to her health problem. However, her immersion in it, despite the danger, highlighted Monica's **fighting spirit**. The native, with white paint—like color of of her doctor's gown—and the rope that bound her to him, represented her ties with medicine, her other life raft together with her willpower.

The fact that she completed her mission was none other than an announcement of the happy outcome of her disease. After six months, she got over it for good. The skulls allude to our **spiritual doubts** about the beginning and the end of life, the concern that Monica felt about her fate. Plants, like skulls, are symbols of life, personal growth, and development. The dream was announcing to Monica that, despite the difficulties, the experience would make her grow, evolve, and better understand herself.

annual cycle, which makes clear the mystery of death and resurrection. In dreams, plants tend to represent our feelings and emotions.

❖ To dream of medicinal plants assures joy and success. To plant them, perseverance in business and your profession.

Plaster ■ Seeing this material predicts a spell of economic difficulty that will cause tension with a couple. If it appears in the form stucco, there is a danger before you.

Plate ■ If you have a great capacity to give to others, probably in one of your dreams you have seen a plate. Not surprisingly, this element says that you are willing to serve your fellows. If the dish is full of foods, it represents the food that is within you (tenderness, solidarity, etc.); however, if the plate is empty, you must find a way to fill it. If you are washing a stack of dishes, the dream may suggest certain boredom and monotony. Dreaming that you break plates is, however, a mechanism of the unconscious to discharge accumulated tension and provide some peace and quiet.

❖ Dreaming of plates is an excellent omen of health and wealth. You will never fail to have a plate on the table.

Plaza (square) ■ The plaza shows the type of relationship the dreamer has with the outside world. An empty square indicates isolation; a square full of people signals the fear of having your privacy invaded and being confused in the crowd (anonymity). However, for this dream's interpretation, the feeling of anxiety or placidly experimented by the dreamer is a determining factor.

Pocket ■ It suggests the existence of unexpected events in a matter that you thought was over. You should check this matter so it reaches a successful conclusion. A torn pocket is a sign of imprecision in your calculations which can generate many difficulties.

Poison ■ Dreaming of poison alludes to the appearance of a negative period in life. To manipulate it foretells that the displeasure will arrive in an unforeseen form; to feel poisoned foretells that you will be very hurt. Trying to poison someone else shows the desire to reach an objective marked by some means.

❖ This dream indicates suffering due to the misdeeds of others.

Poisoning ■ To dream that you poison someone is a symptom of life full of tensions and conflicts with the people around you. You should try a more peaceful communication with them. To be poisoned in dreams, however, alerts of the arrival of bad news about a relative who is in trouble. If you poison yourself it says that in real life you are carrying something out that is harmful to you.

Police ■ Chances are that the dream relates to your own conscience. Perhaps, you are aware that your behavior leaves much to be desired, and therefore you are trying to arrest yourself. Police embody protection, compliance with established rules, structure, and control. Dreaming of the police denotes insecurity and dependence. If the police detain you justly it evidences the presence of guilt. Now, if you are accused of something you have not done it expresses the injustices you suffer in real life: repressions (very often sexual) resulting from norms you must comply to. If you break the rules, however the dream shows that you need to reaffirm yourself and you wish to overstep the limits imposed by others.
❖ According to tradition, dreaming of a police officer portends that someone you love will help you.

Pomegranate ■ It is associated with fertility, sensuality, and pleasure. If it is open in dreams it is an invitation to enjoy life.

Pool ■ Its meaning is associated with WATER and LAKE. However, the pool is more related to leisure and fun. In this dream, it is important to know the depth, how cloudy or clear the water is, and the people who wander around the edges. In this elements, the keys to a correct interpretation are hidden.

Poppy ■ This flower symbolizes serenity and simple pleasures, especially after a period of hard work for the dreamer. However, it may also represent the arrival of a stage of ephemeral pleasures and possible cheating by people around you. In any case, seeing yourself smelling a poppy is evidence of fatigue from fighting the misfortunes and the need to live more pleasant moments, albeit brief and superficial.

Port ■ Shows your desire to escape, to run away from reality, because it represents the beginning or end of a journey. These desires do not involve a genuine desire for change. It also symbolizes security. You may be living a stormy stage and need a little calm and shelter. Resting will help you regain strength and to face things again with renewed energy so everything will "arrive safely." In the event that, besides the image of the port, you undertake a boat trip, the meaning of the dream is the opposite to the one mentioned above. Now it seems that you are beginning a different stage in your life.

❖ Entering a port heralds the arrival of a safety period. But, if you leave the port, one of your friendships will be broken.

Portrait ■ Seeing a portrait of yourself reflects the visible world in reality. A self-portrait allows you to illuminate your true personality or what you desire to be. In general, this type of dream shows a lack of communication with one's interior. If you create a positive image of yourself, it means that you are satisfied with how you are. If the opposite is shown, the dream evidences that you are afraid to discover something hidden in yourself. Lastly, dreaming of making a portrait of someone else manifests feelings toward that person.

Poster ■ A poster present in a dream is often a direct message from the unconscious. It is important to know if you were able to read it and if you remember what was written or drawn; there lies the key for the interpretation of the dream. Sometimes the unconscious uses word play and phrases to tell you something. If an image is displayed instead of words it is necessary to consult its symbolism. Other symbols and the oneiric scene context are also important for the correct interpretation of the dream.

Pot ■ The pot is a symbol of home and family life, just like other similar utensils cush as frying pans, saucepans, etc. If you see a pot over the fire, it will be difficult for you to lead a simple life free from worry. If the dream is not pleasant, the pot could suggest fear of the responsibility to support the family.

Pothole ■ A bumpy road indicates difficulties to be surpassed in order to achieve fruition. It is important to analyze the context of the dream and the rest of the oneiric symbols to determine the kind of situation you face.

Prairie ■ It suggests freedom, spaciousness, and joy. (See GRASS, FLOWERS, and HERB)

Prayer ■ It signals the presence of a feeling of guilt, although also the need for external help to solve a problem that you do not know how to get out of. Despite the apparent helplessness, you trust in that luck will be fair. (See MAGIC)

Precipice ■ See ABYSS

Pregnancy ■ Dreaming of a pregnancy can express your fears about the possibility of upcoming parenthood. But in addition, it can also symbolize all those hidden resources you have inside you but fail to discover. For this reason, this dream is an invitation to self-discovery.

❖ According to some popular traditions, to a woman, to dream she is pregnant denotes she will not be happy with her husband and her children will not be very graceful. To a virgin this dream predicts scandal and adversity. However, if the dreamer is pregnant in real life the dream predicts an uncomplicated birth and rapid recovery.

Priest ■ A priest could represent religion and its traditional norms. You may be in a period of moral self-judgement. On the other hand, the priest could be a manifestation of your own spiritual wisdom. In this sense, dreaming that a priest hears your confession is an invitation to bring yourself closer to more transcendental truths, to connect with your true essence. Only in this way will you be able to find the way to reveal to yourself what it is that you want to do with your life.

❖ Any dream depicting a priest has advantageous omens. It usually signifies the end of a dispute that has been concerning you for a while.

Prince ■ Dreaming of becoming a prince or princesses reveals a desire for primacy, triumph, and conquest of personal values. For this reason, it is a common dream among young people because it shows the dreamer's emerging (not yet materialized) ambitions and aspirations. It symbolizes the hero and heroine, equipped with the most beautiful and desirable qualities. It represents courage, strength, and intelligence, in the male version; and tenderness as well as beauty, in women. Common to both is a strong talent to love with devotion and fidelity.

Printer ■ This indicates a fear that someone will publish secret aspects of your personality, or reveal hidden truths you know. It may be a warning from the unconscious to be prudent and not talk too much.

Prisoner ■ Dreams in which you are a prisoner refer to a limitation of your energy and creativity. They are also related to changes that take place outside, changes you cannot enjoy from your jail. In any case, you must reflect on the causes of this detention. (See JAIL and CAGE)

Prize ■ You may be pleased with yourself and your unconscious is letting you know so. Maybe, you have made great progress in your personal development or your most important objectives have been met.

❖ Money will soon come to your hands.

Procession ■ This dream shows the need to constantly move forward without being attached to earthly affairs. A procession is also reminiscent of Israel's great exodus and the desert journey. Every procession is a ritual that embodies the idea of a cycle because it returns to the starting point. If you dream of a procession it indicates you want to purify yourself, to expiate your sins. It is important to analyze the reason for your journey.

Promise ■ If the dreamer sees herself making a promise, the dream reveals either the need to reaffirm a commitment or fear of breaching it. If someone promises something to you it indicates your distrust and the feeling of insecurity that such promise produces on you.

Propeller ■ This is an emblem of dynamism. To dream of a boat or airplane propeller indicates that you are optimistic, enthusiastic, and impulsive. The faster it turns, the faster you will advance in life. Obviously, this period will not last forever, so you must take advantage of this shot of vitality.

Prostitute ■ Dreaming of a prostitute's company tells you that you are forgetting your principles and this will harm you in the long run. This dream can also suggest that, somehow, you are prostituting yourself: at work, for example, moral or emotionally. For a man, this dream may represent his attitude toward women. Any type of attraction or rejection could be a reflection of your real feeling regarding the dream's topic. Maybe this episode intends to encourage you to reflect on your values.

❖ For a woman, this dream predicts an emotional life full of setbacks and unhappiness.

Puddle ■ If you are splashing in a puddle it marks the enjoyment of those pleasures which later bring you problems. Conversely, to avoid one without getting wet indicates the ability to overcome dangers while keeping calm. To see your own reflection in a puddle predicts quick economic gains; to fall in one, serious setbacks; and leaving a puddle after being soaked, the end of annoyance.

Pumpkin ■ Its figure is associated with domestic wealth and bliss. It is also a symbol of healing and daily wisdom. The rest of the dream's symbols must be interpreted to be sure of its meaning. In any case, pumpkin is a sign of good omens.

❖ Eating pumpkins is indicative of calm, tranquility, and good news.

Punishment ■ Often, this dream is provoked by feelings of guilt for something that has happened or something you have done. No matter if it is you who is punished or the one who punishes, it always reveals a sense of guilt, defeat, or resentment. You may also be punishing yourself. An individual that had traumatic experiences in childhood may constantly blame herself for her actions. In that case, the dreamer must liberate herself from the social or parental pressure that subjugates her.

❖ Gypsy people believe that dreaming that you are punished reveals the guilt you feel for having neglected your personal relationships.

Puppet ■ Puppets have a dual symbolism of opposite meanings. On the one hand, the inconsistency of character, lack of initiative, and inability to make one's own decisions. On the other, the power and the ability to pull the strings, that is, to make others to act under your orders. It's not a positive dream because it shows situations which are not clear or desirable.

❖ The omens of this dream portend happiness thanks to your ability to organize people. To make a puppet dance promises good business and great profit.

Puppy ■ If you do not have children, puppies express a desire to have them; and if you are already a parent, a concern for everything regarding your children. If the puppy is healthy and well-formed it augurs well; but if it is sick or dirty, it raises the possibility that a child gets sick.

Purple ■ A dark red and purple color that denotes dignity, success, honor, and loving happiness.

Purse ■ The purse is a common symbol of female sexuality. It can refer to the genitals of a woman or the uterus. According to Freud, just as purse opens and closes, the woman has the power to give to or refuse others sexually. On the other hand, as the purse usually contains money, it also symbolizes the treasure of your authentic Self. If you dream that you lose it, you may be suffering the loss of your true identity. Dreaming of an empty purse indicates a lack of security.

❖ If you dream that you open your wallet and find money inside, you will achieve happiness. The omen is intensified if it is gold. Similarly, it is good luck to find a purse. But if it is others who find it, it is an omen that soon you will receive bad news.

Pushing ■ The meaning of this dream changes according to the object being pushed. So if it is something heavy, you will need to prioritize your interests over the abuses of others; but if it is light, a tendency to conformity becomes apparent. To push a person reveals your guilt for having acted irresponsibly.

Puppets ■ Puppets are dolls that are controlled by forces outside of themselves. Their presence in dreams indicates clearly that you need to retake control in your life. If you imagine that you are the one manipulating the puppets, the dream advises you that you need to allow others to express themselves freely.

Puzzles ■ Puzzles are challenges that test intelligence and cleverness. If you dream of a puzzle, you may have to face a situation in which you need to use these qualities.

Pyramid ■ In some cultures, the pyramid symbolizes the union between the earthly and the divine, as well as representing the potential energy that flows in favor of the individual to achieve set goals. The good or bad condition of the pyramid, as well as its position (right side up or upside down) are signs of external factors that have a positive or negative effect on the dreamer.

❖ A pyramid is a sign of dignity and wealth; and inverted one, however, indicates ruin. To exit one predicts honors; and to find yourself on top, future glory.

Q

Quarrel ■ Contrary to real life, quarrels in dreams are a positive sign that announces profound lasting friendship. Seeing two people of opposite sexes quarreling foretells the birth of a passionate amorous relationship; but, if the protagonists are two women, a period of tension and dispute is coming.

Quarry ■ Quarries are the result of human activity. Perhaps, you have gotten into such a hole and now you do not know how to get out. Dreaming of a quarry also reveals the desire to explore the unconscious (the earth). Thus, you may be discovering all the fears you hid in the past and now dare to confront. In a social sense, the quarry can represent your concern for the preservation of the environment.
❖ A chalk quarry promises financial difficulties that can be solved by working hard. Stone quarry portends a trip.

Queen ■ The figure of the queen could symbolize the mother of the dreamer or another powerful feminine figure on whom you depend. If an adult woman dreams that she rules as queen, it could be interpreted as a manifestation of excessive ambition, or as the culmination of her process of personal maturity. If the queen is dethroned, it indicates insecurity on the part of the dreamer, despite the apparent authority they have been granted. According to Carl Jung, the strange writings of the alchemists were symbols that favored the integration of all elements of your personality. The queen, in this sense, personified the feminine strengths that are found in your psyche.
❖ Seeing yourself crowned queen assures power to the dreamer, but not happiness.

Quilt ■ Its image refers to cozy comfort. It can be interpreted as the need for affection and protection. A quilt that provides too much warmth is a sign of burden. To cover someone with a quilt indicates the excessive care you provide to someone.
❖ Dreaming of quilts predicts pleasant and comfortable circumstances. For a young woman this dream means that her practicality and boldness will make a man interested in her; he will want to marry her. If the quilt is clean but has holes she will get a husband who appreciates her courage but he will not be the most suitable.

Quinella ■ Dreams in which you make a quinella—or other betting games—do not tend to be premonitions. In every form, this type of scene is positive, as the prize ensures security in life. In case the quinella that you dream of is not a winning one, the message is still advantageous, as it reminds you that what does not happen today could happen tomorrow. If, on the other hand, you are betting your inheritance, the dream advises that you are leaving the resolution of your problems up to chance. (See GAME, LOTTERY, EMBLEM, and ROULETTE)

R

Rabbit ■ Because of its great fertility, it is associated with sexuality. On one hand, it is a symbol of abundance and generosity. On the other, of shyness and innocence. If in your dream a rabbit disappears through a hole, it can mean you are trying to escape from a problem.

❖ The omens are advantageous if the oneiric rabbits run over a field of green grass. If you see them locked in hutches, your fortune will decline. And if they are dead it portends a disaster.

Race ■ If you always are in a hurry, this dream can be an allegorical representation of life. It also reveals the need to compare yourself to others; a very competitive personality. By slowing down you are likely to get more. The slow-moving tortoise beats the impulsive hare. It may also indicate that you are taking too many risks or spending excessive energy.

❖ If you are running or driving a car, the dream states that you will soon receive news. If you win the race, that news will be wonderful.

Radar ■ It is an element that can be interpreted as a symbol of intuition, or of a type of communication that goes beyond words. The dreamer traverses a moment of special sensibility that permits them to perceive situations that escape the senses.

Radio ■ What is played or said on the radio could be messages from the subconscious. You are tuning in to its frequency and should take note of what you hear in order to know what it has to do with your feelings while awake. Frequently you turn on the radio in the background without paying much attention to what it says. So, your dream might be encouraging you to attentively listen something that is currentlybeing told to you, but that you ignore for whatever reason. On the other hand, dreaming that you are interviewed in a radio broadcast manifests the extreme need for communication. The dream may indicate to you that you should externalize your opinions without fear and believe more in yourself.

❖ Recent superstition says that listening to a radio in a dream presages an imminent reunion or encounter.

Radiography ■ Dreaming of radiography is a sign of someone that you strongly believe spreads rumors about you and grossly judges you.

Raft ■ The raft represents a lifeline in a desperate situation. It is a dream of hope. The dreamer has the chance to succeed. However, it indicates the need to find support.

Rage ■ Rage in dreams evidences your state in real life, although sometimes you have not been able to express it. You will have to try to search for the origin of this feeling and try to express it in a controlled manner towards people who have not caused it. Seeing someone raging announces betrayal from someone very close to you. (See FURY)

Rags ▪ Rags tend to denote an excess of preoccupation for one's images and a lack of self confidence. If you don't feel well, seeing yourself dressed in rags indicates personal neglect, moral decline, and misery. When the sensation of the dream is pleasant, it reveals the superiority of intellect over the physical or superficial. (See CLOTHES)

❖ Some oracles predict that you will suffer great losses if you have this dream. Other interpretations consider it a sign that you will make a wise decision.

Rain ▪ A sign of fertility, rain portends abundance and prosperity when it falls heavily: it may be that new stage of life is about to begin. However, it is a sign of obstacles if it becomes a downpour. If it is light but steady, the fruits of your efforts will soon arrive; whereas, if it's muddy, disasters and risks draw near. To see thunderclouds before rain denotes a fear of failure; and to hear the rain from inside, the tendency to delegate to your problems to others.

❖ Generally, dreaming of rain is considered a good omen, unless it falls on livestock. In this case, it announces losses in business.

Rainbow ▪ It is an image of hope and prosperity. After a period of gloom, the rainbow predicts redemption and good news. Soon you will live a time of peace and tranquility in which success will be a constant and your wishes will come true. It is also associated with the pursuit of self-knowledge. The rainbow symbolizes a bridge between heaven and earth, that is, between your earthly self and your enlightened or superior self.

❖ When the rainbow looks bright and colorful in your dreams, gypsies predict an advantageous change. If the color is dull something will deteriorate.

Raincoat ▪ Dreaming of this garment manifests the dreamer's desire to be protected from adversity. Therefore, if you appear without one in a rainstorm, it denotes that you will face dangers without the support of your loved ones. Buying a raincoat is a sign of caution; and taking it off, certainty that a bad spell has ended.

Rape ▪ Dreaming of rape symbolizes the loss of control over your reality. You are living in a situation in which you own love seems damaged. For a man, it could be

a sadistic representation of his sexual desires. It is possible that you harbor feelings of vengeance towards the opposite sex. For a woman, it could represent sexual fears or the manifestation of masochistic fantasies.

❖ Even Victorian books about dreams contemplate this image. According to superstition, if a woman dreams of rape, her pride will be damaged. In the case that it is a close friend who suffers, it is saying that you will hear impactful news.

Raptor ▪ A raptor is, almost always, an alarm that warns of near danger. It indicates distrust and fear of the dreamer towards something that is blossoming over you.

Rat ▪ Rats keep a close relation to sickness and death. In Egypt and China they embodied the evil deity of plague. Dreaming of rats is not exactly pleasant, as they symbolize degenerative passions that are consuming you, such as rancor, jealousy, hatred, avarice, etc. It deals with those thoughts and feelings that you hide or reject, but that you have inside. If in the dream you are aggressive towards the rat it is a sign that you have the capacity to dominate the situation. However, the dream could also reference a certain attitude of the dreamer: you may be behaving like a sewer rat in real life, and your subconscious is reproaching you.

❖ Some superstitions believe that rats have human souls. Generally, their actions should be observed in dreams, and corrected if they are found in your behavior.

Reading ▪ To read in dreams reflects your desire to know the secrets, intentions, or thoughts of others. However, it can also reveal a discovery, surprise, or revelation of a secret. The sensations that you have about reading (if is is boring, interesting, entertaining, etc.) will be important to analyze the dream.

Rebirth ▪ It is often said that to obtain true development, the old has to die. In the space that it leaves something new will be born. The future presents an important change.

❖ The majority of traditions use symbols of baptism to represent the entry into spiritual life. One of the prettiest is phoenix. Although it is consumed in its flames, it is reborn from the ashes. So, this manifests new hopes and a great interior transformation.

Recipe ▪ The type of recipe that you see in the dream will determine the interpretation. If it is a kitchen recipe, it is possible that you need to make more of an effort at work or in a relationship with someone in your environment. If it is a prescription, you will have the need to ask for help from a third party to solve a problem that is getting out of control.

Reconciliation ▪ Dreaming that you are reconciling with some loved one from whom you have distances yourself or fought with in real life indicates that it is a good time to make peace with that person. If you don't have any quarrels with anyone, it is a sign that you are searching to make peace with yourself. Your interior is probably split between opposite tendencies and is not balanced.

Red ▪ This is the color of blood, fire, passion, war, and of sexual instincts. When this color dominates in dreams, it means that you are willing to act viscerally, be it with love or with hate.

Reduction ▪ It may suggest the threat of a loss of prestige or status, as well as the need for affection.

Reed ▪ Due to its characteristic weakness, reeds represent docility, immaturity, and fickleness. If you dream of this element, the oneiric images are reminding you that—even if you are not acting out of malice—you cannot trust yourself, since you are unable to keep your word. Although it can seem contradictory, the flexibility of the reed also represents the value of wisdom.

Reef ▪ It is associated with sea monsters. It is a sinister enemy that comes to meet you. It represents insurmountable obstacles in your way that cause total fear. It also denotes a state of stalemate. In this sense, it relates to becoming petrified, unable to move on or grow.

Reform ▪ If you dream that you are renovating the house, it could indicated the deen for change of aspect or image. There is something in you that has deteriorated and needs a good reform.

Refuge ▪ Searching anxiously for refuge for protection from the inclement environment, or from persecution, indicates a state of insecurity, and the need to search for help and protection. The dreamer could have been rejected socially and feel isolated on the emotional plane, or they may be searching to protect themselves from disloyal and false people that surround them. In the same manner, the dream denotes a great desire to evade problems. Fleeing, of course, reduces the probability that they will be resolved.

❖ Dreaming of displaced peoples, for whatever reason, foretells failure of well conceived plans.

Rehearsal ▪ This dream is recommending you to think before acting. You must organize your thoughts, review them, and avoid rushing. The role the dreamer plays in the rehearsal is significant because it may be advising you how to act. The rest of the casting and the director will help you to relate the dream to real life.

Reincarnation ▪ If, in dreams, you have the sensation of living a previous life (or that you reincarnate as something or someone), it means that you need to go beyond your current circumstances. The curiosity that you have to know the future encourages this kind of dream. In Asia it is believed that once man has reached an appropriate level of spirituality, he can remember his past lives. These come to human memory through meditation and through dreams.

❖ The Hollywood actor Sylvester Stallone is convinced that he lived during the French Revolution; the singer Engelbert Humperdinck believes that in a past life he was a Roman emperor; and a Californian seer told the pop star Tina Turner that she is the incarnation of the wife of an Egyptian pharaoh.

Reins ▪ Represent the possibility of driving a car or horses, like vital forces in your existence. Reins symbolize the relationship that is established between will and intelligence.

Rejection ▪ You may not want to accept an influence or situation that has been imposed on you in real life. If you are rejected, the dream reveals that you have hidden feelings of underestimation or that you have distanced yourself from your environment due to lack of confidence. Sometimes this is produced in the sexual plane. According to Freud's studies, you are the one that rejects yourself: your conscience does not integrate sexual needs of the subconscious. In this sense, it would be as though you were punishing yourself.

❖ Some oneiric oracles believe that the meaning of this dream is the reverse. Generally, rejection foretells successes.

Rejuvenation ▪ This dream reflects the desire to go back to a happy time; or rather, the need to take up issues that were left unresolved in the past. It is also a symbol of vitality, and indicates a moment in which you regain hope and strength that you believed lost. It is a calming dream that reminds the dreamer that they are still young and strong for their age, or that they are not as old as they feel.

Relationships ▪ People that appear in your dreams, especially strangers, tend to represent facets of yourself. In this sense, seeing the truth close to you can be impactful. Relationships and interaction that you maintain with this oneiric group of people shows the harmony that you keep within you. Also, it will manifest those parts of your personality that you do not bring to light. For example, if a man dreams of a woman, it could indicate that he needs to accept the feminine side of his nature. In the same way, if it is a woman that dreams of a man, she may need to behave in a more masculine way. Needless to say, the dream could also be representing a situation from real life and your feelings with respect to it.

❖ The way in which the people act will tell you much about future events. If they are friendly, it foretells happy times; if they have bad intentions, you should be cautious because an disaster could occur in your surroundings.

Relatives ▪ Often relatives symbolize facets of your personality or personal characteristics of which you may or may not be proud. The interpretation of this dream will vary if it is close family members or distant relatives, and based on what they symbolize to you. It may deal with a family reunion due to some event (like a wedding or a funeral), in which you feel strongly sheltered and protected, or, on the contrary, surrounded by distant family member in whom you can identify many defects you detest. (See GRANDPARENTS, FAMILY, SIBLING, MOTHER, and FATHER)

Remembering ▪ A dream in which you remember something that you tend to forget while awake could be a warning from the subconscious not to forget something. Occasionally, you awake in an abrupt manner to make sure that your memory has not fooled you in a way that could bring negative consequences.

Repairing ▪ This dream indicates that you are recuperating from something that saddened you in the past. You are in a period of renovation. The object that you are repairing symbolizes the thing that you need to overcome.

❖ According to some beliefs, mending clothing that you wear in dreams foretells bad luck.

Reptiles ▪ Reptiles symbolize the most primitive, voracious, and slippery aspects of your personality: your base instincts. The cold bloodedness of these animals is synonymous with the lack of emotion and consideration for others. In the case that you dream that a reptile devours you, it means that your instincts are dominating your actions. On the contrary, if you defeat a reptile, it is a sign that you are fighting to dominate your base aspects.

Rescue ▪ Generally this manifests a circumstance from real life that exerts greater force than normal. It is particularly when you have to bring about some type of business or project that the dreamer sees this. On the other hand, the person or thing that you save can be an aspect of your personality that you have previously rejected and are looking for a means of expressing it. If you are rejected, you should analyze the dream scene in its totality. For example, being saved from the jaws of a ferocious animal could indicate that you fear something related to your instincts or nature. If they save you from a storm at sea, it evidences how close you have been to drowning in your own emotions. The person that takes you out of danger probably symbolizes the psychological qualities and attitudes that you should take on in real life.

❖ The most common tradition says that everyone has the potential to be a hero or superhero. Within you are hidden the resources that make you able to get what you want. In this way, nothing is impossible.

Reservoir ▪ Unlike lakes, the waters of a reservoir represent sickness, since their violent movement and stagnant waters are fruit of the artificial. (See LAKE)

Restroom ▪ This dream could have a physiological cause simply because you have to go to the bathroom. The unconscious, in this case, recognizes the body's need and uses the dream to wake you. On the other side, the urge to go to the restroom means that you expect to get rid of old habits and change your lifestyle. In the same manner, the unconscious could be advising you that you are incubating an infection. The act of going to the bathroom would be a way of eliminating toxins.

❖ To dream of the restroom indicates legal problems regarding property.

Retired ▪ When you are young, dreaming of retirement demonstrates a desire to forget your worries and live more peacefully. Probably you are carrying a great tension and the subconscious is telling you you need to enjoy a period of calm. If the dreamer is already retired in real life, it is just a reflection of their current situation.

Reunion ▪ Seeing people reunited signals the fear of not being accepted as you are and being excluded from your social environment. On the contrary, participating in a reunion and expressing your own opinions denotes security in oneself and the ability to reach proposed goals.

Revolution ▪ Dreaming that you are taking part in a revolution manifests that, inside, your attitudes and behaviors are full of irritation. It is a call that you be what you want to be and not what social norms impose upon you.
❖ This dream foretells problems in business. If the revolution is bloody, it means that you are taking too many financial risks.

Rice ▪ Dreaming of rice augurs happy events because it is a symbol of fertility in many cultures. These events can occur at any level: emotional, professional, familial, etc.
❖ Eating rice predicts longevity and abundance; to buy it, increase in equity; to cook it, healing; to harvest it, good luck.

Richness ▪ The meaning of richness is the opposite of what it seems. Everyone knows that dreams of material richness are pleasant and enjoyable. However, you must treat this type of oneiric image with caution. Temporal possession can bring you to think that it is definitive and that it will always last. It is not like this, as reality shows. A dream of this kind can definitely remind you that you should not accommodate a situation of abundance, as it is possible that it will transform into one of shortage.

Riddle ▪ Riddles often indicate confusion and disgust. Attempting to solve riddles denotes you will be part of a company that will test your patience. If you see ourselves as players of a TV contest, there is a possibility you will soon have to answer unpleasant questions.

Rider ▪ Dreaming of a rider predicts you will receive unexpected news or gifts soon. If it is a woman who dreams of the rider, she will have family problems from wanting to marry a man of a lower social status. Seeing a rider fall from the horse is a sign of failure in business and major economic losses. When the rider is the dreamer himself, he will see improvement in emotional and familial relationship as well as in his work.

Riding ▪ Riding in a dream symbolizes the duality between mind and instincts. Therefore, the message that conveys the unconscious will relate to your intellect or, more often, with your sexual activity. So, if you gallop at full speed it means that you should set your senses free. Depending on whether you master the horse or if it bolts, you will know if you are able to keep them under control. (See HORSE)
❖ The dream superstition estimates very good omens for this dream, especially if someone you love is riding with you.

Riding crop ▪ A crop is a symbol of power over others. If the dreamer carries a crop in her hand it can be interpreted as a sign of confidence, but also as an intransigent attitude toward people around her, in her daily life. Conversely, being hit by someone else's crop reflects fear and inferiority complex.

Ring ▪ Like all round and closed figures, the ring symbolizes continuity and wholeness. Therefore, it serves as a symbol of marriage and also represents the bond to a particular affiliation, group, or society. It also provides confidence and power because of the support it symbolizes. The presence of a ring in your dreams portends engagement or a declaration of love, as well as the consolidation of an incorporation. Of course, whatever happens to the ring in dreams it could also apply to what it represents. In this way, a broken alliance foreshadows divorce or separation; losing a ring promises disputes with the person who gave it to you; to put it on someone else denotes the desire to exercise dominion over that person, etc. Rings, in addition to the above, show loyalty to your own principles and ideals. They can also refer to an oath or promise. Finally, by being the symbol of eternity, without beginning or end, the ring represents the true self.
❖ The condition of the omen varies whether you receive or lose the ring. In the first case, the omens are good. In the latter, you will face some challenges. When you find the ring by chance, it means that you will soon have a new friend or a new lover. Finally,

certain traditions assert that dreaming that you receive a ring means the breaking of promise.

Ritual ▪ Rituals symbolize transitions in life. Also, they make up a representation that invites you to escape the limits imposed but the conscience. In this sense, you can enjoy the wide world of your imagination. According to Carl Jung's studies, in dreams, images of fertility rites emerge in the collective subconscious. In this manner, the dream tries to separate the subconscious from the conscience so that you can connect with your most instinctive you.

❖ Shamanic rituals bring the individual to a state where the dreamer develops prophetic and clairvoyant powers. So, it is recommended to take note of the dreams upon waking, in case they contained premonitory information.

Rival ▪ Oneiric thoughts in which you appear fighting against your rivals reflect real life problems in a literal way. In this way, dreaming that you are winning signifies that you have decided to act. In contrast, if you only speak with them, the subconscious is suggesting that you resolve things peacefully. But, if the rival attacks you and you do not fight, it indicates that you not only accept defeat, but you also do not do anything to change the sign of the fight.

River ▪ The current of a river symbolizes vital energy. A river with clear water that flows is a symbol of happiness and satisfaction. If you dream of this element, everything indicates that your emotional side is totally balanced. But, if the waters are turbulent, you may be having emotional conflicts. In contrast, if the river is dry, the dream represents the suspicion that you have been the victim of deceit. According to Jung's psychoanalysis, the river represents life, destiny. If the dreamer is enjoying the shore, it denotes a fear of existence. In contrast, if something pleasant attracts him to the opposite shore, it suggests that to achieve your goal, you should overcome tests and learn to dominate the currents of the spirit. Freudian psychoanalysis, in contrast, associated the river with the father figure. Lastly, crossing a river denotes a change in style of life. (See WATER and FISH)

❖ In his novel *Siddhartha*, Herman Hesse writes close to the river. He says that you can learn a lot from it: how to listen with the heart and how to hope with the soul without passion or desires nor judgments or opinions that trouble you.

Robot ▪ The dream could be telling you that you have a mechanical behavior and that you have lost the ability to express your feelings. You should pay attention to the character of your attitudes: they are probably rigid and cold. On the other hand, automatization could represent the role you play at work. Often the tasks that you have to do at work is mechanical and routine.

❖ Robots do not appear in ancient books about dreams, but they have been converted into modern archetypes. In this technological age, these machines symbolize the fear of dehumanizing yourself. Further, they could reference the fact that death is inevitable.

Rock ▪ A rock symbolizes being, permanence, security, and cohesion with oneself. Its durability is the opposite of living things, submitted to the laws of change, of decadence and death. It symbolizes, in general, unity and strength. If you dream that you are navigating toward the rocks, you may find yourself in a dangerous situation soon. In this case, the best thing would be to change methods when you start your issues. (See STONE)

❖ Sirens that, with their songs, directed seamen to their deaths on the rocks are a symbol of the perverse side of intuition. The danger of the rocks, therefore, reminds you that you cannot disregard too much in real life.

Rocket ▪ It represents momentary and fleeting joy. It also represents the uncontrolled explosion of emotions that overwhelms you in certain situations. Maybe it is time to relax and not to be swayed by euphoria.

Rodents ▪ Rodents usually have a direct relationship with sickness and death. (See RAT and MOUSE)

Roof ▪ A roof is a sign of protection from external circumstances. On the contrary, it could also damage you in a sense: your protection prevents you from enriching yourself with new experiences. Depending on the feeling that you get (pleasant or unpleasant), the meaning of the dream can lean to one or another possibility. In the first case, the subconscious is communicating that you should open your mind to new ideas, but in the other, you will not advance enough.

Room ▪ The room is a symbol of individuality, of personal thought. Each type represents the aspects of our mind and being. The living room is the conscious; the basement or root cellar, the unconscious; the upstairs bedrooms, the spiritual aspirations of the dreamer. It's meaning depends on the state in which you find the room. If it has windows, it symbolizes the possibility of communication with the exterior. On the contrary, a closed room without windows can symbolize virginity or lack of communication. In oneiric terms, there are also established equivalencies between the room and the physical body, so you must analyze the environment in the room. A pleasant room augurs well-being and serenity; if it lacks openness, it reflects isolation, fears, and insecurity. (See HOUSE)

❖ There are many superstitions regarding this. According to one of them, dreaming of your own room means you will visit far away lands.

Rooster ▪ It is a solar symbol, early bird, emblem of vigilance and activity. During the Middle Ages, it was a Christian icon of great importance, as demonstrated by its massive presence in the highest vane of the cathedrals' towers (allegory of custody and resurrection). If you dream of a rooster announcing the dawn you can interpret it as a rebirth, as the beginning of a new stage in your lives. Freudianism identifies it with the pure masculine, aggressive, and proud sexuality. Jungian school recognizes in it a symbol of light, birth, because of its close connection with the dawn.

❖ Overall, the crowing of a rooster is associated with arrival of good news and success in love.

Roots ▪ Symbolize ties with the land, but also, the hidden aspect of the subconscious. Conflicts with others or with one's own personality that need to be attended to.

Rope ▪ General symbol of connection and attachment, like the chain. If the rope is choking you the dream reveals fear of dealing with problems. Similarly, tying objects or people is a sign of repression of feelings. The rope may also symbolize the desire to rise spiritually or to move up both socially and professionally.

Rose ▪ There are many meanings surrounding this flower, as it symbolizes spiritual richness, perfection, delicateness, and emotions. It tends to be fundamentally associated with love and how you feel with respect you your past and present emotional relationships. So, dreaming that someone gives you a rose indicates that you are going through a moment of emotional plenty. However, if the thorns stab you, the dream reflects a fear of sexual relations. Freud, lastly, associated the flower with the form of female genitals, and due to its usual color, with menstruation.

❖ Since roman times, the rose is the symbol of love. The romans believed that this flower would protect the dead from evil spirits. For this reason, there was a tradition of decorating a tomb with roses. In oneiric terms, it foretells security and protection. Many oracles believe that the omens of this dream are all advantageous.

Roulette ▪ Dreaming that you are betting your inheritance in roulette means that you leave the resolution of your problems to chance. (See GAME, LOTTERY, and QUINELLA)

Rowing ▪ Dreaming that you are rowing in turbulent waters is a symbol of emotional confusion. You are consuming your strengths with a passion that does not correspond that may be destructive. If, on the contrary, you row in calm water, the dream is associated—like all with calm water—with an inner state of well-being, confidence, and security.

Ruby ▪ The ruby is the stone of felicity, of vital intensity, and of love. Therefore, dreaming of a ruby expresses the desire to experience a passionate adventure with intense love that will end in felicity.

❖ Red like blood, this beautiful stone, when it appears in dreams, predicts happiness and unexpected gifts.

Rudder ▪ Rudders represent the possibility of driving a ship, or the vital energy that rules your existence. It is a symbol of the relationship that you establish between intelligence and will.

Ruins ▪ The meaning of ruins is literal: they represent destruction, the end of life. Many people experience this vision with a certain amount of melancholy. However, this destruction is mostly necessary to begin to build new and different things. If a monument or temple in a perfect state appears in your dreams, it is a sign that you will have success in your upcoming projects. If you find ancient ruins or sacred relics in dreams, it could symbolize that you have discovered the treasures that you guard inside. So, you have found the ancient subconscious wisdom that you harbor within you. (See ABANDONMENT, COLD, DEATH, and ROCK)

❖ Discovering buried ruins assures comfortable and serene old age. Walking over ruins foretells financial losses.

Running ▪ Dreaming that you run—no matter the cause—without reaching the final line is a sign of anxiety and nervousness. This dream indicates that you should monitor both your physical and emotional health. However, if the feeling is nice, running augurs success. (See DROWNING)

Rupture ▪ If you dream that you break an object or sentimental link, it means that you are leaving a stage of your life behind. Something is coming to an end and you should accept it. Dreaming that you are breaking things in a voluntary way could be a mechanism of the subconscious to discharge aggressiveness and to calm accumulated tension.

❖ Dreaming of mirrors breaking foretells the loss of money; breaking glass, a fight between women; breaking plates predicts indigestion.

S

Sack ■ A full sack foretells good luck, success, and happiness; in contrast, an empty one is synonymous with economic losses and illness. When the sack appears old or in poor condition, it means that there will be setback in the completion of goals. The psychoanalysis regards the sack as an image of the uterus, and by extension, the woman.

Sacrifice ■ If the victim of the sacrifice is you, the dream could be a reflection of your attitude in real life. It is possible that you make a martyr of yourself or that you have self-blaming tendencies. In this case, you probably feel that everyone else makes light of you, forgetting your talents and qualities. If you make a sacrifice, you should consider what it is that you are sacrificing. An animal could signify your natural instinct; a person that you know, and aspect of yourself that you do not want to accept. In spiritual terms, the ego should be sacrificed so that the divine you can enter into the light.
❖ In antiquity, sacrificial rituals were a way to appease the gods and add fertility to the earth. They sacrificed people for the good of cosmic and social unity. In Egypt, Osiris was quartered by his brother, Seth; in Greece, Orpheus was ripped to pieces by a group of women; in Christianity, Jesus was crucified. These acts of divine delivery still exist in modern life.

Sailor ■ If you are a sailor in your dream it means that your emotions are a little off and that, therefore, you want to escape from yourself. Restlessness and a thirst for adventure gets you out of a rut, but you must not let the desire get out of hand. On the other hand, considering that the sea represents the unconscious, the dream may be reflecting your desire to explore it or to begin a long journey. (See WATER, BLUE, BOAT, and SEA)
❖ Dreaming of a sailor who is ashore predicts a new romance; if you are on a boat, news will come from far away. On the other hand, if a woman dreams of being a sailor, popular belief says this is an omen of bad luck.

Saint ■ Dreaming of a saint is always a good omen, as it reminds us that you have the necessary resources to enjoy a happy life. You will not lack in money or friends, so it would be reckless to choose the wrong path. Equally, the saint could be a messenger from the superior you, the guide that you need to value your situation in a more spiritual manner.
❖ For a devote Christian, this dream could be a direct encounter with the spirit of a saint that would like to help you. In the same way, in India it is said that through dreams, a live wise man can equally serve their followers as one who has died can. In a spiritual sense, dreams offer orientation and teaching for real life.

Salad ■ Dreaming of a salad is negative because it predicts conflictive relations with the environment and diseases.

❖ Eating it shows that family life be affected by disputes because of economic issues. To a woman in love, dreaming that she prepares a salad is a sign that her partner is unstable and quarrelsome.

Salamander ■ The image of the salamander is associated with immortality and passion. It is also a symbol that represents the capacity to adapt to unknown situations or circumstances. It signals a high level of self esteem and security in the dreamer.

Saliva ■ Saliva has a fairly complicated symbolism, as its interpretation is not simple. Occasionally, it is linked to gossip and insults that you are afraid to receive. But, it also has positive meanings. For example, if you drool on yourself, it means that you have the sufficient resources to resolve a conflict, despite that you lack confidence in yourself.

Salmon ■ Salmon, able to swim against the current, is an emblem of strength, valor, and courage.
❖ According to an esoteric lecture, seeing a salmon in a dream foretells a litigation; selling it indicates discussions and disagreements in the family.

Salt ■ Salt symbolizes conservation. If it appears in dreams, it could indicate that your ambitions are stagnated and immobile. Generally, it would be convenient to abandon passivity and try to nourish your dreams. The dream reflects that you live too conservatively. On the other hand, salt in dreams could also have other meanings, such as the spiritual essence of life: preservation and indestructibility, what remains after the decomposition of the body. It may also refer to sadness or to the subconscious, as it is in tears and seawater. Lastly, if you are offering or receiving this product, it is a sign of friendship.
❖ Salt has been used throughout history as a symbol of spiritual illumination. When it is mixed with water and the crystals are dissolved, the salty taste remains. The same occurs with the soul: the individual can die or disappear, but the essence remains intact.

Salvation ■ Being saved or someone who saves someone from imminent danger almost always signals the need for approval, acceptance, care, and protection. The dreamer is going through a low emotional period in real life. However, other oneiric symbols and the context will supply important facts to interpret it correctly.

Sand ■ Dreaming of a fine sandy beach promises peace and sensuality. It suggests the soft touch of the sea, of love, and of the mother. In contrast, the desert sand represents aridity and goes hand in hand with the image of the death. Dreaming that you walk over sand reveals you are afraid of not achieving the goal previously set; whereas, if you find sand in food or clothing, it means nervousness caused by an unstable situation.

Sapphire ■ The sapphire is a stone with great celestial meaning. It represents goodness, as well as other positive values, given that it is blue. (See BLUE, JEWELRY, and STONES)

Sausage ■ Seeing this food announces the upcoming reunion with an old friend, which will mark the start of a period of joy and happiness. If you make sausages, the success of your projects will be secured; meanwhile, if you eat it, you will enjoy familial peace. In contrast, if you sell it, you will suffer an unfortunate event.

Sausages ■ Its interpretation depends on the dream's context and conforming elements. It is related to the symbolism of FOOD or DEVOURING, as appropriate. It can also have sexual connotations represented in its phallic appearance. To that extent, eating it or rejecting it is indicative of the dreamer's relationship with her own sexuality.

Savage ■ The figure of a savage half-naked man is frequent in almost all cultures and is related with mythical beings such as "snow men," ogres, etc. This archetype symbolizes, therefore, the savage and primitive component within you, along with your fear of advancement. In this last sense, it could be interpreted as a warning from your subconscious. This reminds you that maybe you are sufficiently mature to bring certain projects that you have in mind to completion. This dream could also refer to your sexuality. It may be trying to tell you that you should behave more diplomatically and tactfully in your sexual relationships.
❖ Although you believe that your primitive and savage side cannot help you in life, it is certain that it could be very useful. More than anything, because it reminds you—from the heart, without materialism or superficiality—the things that are worth it and the ones that are not.

Saw ■ A saw is a manifestation of the desire to cut or to terminate an affair, be it a personal conflict, a work project, or a familial relationship. The dreamer should analyze the negative aspects of life and study the consequences of his actions, because it is possible that the problem has a less drastic solution than what is expressed by the subconscious.

Scale ▪ This instrument symbolizes justice, in other words, the balance between punishment and guilt. In oneiric terms, the scale shows the subject's desire to measure, weigh, test, or judge any aspect of her personality or life. If you are evaluating the pros and cons of a situation, the dream will help you make the right decision. Weighing something important or being on the scale suggests that you must see things from a more balanced view, without being overly emotional. So, it is better not to rush and think calmly before acting. Finally, to see an empty scale in dreams indicates problems of self assertiveness.

❖ Since ancient times, the scale has been the symbol of justice. For the Egyptians, it was the instrument on which the god Anubis weighed the souls of men. The dream may be telling you that justice will come in a particular matter. In any case, the balance is associated with gains, justice, and happiness.

Scalpel ▪ The scalpel urges you to act with precision, determination, and firmness in order to end a worrying situation.

Scars ▪ Scars symbolize moral and physical imperfections, sufferings, and resentment.

Scenery ▪ If your dream takes place on a stage it indicates that you are living some experiences without having the feeling that they are real. If in these oneiric images you are pretending, it means you are playing a role. Therefore, the unconscious is suggesting that maybe it is time you face your responsibility, since, apparently, you try to go through the world marginally.

School ▪ Going back to school you attended during childhood reflects the need to appreciate what you have (in this case, the accumulated knowledge). It is a throwback to the past, but it can help you understand the present. Not surprisingly, dreaming about the school may mean that you are behaving childishly. For this reason, the unconscious is returning you back to that time, reminding you to be over with that stage if you want to look forward and progress in

life. School ultimately urges you to learn and accept the lessons of life. A teacher in this dream represents your own self-censorship and self-control. If the teacher scolds you it indicates that you feel guilty, or you consider yourself inferior compared to others, or your misdeeds will come to light. If the teacher congratulates you it means you trust yourself and your abilities.

❖ If you are the teacher of the school the dream portends good fortune. If you are a student you will suffer a setback in business; it will worsen if, in the dream, you forget the lesson.

Scissors ▪ The presence of scissors in dreams indicates that you want to make an end to or shorten a relationship, activity, or aspect of yourself. Despite that it indicates that you possess an energetic and decisive spirit, you should end the situation as soon as possible, as it could already notably harm you. Although it is not a frequent dream, scissors can also express the start of a team-work project.

❖ Dream tradition interprets dreams about scissors as enemies that will cause you pain. However, in the case that the scissors are clean and shiny, you have nothing to fear.

Scorpion ▪ It is the eighth sign of the zodiac. It points to a danger of death, which is not surprising considering that the sting of a scorpion is fatal in many cases. If you dream that it stings you it means that there is an internal conflict that is poisoning your existence. It can also show that your way of relating to others is extremely hurtful. On a psychological level it also means danger and threat to the unconscious.

❖ Synonymous with poison and silent lethal actions, the scorpion has gone through oneiric tradition since ancient times, as an omen of enmity, deceit, and betrayal.

Scream ▪ Screams you hear or emit during a dream indicate danger. Usually, they refer to the close presence of any threats or anything that would compromise your security (either physical or emotional). In general, when you scream you release a strong inner tension. This dream may be a warning that you are in an extreme situation because of pressures of any kind.

Sculpture ▪ Dreaming that you are sculpting a figure reveals a clear desire to direct or educate someone. It may also indicate the need to engage with your fellow people based on proportion, balance, and ultimately beauty.

Scythe ▪ It symbolizes both the harvesting of the crop and death. Therefore, the presence of a scythe in dream announces the end of a situation or stage that will lead to another. It is recommended that you make decisions at the right time, without precipitation. This attitude will lead you to a happy ending.

Sea ▪ The sea and oceans are considered the source of life and the end of it. "To go back to the sea" is like "to return to the mother": to die. The sea is one of the basic archetypes, as it also represents the collective unconscious and universal love. This dream, therefore, is related to your interior and the interpretation can be almost literal. Thus, a calm sea indicates tranquility; if agitated, it predicts difficulties; if you fall into it, illness or problems caused by unbridled passions; if you let yourself sink, it reflects a pessimistic outlook on life; if you struggle to reach the surface, it indicates that you are fighting with all your strength. The sea also represents the original chaos, the beginning and end of everything. Its fluidity is like the unconscious that can never be fully plumbed, grasped, nor understood. It is the boundless freedom and yet comforting sweetness of the mother's womb. (See WATER, DROWNING, BLUE, BOAT, LAKE, MOTHER, and MOON)
❖ In primitive myths, the sea existed before the world. It was uterus of other living beings. The sea is a symbol of raw materials and is associated with the creative potential of our being. From a spiritual perspective, it can represent the whole. We are each the drops that form part of it. According to some superstitions, falling into the sea ensures good health; and dive into it and emerge just before waking ensures that current difficulties will be overcome.

Seal (animal) ▪ Seeing a seal in dreams points to emotional loneliness, the result of immaturity or inexperience.

Seal (object) ▪ A seal is a sign of personal property, as well as an emblem that marks a difference. It symbolizes authority, protection, and secrets. (See AUTHORITY and CARD)

Sealing wax ▪ Sealing wax is associated with durability of commitments. To seal an envelope with wax shows the intention of keeping a promise to the letter. To open it signifies its breakage, a change in appearance in an unexpected moment.

Searching ▪ What you seek in the dream can be physical, emotional, intellectual, or spiritual. Perhaps, it is about a new solution to a problem. If you dream of looking for someone you know, it indicates feelings of anxiety about the relationship you have with that person in real life. You might want to end an emotional separation. It is important to ask whether what you have been looking for is really worth it. If the answer is negative, the dream reflects your loss of illusion and hope.
❖ This is usually a spiritual dream. Myths such as the one King Arthur is in search of the Holy Grail describe the process of inner transformation of the self.

Seashell ▪ It is associated with female sexuality and fertility. It has been regarded as highly erotic and lies in relation to seawater, the origin of life. It can be interpreted as a repressed sexual desire, or the intention—not yet revealed—to procreate.
❖ Its link to Aphrodite—goddess of love that emerges from the sea on a giant seashell—makes it forecast marriage and travel by sea. A full shell promises success and happiness; empty, however, indicates loss of time and money.

Seashore ▪ In oneiric terms, the shore is the point where the unconscious (sea) and conscious (beach) meet. The dream could also be representing the possibility of a journey. This could be physical (by boat), or symbolic (within yourself). If you find yourself scanning the horizon looking for a boat, you may be worried about not reaching some aspiration or desire. To be on the shore looking for shells or other objects hidden in the sand could reflect your desire to increase your inner resources. (See WATER and SEA)
❖ An empty beach symbolizes an opportunity. A beach with a lot of people predicts that you will feel protected and safe.

Seasons ▪ Seasons are symbolically ages of mankind: spring is for childhood; summer, youth; fall, maturity, and winter, old age and sterility. If you dream that the seasons occur in order it indicates that you need to live one thing at a time. Otherwise, you would have to analyze their meaning separately.

Seasons can represent the state of your mind and the psychological and material conditions that prevail in it. This symbol reminds us that everything is variable and renewable. (See WINTER, FALL, SPRING, and SUMMER)

❖ Since ancient times, the sun, solstices, and seasons have been linked to the human life's stages. In addition, seasons are also associated with the four elements: earth is bare winter; spring is rain; heat and fire are the summer; and air, the fall winds.

Seat ▪ Sometimes, in certain dreams, the protagonist has a sudden urge to sit and relax, as if she were lacking air or feeling her legs go weak. Such condition, rather than physical exhaustion shows certain existential fatigue. Those who experience this kind of dream feel that their life has become increasingly dull and weary; they have little incentive to make the routine more bearable.

Secret ▪ If you dream that you tell a secret that you had promised not to tell, it means that you are going through an uncomfortable time. It is possible that you will not only go through a complicated emotional stage but that you are also involved in something not suited to you.

Sect ▪ If you dream that a sect captures you, it is a clear indicator that you do not have clear ideas. The subconscious is warning you that you should not give in to emotional blackmail from anyone. You should try to conquer the weakness that resides in your character and make your own decisions.

Seeds ▪ Seeds symbolize potential life, projects, and creative capacity. This dream foretells the birth of a project, idea, or circumstance that requires all of your intuition and creativity. It also denotes imminent progress, as much in the work field as in the emotional-personal one. For a married couple, it could be a sign of pregnancy. (See GERMINATION and PLANTS)

❖ According to the oldest books on dreams, seeds foretell an increase in prosperity.

Selling ▪ Dreaming of the sale of many goods signifies that your resources are practically limitless. Because of this, the dream invites you to develop your resources. This type of scene also reveals the necessity of communicating what you now and what you have experienced with others.

Sentinel ▪ Dreams in which guardians or sentinels are present notify your mind so that you are aware of possible deception by third parties. It is also recommended to pay attention to your own actions, as they must be consistent with the commitments that you have established. (See OWL)

Separation ▪ This could be a literal reflection of a situation that the dreamer is going through, but that is not totally defined. It is possible that it brings an emotional relationship that is too narrow or oppressive, and that a break or distancing is necessary.

Sequins ▪ They are always associated with celebration, parties, and costumes. In the dream this could be positive or negative. Parties are generally related to the desire for escape and frivolous moments. Costumes or disguises are related to lies and tricks. However, a party can be the celebration of an event that came to a good end. In this case, they are interpreted as satisfaction of having completed something, or the need for a well deserved rest after too much responsibility.

Serpent ▪ Serpents are one of the oldest figures that have a lot of symbolism. In general, they are associated with phalluses and pagan gods of fertility. Given that snakes live sliding across the ground, they are an emblem of caution of the land and of the dangers that guard the underground world. From a Christian perspective, they are a dark and sinful symbol that tempts men to gain knowledge. On the other hand, these animals could be your hidden fears or the start of a period of internal and external conflicts. In this last case, you will have to suffer unpleasant experiences. However, at the end you will gain wisdom that you would otherwise have been unable to reach in such a small period of time. If you fall in a pit full of snakes, the dream represents the worries that are threatening you. Snakes, lastly, sometimes symbolize venomous words and insinuations from the people around you.

❖ In the representation of the god Mercury (the symbol of the medical profession now) there appear interlaced snakes. For the Greeks, snakes had curative properties. In a similar manner, in India, the cobra is a divine figure of illumination and is associated with the god Shiva.

Sewer ▪ Sewers involve darkness and dirt. Dreaming of them, therefore, predicts arguments and reprehensible

S E R P E N T

Alicia dreamed: "I used to have recurrent dreams in which terrifying snakes would appear. After these dreams, I would awaken drenched in sweat and nervous. If it occurred at midnight I went to get a glass of water with the fear of finding a snake in the kitchen stalking me. During a certain time the dreams stopped, but, shortly after, they would return to repeat themselves in an even more violent manner."

Alicia was raised in a very conservative family that **forbade premarital relations**. She maintained an amorous—though not sexual—relationship for three years, and during this time she was accosted by dreams of snakes. When the relationship ended, the dreams stopped; but later she fell in love again and felt **sexually inhibited**; therefore, the dreams of snakes returned with more intensity.

The snakes of her dreams were clearly a phallic symbol that were warning her of her inability to enjoy her sexuality to the fullest, due to her education. When Alicia understood this, she started to confront her **personal monster** and prepare her path towards a satisfactory relationship. The dreams of snakes began to recede and when they occurred she tried not to distress herself and to understand their meaning.

actions by the people around you. If valuables appear in the sewer it means that someone could get you in trouble by questioning whether something really belongs to you.

Sex ■ Dreams with sexual themes are very frequent and are not always easy to interpret. Often, you have to frame them in the appropriate amorous context. That is to say, if you have problems in your sex life, the dream scenes that you produce while sleeping reflect these preoccupations. In the same way, with sexual themes, the influence of childhood is the most powerful, as it is during this time when you start to conceive of sex as something dirty or sinful. The field of intimate relations offers more recurring dreams. So, sometimes heterosexual people dream that they are making love with someone of the same sex. In most cases, these dreams represent the desire of the protagonist to possess the characteristics of the partner. During the days preceding a wedding, the engaged couple also tend to experience erotic dreams in which they imagine that they are having sex with other people. These scenes are directly related to the fear and anxiety that is produced in many individuals prior to the promise of matrimony. In general, you can say that dreaming that you maintain a sexual relationship with your partner or someone you know could reveal attraction towards these people, but it could also be a result of an anxiety situation. However, if you dream that you are making love to a stranger, it is possible that you are dissatisfied with certain aspects of your life, as you are searching in the unknown for what you have not found in your own heart. (See ADULTERER, LOVE, KISS, HARUM, and INCEST)

❖ A strange superstition says that if you dream that you are in a brothel, your domestic life will improve. If you change sexes, it foretells success within the family.

Shack ■ As the image of a poor and outlawed existence, a shack is evidence of the dreamer's intention of avoidance for not being able to face problems of everyday life. Feeling cheerful inside one means that very difficult times are approaching; but, on the contrary, if you feel unhappy, it will be an incentive to redirect your life and progress.

Shadow ■ Generally, shadows are associated with the dark and malignant. For some psychologists they represent what is hidden in the subconscious, what you do not want to be. It probably comes from emotions and aspects that you have rejected within yourself. It recommends trying to bring to light everything that is hidden. This way, you will see that it is not so difficult to overcome. However, the interpretation of this dream is complex because, despite what has been said, the shadow of a tree could be a positive image that generates relief and protection for the dreamer. In this case, it is a dream of compensation before an adverse circumstance. Other dream symbols and the context in which it develops provide clues as to how it can be correctly interpreted.

❖ Many superstitions believe that the shadow is part of the human soul. Stepping on it or throwing rocks on it is a sign of bad luck and the possibility of causing harm to someone. If it is about one's own shadow, you should be cautious.

Shame ■ The dreams often demonstrate our weaknesses and hidden fears. Maybe you feel lacking in self-confidence or doubtful towards our sexual life, and this feelings has transcended to our dreams.

❖ Some ancient superstitions say that this dream represents just the contrary of what it appears. So, the more shame you feel, the better your successes and decisions will be.

Shark ▪ The shark has always been considered by western culture as an enemy of man. Dreaming of one represents imminent danger. It is a call from the subconscious to be cautious and deliberate toward external agents that negatively affect your life.

Sharpener ▪ The sharpener makes knives sharp, it gets weapons ready for combat. Its appearance in dreams can be interpreted as the approach of fights and disputes. However, it also has a positive meaning because it denotes security and preparedness to face difficult situations.

Shaving ▪ Dreaming of a shaved person means that, in real life, you strive to make a nice impression.

❖ Shaving oneself represents the oneiric prediction of a major economic loss; shaving another person indicates marital bliss.

Shawl ▪ The shawl represents hiding your personality. Dreaming of it announces protection from a friend. Losing it means being naked in front of others and being victim of their gossiping.

Sheep ▪ It is a sign of passivity, conformity, and lack of initiative. We tend to delegate responsibilities that affect us to others in order to avoid commitments. Or, we give only what is expected of us. Dreaming of this situation (although it is presented metaphorically) indicates that your attitude, deep down, is unsatisfactory. On the other hand, the sheep also means purity and innocence, two positive attributes. However, it may also represent ignorance and blindness. In the event that a shepherd appears, the dream may refer to the power of love to unify divergent forces.

❖ To see many sheep is a sign of calamity; but if they belong to you it promises great riches. A white sheep is a good omen; a black sheep, a bad one.

Sheets ▪ Clean or new sheets denote success in business and prosperity; meanwhile, if they are dirty or broken, it foretells economic ruin and emotional failure. Cleaning sheets shows the desire to establish new and better

friendships, and covering oneself with sheets shows the desire to avoid some type of rift in the environment.

Shell ▪ The shell symbolizes fertility and eroticism. Do not forget that on the one hand, two female characters of great mythological importance, such as Venus and Aphrodite, were born into a shell; and, second, in Argentina, it represents the genitals of a woman. Consequently, this dream can have a clear erotic reading. In another sense, the heavy shell of a turtle can express your desire for protection. Something similar happens with the eggshell, whose fragility indicates that your feelings are too vulnerable.

❖ Shells that appear in dreams predict that something very strange will happen.

Shelves ▪ To see them filled up promises great opportunities to increase your assets, whether material or spiritual. Empty shelves, however, warns against losses or frustrations.

Shepherd ▪ The shepherd symbolizes the guide of souls, since he directs a flock. When one appears in your dreams, the unconscious is calling your attention to the potential you have as a leader or director.

Ship ▪ An oneiric ship can represent our life course and, depending on how it appears, will reveal the state of our mind. If it is a cruise ship, the dream alludes to the pleasant calm that you are going through. If it is a warship, you may be showing too much aggression. The appearance of a lifeboat at the scene indicates your need to escape a storm of feelings and problems in real life. If, however, is a submarine, the dream indicated your desire to explore the unconscious. On the other hand, ships also symbolize the ability to communicate with people who are far away, whether geographically or in their way of thinking and feeling. For this reason, a journey by sea means you have begun a new life stage or a new relationship. By contrast, in this sense, a ship that sinks warns of the danger of a breakup. (See WATER, BOAT, and SHIPWRECK)

❖ A ship docked at the pier or sailing a calm sea predicts great happiness in love. If you dream that there is a storm, this happiness will be delayed. In the case of a shipwreck, you will receive bad news.

Shipwreck ▪ To drown in a shipwreck reveals a feeling of distress, which has lasted some time, due to a project that has not prospered or a personal relationship that has failed, leading you to believe that "all is lost." Normally, a dream of this kind indicates that you have taken on too many responsibilities. Therefore, it can be interpreted as a warning that you should rest or take a short break. You have reached the limits of your strength and you need to recharge. (See WATER, BOAT and SHIP)

Shirt ▪ A shirt, because it is permanently touching the skin, indicates a need for communication and affection. For this reason, dreaming that you wear a ripped shirt means that chances are you will suffer a sentimental loss. On the other hand, this piece also reveals the way in which you appear in front of others: your image. If it is too ironed and fully buttoned it will show your conservatism, whereas if it is open and not tucked in it will express your free and unconventional spirit.
❖ Gypsy tradition considers that the more colorful the shirt is in your dream, the luckier you will be.

Shoes ▪ Shoes symbolizes the "low" things, as much as for humility as for pettiness. If you dream that you are buying shoes, it shows that you need protection. If the shoes are small or cause you harm, it shows that you are not ready to give everything that is expected of you. In contrast, if the shoes are big, it shows that you have many resources within your reach, but that you do not know how to funnel them appropriately. Clothing that introduces a certain part of the body were for Freud sexual symbols. In this sense, fairy tales use the same language. When Cinderella puts her foot in the shoe, it shows her sexual desire for the prince.
❖ According to popular superstition, losing a shoe precedes an illness. It is possible that this belief come from an ancient English custom which consisted of burning an old smelly shoe in the fireplace to drive off possible household infections. Lastly, shoes covered in dust foretell an unexpected trip; shining shoes foretell felicity and love.

Shop window ▪ Shop windows symbolize the way in which you go through life, often without finding yourself. It may point to the loss of part of your identity. This dream reveals the anguish of not knowing where to go.

Shopping basket ▪ This basket can predict wealth in a broad sense. If it is empty it indicates material, emotional, intellectual, or spiritual poverty.

❖ A basket full of fruit promises romantic pleasures; full of flowers, happiness in love; a basket full of gold, abundance and fertility; an empty one, loneliness and unrequited affections; a closed one, secrets.

Shortcut ▪ A shortcut reflects anxiety related to achievement of objectives. They lay doubts and obstacles hard to overcome, but if the dreamer is able to surmount them she will have the ability to reach any proposed goal.

Shoulders ▪ They represent strength and the human capacity for self fulfillment. If they are broad and strong, success and self confidence; but if they are narrow and weak, they indicate a lack of vitality, pessimism, and emotional dissatisfaction.

Shower ▪ This dream represents the spiritual energy and purification. You are finally clean, washed, and ready to begin again. Down the drain go pain, sickness, and worries.
❖ Showers can be a symbol of healing. There is a technique we can all practice: imagine yourself under running water that washes you outside and inside. Next, you are filled with light, from your feet to your head. It is quite possible that this dream has given you clues to carry out your own self-cleaning. It is worth trying it in real life.

Shrink ▪ When you cringe in dreams it is interpreted as the fear of facing reality or the desire to become small to the point of invisibility so you can avoid reporting to anyone. It is the fear of failure or making commitments that imply responsibility.

Sibling ▪ Siblings symbolize very clear tendencies in your personality. Dreams in which siblings appear— although the dreamer is an only child—foretell the need to integrate certain qualities that the dreamer lacks and are necessary for communication with others, into their deep Self. Consequently, this dream is trying to say that you want to find someone to share experiences with. Additionally, you must keep in mind that traits or defects we don't like to accept in ourselves tend to be projected on siblings. In this case, a correct interpretation can be very helpful to know yourself better.
❖ Dreaming of a sibling may represent that you've found a guide to bring you to your deepest Self. So, you can more easily resolve the problem that is worrying

you. The oneiric images of the sibling is, for some superstitions, a sign of betrayal and hypocrisy.

Sidewalk ■ The sidewalk is a safety zone. If you step onto a sidewalk in dreams it can symbolize a job promotion. However, this symbol may also mean the opposite of what seems to manifest at first sight. Thus, if in a dream you walk on a sidewalk, you must not trust in the security you felt before; you could soon go through a difficult period. On the other hand, stepping off the sidewalk indicates that you are about to lose your current position. If you act quickly, you still have time to rectify this.

Sieve ■ Sifting is synonymous with purifying and perfecting: integrating the chosen and looking down upon the superfluous. The dream generally invites you to select those issues and people that truly interest you. It includes, therefore, your thoughts, desires and projects. (See FLOUR)

Sign ■ Many dreams try to help you resolve your problems. In this case, it shows you what direction you should take in life. According to the destination the sign indicates, you will gain valuable clues. The sign in your dreams could also be a direct message from the unconscious. It is important to know if you could read it or remember what was written on it, since this will be key to interpreting the dream. (See POSTER)
❖ Gypsy tradition claims that dreaming of a wooden or stone sign denotes that soon you will overcome a period of indecision.

Signature ■ A signature is a symbol of commitment. Signing a document emphasizes the need to strengthen an uncertain situation. Not signing it indicates insecurity and fear of commitment. Wanting to sign but failing to do so can be interpreted as a sign of dissatisfaction with your own intellectual abilities.

Silence ■ This is not a frequent dream. It denotes interior peace and emotional maturity. Silence also reflects detachment from material interests and can be a fruit of anxiety.

Silk ■ This dream is associated with sensuality and has important erotic connotations. It also alludes to narcissism and fetishism. According to the color and other characteristics of the fabric, it could signal purity, passion, perversity, or attraction.

Silver ■ It is related to the moon, the color white, water, passivity, femininity, and sincerity. It represents something of value to the dreamer: it could be her economic needs, or her emotional resources. Its presence in dreams is positive except when it is tarnished, since in these circumstances is augurs serious losses. (See WATER, WHITE, NUDITY, MONEY, and WOMAN)
❖ Silver is not considered a very lucky metal. If you find it in your purse in a dream, it augurs economic losses.

Silverware ■ Dreaming of pretty silverware that is well conserved denotes good familial relations and feelings; while if it is dirty or broken, it indicates a period of conflict. ‖ Buying silverware shows the desire to grow your circle of friends; cleaning it signifies catching up with old friends; breaking it, the expression of your feelings toward someone who has done you harm. For a woman, dreaming of silverware is a sign of a happy marriage.

Sin ■ Setting aside the religion or beliefs of the dreamer, dreaming of sin is almost always indicative of a feeling of guilt. Although upon waking you don't feel at all guilty, your subconscious accusing you, so it is a good idea to investigate the causes to get rid of this sensation.

Singing ■ The dream is expressing your feelings at the moment. The lyrics and the type of music will give you plenty of information about you. (See SONG)
❖ Singing can be a spiritual act. Tagore said, "God respects me when I work, but He loves me when I sing."

Sinking ■ On occasion, this denotes that feelings and worries monopolize our whole being. Or, perhaps, you fear something that means a lot to you will end. For example, a relationship or a business. This dream could be showing your deception regarding some aspect of your life.
❖ Some astrologists assert that dreaming of sinking means you have spent too much on purchases.

Siren ■ A symbolic figure incarnated by the mermaid. The myth of sirens is one of the oldest, as already in ancient Greece there existed stories about them. They represent the feminine side of the mind and evidence the mystery that surrounds the human psyche. Sirens bring secret wisdom from the depths of the subconscious (the sea). If a man has this dream, he may be afraid of his femininity or of his dark thoughts. For a woman it manifest the doubts about the nature of her own sex. Further, thanks to the seduction that a siren's song exercises over masculine energy, it represent the temptations or passionate desires. Dreaming of the siren's song foretells possible deceit in love.

❖ Mythology offers many figures that are part human, part animal. The major part includes the conscious mind; the minor part, the primitivism and irrationality that the conscience needs. Originally, these symbols were conceived to demonstrate that human nature and animals are inseparable.

Sitting ■ The dream could indicate that you are behaving too passively against a real issue. This indifference in action could end up causing you problems.

❖ If you dream that you are sitting on a tall seat, you will have good luck. If it is short, it foretells disappointment.

Size ■ The increase or decrease in the size of things or people that appear in your dreams signals the importance that they have to you. Seeing a person reduced to invisibility indicates the fear that you have of losing them. Seeing that such person's size increases in an exaggerated manner is a sign of the excessive influence that she exercises on you.

Skating ■ To dream that you are skating predicts that you are entering an unstable situation, since this type of dreams symbolizes risk. If the sensation is unpleasant, it is from your real life fear that this instability will end badly (for example, in serious economic loss). On the contrary, if the scenes of skating are pleasant from an esthetic point of view, you will probably emerge from the conflictive situation stronger. And more importantly: you will distinguish with greater clarity your existential direction from this point on.

Skin ■ Your skin is an essential part of the image of your body that you project to others. If you dream that it does not look very good, it might suggest a fear of giving a bad impression or even that you are ashamed of something and harbor the illusion of being able to hide it. Also, it is associated with the idea of time. Therefore to dream of wrinkled skin is expresses your fear of aging and loss of physical attractiveness. But if the skin is soft and smooth, this suggests sensuality, delicacy, caresses, etc. In short: the need for affection.

❖ Some Omani women believe that a dream about pale skin portends the arrival of a lot of jewels. To dream that you change your skin is omen of troubles.

Skirt ■ The meaning of this dream depends on the sex of the protagonist. For a man, a skirt in dreams denotes his attraction to a woman; a short or tight skirt advises caution with certain companies; a long or wide one represents excess of morality; and if he is wearing it, gossip and public humiliation. If a woman dreams in skirts it means that she will soon receive an unexpected visit; if it is beautiful, success in her relationships will be assured; if it is too short she should be aware of bad companies; and if it is too long she will be the subject of acquaintances' gossiping.

Skull ■ Carl Jung decided to become a psychologist after dreaming that he found a skull in the basement of his house. The skull represented his desire to discover and explain the secrets of the mind. Dreaming of a skull also refers to mortality and to your spiritual contemplation about the beginning and the end of life. It can also express things that are coming to an end or whatever you are just unable not reach.

❖ For gypsy people, skulls are the wisdom of their ancestors. Drinking from one of those means sharing this old knowledge. In Ireland it symbolizes the truth because it is said that if an individual takes false oath with a skull, she will die soon.

Sky ■ It symbolizes your aspirations, your deepest desires, the ultimate meaning of your actions. Not surprisingly, except in Egypt, the sky has always been associated with the masculine, to the active and to the spirit (the land, however, is linked to the feminine and passive). If in dreams you look at the sky during daylight, it is a sign of openness and clarity in your aims. The night sky, in turn, indicates order, and balance when it is starry. For Jung, at nightfall, the sky was the most appropriate place for the subject to project her unconscious. The symbolism of the constellations and zodiac signs, therefore, are archetypal expressions of the subject's inner world.

❖ Many oneiric superstitions agree that dreaming of a blue sky heralds good luck. If it is cloudy, quite the opposite. On the other hand, some believe that a red sky in dreams portends a national disaster.

Slander ■ Being slandered in dreams alerts that, in real life, people very close to you might betray you. On the other hand, to slander others evidence a thoughtless action that will bring you serious trouble.

Slap ▪ When the one slapping you in dreams is someone known it suggests the need to analyze the relationship you have with this person. Things are not very clear and, therefore, you must be sincere with her. You have to prevent the situation from worsening and amend what is deteriorated. If it is you who slaps someone else you are expressing frustration of your desires.

Slapping ▪ A slap always indicates a drastic reaction. It can be interpreted as a warning from the subconscious to rectify a judgment or an attitude. Maybe, the time is right to take a break along the way and reconsider. It may also warn against an illness that you have not yet noticed any symptoms of.

Slavery ▪ If you dream that you are held captive, you may be controlling some aspects of your psychological dimension too much. Perhaps, you are preventing your self-expression or feel prisoner of your circumstances. You may also be rejecting your hidden potential or your true feelings. The cause can be that you have to face a new job, marriage, birth of a child . . . In any case, these things, for worse or for better, restrict your freedom. On other hand, maybe you need to show that you dominate others, especially your family and friends. You force them to act according to your will. Clearly, in this way, you will never reach happiness.
❖ Dreaming that you are bound up expresses you will harvest love in your life.

Sleeping ▪ Looking at yourself asleep in dreams reflects a lack of attention on the activities that you carry out during wakefulness. If in your dream you struggle to wake up it is a warning that you are not complying with commitments you have taken on and want to escape reality. From a philosophical point of view, this dream represents human nature; being asleep is ignorance; waking up is tantamount to understanding the reality around us.
❖ In these cases, the concept of "astral travel" is referred. It means that you have abandoned your bodies and you are looking at it lying in bed.

Sliding ▪ It is a manifestation of insecurity and fear. Sliding in dreams tells you that you are entering into an unstable situation that is full of risks. If the sensation is unpleasant, it is the fear that a period of discomfort will come about (for example, of important economic losses).
❖ Sliding on ice means a short period of happiness followed by sudden sadness.

Slingshot ▪ As the biblical tale of David and Goliath shows, the slingshot is a symbol that the strength of the weak can conquer the powerful. This type of dream invites you to have more confidence in yourself.

Slippers ▪ They represent the most intimate feelings and emotions of the dreamer. To walk around the house in slippers could be a sign of physical or mental exhaustion, but also indicates a relaxed state of comfortable intimacy. To find yourself in the street with slippers instead of shoes reflects insecurity, embarrassment, or fear of ridicule. The dreamer is afraid of not being up to speed in real life.

Slope ▪ Climbing a slope is a sign of the effort that the dreamer in real life is doing or should do in order to achieve a desired goal. Thanks to the context of the dream and the interpretation of the other oneiric symbols of the scene, it is possible to understand the message the unconscious is trying to convey.

Sludge ▪ Sludge has two opposing interpretations. On one hand, it symbolizes dirty and undesirable aspects at moral and material levels. Dreaming that you walk through a muddy field signals the dreamer's difficulties in real life. If you dread getting stained by mud it indicates fear of becoming involved in matters that are unpleasant or turbid. In addition, clay combines soil and water. It is a soft and malleable material, suitable for the manufacture of household utensils and for the development of creative activities. This dream's interpretation depends on the context of the oneiric scene, the events that it unfolds, and above all, the sensations and feelings it produces on the dreamer (pleasant or unpleasant).

Smells ▪ Rarely we dream of scents that are not from the physical space where we are sleeping. Otherwise, the smells in dreams have a highly sensuous connotation. It is possible that the unconscious has launched a compensation mechanism in response to lack of satisfactory sexual intercourse. Although sharp and unpleasant odors are very rare, if you perceived one, it means that you are reacting to the attitudes of others.

❖ Each scent has a specific meaning. Mothballs allude to scandal; ginger, to love affairs; jasmine, to true spiritual experience; lavender, happiness in relationships; and nutmeg, deception. In general, a bad smell means disease; and a good one, health. Perfume denotes beauty and pride. To notice a good smell emanated by someone promises new friends; but if someone detects your odor, it is indicative of lost friendships.

Smile ■ The dream could be expressing your approval with respect to decisions that you have made. It is possible that you feel satisfied with your successes and achievements. The future will bring you happiness, you should seize it.

❖ Perhaps the dream is telling you to smile a little more. An Indian guru named Paramahansa Yogamanda in his book titled *The Search for Eternity* encouraged his readers to make millions of smiles, as in front of others the face is very contagious.

Smoke ■ In some cultures, beneficial power is attributed to smoke, since it supposedly possesses a magical quality to scare misfortune away from humans. If in the dram you imagine this smoke as a white column, light and subtle, that rises up to the sky, it is a sign that you will be spiritually elevated. On the contrary, if the sensations it causes are unpleasant, this could point to a state of mental confusion. Not in vain, this impedes us from seeing clearly and consequently makes it difficult to solve problems that arise.

❖ If the smoke bothers you, the omens are unfavorable.

Snail ■ The image of a snail is related to several meanings: the upward spiral, female and male sexuality, the notion of slowness in the course of things, and also infidelity. However, a snail in dreams can be interpreted as an indication of introspection and shyness.

❖ If in the dream the snail eats plants and flowers, it announces the loss of job due to negligence or laziness; if it shows its horns, infidelity; if it stays in the shell, sympathy for the characters that presented in the episode. If, however, it moves towards the dreamer it suggests delays in business.

Snake ■ This type of serpent without poison shows that everyday problems, though not serious, may become very annoying. These issues come to an end when you kill the snake in the dream.

Sneezing ■ Sneezing is the arrival of something unexpected, so this dream denotes that you will receive a surprise that will change your plans. If you struggle to sneeze, the dream predicts a great disappointment; but if it is easy, good luck will come for sure. Seeing others sneezing provides tedious family visits.

Snow ■ The snow covering the ground symbolizes the sublimation of the latter. Along with the sky, it forms a white and blue mystical axis. In general, the presence of snow in your dreams shows little enthusiasm and excessive rigidity. You should live more intensely and show more warmth toward loved ones. The snow is also related to the human longing for solitude or elevation. Do not forget that its whiteness, as well as being a symbol of life and death, is also associated with purification and transformation. This may represent a new beginning that lies ahead. If the snow melts, can mean the dissolving your fears and problems in real life. If you endure an avalanche, maybe you are overcome with the emotions that you have kept repressed for a long time.

❖ If you dream that you are watching the snow fall, soon you will receive a letter. According to some beliefs, the letter will be from the person you will marry in the future. Many believe that this dream brings good luck.

Snow plow ■ Imagining a machine of this sort is a good sign, as it expresses the arrival of resources with which to achieve objectives. However, if the snow plow is damaged or unable to do its job, you will fail despite having planned appropriately.

Soap ■ To imagine that you wash yourself with soap indicates that you need to "clean" certain aspects of your life. On the contrary, this image could also mean that the matters that worry us begin to clear up. An important nuance: if you wash clothes or a personal item, it is your emotional relationships that need a "cleaning" treatment.

Socks ■ They are a garment that is closely related to the individual's welfare or comfort. If they are torn and dirty it is a sign of waste: the dreamer spends more than she can afford. If they are new and clean they indicate a comfortable and wealthy situation. To take the socks off is interpreted as the need for a change that is getting imperative.

Soldier ■ Soldiers symbolize duty, obligations, and social hierarchy. They reflect a feeling of submission from which you would like to liberate yourself. Soldiers are also associated with aggressiveness and a spirit of conquest. In this sense, this dream can indicate how you impose your feelings over others in real life. On the other hand, you may be getting ready for a battle regarding some issue, or you may be needing to defend yourself against an emotional attack. You must be really careful when using your power. (See BOOTS, ARMY, ENEMY, and WAR)

❖ For a man, this dream means that he will change job. For a woman, it is a warning of a casual relationship. According to some oracles, it foretells a law suit. For the gypsies, on the other hand, it means that you will be honored soon.

Song ■ Music in general and songs in particular help to resist sorrows with more composure. Dreams, in this case, invite you to use these elements to sublimate the misfortunes and to share the joys. If you forget the lyrics or go out of tune it may be warning you to avoid dismissing the difficulties of a task that will begin shortly. Of course, what we sing (either something with rhythm, sad, funny . . .) is greatly important because it will give your a very reliable clue of your mood in real life. If it is a song you learned in childhood, perhaps it refers to an old problem or inhibition. Humming while you sleep is, however, a sign of grief; your inner self is lulling you in order to calm you with a soft melody.

❖ Although, in general, songs are a prediction of serene happiness, to listen to someone singing promises safe businesses.

Soothsayer ■ This figure is related to the ABBOT, the SAGE, and the POWERFUL. It could be our unconscious call for attention, asking for someone else's help in order to overcome a difficulty. If the one who guesses is the dreamer himself, the oneiric image shows a status of high self-esteem and self-confidence.

Sores ■ To dream of sores or ulcers is a sign that soon you will suffer some illness or emotional tension. However, if they heal, it means that a difficult time is coming to an end.

Soul ■ Seeing the soul leave your body during sleep is warning against the danger of losing your identity due to petty-minded interests. If, on the contrary, your soul does not flee and it is a different one that overtakes you, then it predicts the arrival of a friend you have not seen in a long while. Discussing in dreams about the immortality of the spirit signals that the subject will soon acquire new knowledge due to the actions of other people.

Sounds ■ If the sounds that you hear are loud, it is probably that your subconscious is trying to call your attention to a certain issue. The sound of a bugle, for example, represents a warning to be more combatant and alerted to the importance of problems. A whistle, on the other hand, indicates that someone has revealed your clandestine plans or that you are too obedient, like does who follow the calls of their masters. Hearing muted sounds or almost imperceptible voices suggests that you should lend yourself more to what your inner wisdom is telling you. However, sometimes dreams incorporate sounds from real life, like the sound of an alarm or traffic from the street.

❖ According to those that believe in astral voyages, after the first experience one hears a loud and irritating click, mostly when the return to the physical body is too fast. With time and practice, this disappears.

South ■ The south represents illumination, success, and glory, as it is the cardinal point in which the sun reaches its maximum splendor. (See CROSS, CROSSROADS, and ORIENTATION)

Sowing ■ This dream symbolizes a new stage in your life. You have the necessary means, although you will have to learn to use the tools. The work will be hard, but if you apply yourself with all of your potential, you will await satisfactions of every kind. If you are sowing arid land, it indicates that you have not chosen the work that best suits you, and, in general you should re-think your profession.

Spark ■ To see sparks in your oneiric thoughts announces the rapid improvement of social and professional relations. However, it also warns against the possibility that some of your properties could be set on fire.

Sparrow ■ Sparrows express inconsistency and futility, either in ourselves or those around us. In the latter case, dream images alert you of someone close trying to profit at your expense.

❖ This humble and friendly bird, perhaps because of the damage it causes to the fields, holds a negative connotation in the dream. If it flies, it announces unpleasant events and empty promises; if it is in a cage a loving conquest will prove to be a huge mistake. To see many of them together is a sign of ruin; to hear them chirping is sign of nasty gossiping.

Speaking ■ Speaking in dreams reflects the need to communicate. If what you say does not make any sense, it means that you are trying to attract others' attention, which is evidence of an emotional dissatisfaction. On the contrary, speaking with logic and common sense is a way of organizing thoughts. To dream that you communicate in a foreign language that you don't know could suggest a need to analyze your projects from different points of view. Finally, if you don't understand the words you hear, the dream is manifesting your fear of rumors. (See MOUTH, YELLING, and TONGUE)
❖ To talk to animals in dreams is an omen of suffering; with other people, of risk and danger; with superiors, of happiness; with enemies, of health. To speak to your mother is a good omen. If you dream that someone speaks badly of you, this predicts beneficial projects.

Speed ■ To dream that you are moving at high speeds could express a hidden fear of death, which, very probably, comes from the recent death of a loved one. However, it could also allude to the rushing rhythm of your life; maybe you need to slow down a little.

Sphere ■ Symbol of wholeness. The sphere is identified with the globe, thus by analogy, with the celestial bodies. it is considered an allegory of the world. (See CIRCLE)

Spider ■ In the spider three different symbolic meanings converge, and sometimes overlap: creative capacity (the spider weaving its web), aggressiveness (having a predatory instinct), and the fabric itself (such as a spiral net equipped with a center). That said, dreaming of a spider is interpreted in various ways. In most cases, it is a negative dream because the web it weaves symbolizes the trap in which your are about to fall. It also represents loneliness, isolation, and disputes. On the other hand, if the spider has woven a beautiful fabric that produces admiration, it means that the forces of the universe will act in your favor. It is time to intervene because you are at your full potential. The oneiric spiders can also represent the subject's fears. Perhaps you feel trapped into a web of deception or agitated emotions. Sigmund Freud believed that spiders were

overprotective mothers holding their children (innocent victims) under a sense of possession (web).
❖ Arachnophobia is an instinctive effect for humans since ancient times, the time when poisonous spiders were common. Such a dream merely reviews that fear to express that there are things in real life that cause sadness. Other ancient superstitions, however, consider that dreaming of spiders is a positive omen.

Spilling ■ Something spilling is indicative of wasted resources. It may represent the anguish over losing time or having squandered goods you will miss later. In any case, it reveals a sense of guilt for reckless behavior.

Spinning top ■ The top could illustrate how you take life: going around in a thousand circles with each decision you must make. This dream recommends serenity and simplicity.

Spiral ■ A spiral upward may represent progress and advancement. If it is downward, however, it expresses despair and failure.
❖ According to Chinese feng shui mystical tradition, the spirals are auspicious symbols that encourage health, wealth, and happiness. Also, if the life energy (Chi energy) moves in spirals then nothing can be better.

Spitting ■ Maybe you need to get rid of something, or think it is time to have a spiritual washing. Spitting can represent fury and contempt.
❖ Dreaming of spitting predicts the sad ending of what seems to be good business. To look at others spitting predicts disgust and disagreements. The most superstitious people believe that after a dream that predicts bad luck, if you spit three times right after waking up the harbinger will disappear.

Splashes ■ Generally, this is a warning from the subconscious. A call for precaution when expressing opinions or judgments that could come back against you.

Spool ■ In the case that a spool of thread appears in a dream, this may indicate that your ideas are a bit tangled. You should let them flow without trying to limit them or solve them. The dream reflects a lack of clarity regarding a project we are about to undertake. (See THREAD and WOOL)
❖ A silk spool is a sign of inner enrichment for the dreamer; cotton denotes poverty and complicated matters.

Spoon ▪ The spoon is interpreted as a promise of well-being and happiness. Losing it indicates fear of going through penalties; and sharing it, a good emotional time, but also the fear of revealing your most intimate secrets. Finally, a ladle may signal the desire for generosity toward the people around you.

Spouse ▪ References in this dream may be literal. Perhaps you are concerned about your relationship or have unconscious feelings about it. However, you may be projecting other thing in this dream. Your dream husband, perhaps, represents your father or the masculine side of your nature. Dreams about husbands and wives may refer to an aspect of your personality that you see reflected in your partner; therefore, if a woman dreams about her husband, surely this dream refers to the masculine, energetic aspects of her nature and the actions of the husband in the dream are actions that she herself would like to accomplish. If a man dreams of the husband of another woman, that man should question what the husband represents to him and what his true feelings are about the woman. As always, the context of the dream is of great importance for interpretation.

❖ If you dream that you're married and you are not in real life, popular superstition predicts problems. However, being next to an unknown spouse is an omen that promises marital bliss.

Spring ▪ It symbolizes happiness, optimism, and rebirth. This dream usually occurs when, after suffering a crisis, the unconscious reminds you that the future is always synonymous with hope. New projects and attitudes will show up in your life. This season also reveals the happy state of your spirit. (See FLOWERS and PLANTS)

❖ Dreaming that spring is close is a sign of lucky business and happy companies. However, dreaming that spring occurs unnaturally presages concerns and losses.

Spring (water) ▪ Dreams in which a spring appears highlight your desire for renewal and purification. The appearance of its water will reveal the state of your emotional relationships. Therefore, to drink from a clear spring indicates that you will satiate your physical, spiritual, or emotional needs and attain success. But if the spring is dry or its waters are cloudy, your love grows weak. (See WATER, FOUNTAIN, and GOD)

Sprinkler ▪ They are related to the fertility of water. It also reflects laborious work expecting large rewards in the long term. On the other hand, its image is associated with uncontainable crying. In this sense, its meaning would be similar to RELIEF and OVERFLOW.

❖ Following esoteric symbolism of water, dreaming of a sprinkler is translated as an omen of gainings. In particular, if it deals with flowers it indicates the imminent arrival of a new and happy love for the dreamer.

Squirrel ▪ The squirrel symbolizes lightness, trivial and superficial concern. It relates to flirtation.

❖ It is prediction of sacrifice, although successful at the end. Watching the squirrel eat predicts domestic joys; to capture it denotes danger. Being bitten by a squirrel indicates altercations with partner or child.

Stabbing ▪ If in dreams you stab someone it means you must solve an emotional conflict that has been postponed for too long; it has consequently taken on exaggerated proportions. Therefore, if you interpret it correctly, you need to urgently approach the person or the emotion stabbed in order to solve this problem in a positive way. In this case, dreams validate the premise that there is a thin line between love and hate. Not surprisingly, it is common for oneiric images to display scenes in which the subject attacks those whose affection is most needed.

Stain remover ▪ Stain remover means that you should not hold a grudge towards someone with whom you have had a confrontation.

Stains ▪ Stains are a sign of guilt. If you discover a stain on clothing, it shows that you need to conduct a thorough cleaning in your daily life. The stain might be related to some shady affair in which you have participated or intend to take part.

Stair ▪ The essential ideas tied to the ladder's image are: ascension, gradation, and communication between the various levels of verticality. The dreams in which stairs appear are very common and have great symbolic significance. If you climb the stairs it means the need to move up in life, either at a personal or professional level. It suggests that although it takes a lot of effort, you ultimately achieve your reward. It also indicates a desire for spiritual and social elevation, an attempt to reach the light of consciousness and remain there. If, however, you are going down the stairs it reveals a retreat from your goal or your responsibilities. But also a desire to dig into the unconscious. A step that is missing demonstrates psychic fractures. In particular, the spiral staircase indicates tortuous mental processes; the weight of life. The biblical story of Jacob's ladder symbolizes communication between this world and the spiritual. In psychological terms, it would be the means of contact between your true self and your ego. (See GETTING DOWN and GOING UP)

❖ Any staircase, but especially a marbled one, represents a state of joy and achievement in life. According to the reverse symbolism, to climb it predicts ruin; but if we follow a criterion of analogy it is a sign of happiness. To descend the stairs reveals treasures. And falling down the stairs means loss of fortune, risk, or failure.

Stalk ▪ A stalk of grain represents growth, fertility, maturity, and wisdom. Usually, this symbol is associated with sunlight. (See SUN)

Stalking ▪ Being stalked reveals a life of insecurity and danger, probably by adversaries who wish you failure using all means possible. If you are the one who stalks someone, this implies you do not trust others to solve a problem that affects you.

Standard ▪ See FLAG

Star ▪ As a glow in the dark, the star is a symbol of the spirit. This represents an option only reserved to the chosen one (in the rites of Mithras, for example, it is stated: "I am a star that shines and walks with you from the deepest"). The pentagram is the most common. In the Egyptian hieroglyphic system it means "elevation to the beginning." Consequently, dreaming of stars symbolizes ideals and hopes. However, if you imagine them falling rapidly or if they are very pale, it rather means a future misfortune.

❖ Formerly it was believed that when a person died, she or he would become a star. Dreaming of stars, therefore, implies that wise spirits guide the sleeper.

Station ▪ It is a place of passage symbolizing the many choices we have in life. It is related to travel and existential projects. If it is a railway station, the straightness of the rails take you directly to the fulfillment of your purposes. A station is also a public place, so it may be stating your social role. If it is empty and you walk without knowing where to go it reflects your lack of determination regarding a decision you have to

make soon. (See BUS, AVENUE, PLANE, BOAT, and CROSSROADS)

❖ This dream is considered lucky if you run into someone you know at the station. This shows that you will receive support in your endeavours, exerting a beneficial influence on you. In addition, this dream can mean future news.

Statue ▪ The image of a statue or a bust usually symbolizes the need to idealize something or someone. If you put someone on a pedestal it reflects scarcity of resources to achieve your goals.

❖ If the statue comes to life in the dream it means that you will recover a friendship that was broken. Some oracles also say that sculptors are promising omens. If, in a dream, you see one working your fortunes will improve.

Steal ▪ Seeing a thief stealing your things means that you are afraid to lose your possessions. On the other hand, if it is you who is stealing, it indicates resentment towards someone. You may be trying to take ownership of foreign goods or feelings; or you may have set goals so high that now you have to break the rules to reach them.

❖ Some superstitions associate this dream with love problems.

Steel ▪ Hard, resistant, inflexible, this metal in a dream plays the symbolic role of perseverance and strength in the face of difficulties. In general, images with steel in them are generally positive for the dreamer denoting success and the achievement of goals.

❖ Dreaming that you touch steel promises safety in life; to melt it reveals perseverance; to break it promises victory over powerful adversaries; to sell it is a harbinger of inheritance; to attempt to bend it unsuccessfully represents the dreamer's mistrust at overcoming a challenge.

Stepping down ▪ Stepping out of a vehicle (or a high place) voluntarily can mean the end of a path or activity. It thus closes a stage in your life. If the action is done involuntarily it means that you are in a situation of deterioration that is difficult to solve.

Stick ▪ The stick is an instrument of power and, therefore, a symbol of wealth and action. If you see yourself holding firmly to a stick in your dream, the scene suggests that you have decided to get to work to resolve a problem; if, however, you are hit with one, the scene could announce conflict due to a lack of initiative.

Sting ▪ Stings, no matter the insect they come from, represent small disappointments of daily life, those that can destabilize the subject at the least expected moment. So this oneiric thought advises caution as the best way to prevent these small disputes from becoming major trouble.

Stockings ▪ A symbol of erotic seduction. The context of the dream will clearly indicate its meaning. Stockings are a sign of prejudice and financial loss. To put them on reinforces this forecast of loss; to remove them, however, denotes luck. Holey socks reveal vain hopes and mismanagement at home. Silk stockings announce luxury that is fleeting, as well as losses; cotton, modest well-being. To see stockings hung up expresses a false appearance of wealth; to wash them promises profits.

Stomach ▪ In oneiric terms, dreaming of the stomach may have a physiological origin. Otherwise, this is often related to your refusal to "digest" the events that disturb you. The message of the dream is clear: you must take things more philosophically. (See EATING and HOUSE)
❖ Symbolizes maternity and the need for care and protection. Dreaming that you have a swollen belly indicates that you are saturated by responsibilities. If it hurts, it signifies that you are trying to evade a problem or situation that you believe has nothing to do with you.

Stone ▪ The stone is a symbol of being, of cohesion and consistency with yourself. Its hardness has always been seen as the opposite of the biological, subject to the laws of change, decay, and death. Despite appearances, the stone also has an inverse meaning to SAND. This element, in short, is an emblem of resistance, tenacity, perseverance, and eternity of being. Similarly, these qualities can lead to coldness, stubbornness, and the refusal of renewal. As a heavy element, a stone can symbolize the harsh burdens and responsibilities you have in real life. On the other hand, when broken into many pieces a stone represents dismemberment, mental disintegration, illness, death, and defeat. If you dream that the stones rain down from the sky it means that your heart is hardened. Finally, gemstones

symbolize transmutation from opacity to transparency, from imperfect into perfect. (See ROCK)
❖ Stones in the road may be a reference to the clumsy and difficult-to-handle people who impede your progress. If you throw stones, the dream indicates accusations. According to some oracles, if you collect them, you will inherit properties. Finally, to find precious stones augurs good luck.

Stool ▪ Given its usefulness (as much to sit down as to raise yourself to higher places) despite its small size, this dream announces that you will receive some help that will be very beneficial to you.

Store ▪ A store can symbolize the assortment of opportunities and rewards that life offers you. However, dreaming that the store is closed or that you do now have enough money for your purchases indicates that you feel incapable of reaching what you want. In this sense, the dream recommends that you not make too high of goals and that you be more realistic. If the store is a countryside store, it symbolizes evasion and protection. It is possible that this dream also foretells discomfort, but in this experience you will gain knowledge. The store could suggest that you should isolate yourself so as to know your inner self more.
❖ For the merchant, dreaming of a store is a sign of bad luck. It is saying that you will suffer the pressure of creditors. For everyone else, the dream predicts prosperity, even when you do not buy anything. In this fashion, if you dream that you are working in a store, fortune will smile upon you.

Stork ▪ Symbol of fertility and motherhood, a couple of storks flying portends family happiness and births; if it flies alone, probable failure of your projects; and if dead, good end after a dangerous threat.

Storm ▪ A storm, like everything that comes from the sky, has a sacred character. In dream terms, a storm suggests the possibility that difficulties will arise in your personal relationships. You should try to catch the self-destructive impulses that you occasionally try, as the conflict could occur at any moment. In whatever case, you have to search for the way in which to reconcile with your inner self. Only this way will you find calmness.

Stranger ▪ The dreams in which unknown individuals are present, playing a role in the oneiric scene, are often messages that the unconscious uses to represent aspects of your personality. Sometimes, it portrays person who behaves as you would like to yourself. In other times, strangers have negative characteristics that are nothing but facets of your personality that displease or disappoint you.

❖ If in dreams you talk to a stranger it means that you will receive news from some distant place. According to some oracles, the interpretation of this dream is reversed, namely, your friends will come to help.

Strangling ■ If someone strangles you, maybe there is something in your life that restricts you emotionally. If you strangle someone, it is probably the way to show your frustration toward that person. Also, that person can be an aspect of yourself that you do not let emerge.

❖ Tradition says that if you ask for a wish after having this dream your request will be fulfilled.

Straw ■ If you dream of a great quantity of straw stored, it indicates abundance. If it appears scattered, it reflects poor organization that could cause economic problems.

❖ To sleep on a pile of straw is an omen of sadness and injustice. In the same sense, to have sex on it is a warning of misery and bad relationships.

Strawberries ■ Strawberries symbolize feminine sensuality. Eating strawberries augurs the beginning of a loving relationship. Passion and desire are the keys expressed through these fruits. If during the dream you do not taste this delicacy at all it seems clear that you are repressing yourself. Keep in mind that unfulfilled sexual desires do not disappear and, therefore, the unconscious sends you messages reminding of an inhibited erotic load.

Stream ■ A stream of clear water flowing symbolizes joy and satisfaction. Dreaming of this element indicates that your emotional dimension is perfectly balanced. However, if the water is turbid you may suffer emotional distress. A dry stream, instead, represents the suspicion derived from a disappointment you had in the past.

Street ■ Streets symbolize the path that each person follows in everyday life. The turns and curves they have represent the difficulties that you find on the way. ‖ If the streets are wide and lined with trees, it indicates that you

have a very definite orientation and you are satisfied with it. The narrower the street the scarcer your life's projects will be. If it is a dead-end street, the dream clearly warns that you should reconsider your options and take another direction; this type of street is associated with depression and discouragement. (See AVENUE)

❖ The ancient books on dreams portend success if you dream of streets lined with trees and flowers.

Strength ■ It symbolizes the ability of the person to successfully perform those tasks that, at first, she did not believe possible. Dreams bring out the authentic potential that lies at the bottom of your psyche, often buried under a thick layer of prejudice and excuses that prevent you from doing what you really want to accomplish.

Stretcher ■ It announces illnesses or accidents. The dream gives you clues so you can take appropriate precautions in order to avoid both circumstances. To see yourself using a stretcher indicates concerns and moral distress.

Strike ■ A strike indicates that something in your personality is rebelling against a certain situation. It symbolizes boredom and rebellion against your real life. It is evident what this dream is advising: you should change what you don't like.

Suffering ■ Dreaming of suffering—as much your own as someone else's—is a bad omen, as it signals tensions and disputes with loved ones. Further, it denotes betrayal in the work environment that could be very harmful to your interests.

Sugar ■ To add a lot of sugar to a meal reflects great anxiety, probably motivated by lack of affection or tenderness. This dream indicates a clear need for affection and may suggest that your emotional state is somewhat hurt because of recent events.

❖ Sugar is, for many traditions such as the Arabs, a harbinger of deception and bad intentions. However, buying it is a sign of happiness and honor; to sell it promises success in the face of danger. Eating it predicts success in business but it does not exempt the dreamer from adultery and false friends.

Suicide ■ Since its existence, suicide is a symbol of the destruction of the world. As widely popular Sartre's doctrine preaches it, the value of reality is exclusively the scope of existence. However, in some cultures, like

Japanese, suicide for ethical reasons is considered an honorable action. Dreaming of suicide could symbolize an aggression against your person which you punish for some motive or need to remove an aspect of your character with that which you do not like. It also indicates, in some form, that you resist accepting the problems that are affecting you or living in a way against your desires. You should interpret this dream as a severe warning: you are not upholding your commitments and you try to avoid reality. Lastly, the act of destroying an object with which you identify could be a sign of the latent desire to suicide.

❖ Oneiric oracles say that this dream foretells deception.

Suit ■ A suit could represent your desire to impress someone. It is possible that it hints at the good state of your self-confidence or the side that you show in the professional sphere.

❖ According to gypsy tradition, wearing a suit foretells successes.

Sulfur ■ For many, sulfur has evil connotations because this substance is usually associated with the devil. If this is your case, the dream suggests guilt. But, at the same time, sulfur is a symbol of purification and improvement. And sometimes it is also associated with love, passion, eroticism, and wisdom.

Summer ■ The summer symbolizes plentifulness and richness, and this dream foretells being able to collect the benefits of your work. It is the season of happiness, satisfaction, and pleasure; unless the dreamer experiences unbearable heat. (See SEASONS)

Summit ■ It marks a goal, an objective. Its importance is proportional to its height. (See HILLTOP)

Sun ■ The sun symbolizes the conscious activity and rational governing of your life. The observation of your path invites you to consider the distinct cyclical phases of your existence. So, dreaming of a rising sun reflects the start of a stage of happiness and prosperity; if it gives off a lot of light and heat, it presages economic abundance; but, if it is hidden or not bright, it foretells losses; if it is dark between the clouds, it is a sign of sadness and unexpected problems; lastly, a sunset announces the end of a period.

❖ The first god of the human species was the sun. It was able to end the darkness and the dangers of the night. If has always been considered a blessing. In the Tarot, the sun card represents happiness and exuberance. In general, every dream tradition says the same thing: this dream foretells the arrival of happy times.

Sunflower ■ Sunflowers indicate that you are in a position to get all the energy and strength necessary for your projects though this winning streak will have a short duration. You must then bear in mind the main objectives and take advantage of moments of "glory." (See PATH)

❖ Clytie—who because of her jealousy made her sister be condemned to death and be transformed by Apollo to incense—also suffered her own metamorphosis; she transformed into a sunflower, always forced to turn her head to the god with whom she was madly in love and who had abandoned her in order to take her rival.

SUITCASE

Carlos dreamed: "I was looking for my bag and could not find it anywhere. I was at the airport and my plane was about to take off. They announced the last call to board, and I could not remember where I had left it. I was very distressed, it had all my documents, valuables, and money. But I could not miss the plane because an important business meeting awaited me. I spent the whole dream running back and forth, searching every corner of the airport, but nothing, the suitcase did not appear and I couldn't leave; the tickets were inside."

When Charles had this dream he was suffering the first symptoms of mild depression. He felt very sad, insecure, and uncomfortable in his life, but did not know how to improve it. Searching in dreams alludes to a lack, something that we need for our **emotional stability**. The suitcase full of important things reflects the values that guide us in life, without which we would feel lost, like Carlos. The plane shows our desire to excel, to rise or transcend our daily concerns. The fact that he missed it indicates that he felt unable to move forward, despite his continued attempts (running from back and forth, looking everywhere . . .). A month later, Carlos began treatment with a psychoanalyst to overcome his sadness. After a few days, he found his oneiric suitcase in a dream and managed to catch the plane. In his waking world, he began to understand the causes of his discomfort and feel more satisfied and confident in himself.

analysis of a dream

Sunrise ■ Contemplating the first lights of the day represents triumph over doubts, sorrows, or tribulations. A sunrise indicates the beginning of a happier period in which you should be able to guide your own actions willingly. This dream signals hope and optimism.

❖ In ancient Egypt, sunrise was associated with New Year's day and the beginning of the world. Since the beginning of the times, humanity has paid tribute to the rising sun as divine symbol of hope and rebirth.

Surrender ■ Surrender occurs due to a loss of orientation. The dream recommends restarting the jobs that are being completed in the present. The problem is that this dream, occasionally, is not very pleasant. Surrendering is equivalent to stopping to fight, resigning yourself to what others decide for you, so to say, taking external orders.

Swallow ■ The swallow is an allegory of spring. Swallows embody purity and holiness because they always remain high in the sky; and solitude and freedom because of their migratory habits. (See SPRING)

❖ According to gypsy tradition, it is a sign of prosperity and fun. In the nest it forecasts fortune and happiness.

Swan ■ For some anthropologists, it represents the naked woman due to its elegance, its rounded and silky body, and its immaculate whiteness. Therefore, the swan usually refers to the fulfillment of a wish. Dreaming of swans also invites reflection on the harmony and serenity of yourself.

❖ Because of its long neck, swans in a dream may have sexual connotations. In Greek mythology, Zeus seduced Leda, the Spartan king's wife, by transforming into a swan.

Sweat ■ It could be the result of a feverish state of the dreamer. But, if not a physical ailment, it is generally a positive dream that alludes to purification through hard work and bodily strength. It can also be interpreted as the fear that an aspect of your personality will be brought to light and will cause others to reject you.

Sweeping ■ To sweep in dreams is equivalent to getting rid of old ideas and attitudes. You must set aside what is worthless to begin a new life stage. Dreaming of sweeping has different meanings depending on where it is done. If it is the subject's room, it predicts a good end to romantic projects; if it is the house, it signals the need to address an everyday problem; and if it is a business space, exhaustion due to work overload. In the case that you need to sweep and have not done it yet, you could suffer great upset soon.

❖ According to a superstition, to sweep what is unnecessary out of your house, you run the risk of sweeping out good luck. Thus, these dreams have negative connotations.

Sweets ■ The oneiric thoughts in which you eat sweets announce not only pleasures but also the need to take care of expenses caused by some superfluous whims. If the candies are stale you must be cautious with your health, as there are great chances of becoming ill. Receiving sweets is a warning that you will be flattered by someone you are not sure about her intentions, so you must be attentive to her movements; but if, on the contrary, it is you who make them, then it becomes evident the profit after hard work.

❖ In general, sweets are an omen of good business; but to receive them indicates deceit; and to buy them, some minor trouble.

Swelling ■ This almost always indicates the disproportionate exaggeration of something. A swollen body part, for example, may be the reflection of an illness, but it also manifests that you pay too much attention

---

SWEEPING

analysis of the dream

Claudia: "I was energetically sweeping my house; but the more I swept, the more dust and dirt appeared at every corner. I struggled a lot and I spent the whole dream with the broom; but as much as I insisted, I could not get the floor clean at all. I woke up exhausted."

It is an exhausting dream indicating that you are unmotivated or **waste your energy** in worthless issues. When Claudia had this dream she was investing every effort to restore an old family house that was in pretty bad shape. Despite the recommendations of the architect and her children to tear it down and do it again, Claudia had no money for such an expensive reform and invested all her savings in restoring it superficially. After a few months, cracks began to appear everywhere and, fearing a collapse, the work was stopped.

to what that specific part of the body symbolizes. However, seeing a swollen object signifies the excessive importance you give its meaning. To blow up a ball is a warning that you are taking a certain situation to unsustainable limits.

Swimming ▪ Water symbolizes the unconscious and thus swimming means that you trust it and are open to its path. You are sure of what you do and you are receptive to the creative power of the mind. If you dive, it denotes that you and your unconscious form a team. This conjunction is strengthened if, in the dream, you are able to breathe underwater.

❖ To swim strongly in clear water foretells success in love and business. If, on the contrary, you sink or fight to stay afloat, it means the opposite.

Swing ▪ Psychoanalysis tend to relate the swing with auto-eroticism, and interprets the fear of rolling or of seasickness, produced by the swing, as inhibitions from childhood.

❖ Dreaming that you swing with your partner predicts a happy marriage and a large family; if you swing alone it denotes selfishness and infidelity; and if the chain is broken a birth of a child will be coming soon. A stationary swing is indicative of intense but brief joy.

Sword ▪ The sword has received special reverence by many peoples. Generally it represents courage, power, and justice, especially in the Christian tradition, when it was reserved only for knights. In parallel, the sword is also a spiritual symbol. Its presence in dreams indicates that you should try to behave according to the attributes that are linked to this weapon. Only then you will triumph. On the other hand, dreams in that contain swords can also have sexual connotations, since these are considered phallic symbols. Consequently, if you are fighting with a sword it may indicate your sexual desires.

❖ It is the symbol of truth. It is the conscious liberates itself from the unconscious part of the mind. This process of individualization usually appears in many myths and legends, when the hero fights dragons and demons with his sword.

Syrup ▪ Extremely sweet and cloying, it can be a reflection of the attitude that someone has toward you, or your own. Taking a syrup also shows you that, after a period of misfortunes, you will be able to solve all your problems and live with certain peace. According

S W I N G

analysis of the dream

Joana dreamed: "I was ten and I swung on a swing in the park. My father pushed me and I drove myself forward strongly, stretching my legs. With my toes I could almost touch the clouds. I was happy. I felt light and powerful. Suddenly, I turned around and I no longer saw my father. I felt fear and dizziness. I called him with all my might, but he did not appear."

Joana had this dream two days after receiving a marriage proposal. She was still undecided. She knew her boyfriend very well and was truly in love, but the idea of marriage made her feel too grown up, despite her youth—she was only 20 years old. This also made her **long for her childhood**. Swinging on the swing and the pleasant feeling from getting high up are related to her desire for freedom. But the fact that it was her father who pushed her and watched her closely, so that she would not fall, revealed her insecurity and her desire for protection.

In dreams, swinging yourself in the swing is also interpreted as a symbol of indecision; your issues are on the tightrope and sway from side to side without ever landing on site. Joana's unconscious was encouraging her to be in charge of her life and to decide for herself, breaking family ties—her father disappears in the dream—and accepting her maturity.

to other interpretations, this dream denotes excessive sentimentality and nostalgia.

❖ Some superstitions associate dreams that contain sweet things with all things "sexy." This comes from the fact that the human mind, when an individual is sexually excited, produces a chemical substance also found in chocolate.

T

Table ■ The table symbolizes friendly fraternization. In dreams, it represents your relationship with your environment. If it is rectangular, it shows a hierarchical structure based on a leader, who is usually on one side or in the middle. Your position indicates where you are on the ladder. However, if the table is round, it means that all those who sit around it have the same rank. But apart from indicating your "status," the table can also mean other things. What is on it refers to what will soon enter your life. Thus, if it is filled with delicacies, the dream predicts prosperity; if it is empty, problems at home; and finally, if no one has sat around, it suggests that you need to feel more closer to your family.

❖ The table predicts domestic comfort and happiness in the marital relationship.

Tablecloth ■ A tablecloth on the table indicates a tendency to be overprotective. You attach great importance to material things. It also expresses a certain inertia in everyday life. You are conservative and changes frighten you. If the cloth is stained and creased, it reflects domestic problems.

Tail ■ If in the dream you grow a tail it represents your animal nature. The fact the tail is on your back can also mean rejection of part of your sexual dimension.

❖ If you cut off an animal's tail, the dream predicts you will not receive care and affection.

❖ If you grow a tail, your dream could allude to a bad action that you have done, such that the subconscious perceives you as a demonic being. It could also be interpreted as a phallic symbol or be a masculine sexual allusion.(See PHALLUS)

Taking shelter ■ Dreaming that someone favorably welcomes you means that you will receive necessary protection. But if you are not welcome, you should distrust advice you receive in the coming days.

Tamer ■ If you dream of taming beasts it is very possible that you are living the opposite. That is, it could indicate that you are dominated by certain situations that do not allow you to freely express yourself. The dream is confirming your desire to take control and to take charge of your own life. Other interpretations claim that taming animals in dreams means you have learned to control your emotions.

❖ If you dream that you tame a lion you will be successful. According to some oracles, this dream also predicts that you will marry an intelligent person.

Tapestry ■ Dreaming that you are weaving a tapestry indicates that you are living in agreement with your plans, using much patience and constancy with them. If the tapestry is very light, it indicates that you are going through life superficially; meanwhile, a thick and beautiful tapestry shows the exact opposite. This tapestry reminds you that your way of existing is abundant and rich. (See PICTURE and THREAD)

Tattoo ■ Getting a tattoo could indicate an important amount of dependency with respect to the image that you have tattooed. In parallel, this dream also manifests the need to do different things than usual. In every form, although you desire a change in your life, you do not know just what it is that you want to change. This dream reflects confusion. On the one hand, you yearn to live like others, but on the other, you would like to be different. According to other interpretations this dream references an emotional situation that you have noticed and you cannot forget. In the same fashion, it may concern a behavior pattern that you have fully integrated into your personality.
❖ The dream could be of a sexual nature. "Tattoo" is a Maori word and was considered by the Maori people as a beautiful and sensual ornament. In Polynesia, many people had their entire body tattooed (except the eyes). For many cultures like this one, tattoos are a symbol of sexuality and virility.

Tavern ■ Managing a tavern in dreams shows that, in real life, you are using dishonorable means to reach your goals. Entering into an establishment of this sort evidences the desire to avoid daily problems and the abuse of pleasures and superficial things.

Taxi ■ Dreaming that you are driving a taxi expresses your need to share projects and ideas with others. You probably feel that you are not paid attention to, and that you have the impression that something does not work in your emotional relationships.

Teacher ■ The figure of the teacher is very important. It represents the values of knowledge, experience, and wisdom. This dream, however, can have many nuances. For example, if you are a strict school teacher, inclined to punish students, it is a sign that you lack security. The cause may be from a latent inferiority complex that is balanced out by a controlling and dictatorial attitude. In most cases, having a dream of this kind does not speak well of your maturity. If the teacher is a serious, formal, scholarly person, it means that you are at a formative stage of intellectual development. If the teacher inspires respect and admiration (a father figure), the dream expresses emotional maturity and stability. (See GRANDPARENTS, ACADEMY, AUTHORITY, LIBRARY, and HERMIT)

Team ■ If you dream that you work in team, or that you are part of a sports team, the unconscious is transmitting you the need to be more sociable in the professional field. Therefore, if these images coincide with an offer to participate in a business, a priori, the dream would be encouraging you to be part of such project.

Tearing ■ Tearing garments is something that, in many religions and cultures, is a symbol of pain or humiliation. This dream portends slander and abuse. If others are tearing your clothes, it would be an offense caused by rumors in your social circle.

Tears ■ Surprisingly, tears in a dream bodes well: you can resume old projects and through them enjoy economic prosperity and social success. Similarly, the innermost desires will be satisfied and you will experience a time of happiness and joy. Associated symbolically with sperm and the fertility of water, in the psychoanalytic field, tears correspond to fecundity.
❖ The Egyptians related tears with fertility, based on the myth of the flooding of the Nile (their means of fertilizing the fields); thanks to the tears shed by Isis in search of her murdered husband.

Teeth ■ Although it might be telling you about a physical pain you are not yet aware of, one of the most recurrent and universal dreams is one in which you lose your teeth. Many psychologists agree that this is a clear sign of fear and insecurity. They usually take place during the transition from one stage of life to another, reflecting your concern for growing up or sex appeal. Ultimately, you are feeling equally as helpless as when you were a kid and lost your baby teeth. Teeth also represent your capacity to respond aggressively, both for defense and for attack. In this interpretation you want to know about the condition of the teeth in the dream (if they are sharp, if they move . . .). On the other hand, growing your teeth is an omen of prosperity of all kinds. Healthy teeth indicate a good physical and mental health. Instead, dirty or damaged ones mean that someone around you is not acting properly. False teeth denote excessive importance to physical appearance.
❖ In a region of Sudan, if a woman smiles by completely showing her teeth it is a bad omen. It symbolizes the jaws of a wild animal that scare the cattle. African sorcerers believe that this dream augurs upcoming prosperity. However, according to popular tradition moving teeth indicate illness or loss of affection. And losing them predicts pain and death. However, if the tooth

falls on your hand, it is an opposite omen: you will have a son or will receive good news.

Telephone ■ The telephone embodies communications with your loved ones. Therefore, the conversation in the dream reflects the quality of your relationship with the person in question. On the other hand, dreaming that you do not respond to the telephone despite its insistent ringing reveals that you are ignoring the advice of your subconscious. You should be attentive to what it communicated to you, because it could contain a lot of information about your fears and hopes.

❖ Many people believe that dreaming of a telephone call is a sign of good luck, as is announces advantages in business. However, if it is you who is making the call, and important appointment will be postponed. Long distance calls foretell happiness.

Television ■ The television could represent your mind with its flow of thoughts. It is possible that you are observing yourself in an objective manner. In this case, what appears on the screen will tell you a lot about your subconscious. On the other hand, dreaming that the television is on while you are sleeping signifies that you do not control your energy in an appropriate manner. You have a lot of information, but you do not manage to process what is truly important. (See THEATER)

❖ Modern oneiric superstition says that if you enjoy watching television in dreams, you will achieve success. If, on the contrary, the feeling is unpleasant or it bores you considerably, there will be people who will lead you astray.

Temple ■ The temple symbolizes the sacred, everything that is out of your power, and generally, seeing a temple in dreams foretells tragedies in the short term. For people in love, it is a sign that if you marry, your marriage will be short and miserable.

Test ■ This is a negative dream that reveals your social vulnerability, that is, what you are afraid of showing or communicating to others. Perhaps, you feel that your vital role is going through an ordeal or being evaluated. Dreams of this type usually take place after the start of a new job or after taking new responsibilities that overwhelm you. It is also possible that, in the dream, people laugh at you, you are not able to make yourself heard, or you have a premonition of an impending disaster. These images demonstrate your fragility at

getting involved with others. If, while you perform the test, the people watching you stir in their seats and talk it means you do not know how to take your ideas forward. If you have no audience at all it denotes the lack of recognition that you receive.

❖ Many dreams related to actors, actresses, and stages are advantageous omens. But if they are poor and appear disoriented, the good luck will vanish. Dreaming that you speak in public is very positive but if you do it from a podium it predicts diseases and failures.

Thawing ■ It means returning to life. It can be interpreted as a time when conditions are favorable for resuming relations or projects that were stagnant or distant. It is a positive dream because it indicates a desire to re-energize and move on.

Theater ■ The dreams are, in and of themselves, works of theater represented by the fears, problems, and hopes of your imagination. Theater, overall, is a dream within another dream. The plays are the staging of morals, critiques, and observations that will help you reach the desired emotional and psychological equilibrium. Since the Greek tragedies, there has always been the desire to portray intimate emotions through theater with the end of gaining wisdom, resignation before the inevitable, etc. So, dreaming that you see a play foretells a period of benefits and satisfaction in general. In the same fashion, you should try to decipher what each element of the piece means. If you are not participating in the performance, it denotes that you are living too passively. On the contrary, if you are in the scene it signifies the desire to take the reins in your life. To do so, you should analyze and pay attention to what occurs during the play, as the plot will reveal the essence of the dream. Further, the role that you play in the piece could be very revealing.

❖ Those wise men who have reached a high level of consciousness assure that life is like a play. You play a small and short role within the entirety of the cosmic game. When you die, you take off the costume and return to your true identity. A curious superstition says that, if you dream that your teeth fall out, you will give birth to a boy who will be very famous in the world of theater.

Thermometer ■ This dream could be a warning of your physical state: You may be cold and have a fever. But it could also signify that your temperature, metaphorically speaking, is too high; perhaps due to attraction that you feel for someone. It is also possible that the presence of a thermometer in dreams reflects a concern with determining specific facts, or perhaps it alludes that you are trying to "take the temperature" of some new project or idea that you have in mind. On the other hand, you should not forget that the thermometer contains mercury, so it may be interesting to investigate the role of this god in Roman mythology or the influence of the planet in astrology.

Thicket ■ Its meaning is similar to that of UNDERBRUSH in that it represents obstacles to be overcome. It also alludes to situations or bits of the personality that are dark and mysterious. To go into the thicket to discover what is inside, or avoid it and go around, will be keys that reflect the attitude of the dreamer with respect to her life circumstances at the moment.

Thief ■ To see a thief stealing your belongings in a dream means that you are afraid of losing your possessions, whether sentimental, material, or work-related. For example, a work mate could have taken all the credit for your work. However, if it is you who is stealing, it could indicate jealousy toward someone. It's possible that you're seizing onto others' goods or feelings. If in the dream you find the thief in the precise moment of stealing, the item being stolen will be extremely important for a correct interpretation.
❖ Gypsies believe that to dream of theft means you have a guilty conscience. However, if you are part of a gang of thieves, it denotes that you trust your friends.

Thirst ■ This could reflect a real physiological need, especially when fevered. Contrarily, thirst symbolizes a clear spiritual yearning, as well as mystical. However, if in the dream you sate this thirst by drinking cloudy or hot water, the image announces delusion, deceit, and general disappointment.

Thistle ■ This flower, whose petals are thorns, symbolizes irritability caused by bad experiences; an attitude that can lead to the departure of your loved ones. On the other hand, if they give you a thistle it is evidence that you will suffer abuse and rejection from others; and you could even see your businesses ending up in misery.
❖ To see a thistle indicates annoyance, discussions, and betrayal; planting it, pain; and consequently, to pull it out, joy; watering it expresses ingratitude; to grab it, stupidity and laziness.

Thorn ■ Freudian psychoanalysis identifies thorns with painful events of sexual life; Jungian, with sentimental disappointments. Thorns also represent the pain always linked to pleasure, "there is no rose without a thorns." This dream can also be caused by rheumatic pains or nocturnal insect bites. (See HEDGEHOG)
❖ Dreaming of thorns announces fights and disputes with neighbors. Getting pricked by them portends dangers concerning, in particular, money and career.

Thread ■ This is one of the most ancient symbols of humanity. The thread represents the essential connection on the spiritual, social, biological planes, etc. Because of this, you can interpret the thread as the chain of circumstances that happen in your life, making up your destiny. So dreaming of thread that doesn't end predicts health and many years of life. On the contrary, if it is broken, it announces illness or physical problems. The same interpretation is applicable to your emotional relationships or job. Threads of noble metals, such as gold or silver, predict success earned thanks to intelligence and subtlety.

Threat ■ If you dream that you are threatening someone, it may mean that you need to impose yourself in real life. However, if you are the one being threatened you must discover the cause of this situation. Some dreams have a climate so disturbing that it is difficult to find out who or what causes them. Chances are it is all derived from the problems you have in your relationships. You might be emotionally threatened by your partner, your parents, or your boss. Finally, those feelings the individual tends to repress—such as resentment, anger, fear, and eroticism—can also be fighting to become visible.
❖ Some oracles consider the meaning of this dream is suggesting the opposite. So, everyone will behave in a sweet and affable manner towards you.

Threshold ■ If, in dreams, you cross the threshold of a door, you will soon start a new stage in your life. Given that it could be transcendental for you, it is important that you meditate thoroughly whatever decision you ae going to make. Once you cross this threshold, there is no turning back. In the case that you cannot pass the threshold, it is a sign that you should not change your situation at the moment. You are probably not yet prepared to do so.

Throat ■ Through the throat we swallow what comes from the outside. If, like ostriches, you gobble without chewing it means that you do not understand what is proposed to you. Excessive rigidity indicates the presence of a strong repression.

Throne ■ Seeing yourself seated on a throne indicates that you are in a position that does not suit you. You are living above your possibilities and you are not acting accordingly.

Thunder ■ Thunder represents our feelings of fury. It could be that you will have a discussion. It is very possible that your relationships are too stormy. Hearing thunder also foretells the imminent approach of some danger in your life. If the thunder is accompanied by lightening, you could suffer betrayal by a friend.
❖ In ancient Greece, it was believed that the cause of storms was the disputes between Zeus and his wife Hera. In Sumerian mythology, the storm was associated with the roar of the bull and rites of fertility. The dream represents your indomitable and powerful psychic strength.

Ticket ■ A ticket may represent the beginning of a whole series of psychological events; perhaps, you have allowed yourself to explore your unconscious. It also symbolizes that you have approval for a new project. You know the direction your life needs to go. If you lose the ticket, you may feel insecure and confused regarding your destination, or you may not consider yourself sufficiently prepared. However, depending on the type of ticket in the dream, the oneiric sense will vary: if it is from a bank it announces incidentals and litigation for economic reasons that you will likely lose; if it is a lottery ticket, danger by leaving your affairs at random; a train ticket, patience when social climbing; and a theater ticket, willingness to escape everyday reality. If the dreamer is traveling in economy class with a first class ticket, it indicates the dreamer's perception of her social or work position as being well below the one she really deserves.
❖ You will receive news that will clarify your situation.

Tide ■ The high tide denotes disappointments and disturbances; the low tide, peace, and tranquility. (See SEA)

Tie ■ As a male garment, the tie is a symbol of virility and also of slavery.

❖ According to an esoteric interpretation, the tie is a symbol of debts. To tie it can also reveal a desire to escape from too rigid rules.

Tiger ■ The tiger almost always represents hidden aspects of one's own personality, normally those that frighten you. It is also the symbol of strength and aggressiveness. Because of this it is associated with the liberation of the basic instincts: plenty of energy that could turn against you. A domesticated tiger, in contrast, reflects the triumph of reason over passion.
❖ In the children's poem "Tiger" by William Blake, the animal represents material existence. Its frightening character is the suffering that people experience when they lose their innocence.

Time ■ Many terminally ill people dream of clocks that are marking the passage of time which, inexorably, brings them closer to death. On the other hand, the feeling that you are running out of time during the events of a dream is a clear indication that you are living too rushed. If time stops, it reveals the need to deliberate deep within yourself. In contrast, in the event that you dream that you have too much time, it signifies that you are little motivated and that you strayed from your main objective.
❖ As you approach spiritual truth, time will be of less importance. Sometimes, in dreams, the past, the present, and the future mix within themselves to offer a unique feeling. When you concentrate, the same occurs. The less consciousness you have of the passage of time, the more profound the meditation of the mind will be.

Tiredness ■ Feeling tired in dreams is often the literal reflection of a situation in real life. It is important to try to remember what the cause was in the dream and then interpret its symbolism. Perhaps, you have not yet noticed the real reason for the excessive fatigue that you suffer.

Toad ■ This dream has the same meaning as that of FROG, but only in its more negative aspects.

Toasting ■ As in real life, toasting in dreams is synonymous with joy and celebration. However, this joy may be hiding the hypocrisy of those who toast with you. If they are strangers, you must be even more alert, because they represent the closest people in real life.

Tobacco ■ Smoking tobacco forecasts success in business and in studies, although little luck with love. Seeing it dry alerts you of gossiping from close persons; as a plant, it signals that it is not a good time to make new friendships.

Toilet ■ These dreams allude to the intention of cleanliness and purification. They tend to be very positive in those where the dreamer searched for ways to discard the superfluous, to get rid of all of the extra, not only physically but also spiritually and emotionally. Finding yourself on the toilet could indicate the best moment to rid yourself of and overcome old fears, complexities and guilt. (See BASIN)

Tomb ■ Something inside you has died and you should find out what it stands for and why it has appeared in the subconscious. Also, this dream invites you to reflect over a terminal state, about what it means for your mortality. If it repeats a lot, it could be an indication of neurosis. Assuming that you see your own body in the tomb, it means that you are restructuring your life. Generally, the dream foretells a profound change in your existence.

❖ Superstition says that you experienced a loss, but not necessarily death. Maybe you are dying spiritually and you will later be reborn. The celtic people considered cemeteries the uterus of Mother Earth, and that in

them new spiritual life is born. Other interpretations claim that this dream foretells deception, and, curiously, news about a marriage.

Tombstone ■ This dream indicates the person's insecurity about their future. It expresses a desire to find transcendental answers. You do not know where your life is going and you want to know. You are in a crisis of identity. However, this dream is positive because it indicates that you are maturing.

Tongue ■ In general, to dream of a tongue means that you talk too much. If you bite it, it should be read as a call for prudence. this type of dream tends to indicate that you are starting to realize your failures and regret some things. If the tongue stutters, it denotes that you don't know how to express your needs in a coherent manner. If it hurts, the dream probably alludes to the fact that you have been speaking badly of someone or telling lies. For Freud, the tongue had a clear sexual meaning. Because of its shape and erotic function, he compared it to the penis. (See TALKING and MOUTH)
❖ if the tongue you dream about is your own, it means that you will tell lies. If it's someone else's, others will lie about you. To dream that you don't have a tongue denotes the inability to defend yourself against slander. Finally, an infected tongue means that you speak too carelessly.

Tools ■ Dreams in which tools appear have clear positive meaning. These usually don't evoke unpleasant activities. But, if you don't like the work you are doing with tools, you should interpret the dream as an invitation to overcome your own limits.

Toothpaste ■ This dream is positive, since it announces improvement of affective relationships. You will have to address, however, the color of the toothpaste to better clarify its meaning. (See COLOR)

Topple ■ It represents overcoming a major obstacle you were not sure you could avoid.

Torch ■ Carrying a lit torch indicates the protagonist's desire to share the light, that is, her joy and vitality. However, if the torch is extinguished, the dream means that your enthusiasm level is not precisely at its prime.

Torpedo ■ An explosion is an alarm, either warning of imminent danger or expressing the desire to end a

TONGUE

analysis of a dream

Julio dreamed: "I dreamt that my tongue itched a lot and I could not alleviate it. I tried to scratch it with my teeth but the taste buds, which were like enormous pink pimples, popped in my mouth, leaving a horrible bitter taste. I looked in the mirror and was shocked to see it so purple. It was a very stressful dream that left a bad taste in my mouth when I woke up."

The tongue is strongly associated with the act of speaking. In Julio's case, the dream was a warning for him to **stop lying**. At the time of the dream, Julio had problems with some friends because of his tendency to lie and talk badly about them. His unconscious was warning him of the "dirtiness" of his tongue and that he should solve it as soon as possible. The bad taste in his mouth is a reflection of the problems his attitude could cause.

situation that has become unbearable in a violent manner. It is also possible that there is a loud noise where you are sleeping and the subconscious assimilates it as part of the dream scene that is developing at that moment in your dreams.

Tower ■ Towers symbolize ascending. In the Middle Ages, towers and bell towers could serve as watchtowers, but they had a meaning of a staircase between earth and heaven (in those times, material height was associated with spiritual height). On the other hand, towers also symbolize isolation from the world in which you live, so to speak, the defense from external aggressions. A solid tower signifies that you are confronting the challenges that are thrown at you in life perfectly; a half-demolished tower, in contrast, represents the opposite.
❖ Seeing a very tall tower foretells good luck. But, if you are coming down from it, it predicts failures.

Toys ■ Dreaming of toys is interpreted as a repressed desire to return to childhood. It indicates a fear of commitment and adult responsibilities. The dreamer feels overwhelmed by the weight he carries and seeks refuge in a safe, happy time, free from obligations and responsibilities. If this dream is an unconscious way of expressing your hidden feelings, you should ask yourself which aspect of your life is represented by each toy. On the contrary, it could be that the dream is advising you to stop playing with your life and that you need a more practical, grounded point of view.
❖ In general, this is a favorable dream, since it augurs happiness for children and their families.

Traffic ■ A traffic jam could express that your life is not going as you would like. You feel blocked. If you dream that you are a traffic director, it shows your desire to impose your own norms on society. On the contrary, you likely believe yourself to be in a role not meant for you, and that others isolate you. In this case, you should confront the problem.
❖ If you dream of a big traffic jam, it means that you will resolve your problems through a lot of patience.

Traffic light ■ Like in real life, the traffic light in oneiric thoughts is a sign of warning; especially if it is red or orange. In this case, it warns of the arrival of imminent danger and the need to stay alert. If it is green, it announces that now is the favorable moment to start new projects and establish more profound relationships. But, the traffic light can also represent the moral and social code, with all of the resistance, inhibitions, and obstacles that hinder the evolution of people and their understanding. The dreamer should decide, in this case, if he should disregard this sign or not, and if it is prudent to run the red light.

Trap ■ Dreaming that you fall into a trap indicates that you trust too much in providence, which is why you sometimes lose control of your life. At the same time, this trap could also be the result of incoherence, as you tend to talk about things you dont know. Evidently, in this case, you are the one who makes the trap.

Train ■ Your future is going forward. Given that the train follows a fixed route, this dream suggests that you are receiving help and direction in your vital life. As a means of collective transportation, on the other hand, this image symbolizes the need to share projects, ideas, and thoughts. From it you can deduce the need to speak more often with your loved ones, fleeing from the isolation that threatens you. On the contrary, being the only occupant of the train is a sign of great timidness or ego. If you miss a train, it indicates the frustrated hope for change or the desire to leave a real situation, but without a clear sense of direction. For Jung, the figure of public vehicles expresses that the dreamer has not found her own way yet, and that her behavior is the same as everyone else's. According to Freud, dreams that imply movement represent sexual relations. In fact, Freud believed the train to be a phallic symbol.
❖ In antiquity, dreaming of voyages presaged a change in fortune. This would be better if the destination were at the top of a hill or of a mountain. And if the voyage continued at large in a straight line, the good luck would appear very soon in your life.

Trampoline ■ Trampolines represent a means to reach objectives that you have proposed. Jumping on a trampoline indicates favorable conditions for launching a new project. They are almost always positive dreams that reflect the trust that the dreamer has in him- or herself and that which surrounds him or her.

Trapeze ■ A symbol of coming and going fortune, dreaming of a trapeze foretells the arrival of a happy and calm period after going through many setbacks. Finally, you will obtain the fruits of your strength and hard work.

Trapped ▪ This dream is probably expressing how you feel in real life. Perhaps, you are trapped by marriage, dependance on your parents, or in a job without future. In this case you need to reformulate some aspects of your own situation. On the other hand, you might be trapped on your own conservatism or obstinacy. If you change the way you do things, you will surely experience a feeling of liberation.

❖ Gypsy tradition says that if you dream that an animal is caught in a net you must act with caution. Otherwise, your plans will fail.

Travel ▪ Sleep is already, of a fashion, a trip to the center of oneself. Consequently, there are many meanings associated with this dream. In general, it represents your vital travel. Finding yourself in the middle of a wide road suggests the well-being of your progress. If, in contrast, the road is full of rocks, it is trying to say that the path is arduous and difficult. A luxurious environment, on the other hand, indicates that you are pleased with your situation; but, if it is an arid desert, it expresses loneliness and lack of creativity. The hardness or smoothness of the path will manifest the tenseness or relaxedness that you are, respectively. The destination of the trip could be to find one's true self. If the lands that you encounter on you path are strange and unknown, everything could be an invitation of the subconscious to explore. In mythology, a trip to the west signifies a return to your ancestry, while a trip to the east denotes rejuvenation. The interpretation of the places, cities, or countries that you visit will add valuable information.

❖ The ancient interpretations of dreams coincide with the modern ones. For example, the ease with which you realize the trip will be the same that you will find, in some future, in real life. In addition, the medieval mystics said that dreaming of a happy group of friends taking a trip signifies that you will soon experience a happy existential period.

Treasure ▪ Discovering a treasure or finding money symbolizes a rediscovery of some part of yourself. It could be something that you have hidden or put away previously. This may be the appropriate opportunity to return to pursuing your aspirations. Treasures always symbolize something for which it is worth fighting, despite the difficulties that will arise along the way. With it, you should try to achieve you objectives, although the effort will cost an important sacrifice. At the end you will be compensated and will obtain great satisfaction. The patience and constancy should be your virtues. (See

MONEY, DIAMOND, FOUNTAIN, GARDEN, JEWELS, OASIS, GOLD, PARADISE, and PINK)

❖ Old superstitions, in this dream, do not coincide with the modern ones. If you uncover a treasure it indicates that someone that you love and in whom you confide does not totally deserve you. However, if you find gold in whatever form, then everything will go well.

Treasure chest (object) ▪ It is an intimate place where we keep the most precious treasures, either of material or spiritual nature. It is also related to the woman's uterus and therefore maternity, dependence, and overprotection. To open a chest indicates discovery of important secrets. If someone else opens it you fear the disclosing of your secrets. If you find it empty it indicates disappointment.

Tree ▪ The tree represents, in the broadest sense, the life of the cosmos: its density, growth, proliferation, etc. In oneiric terms, it is the embodiment of the subject's personality. Thus, the type of tree and its condition will indicate the state of mind and spirituality. If any of its parts have been damaged, some dimensions of the subject will have suffered as well. In this sense, the branches represent your superior functions; the trunk, your social role; and the roots, the foundations of your personality and your unconscious. A leafy and strong tree therefore symbolizes self confidence and creativity, as well as material and spiritual protection. But if the tree is weak and without leaves, you are not on track and you lack sufficient experience to undertake your life's purpose. On the other hand, if you dream of planting a tree or if it is in bloom means a sign of fertility or inner maturity.

❖ According to tradition, the tree symbolizes time: roots represent the past while branches the future. Perhaps the dream portends a premonition or your future hopes and fears. In the event you dream that you climb a tree, you will be lucky.

Trench ▪ A trench symbolizes the need for protection. The dreamer feels set upon by people or events that they cannot control and is looking to defend their self. In any case, it is not a negative dream because it indicates that you have not tired in the face of the danger, and there is the intention to act against it. The dreamer could come out well from a turbulent situation.

❖ Walking along the edge of a trench indicates the fear of being in a dangerous situation that is out of control. It can be interpreted as a warning of caution to the dreamer against her current difficulties. Falling into it indicates loss of control over your issues. Deliberately jumping into it is a sign of bravery and courage in the face of the unknown.

❖ Dreaming of a trench is generally a bad omen. It portends dangers, misery, and an unhappy marriage.

Trial ■ If you see yourself sentenced to a trial in your dreams, it symbolizes the need to review your behavior, your way of treating people, or the way you focus your life projects. The trial indicates that you are not satisfied with your own behavior. In and of itself, the trial is a symbol of the fight between good and evil. If you are in the role of judge rather than the accused, it means that soon you will take on a great responsibility.

❖ The majority of oneiric oracles agree that this dream foretells legal disputes.

Triangle ■ Triangles symbolize perfection, the total integration of the body, mind, and spirit. For this reason, dreams in which geometric figures appear should be interpreted as the antecedent to a period in which you could enjoy great abundance in every sense. Triangles also reveal to the dreamer that their objectives will be achieved due to how high they are.

Tribunal ■ If you see yourself in front of a judge, the presence of a tribunal indicates that you are rigorously analyzing your acts. You should try to be less hard on yourself.

Trophy ■ Seeing that you give a trophy to someone in a dream signifies that you know how to recognize other people's merits. It is a clear sign that your professional relationships are improving. In case you are receiving the trophy, it indicates that it is advisable to be more humble (despite that you deserve the recognition).

Trough ■ An animal quenching its thirst at a trough is a symbol of tranquility and the announcement of good news, especially financial. On the other hand, if the trough is dry it means you are about to experience a loss of capital. If you are the one drinking from it you should deduct that is not the best place to satisfy your thirst, and you will have to change the methods you employ to meet your needs in real life. That indicates, therefore, that you must seek other sources more appropriate for drinking.

❖ According to tradition, dreaming of a trough predicts an inheritance is coming soon. If it seems dirty it indicates a child will be born soon; if it is dry, it indicates

some mysteries will be unveiled; and if horses are drinking from it, future happiness.

Truck ■ A new and well maintained truck indicates the possibility of receiving an inheritance, although it will be small; but, on the contrary, an old and dirty one means economic losses.

Trumpet ■ The trumpet symbolizes the longing for fame and glory. It could announce any sort of event that will be of great importance. If the trumpets are sounding, you should interpret the dream as a coronation of your efforts. You will probably experience an important change in your life soon. If the sound is stronger than normal, it may be the subconscious trying to call your attention. In this sense, you should revise your ideas and behaviors or fix your sight on what you normally ignore.

❖ If you are playing or listening to the trumpet, oracles say that the dream foretells deception.

Trunk ■ See CLOSET

Tube ■ This is the conductor for where things flow. In this sense, it could symbolize a means of obtaining richness or intellectual growth. If you see yourself inside a tube, on the other hand, the meaning is very similar to that of a corridor: You are in a time of transition. The path could end well or poorly, depending on the feeling that you experience in the dream.

Tulip ■ The tulip indicates hope of a happy and lasting period. On the other hand, like almost every flower, tulips have a high sensual connotation. They could be the expression of a compensation mechanism of the subconscious due to dissatisfaction or lack of sexual relationships.

Tumor ■ Its interpretation is similar to that of ABSCESS. It indicates an interior or exterior burden that makes you heavy and resentful. It tends to be a distressing dream in that you see your body deformed or grossly exaggerated. It would benefit you to analyze your life to discover what is bothering you so much and to be able to solve it in the most appropriate manner.

Tunic ■ The tunic symbolizes the self and the soul, or the area most directly in contact with the spirit. Given that it represents personality, it is important to analyze the color of the tunic, as well as its texture. (See STAINS, CLOAK, and CLOTHING)

Tunnel ▪ A tunnel incarnates your interior world. For this reason, if you dream of a tunnel in which there is only darkness, it means that you should pay attention to your feelings to get out. Your existential distress is keeping you from seeing the light. If, in the end, you are able to glimpse a flash of clarity, it indicates that you will overcome the obstructions on the way through your strength of will. Your conscience is amplifying your range of action. (See LIGHT, BLACK, and BRIDGE)

Turnips ▪ Its symbolism has contradictory meanings. For some, it is a sign of mediocrity and laziness. For others, however, it represents immortality. The life circumstances of the dreamer and the analysis of other elements of the dream will be crucial for a proper interpretation.
❖ To dream of turnips augurs wealth, a good paying job, and emotional fortune. It announces healing for the sick.

Turning to someone ▪ The interpretation of this dream can lead the dreamer to realize that there are issues or persons demanding his attention. On the other hand, it also indicates his desire to be cared for and needed by others. Almost always, it is associated with a need for affection.

Turnips ▪ Its symbolism has contradictory meanings. For some, it is a sign of mediocrity and laziness. For others, however, it represents immortality. The life circumstances of the dreamer and the analysis of other elements of the dream will be crucial for a proper interpretation.
❖ To dream of turnips augurs wealth, a good paying job, and emotional fortune. It announces healing for the sick.

Turquoise ▪ Dreaming of this precious stone announces peace and harmony in the family scene, as well as prosperity in business. However, if the turquoise is stolen, there exist disagreements with friends that you will not be able to overcome. For a woman, dreaming that someone gifts you with turquoise could be a sign that your possessions will notably increase thanks to an advantageous marriage.

Turtle ▪ This is related with slowness, longevity, and protection. Due to its slow speed, the turtle could represent natural evolution, in contrast to spiritual evolution. In some ways, this animal is the opposite of another

symbol: wings. Wings represent flight as spiritual and elevating, while the turtle is associated with values such as heaviness, convolution, obscurity, and stagnation, etc.

Twin ▪ Twins represent your psyche's polarity, like extroversion or introversion, and your masculine and feminine sides. In oneiric terms, if you dream of a person who looks just like you—either a double or a twin brother—it means you need to return to your essence and to restore internal harmony. It can also reveal problems of identity or serious personality imbalances.
❖ Many ancient cultures believed that twins were divine characters. According to another superstition, they had different fathers; one of them was a god or a spirit. The dream may be showing you, in this sense, your spiritual side. If a woman dreams of delivering twins it is omen of cheating.

Tying ▪ When tying something, you are acting out the desire to hold something so it will not leave you. In general, the subject tries to tie people that they depend on. Sometimes, the subject also ties herself through repression of all kinds.

Tyrant ▪ This could be the negative archetype of the paternal figure. You may fear being like this. ‖ It could equally signify that you are obligated to do things against your will. The tyrant, in this case, is the person or situation that is restricting your liberty in real life.
❖ Oneiric oracles say that the meaning of this dream is the contrary to what it suggests. You will soon meet someone who is very kind and happy.

U

Udder ▪ Dreaming of a cow's udders expresses plentitude and lushness. In the case that in the dream you are drinking from the udders, the image indicates that you have a lot of energy to live life with intensity.

UFO ▪ Carl Jung believed that UFOs were figures with a similar meaning to the resurrection of Christ: they represented hope in the age of technology. According to him, the form of UFOs was circular because, like other symbols, they referred to the totality of the higher Self. So, considering that the unconscious possessed the ability to show up through many different images, UFOs could be one of them. In oneiric terms therefore, UFOs are perhaps expressing your desire to reach true spiritual purpose of life.

Ugliness ▪ This feature always denotes something negative: on one hand, if you look ugly in the dream it involves physical disgust with yourself or your intellectual abilities. It also highlights the impact bad experiences have made on you. On the other, If others look ugly in dreams it indicates that someone will want to betray you and that you must be very careful.

Ulcer ▪ You have difficulties managing certain experiences, which is what is deduced from a dream in which you have an ulcer. Furthermore, these difficulties increase through your inability to outwardly express your situation. You should fight against your inner

ghosts. The first step will be to express your feelings. Only this way will you be able to purify yourself.

Umbrella ▪ In general, this is a sign of immaturity. To dream that you take shelter under an umbrella indicates that you avoid the difficulties of life, that is, that you do not face them. In other words, the umbrella suggests that you are shirking responsibilities. In more specific interpretations, it is said that the umbrella symbolizes inner self-protection. Rain is the escape route through which your emotional stress is expressed and you are prepared to face it.
❖ If you dream that you lose the umbrella, the omens are good: it predicts a valuable gift from a relative. However, if you find it, you will experience a great loss in business.

Uncovering ▪ Throwing a blanket away or uncovering a pot can be interpreted as the need to clear out dark affairs, which will have a positive impact on your lives. It also indicates curiosity and desire to learn.
❖ The fairy tale *Beauty and the Beast* illustrates the theme of internal beauty. You should not judge based on appearance. Also, something that at first frightens you may be hiding your true and beautiful self.

Underbrush ▪ To pass with difficulty through the underbrush is a sign of a confusing and perilous situation, full of obstacles that must be overcome to successfully finish projects. To get lost in the underbrush can be interpreted as an unexpected situation in which the dreamer has lost control and needs outside help.

Underground ▪ The underground normally symbolizes the subconscious. Things that are covered, interred, or that emerge from the ground represent qualities that come from the deepest part of your personality. It could be a positive or negative dream. Digging in the ground could be frightening, but sometimes it is useful in order to know secrets and hidden truths that you would otherwise miss. Further, exiting an underground tunnel and reaching the light represents a triumph over adversity. To interpret this dream it is important to pay attention to the sensations that you feel, and to the events that occur therein.

Underpants ▪ It is closely linked to desires, fears, and sexual fantasies. If the dreamer is a man, the condition of his underwear indicates the relationship he has with his sexuality. Showing up in underwear at a wrong time or place is interpreted as fear of embarrassment or fear of not being prepared for the circumstances. ‖ In general, underwear represents your attitudes and hidden prejudices. Depending on its color, it has different meanings. Red, for example, denotes passion and yellow, a secret fear. Clean underwear indicates good behavior; Instead, dirty or torn may suggest that you are not comfortable with yourself or your sexuality.
❖ The oracles say that dreaming of wearing underwear portends stolen pleasures that will turn against you.

Underwear ▪ In olden days, underwear was related to wealth but today it is interpreted according to how it appears in the dream. If it is clean, you will receive an unexpected sum of money; if it is dirty, there is danger of public humiliation; and if it is black, it is a sign of deprivation and unsatisfied desires. To wash it shows insecurity and excess attention paid to the opinions of others; to dry it manifests a desire for novelty; and to put it away, the arrival of economic gains in the long term.

Unearthing ▪ This dream states, in general, the advent of a bad time that will test you. However, if you find the extracted object is pleasant, what lies ahead are positive surprises. To exhume a person who is alive, in real life, marks the departure of a loved one. Probably because of a breakup; but if the person is dead in real life it is evidence of nostalgia for that person.

Unemployment ▪ This dream does not necessarily have to do with the dreamer's work situation. It indicates a period of stagnation, voluntary or otherwise, that you experience with impatience and anxiety. It would be beneficial to study the circumstances that generate this type of distress in order to get out of this limbo that the unconscious shows in dreams.

Unfasten ▪ It can be interpreted as a sign of eroticism or extreme shyness. It also indicates a pleasant relaxation of tensions, recovery of self-confidence, and trust in the people around you.

Unicorn ▪ Tradition represents this symbolic animal as a white horse, or multicolored, with one horn that comes from the forehead. Unicorns harbor the combination of variety and demonstrate that the essence of everything is in unity. They are the mythical incarnation of your inner imagination. They equally represent power, gentleness, and purity. This dream may announce inspiration wonders that you keep inside. It could also be a sign of an interesting offer, because they are sometimes related to abundance.
❖ The oneiric oracles claim that unicorns predict interaction with official affairs.

Uniform ▪ The dream could be manifesting your conformist feelings. Or, contrarily, it may alert you that you should be less individualistic and consider the needs of the group that surrounds you. If you dream that you are wearing a military uniform, it indicates that you are trying to reduce your responsibilities in your community. In the case that the uniform is full of medals, it denotes that you are authoritarian: you impose your standards by force without allowing others to express their opinions.
❖ According to popular superstition, this dream foretells a trip full of adventure and of special interest for your marriage problems.

University ▪ Dreaming that you are going to the university signifies that you want to increase your knowledge by developing your capacity. The dream indicates that you may be wasting time in little things, when in reality you have a scope of experience that could enrich you.

U N I F O R M

Ricardo dreamed: "I was wearing a military uniform and my family marched according to my orders: 'One, Two, Three, and! Turn, and!' They were all very firm, rigid and obedient, and I felt proud of my control. We marched through the street and the neighbors watched us from the windows with expressions of admiration."

Ricardo had this dream in a time in which his family disintegrated. His wife was being difficult in the divorce negotiations, and his adolescent daughter threatened to go live with her boyfriend and leave her studies. The dream reveals his **desire to put his family life back in order** and avoid the circumstances that had escaped his control. His subconscious was recommending that he be more strict and energetic in enforcing his opinions. Up until then Ricardo had always given in to his wife's and daughter's desires, and his life was uncontrolled. The fact that the neighbors approved of his conduct from the windows reflects **his need for recognition**, which he only felt in this important moment of his life.

Unstitching ▪ If you are unstitching something it can be a disappointment or letdown. It is also interpreted as a need for amendment. You have taken a wrong road and would like to go back and start again in the right direction.

Urine ▪ In many cases, to dream you have the urge to urinate stems simply from the physiological needs you experience while you sleep. Sometimes this dream also refers to sexual desires. The urine, however, can represent all the things we get rid of or reject. You are trying to clean up your Interior, so you leave behind all you think is not worth it. (See DEFECATION)

❖ For many centuries, urine has been considered the ultimate protection against ghosts and evil spirits. It was also believed that if a girl urinated in the shoes of a man, he would fall head over heels in love with her.

Urn ▪ An empty urn suggests a certain egocentrism with respect to the relations between a couple. You are enclosed in yourself with allowing anyone—not even that person with whom you share your existence—to see what you have hidden inside. In contrast, an urn full of papers indicates the tendency to leave your projects unfinished.

Usurer ▪ Seeing a usurer in dreams warns of the possibility of earning a lof of money, although in a dishonest manner. In contrast, if you are the usurer, it foretells bad relations with your relatives and the possibility of enduring great humiliation.

Utensil ▪ Utensils usually predict the failure of project due to inappropriate usage of the available materials. When they are broken it announces the illness of loved ones. In contrast, if they are made of wood or metal, they foretell prosperity and happiness in some scope.

Uterus ▪ According to some psychiatrists, dreaming that you are back in a mother's womb signifies that you have a great need for protection. Uteruses are also symbolized by caves, rooms, or safe places. They provide a retreat and adequate isolation from daily problems.

❖ This dream could be very spiritual and could express the awakening of the conscience.

V

Vacations ■ Dreaming that you are enjoying a vacation shows the need for relaxation. The subconscious is advising you that, if you do not take a break, you will end up exhausted or ill. This type of dream often also shows itself through images of anxiety, like missing a flight, excess baggage, or a disaster during a vacation. Without a doubt, you need to learn to take things with more calmness.

❖ If a young woman who has been rejected by her significant other in real life dreams of vacations, she will soon get over that person.

Vaccinate ■ In dreams, vaccinations alert of problems that will arrive in the life of the dreamer. It is necessary, therefore, to pay attention to this type of dreams to avoid some type of disgrace. However, the dream references a problem with a solution, that you can prevent with some caution.

Vagabond ■ Although it might suggest the opposite, dreaming that you have become a vagabond does not necessarily have to relate to failure. This image could also indicate a profound desire to leave everything and avoid one's responsibilities. You want to feel free, and a vagabond illustrates this yearning perfectly.

Valley ■ Due to its fertile character, opposite to the desert and to the tall mountain, the valley is the symbol of life, the mystical place of shepherds and monks. It represents the homey character of Mother Earth. As it is situated between mountains, it defines your direction and limitations. Traveling to a valley usually symbolizes the step from one circumstance to another. It is possible that you will encounter difficulties during this transition, but in the end you will find beneficial spiritual changes. In terms of dreams, the valley also represents the place where our soul recovers its energy. Therefore, it announces a period of tranquility and happiness.

❖ As a spiritual-dream symbol, the valley represents the wisdom and importance of modesty.

Vampire ■ Dreaming that you are attacked by a vampire signifies that someone close is trying to profit off of you. However, if it is you yourself who plays the role of the vampire, this is a sign that you get carried away by passions and instincts that are each time more voracious. You will have to try to conquer them, as your internal equilibrium could resent it. (See MIDNIGHT, FEAR, and BAT)

Vapor ■ If vapor appears in your dreams, it is probable that you have to take an impromptu trip to solve a professional problem. If you see yourself engulfed in vapor, it alerts of a close friend's plotting for your ruin.

Varnishing ■ Dreaming of varnishing furniture, a door, or any object is a sign that there is something you want to keep secret. Frequently, it refers to defects, shortcomings, or attitudes that do not make you proud. There is something in the self that you do not fully accept and, therefore, you cover it with layers of varnish.

Vase ■ A vase full of water indicates the start of feelings. Offering a vase indicates your desire to share love and happiness.

Vault ■ It represents the unconscious, so what you find inside can be of utmost importance for you. If it is a crypt, the bodies represent parts of your personality that are no longer active or matters that have been relegated to rest. If the vault is a safe, it symbolizes happiness and opportunities for spiritual unfolding. Treasures contained are your spiritual potential: the reward for having explored the unconscious. Depending on its shape, the vault is also associated with the womb. Its appearance in dreams, in this case, points to the need for feeling protected. You must pay attention to the condition of the vault in the oneiric image because it represents the environment around the dreamer in real life. If it is high and illuminated it indicates well-being; if it is dark and low, confinement; if it is in ruins, material or spiritual poverty.
❖ An old book on dreams says that if a man dreams of walking under a vault of black color, he will marry a widow, and will become the slave of her cruelty.

Vegetable garden ■ The garden where crops are grown symbolizes everything related to your small, often inconfessable, desires. To dream that you plant a garden indicates that you are achieving, little by little, the small goals that give life meaning. Additionally, if you pick fruit from the orchard, there is a possibility of receiving an unexpected prize. (See AGRICULTURE)

Veil ■ This is an invitation to knowledge, but serves to hide the face and suggests, at the same time, that which it hides. In parallel, to dream of a veil should also encourage you to fight against that which shames you. For a woman, it denotes an erotic game and seduction. Additionally, according to Freud, it symbolizes the female hymen and the fear of sexual relations.
❖ The monks occasionally wear veils. In spiritual terms, this dream could represent a rejection of mundane things. On the other hand, oneiric superstition says that dreaming of a black veil predicts a break in love. A white one, in contrast, foreshadows marriage.

Velvet ■ Velvet is a symbol of richness and sensuality. Many people link it with eroticism. This dream reveals an evident emotional need.

Vengeance ■ Harboring dreams of vengeance does not speak well in favor of the dreamer. However, it is not necessary to exaggerate; this type of image only indicates the disability that the individual feels due to his own limitations.

Venting ■ Sometimes you dream that you weep, argue, or reveal a secret truth. These dreams indicate that the mind can no longer resist this pressure and needs to be relieved consciously. It is important to be alert to such dreams because they show an extreme situation that must be resolved in a peaceful manner. They can also be signs of a physical or emotional loss that the dreamer has not completely assimilated.

Ventriloquist ■ It is possible that, in real life, you are putting your own words into others' mouths. Or, perhaps you only hear that which you would like. The act of projecting one's own voice symbolizes one's desire to influence the opinions of everyone else. On the other hand, the image of the ventriloquist would suppose a lack of communication between one's true self and that which one presents to the world.
❖ You will soon suffer a betrayal. According to oracles, you should be cautious in the deals that you make.

Vertigo ■ Vertigo symbolizes, clearly, the fear to know one's true self. If the lands that you find on your way seem strange and unknown, everything could be an invitation of the subconscious to explore. ‖ In mythology, a protagonist encounters a situation that is unknown or that is out of his control. You should take certain risks, since insecurity is paralyzing you.

Vest ■ Wearing a vest portends a good social position after hard work. But if it is dirty or torn it means you want to achieve a level for which you are not ready yet.

Victim ■ The dream develops the feelings that already exist in real life. It is possible that there are people who damage you. Or, on the contrary, maybe you are the one who has damaged others, and now the dream is turning the tables on you. In this case, it is about the expression of your guilt.
❖ According to the majority of dream oracles, the significance of this dream is the reverse. You will be the

victim if you dream that you victimize others, and vice versa.

Village ▪ A village denotes, in general, a desire for peace and tranquility; you may be looking for closer ties with the people around and to enjoy a more relaxed family life. However, if the village is abandoned it signals that the subject cannot solve their problems and must find new ways to reach fruition. If quaint and sunny, then an honest and straightforward personality of the dreamer transpires. If it is abandoned in favor of the city there is the possibility of professional improvement (although, at present, job matters are not the first concern in the protagonist's life).

Villain ▪ This figure could represent a part of your personality that you need to reform. The villain symbolizes your rebellious side and your hidden desire to abandon societal norms. On the other hand, it could show feelings of vengeance that you harbor, or your craving to interfere with someone's plans. Equally, the dream could be caused by the desire to overcome a vice, like smoking or drinking.
❖ Dreaming of a victim predicts that you will receive a gift or card from the person that you love.

Vine ▪ A symbol of plenty, it represents the sensuality and indulgence of the dreamer. In a similar fashion, it can represent the harvest, and with it, a period of prosperity. If the dream is related with health items, then the vine may represent the nervous system.
❖ Each dream related to a vine or with the grape is considered advantageous while they bloom. A vine that is still green, but not full of bunches signifies that your biggest dream will become reality.

Vinegar ▪ Vinegar in dreams always has a negative connotation, as it predicts disputes and any sort of unpleasant situation. Drinking vinegar expresses familial disagreements over material things; emptying vinegar shows the insignificance of your personal opinions in the situation. Flavoring food with vinegar is a sign of bad luck: if you do it with red vinegar, the problem will arise in the love life; meanwhile, if it is white, the problems will be related to the economic sphere.

Violence ▪ If you dream that you have violent behavior, it could be that you are harboring hidden feelings of resentment towards someone who is impeding your progress. On the other hand, you could be denying something inside you. This dream shows you that you should be more tolerant of your feelings and accept the failures that occur to you. Contrarily, you will repress too many emotions. If you are the victim of violence in the dream, it is trying to say that you are punishing yourself and you consider yourself guilty of something in real life. In the case that it gives you the sensation that everything is going against you, you should not lose hope, because your luck will change soon.
❖ The significance of this dream is the opposite as it suggests. If you are violently attacked, superstition foretells better times.

Violet ▪ This flower symbolizes modesty. The color violet is related to autumn, and is related to the transition of life to death.

Virgin ▪ This dream could the effect of nostalgia. Maybe you are observing the past, when you experiment for the first time the pain and complexity of human relationships. In the same manner, a virgin could represent something pure and innocent in real life.
❖ In dreams, the Virgin Mary represents the soul. It is the spiritual guide that brings personal plentitude to man.

Visit ▪ To dream that you are going to visit someone's house expresses your need to communicate yourself to others. You are interested in community activities and want to share things with those surrounding you. However, a visit could be as much as pleasure as a bore, and our dream could show you either position. The dream could also draw your attention so that you worry more about someone that you disregarded.

Voice ▪ This dream could have different connotations. So, if you hear a voice that you do not recognize, it could mean that your subconscious is trying to tell you something of vital importance. All that you can be found inside you: you should simply learn to listen at the appropriate moments. On the other hand, dreaming that you are losing your voice reflects a notable lack in determination and security in yourself. (See SCREAMING, SOUNDS, and CALLS)

Void ▪ Dreaming of the void (an abstract idea) indicates the state that you are in mentally. It expresses the lack of motivation at the time to do things. You should try to fill this void with new projects, objectives, and hopes. If you dream of a room, a box, a house, or empty spaces, it expresses an emotional deficiency. According to Freud, the origin of these feelings is in one's own repression.

❖ The things you propose to do in moments like this will be futile.

Volcano ■ Represents the explosion of hidden and repressed passions. Depending on the context in the dream, you could determining if this eruption will be positive or negative. In either case, you should take caution that your aggressiveness and the depart of your destructive feelings could play tricks. In this sense, it is important not to inhibit your own emotions for too long. Contrarily, before or after, the will explode. If the volcano is extinct, it means that you are regressing. (See CATASTROPHES and EARTHQUAKE)

❖ Dreaming of a volcano preludes a period of peace and happiness. Superstition also says that if you are nearly engulfed in flames, this happiness will increase.

Vomiting ■ Seeing yourself vomit in a dream is a sign that you want to eliminate some aspect of your life that you cannot bear. It definitely deals with the feelings that upset you: a situation or alien behavior. In some cases, vomiting expresses that you are not pleased with yourself. Something from your life or from your attitudes

repulse you such that you are unable to continue forward. You should do an internal cleaning.

❖ According to ancient texts, this dream announces that the poor will gain benefits from the losses of the rich.

Vulture ■ Although it may seem surprising, the vulture is a symbol that, throughout history, has always had positive connotations. Not surprisingly, many people believed that because its diet is carrion, the vulture had a special relationship with Mother Nature. Thus, the Parses—followers of Zoroaster—expose their dead on the top of tall towers so the vultures devour them in order to facilitate their rebirth. Likewise, in India the vulture appears as a symbol of protective spiritual forces that substitute parents: an emblem of devotion and spiritual advice. In Western culture, this bird has, however, negative connotations. The presence of vultures in dreams indicates the possibility that some people are waiting for a mistake to take advantage of the situation.

❖ For the gypsies, oneiric vultures warn you against corrupt people around you.

W

Waiter ▪ Dreaming of a helpful waiter is a sign that you can count on the help of friends or someone unexpected; but if the waiter is rude or careless, then, you could suffer abuse and slander from people close that you used to trust.

❖ If you dream that a waiter serves you in a hotel or a restaurant, you will have good luck. Conversely, if you are served in your own home the omen is exactly the opposite.

Walking ▪ If you are walking in dreams it means that you are ready to face present and future experiences. This type of dream reminds you are a person of action and, therefore, when something concerns you, it is better to make a decision instead of beating around the bush.

Wall ▪ The general meaning of this symbol is that of protection and transcendence. The status of the wall as solid strength allows introspection, creativity, and spiritual contemplation. In general, dreaming of walls is evidence of a need for isolation.

Wall ▪ A wall is an obstacle that prevents you from achieving what you want. This blockage can be found in real life or within yourself. You may be behaving like a real brick wall, rejecting any display of affection. On the other hand, it may symbolize a problem you cannot solve yet. In these cases, it is best not to obsess and just wait patiently. In the event that you see yourself building a wall, the dream trying to warn you that you need additional protection to defend against the setbacks of daily life. If, on the contrary, you are knocking it down, perhaps you crave more freedom or need to escape a claustrophobic atmosphere.

❖ The wall foreshadows difficulties and obstacles related to money. However, all will be well if you find a door or a hole to pass through.

Wallet ▪ (See BAG)

Walnut (nut) ▪ The shape of this nut suggests a human skull and brain. It also symbolizes the effort needed to achieve what you desire. The walnut shell, on the other hand, represents the ego that must be destroyed for the emergence of the spiritual self (the fruit). If the nut is green, it is impossible to open. But if it is ripe, a small tap can open it. Similarly, spirituality emerges when the person is truly ready.

❖ According to popular superstition, this dream portends that you will receive money.

Walnut (tree) ▪ Its symbolism is related to premonitions and the ability of divination. The fruit that guards a secret treasure can be interpreted as the reward of risk and hard work.

War ▪ Every war concerns the struggle of light against darkness, of good against evil. At the psychic level, it symbolizes the struggle between the subject's actions and thoughts, because we always have the tendency toward inner unity. According to Jung, this dream reflects an inner conflict; war is being waged between your conscious and unconscious part, between the instinctual impulses and social norms. In oneiric terms, this dream reflects insecurity and fear of the events of life, but it also shows your desire for rebellion against inner oppression. When you see no end of the fight, it indicates that the conflict is not exactly about to be resolved. (See ARMY and ENEMIES)

❖ A time of difficulties and dangers is announced. The dream also predicts family discussions.

Washing ▪ If you wash yourself in dreams it means you need to "cleanse" certain aspects of your personality, since you harbor feelings of guilt. On the contrary, these images could also mean that matters that are worrying you are beginning to clear up. An important detail: if you are washing clothes or a personal item, it is your emotional and intimate relationships that require cleaning. If you wash dishes, it indicates spiritual purity that nourishes you. If you was someone else, it shows your desire for that person to heal. (See WATER)

❖ To wash clothes or rags of white linen is a very promising dram. To wash yourself is also a good omen, as long as it is with clear, clean water. Stained clothing, however, predicts bad luck. If you take a bath while clothed, it signifies coming deceptions.

Wasps ▪ Dreaming that wasps sting or chase you suggests the presence of discomfort, obstacle, or sorrows in real life. These are not too major, but very painful. If you kill them, the dream reveals you are overcoming these problems.

Water ▪ Psychology attributes water to the unconscious desire to return to our mother's lap.

Water symbolizes life, feelings, fertility, and abundance. Thus, this type of dream plays an important role, though the meanings attributed to it vary. Water quality, therefore, reveals your emotional state. If water is clear, your feelings are pure and you enjoy a blissfully peaceful period. But if it is muddy, you will suffer personal or health complications. If there is water in the form of large ground-breaking waves, you might feel out control. If it is a river, the flowing pace will express the calm or anguish of your emotions. Likewise, to see dirty and stagnant water reveals insincerity in your feelings. If the water comes from a lake or a stream, it is indicative of

WATER

Lucia dreamed: "I was sunbathing on a paradisiacal island of fine sand and crystalline waters. The sun was warming my body up while I was listening to the waves gently lapping. I felt really good, confident, and happy. Suddenly, I saw a huge wave coming, and before I could react, it invaded the whole beach. The sky turned black and a strong storm completely changed the landscape. At that point, there was no island, no sand, no firm land, and I was floating in the water frightened. I suddenly remembered that I did not know how to swim."

When Lucia had this dream she had just begun an **affair** with a man; she had long been in love with him. The calm sea and the idyllic landscape reflected her confidence and initial joy. However, the water fiercely flooding the beach was warning her against the risk of drowning due to **excessive enthusiasm**. Any dream in which the water is stagnant is a warning sign indicating that we should give more freedom to our emotions. In Lucia's case, the sea flowing freely—first in gentle waves and then stormy—is an indication that she was letting her feelings blossom.

By analogy of uterus and birth, dreams in which water appears may relate to feeling like getting ready for a new life or the desire to change old habits. The island represents Lucia's **individualism**, her independent and safe live that was threatened by the arrival of romance and the overflowing torrent of emotions that it implied. The effect of drowning announced a condition of **emotional tension** due to a new situation.

emotional passivity. Similarly, fine rain is usually a symbol of fertility, which predicts success in your projects. Heavy rains, however, announce unattended desires and disputes. (See BOAT, SHIPWRECK, and SHIP)

❖ Water, depending on its condition, may portend very different situations. When fresh, it denotes fortune and health. Boiling: anger or illness. Mild: temporary discomfort. Muddy water indicates obstacles in business. Stagnant and putrid water: illness or death. Flowing water: good luck and good health. Saltwater portends tears. Looking at water ensures safety from a danger. Bathing is a sign of innocence. To pour it: litigation. Walking on water represents triumph. To see a spring:

improvement of a distressing situation. The water of a bathtub means happy old age.

Water Lily ▪ A pond full of water lilies can predict a very pleasant romantic experience. It means that your relationship with a partner will go through a time of great comfort, tranquility, and harmony, but also that you may fall in love suddenly. Considered by some civilizations as a sign of good fortune, the water lily represents the force of passion.

Watercolor ▪ Related to murky colored water, watercolor shows that we have a very distorted perception of ourselves, possibly caused by emotional confusion. In order to overcome the impasse, you must not complicate your life, and act more spontaneously and simply.

Waterfall ▪ It is a sign of abundance and vitality. A continuous flow of elements that are renewed. It indicates events that develop in healthy and enjoyable manner. Everyday life is cheerful and without monotony. However, the context of the dream and the conditions of the waterfall are crucial for interpretation. In this sense, if in the dream they push you into a waterfall while on a boat, it means you do not control your excitement and emotions. Perhaps you have gone beyond your limit.
❖ This dream refers to two traditional interpretations: you will be invited to a fun place or rumors about you will be spread.

Watermelon ▪ A sign of fertility. It is an affirmative signal when you are involved in a negotiation.

Waves ▪ Waves represents the threatening and sometimes stormy activity of the conscious, but also symbolizes a transcendent, open, and expressive emotion. To notice that you are being carried away by the waves indicates a passive attitude toward the circumstances, as minutiae easily distract you from your goals. By contrast, choppy waves announce a possible emotional conflict. Everything indicates that will jealousy and envy arise, and that aggressive outburst could occur at any time. However, this situation will be temporary. On the other hand, to dream that you walk over the waves predicts you will overcome the obstacles that separate you from your goal. (See WATER, LAKE, and SEA)
❖ Dreams of waves denote, according to some superstitions, a need for inner cleansing.

Wax ▪ It is an element full of magical connotations. Its malleable character and the form it reacts to heat symbolize transformation processes. The interpretation depends largely on what happens to the wax. It may mean union, passion, curing diseases, willingness to creative activities, or feelings of loss and grief.
❖ The interpretation is significantly influenced by the color. White wax promises marriage and good health; yellow, deception and the possibility of having to attend a funeral; red, the sale of a current asset. To see melted wax is a sign of financial loss and mourning.

Weapon ▪ Possessing a weapon denotes personal insecurity. You are not trusting yourself or your own strength to cope. If the oneiric weapon is fired, it shows a marked tendency to solve problems aggressively. Although you have a lot of energy, you are using it for negative purposes. The dream is an invitation to stop considering life as a constant struggle. Arms also express anger, resentment, and conflict. When used against someone you know it means that you hold emotions such as anger or rancor. Perhaps you do not dare to speak frankly with that person. In case you do not know such individual, it may represent undesirable aspects of yourself: you are having internal problems that need to be resolved. Furthermore, swords, arrows, knives, pistols, and daggers are phallic symbols denoting male sexual aggression.
❖ Dreaming of weapons is an indication of ferocity and honor. Holding them with your hand is an omen of glory and success. Making them represent convalescence and recovery of energy. To see someone armed fleeing portrays a probable victory. Watching the latter person getting away means safety; the dreamer has nothing to fear. A fired shot predicts unexpected profit.

Wedding ▪ Dreaming of your own wedding signifies the desire to unify criteria, obtain concessions or professional alliances, and find allies to support projects. It also indicates the search for inner harmony, communication with the inner self, and the union of two formerly conflicting aspects of your personality. Wedding dreams are recurring for couples who are about to get married. In fact, some studies indicate that forty percent of all oneiric activity during the prenuptial period contains references—either direct or indirect—to the marriage ceremony, to the future spouse, and to marriage in general. It is often common to dream of disasters occurring in the ceremonies, scenes of sexual rejection, images of infidelity, etc. But these prenuptial dreams should not be cause of alarm because, for example, dreaming of a sexual adventure can reveal fear of abandonment; and being naked at the wedding, fear of performing badly.

❖ Not all old dream books agree on the interpretation of this symbol. Usually, it is seen as a good omen and as a premonition of a future marriage. However, to attend someone else's wedding is a prediction of damage, loss, and infidelity.

Wedges ■ Tearing wedges of orange, garlic, or other food indicates an unstable economic situation. It may be a warning that you should be cautious about spending money.

Weeping ■ Tears are associated with rain and therefore also with vitality and fertility. But to cry in dreams can have a less favorable interpretation. Almost always, it is a compensatory mechanism of the unconscious, which releases repressed emotions. In this case, the meaning alludes to that of RELIEF. The origin of this dream, therefore, may be an overly tense situation has stretched you to your limits; or the grief over a spiritual or material loss that the dreamer has not assimilated entirely.

Well ■ The well symbolizes communication established with the subconscious; therefore, its condition will denote how your interior is doing. If it is properly maintained and filled with water you will feel self-confident; but, if it is poorly constructed or spent, you will feel undervalued and depressed. Emblem of the uterus, the well indicates your desire for regression, for returning to the origin in search of a complete emotional satisfaction. To collect water from it announces the encounter with a person who will help you fulfill your desires; and to fall in the well means the arrival of a of great tension that could frustrate your projects.

❖ The images of the I Ching believe that dreaming of a well brings good luck. Jung was inspired by this Chinese oracle for one of his psychological theories.

West ■ This represents rest and the fall of twilight, which announces peace and tranquility. This dream urges you to relax and get over the problems you are going throught. (See CROSS)

Whale ■ Whales are a symbol of gigantic but selfless strength whose protective power is beneficial. In this way, dreaming that a whale is approaching you portends a great event that will change any aspect of your life, either at personal or professional level. If you fall into the sea and a whale gobbles you up, it means that you are going through a difficult situation, though it will end shortly. It indicates a positive rebirth in some aspect of your life.

❖ Related to birth, this whale seen in dreams announces a joyful event.

Wheat ■ Dreaming of a field of wheat foretells richness, as well as the culmination of your projects. The well-being will be proportional to the amount of wheat that appears in the dream. This type of image shows you that your efforts always pay off.

Wheel ■ This is a symbol that is linked with perpetual movement, which once initiated proceeds on its course inexorably. Due to its circular form, it symbolizes something finished that offers security and protection. Further, its rotating movement is linked to your psychic evolution and the arrival at a new stage. Generally, if the wheel rotates without problems, it is a sign of success and of favorable personal evolution. If it is punctured or encounters obstacles while moving, it evidences that things are not going as you would like.

❖ This dream could be an invitation to enter the true nature of reality.

Whip ■ The symbolism of the whip is directly linked to that of the CLUB and the LASSO, linked to the concepts of domination and superiority. It expresses the idea of punishment, like the club and the mace, as well the power to dominate. Logically, whips are also related to the rituals of flagellation. In general, using a whip means that you should review your attitude toward others, because all signs point to you being somewhat tyrannical. So, if your romantic relationships are not in going well, you should reconsider your position. On the contrary, if you are the one who receives the punishment, it means that you feel humiliated.

❖ Dream oracles say that he who dreams of using a whip on someone will soon have problems. However, if the dreamer is the recipient of the lashes, he will lend his services to someone.

Whirlwind ■ Depending on the meaning, the movement in a spiral that characterizes the whirlwind represents the creation or destruction of the world. When its speed overtakes you, it means that the circumstances are dominating you, and there is nothing you can do. Certain circumstances could be familial, social, or professional. The dream tasks you with reversing this force, such that it is you who has control in your life.

White ■ In dreams, the color white can be a symbol of life or death. In the first case, the white represents purity, virginity, and hope. On the other hand, painting the house white symbolizes the need to purify and recover something you have lost. Dreaming in black and white indicates shortsightedness and low enthusiasm. You should try to live more intensely.

Wicker ■ Wicker objects in dreams are a symptom of poor progress in business and the likelihood of failure. Thus, it is advisable to all the means possible to prevent this from happening.
❖ To weave it predicts indigestion.

Widower ■ This does not have to be a prophetic dream. It may be warning of a situation of neglect or abandonment on the part of your partner. Although it sometimes signifies that you should learn to develop yourself alone and be more independent.
❖ Seeing yourself as a widow or a widower announces moments of suffering by gossip that originates in the environment and could create enemies with third parties. You should try to discover who is trying to cause you harm so that your relationships with others are not harmed.

Wife ■ This dream could refer to the real dreamer's wife or certain feminine traits. Freud's studies suggest that your behavior toward her can be reminiscent of the relation you maintained with your mother during childhood.
❖ Dreaming of a single man walking next to a woman claiming to be his wife predicts unexpected news.

Wig ■ Unless you tend to wear a wig in real life, to see yourself wear one in dreams indicates an alteration of your self image. Some of what you project to the exterior does not reflect your true desires, feelings, or emotions. It points to the intention to conceal, disguise, or distortion. To see someone else wearing a wig expresses a feeling of distrust toward them, or the fear that their attitude or feelings will change. For men, baldness is often the companion of a fear of impotence. A wig can be, in this case, a sign of the desire to hide a feeling of insecurity or disguise some other facet of his personality that he may be ashamed of.

❖ There are many interpretations of this figure. A blonde wig, for example, predicts that you will have many admirers; a dark one brings loyalty; a white one, wealth; and a brunette one predicts that the person you marry will be poor.

Will ■ Dreaming that you are writing a will announces a period of familial disputes due to economic interests. The rifts could be so big that emotional relationships will break.
❖ Losing a will is a sign of misery and setbacks of any kind; destroying one is a sign of suffering by a possible betrayal.

Willow ■ This tree symbolizes sadness and immortality; by analogy, it foretells pain and tears.

Wilting ■ To see flowers wilting indicates a state of sorrow in which the dreamer feels nostalgia or frustration at the end of a time of well-being.

Wind ■ A violent wind could be synonymous with a threat to your plans. Your projects are not stable and are fighting a war that was lost from the start. If, in contrast, you dream of a light breeze, it is a sign that your conscious is changing in an appropriate manner. The wind blows in your favor, which signifies that your objectives are being accomplished and that you have gained recognition with others. On the other hand, the wind can also be a manifestation of imbalance and the inconsistency of your emotions. It is possible that you need a change.
❖ Dreaming of wind foretells problems. However, as a result, you will bring happiness to someone.

Windmill ■ The windmill is one of the classic symbols of constant, disciplined work. If it is still, the dream is warning you that you are being dragged down by laziness.
❖ To see many women in a dream will bring fame and wealth. More specifically, an ugly woman predicts worries; a pretty one, however, happiness. If a woman dreams that she is pregnant, she will soon receive good news; If she dreams she is a man, she will give birth to a son.

Window ■ The window is an opening to the outside world and, as much as the view that it shows, like the light that shines through it, symbolizes the future that we hope for. So, a pleasant and bright view reveals that you will need the energy and motivation necessary to complete your projects. However, if it is dark, it shows us a more uncertain future. On the other hand, being afraid to look out the window indicate insecurity and fear of the consequences of something that you have done. Dreaming that you are spying through the slits of the blinds is a sign of repression and curiosity. Finally, if you enter or leave through a window, instead of doing so through a door, it shows that you have made a wrong decision. For Freud, windows were feminine sexual symbols.

❖ If you observe a happy scene from a window, the dream foretells happiness. But, if you witness a horrible event, you will have problems. A broken window predicts deceptions.

Windshield wipers ■ This is a dream that manifests your need to see things clearly. It may be that you are going through a confusing situation in real life that is uncomfortable and stressful. It is best to analyze what aspects of your life are unclear and difficult to understand.

Wine ■ Represents the liberation of the subconscious, and in addition, of repressions. So, dreaming of drinking wine in moderation reflects the yearning to reach a higher spiritual level. However, if you see yourself drinking too much, or intoxicated, it signifies that you want to realize your ambitions for power and richness at any price. On the other hand, red wine represents blood, and consequently, vital strength. Drinking it foretells health and the start of a more satisfactory phase. Equally, the red color is associated with passionate feelings. An old bottle of wine symbolizes maturity. (See GRAPES)

❖ In France and California, it is believed that passing wine around the table in the same direction as the points of the clock gives bad luck. In dream terms, drinking wine is a sign of a comfortable home. If you pour it, someone will get wounded. If you get drunk, you will soon achieve a great success.

Wings ■ Wings symbolize, since immemorial times, spirituality, imagination, and freedom. Therefore, already in ancient Greece, they appeared in some fabulous animals such as Pegasus or the snakes of Ceres. On the contrary, according to Christian symbolism, wings are the sun that always illuminates the intelligence of the just. In oneiric terms, wings predict success, achieving goals, and overcoming difficulties. Therefore, such images should encourage the person to jump into action (it is time to

take flight). Finally, wings are also a symbol that appears before great travels. Since they also represent the imagination and knowledge, dreaming of wings predicts positive results on upcoming tests or examinations you face.

Winning ■ Dreams that reflect the need to win symbolize anxiety, and sometimes fear, because you assume that you do not have what it takes. If, in the dream, you get hurt for wanting to win, it means that the ambition is harming your health. You must limit your activity and stay away from any competition.

❖ The oneiric oracles claim that the meaning of this dream is the opposite of the literal reading.

Winter ■ The winter symbolizes sterility, sleep. The message is simple: you should reflect and plan for your future activities, taking advantage of this time of isolation. (See DESERT, COLD, and ICE)

Wise scholar ■ If you dream that a wise scholar lectures you, it is trying to say that you are in a period of growth and intellectual development. In case the professor figure inspires respect and admiration, the image suggests emotional maturity and balance. You should listen to the advice that the dream gives you. It is your subconscious guiding you. (See ABBOT, GRANDFATHER, ACADEMY, AUTHORITY, LIBRARY, and HERMIT)

❖ For some oracles, this dream foretells that you will receive news soon.

Witch ■ Originally, witches were priestesses who possessed great wisdom and healing powers. With Christianity, witches began to get a bad rap, so, in dreams, they are associated with the destructive part of the unconscious. That is, with those feelings caused by the repression of your true self (moodiness, disappointment, jealousy . . .). For children and adolescents, this dream reveals unfulfilled desires and a fear of the unknown and mysterious aspects of life. In turn, for an adult it indicates the possibility that someone close attempts to take advantage of you for their own benefit. In general, this dream is a warning that obstacles and problems will soon appear in your environment, whether at work or in your personal relationships.

❖ Witches often presage diseases.

Wolf ■ It is associated with ferocity and cruelty. The presence of a wolf in dreams is a warning that you should distrust those around you, since someone could betray you. The wolf may also symbolize those tendencies you fear in yourself, such as aggressiveness and sexual desire. If a pack of wolves threatens or attacks you, it is an indication that your repressed instincts and emotions are trying to come to light.

❖ In the story *Little Red Riding Hood*, the wolf represents the cruelest part of man and the fear of sexual contact. In olden days, this story was told by mothers to their daughters to warn them of the danger of premarital sex.

Woman ▪ The interpretation of this dream varies depending on the sex of the dreamer. If a woman has this dream, it reveals her own personality. Thus, if the protagonist is an unknown woman, it indicates the dreamer's unconscious desires and tendencies. The woman of her fantasies, therefore, embodies the model of herself that she would like to project. At other times, the female figure refers to the mother of the dreamer: how you interact with her in the dream will provide much information about your mother-daughter relationship in reality In a man, contrary to common belief, dreaming of strange women or seeing himself as a woman does not always have sexual connotations or mean a conflict of identity. It may be representing the more intuitive and sensitive side of his personality. (See MOTHER)

Wood ▪ Wood symbolizes the raw material from which you can make new shapes without losing its resilience. Wood is therefore the formation of your personality throughout life. The meaning of the dream varies depending on the type of wood. Dry branches reflect a diluted personality and predict illnesses. Carrying branches on your shoulders is an omen of fruitless effort and suffering. On the contrary, to see the wood cut and ready to use (whether as firewood or for the construction of furniture or sculptures) indicates maturity and preparation.

Wool ▪ It symbolizes simplicity, peaceful happiness without ambition. Moreover, the presence of wool in dreams may also indicate a need for love or protection. If you are the one to spin it, you must soon be willing to help someone who is sick or in trouble. Finally, if one of your friends gives you wool, is an invitation to become something more than friends. This friendship can bring great satisfaction in every way, but mainly will provide the tenderness you were looking for.

Work ▪ Dreaming of searching for jobs denotes the need of the protagonist to feel useful. It is possible that you are dissatisfied with your current activity and you are trying to find a way to change it. If you succeed in finding a job, it foretells a possible change in profession.

Workers ▪ Workers in a dream may represent parts of your personality that you have not taken advantage of yet. The attitude of the workers will be very important to the interpretation. Were they efficient in their work, or were they lazy and inefficient? To see workers working is also a sign that a time of hard work and suffering is approaching, after which you will enjoy great benefits.

❖ If the workers go on strike or their attitude toward you is negative, this makes it clear that you should change strategies to reach your goals.

Workshop ▪ It could be that you are assuming some new position at work and the dream is giving you the necessary indications and tools so as to improve your methods. On the other hand, dreaming of a factory full of workmen signifies that you will soon complete your most ambitious projects; meanwhile, if it is empty, you should put more interest into the job. If it is you who is occupying the factory, you will arrange a way to leave the situation.

❖ Dreaming of workmen or of a factory is a very good sign. It foretells happiness in business and in love.

Worm ▪ Jung defines it as a negative figure. Its underground character and creeping locomotion have not given it a really "good reputation." Worms, therefore, symbolize what has been corrupted. Dreaming of them is often quite unpleasant. It should be added, however, that worms are also good for the garden and its fertility because they aerate the soil and eat up many unfavorable insects. In addition, as it is known, even the most horrifying caterpillars can become butterflies. As a result, this image advises you to not be depressed because of your defects; deep inside every creature, there is a huge potential for transformation. (See BUTTERFLY, METAMORPHOSIS, and CATERPILLAR)

❖ In traditional books on dreams, worms predict infectious diseases. And if you dream that you wipe them out, the harbinger says you will receive money.

Worry ▪ To feel worried while you sleep reveals physical discomfort and possible malaise. The dream wants you to understand that you must pay more attention to your health. Some aspect of your private life is affecting you physically, you are externalizing all the negative influences that overwhelm you in daily chores.

Wound ▪ Manifests psychic wounds (to your pride, dignity, sensibility, etc.) suffered before the eyes of others. That is where the cause of your fear dwells: you dread that those around you discover your wounds. If you resign yourself to remain silent, the only thing you will achieve with that attitude will be feeding your bitterness and resentment. (See SCARS)

❖ Dreaming of being wounded by a knife means a danger of suffering attacks, or perhaps a surgical operation. However, with a sword promises benefits. If the wound is inflicted by a stranger, unexpected problems will come up. But if it scars quickly, it indicates you will return to good graces through your own strength. If it is inflicted by an acquaintance, it portends an inheritance.

Wrapping ▪ Dreaming that you wrap an object reflects your desire to hide something; usually some aspect of your personality that is repressed. The opacity of the wrap indicates whether this rejection is deep. The act of unwrapping, however, indicates otherwise; It means that you begin to be more open.

❖ Receiving a wrapped package in dreams is considered a lucky omen. Unwrapping it, however, brings bad luck.

Wrinkles ▪ Wrinkles mean that your unconscious is telling you about the experiences acquired throughout your life. For some people, wrinkles are also linked to fear of aging and loss of physical attractiveness.

❖ Seeing yourself with a face streaked by wrinkles predicts pain and death at an early age. If wrinkles furrow someone else's face, they are a good sign for that person.

Writing ▪ The dream may be revealing your deepest feelings and what you really think about a given situation. The person to whom your writing is addressed, in this case, represents the nature of what you want to express. If the writer is someone else perhaps one aspect of your true self wants to get your attention. The contents of the letter can reveal valuable messages from your unconscious.

❖ The mystical tradition, in this case, stresses the importance of the silence of words. Dreaming of writing portends good news from relatives and friends. If in the dream you write with difficulty or pain it portends unjust accusations.

X

Xenophobia ▪ Acting xenophobic with a stranger shows your own fears and insecurities, and could be in the working field or in amorous relationships. Being rejected by this type of attitude denotes your fear of not being accepted as you are.

X-rays ▪ This dream demonstrates that you have clearly seen the intentions of a problem or issue that preoccupies you. It tends to reference you capacity to perceive, to intuit what truly motivates and moves people. On the other hand, the dream could be a manifestation a health problem of which you are not yet aware.

❖ There is no traditional interpretation of X-rays. However, it is interesting that Marie Curie, the discoverer of radioactivity, was very interested in spiritualism, mysticism and the world of dreams.

Xylophone ▪ If you dream of this instrument, you will experience happy and grandiose moments. However, if it appears broken or in poor repair, you could suffer some sort of setback from not having listened to the advice of an expert.

Y

Yacht ■ Dreaming that you are on a yacht signifies that you want to escape responsibilities to enjoy an easy life. The consumerist environment surrounding you is hurting you, and prevents you from being yourself. Given that, you need to draw on your essence to advance spiritually.

Yawn ■ To imagine that you yawn in dreams shows you are careless about those around you, about the problems that it will provoke in your relationships. On the contrary, seeing others yawning predicts disease and poverty for your loved ones.

Yeast ■ Although the meaning is similar to that of SWELLING, generally this is a positive dream that reveals a dynamic state and well-being manifested in the positive results of a task. It is also related to maternity and the desire to procreate.

Yellow ■ Yellow is the color of intuition, intelligence, thought, and mental clarity. This color helps to fight anxiety while awaking creative talent (despite this, yellow is often hated by actors and other artists).
❖ Dressing in yellow in dreams promises future happiness caused by an unforeseen event. According to gypsy tradition, yellow indicates a solar nature able to discern the best of each person and every single thing.

Yogurt ■ Eating yogurt in dreams is indicative of unsurpassable health, after having passed delicate moments.

Yoke ■ The yoke is a symbol of impositions, servitude, and discipline. It represents a vital circumstance that obligates you to do something that you don't want. The subconscious reminds you that you can try to change the situation by searching out new initiatives. However, the things that impose this yoke on you could equally be internal as external.

Youth ■ The age you are in dreams is like a thermometer that marks your psychological age. If you see yourself as younger than you are in real life, it is a sign that you are full of energy and new ideas. On the contrary, dreaming of being older than you are reveals a lack of enthusiasm. Pessimism is undermining your life, so you must act to eradicate this negative feeling.
❖ If in your dreams you see a young person, there will be a reconciliation in family disputes. If a mother dreams that her child is young again, she will experience a period of vigor and renewed hope.

Yolk ■ If the yolk of an egg appears in your dreams, it signifies that you are enjoying or will enjoy good health, especially if you have recently suffered from an illness.

Z

Zero ■ Zero is represented by a circle, meaning the totality of being. Furthermore, it can manifest vital emptiness.

❖ Dreaming of nothing is synonymous with a waste of your energy. You must act and change direction. Drawing a zero in dreams predicts uncertainty and unrest.

Zipper ■ This dream may have sexual connotations. A broken zipper, on the other hand, can symbolize your inability to solve a problem.

❖ If you dream of a broken zipper it means that others will exercise their power over you.

Zodiac ■ The zodiac is always a positive dream: it announces peace and bliss in all personal spheres. Studying the zodiac will result in great benefits by establishing relations with influential persons; by dominating the zodiac, a social and occupational rise without precedent in life. If you dream of your own zodiac sign, it is likely a representation of yourself. If the other figures appear, you should pay attention to the qualities that they symbolize and their relationship to your own life or personality.

❖ Some oneiric oracles claim that dreaming of zodiac signs foretells that you will soon emigrate.

Zoo ■ Visiting a zoo denotes pleasant surprises and good luck in any sort of project. If you are a woman, there will be a passionate romance that results in marriage; for a man, he will succeed in winning over a woman that he wants. On the other hand, depending on the animals included in the dream, it could represent your nature. Every animal that appears will be an aspect of your nature. You need to assess which feelings appear represented.

❖ The zoo dreams predict trips and pleasant stays in foreign countries. If a child accompanies you in the dream, it signifies very good luck.

Bibliography

ALMUTH, Huth, *Sueños*, Abraxas, 1998. (*Dreams*)

ARANCIO, Angiola, *Cómo interpretar los sueños*, Editorial de Vecchi, 1998. *(How to Interpret Dreams)*

ARTEMIDORO, *El libro de la interpretación de los sueños*, Ediciones Akal, 1998. (The Book of Dream Interpretation)

BARRET, David V., *Sueños*, Editorial Juventud, 1997. (*Dreams*)

BECKER, R. de, *Les machinations de la nuit : Le rêve dans l'histoire et l'histoire du rêve*, París, 1965. (*The Machinations of the Night (Famous Historic, Religious, Political, and Cultural Dreams*)

BENTLEY, Peter, *The Book of Dream Symbols, Edition B*, 1998.

BORILE, Silvana, *Sueños premonitorios y presentimientos*, Editorial de Vecchi, 1996. (*Premonitory Dreams and Premonitions*))

BULKELEY, Kelly and Alan SIEGEL, *Cómo interpretar los sueños infantiles*, Espasa Calpe, 2000. (*How to Interpret Childhood Dreams*)

CARDANO, Gerolamo, *El libro de los sueños*, Asociación de Neuropsiquiatría, 1999. (*The Book of Dreams*)

CARRANZA, Armando, *Enciclopedia de los sueños,* Planeta, 1996. (*The Encyclopedia of Dreams*)

COWAN, James, *Aborigine dreaming*. Thorsons, 2003.

COXHEAD, David, and Susan HILLER, *Sueños*, Thames & Hudson, 1976. (*Dreams*)

DELANEY, Gayle, *El mensaje de los sueños sexuales*, Robinbook, 1995. (*The Message of Sexual Dreams*)

DUDLEY, Geoffrey A., *Los sueños*, Editorial El Ateneo, 1997. (*Dreams*)

FONTANA, David, *Aprende a soñar*, Ediciones Oniro, 1997. (Learn to Dream)

FONTANA, David, *El libro de los sueños; cartas oníricas, almohad- illa onírica; diario de sueños,* Ediciones B, 1998. (*The Book of Dreams: Oneiric cards, oneiric pillow; Dream Diary*)

FONTANA, David, *El poder secreto de los sueños,* Oceano, 2000. (*The Secret Power of Dreams*)

FONTANA, David, *Sueños,* Ediciones B, 1998. (*Dreams*)

FOURCHE-TIARKO, J.A and H. MORLIGHEM, *Les communications des Indigènes du Kasaï avec les âmes des morts,* Inst. royal colonial belgue, *Brussels,* 1939.

FRANZ, Marie-Louise von, *Sobre los sueños y la muerte,* Editorial Kairós, 1999. (*On Dreams and Death*)

FREUD, Sigmund, *La interpretación de los sueños,* Alianza Ed., 1997. (*The Interpretation of Dreams*)

FREUD, Sigmund, *Los sueños,* Editorial Tecnos, 1988. (*Dreams*)

FREUD, Sigmund, *Nuevas aportaciones a la interpretación de los sueños,* Alianza Editorial, 1986. (*New Contributions to the Interpretation of Dreams*)

GIMÉNEZ, Quiona, *Diccionario esencial de sueños,* Oceano, 2000. (*Essential Dictionary of Dreams*)

GOOGISON, Lucy, *Los sueños femeninos,* Integral, 1999. (*Feminine Dreams*)

HEARNE, Keith, and MELBOURNE, David, *Understanding Dreams.* New Hollander, 1999.

INDMAN MILLER, Gustavus, *10.000 sueños interpretados,* Ediciones Scriba, 1998. (*10,000 Dreams Interpreted*)

HOLZER, Hans, *Interpretación práctica de los sueños,* M. Roca, 1981. (*Practical Interpretation of Dreams*)

JULIEN, Nadia and Luc UYTTENHOVE, *Diccionario de sueños; Diccionario de supersticiones y presagios,* Salvat Editores, 1999. (*Dictionary of Dreams; Dictionary of Superstitions and Omens*)

JUNG, C.G., *Recuerdos, sueños, pensamientos,* Editorial Seix Barral, 1999. (*Memories, Dreams, Thoughts*)

JUNG, C.G., *L'homme à la découverte de son âme (estructura y funcionamiento del inconsciente).* 2ª ed., Ginebra, 1946.

JUNG, C.G., *L'âme et la vie,* París, 1963.

JUNG, C.G., *Types psychologiques,* Ginebra, 1950.

LAVIE, Peretz, *El fascinante mundo del sueño,* Crítica, 1997. (*The Fascinating World of Dreams*)

LÓPEZ BENEDI, J.A., *Cómo interpretar los sueños*, Obelisco, 1996. (*How to Interpret Dreams*)

MANIN MORRISSEY, Mary, *Construye tu campo de sueños*, Ediciones Obelisco, 1999. (*Construct Your Field of Dreams*)

MARSHALL SMITH, Michael, *Sueños*, Grijalbo Mondadori, 1998. (*Dreams*)

MICHELAZZO, Maria, *Cómo recordar los sueños*, De Vecchi, 1998. (*How to Remember Dreams*)

MONNERET, Simon, *El sueño y los sueños*, Mensajero, 1996. (*Sleep and Dreams*)

MORIN, E., *Le Cinèma*, Paris, 1960.

MULLER, Werner, *Les religions des Indies d'Amèrique du Nord* (*Les religions amèrindiennes*), París, 1962.

NELSON, Susy, *Guía práctica para interpretar los sueños*, Editorial de Vecchi, 1997. (*Practical Guide for the Interpretation of Dreams*)

PAPUS, *El Tarot de los Bohemios* (París, 1889), Kier, B. Aires, 1957. (*Tarot of the Bohemians*)

PARKER, Julia, El mundo secreto de los sueños, Paidós, 1998. (*The Secret World of Dreams*)

ROJAS GONZÁLEZ, Margarita, *Taller de sueños*, Pirámide, 1999. (*Dream Workshop*)

RUIZ, Celia, *Pesadillas y sueños infantiles*, Susaeta, 1999. (*Nightmares and Childhood Dreams*)

SALAS, Emilio, *El gran libro de los sueños*, Martínez Roca, 1997. (*The Big Book of Dreams*)

SALOMON, Marcus, *La nueva enciclopedia de los sueños*, Ediciones Robinbook, 1999. (*The New Encyclopedia of Dreams*)

SCHOLTEN, Max, *Interpretación de los sueños*, Ultramar Editores, 1996. (*Interpretation of Dreams*)

SERGIO, Jorge, *Qué son los sueños*, Ediciones Continente, 1996. (*What Are Dreams*)

SIEGEL, Alan B., *Los sueños que pueden cambiar su vida*, Tikal ediciones, 1995. (Dreams That Can Change Your Life)

SHANKAR, *Indira Diccionario de los sueños*, Editorial Acervo, 1990. (*Dictionary of Dreams*)

TANOUS, Alex, *Sueños y poder psíquico*, Booket, 1998. (*Dreams and Psychic Power*)

TAPIA, Javier, *El mensaje está en los sueños*, Abraxas, 1999. (*The Message Is in the Dreams*)

THYLBUS, *Los sueños y su interpretación profética*, Iberia, 1983. (*Dreams and Their Prophetic Interpretation*)

TOFFOLI, Angela, *Los secretos de los sueños*, De Vecchi, 1998. (*Secrets of Dreams*)

TOSCANO SÁNCHEZ, Estefanía, *100 mensajes a través de los sueños*, Olalla Ediciones, 1997. (*100 Messages Through Dreams*)

TUAN, Laura, *El gran diccionario de los sueños*, De Vecchi, 1998. (*The Big Dictionary of Dreams*)

VV.AA., *Le rêve et les sociètès humaines*, París, 1967.

VV.AA., *Sources orientales II, Les songes et leur interprètation*, París, 1959.

VIREL, André, *Histoire de notre image*, Ginebra, 1965.

VON DER WEID, Jean-Noel, *El sueño y los sueños*, Acento Editorial, 1994. (*Sleep and Dreams*)

WALKER, J.F., *Los mil y un sueños de la A a la Z*, Editorial Sirio, 1996. (*A Thousand and One Dreams from A to Z*)

Images in this book

2 "The Virgin," Gustav Klimt (1913), Národní Galerie, Praga;

6 "Sweet dream," John William Godward (1901);

15 "Danae," Gustav Klimt (1907), Galería Welz, Salzburg;

21 "Starry Night," V. Van Gogh (1889);

34 oil on canvas (Joan Ponç, 1974);

47 "The splash" (fragment), David Hockney, 1966;

48 "The Room," V. Van Gogh (1889), Art Institute of Chicago; "The Scream," Edvard Munch (1893) The Munch Museum/ The Munch Ellingsen Group, © VEGAP, Barcelona 2003;

51 "Little Nemo," Wilson McCay (1905);

54 Cover of Hipgnosis for the album "Elegy," by The Nice (1971);

55 psychedelic posters: "Blowing in the Mind" (1967, Martin Sharp), "Middle Earth Club" (1968) and "5th Dimension Club" (1967), Hapshash and The Coloured Coat;

56 painting for M. Slam; huichol art;

57 "Bond of union," M.C. Escher (1956) © Cordon Art BV, Baarn, Holland;

58 "Philippino Food," comic by Ed Badajos (1971);

59 "Wish you were here," image by Hipgnosis for the album of Pink Floyd (1975);

62 "Sleeping Beauty," Edward Frederick Brewtnall. Between 1846–1902;

73 "Puddle," M.C. Escher (1952) © Cordon Art BV, Baarn, Holland;

76 "The Sleeping Gypsy," Henri Rousseau (1897);

78 "A Little While After Death," (1989), oil by Vicente Pascual Rodrigo (private collection);

81 "A Garden for Venus," Ljuva (Popovic Alekes Ljubomir);

84 "Shaft n.° 6," H.R. Giger (1966–1968);

86 "Pallas Athenea," Gustav Klimt (1898);

87 Cover by Hipgnosis for Misplaced Ideals, album by Sad Café;

96 "The Kiss," Gustav Klimt (1907–1908) Österreische Galerie, Vienna;

98 "House of stairs," M.C. Escher (1951) © CordonArtBV, Baarn, Holland;

100 "Flaming June," Frederic Leighton(1895) The Maas Gallery;

106 "The meaning of life/Swimmer in the desert," Hipgnosis (1973);

107 "Mirón," Carles Baró © Carles Baró, Barcelona 2001;

110 "The Tree of Life," Gustav Klimt (1905–1909) Österreische Galerie, Vienna;

127 Publicity collage by Japanese designer Tanadori Yokoo for Dartimon (1976);

128 "Forks in the back," Hipgnosis (1982) Österreische Galerie, Vienna.

Other drawings, images, and photographs: Age Fotostock, Stockphoto, Cordon Press, Dreamstime, Océano archive. © Editorial Océano, S.L. 2003